Volume 8

I0028280

PRIVATE RENTED HOUSING IN THE UNITED STATES AND EUROPE

PRIVATE RENTED HOUSING IN THE UNITED STATES AND EUROPE

MICHAEL HARLOE

Routledge
Taylor & Francis Group

LONDON AND NEW YORK

First published in 1985 by Croom Helm Ltd

This edition first published in 2021
by Routledge
2 Park Square, Milton Park, Abingdon, Oxon OX14 4RN

and by Routledge
52 Vanderbilt Avenue, New York, NY 10017

Routledge is an imprint of the Taylor & Francis Group, an informa business

© 1985 Michael Harloe

British Library Cataloguing in Publication Data
A catalogue record for this book is available from the British Library

ISBN: 978-0-367-64519-9 (Set)
ISBN: 978-1-00-313856-3 (Set) (ebk)
ISBN: 978-0-367-68010-7 (Volume 8) (hbk)
ISBN: 978-0-367-68015-2 (pbk)
ISBN: 978-1-00-313384-1 (Volume 8) (ebk)

Publisher's Note
The publisher has gone to great lengths to ensure the quality of this reprint but points out that some imperfections in the original copies may be apparent.

Disclaimer
The publisher has made every effort to trace copyright holders and would welcome correspondence from those they have been unable to trace.

PRIVATE RENTED HOUSING IN THE UNITED STATES AND EUROPE

Michael Harloe

CROOM HELM
London & Sydney

© 1985 Michael Harloe
Croom Helm Ltd, Provident House, Burrell Row,
Beckenham, Kent BR3 1AT

Croom Helm Australia Pty Ltd, First Floor,
139 King Street, Sydney, NSW 2001, Australia

British Library Cataloguing in Publication Data

Harloe, Michael
    Private rented housing in the United
    States and Europe.
    1. Rental housing
    I. Title
    363.5'8   HD7288.8
    ISBN 0-7099-3714-8

Printed and bound in Great Britain by
Biddles Ltd, Guildford and King's Lynn

CONTENTS

Contents

Contents

TABLES AND FIGURES

Tables

Figures

FOR KATHERINE

ACKNOWLEDGEMENTS

The research on which this book is based was
initially funded by the British Department of the
Environment and later by the Nuffield Foundation.
The support of these bodies and the assistance of
their officials is gratefully acknowledged.
Dr. Christine Whitehead acted as economic
consultant during the early stages of the project.
She provided much valuable advice on all aspects
of the project and particular assistance with the
work on French private rented housing. The research
depended greatly for its success on the
contribution made by several consultants which is
described elsewhere in this book. They were
Professor Emanuel Tobier (New York University),
Lars Østergaard (Boligministeriet, Copenhagen),
Jan van der Schaar with the assistance of Professor
Hugo Priemus (Technische Hogeschool, Delft),
Christian Topalov (Centre de Sociologie Urbaine,
Paris), and Eberhard Mühlich (Institut für Wohnen
und Umwelt, Darmstadt). In addition, Professor
Peter Marcuse (Columbia University) provided
considerable additional help with the analysis of
rental housing in the USA. I have benefitted
greatly from the discussions and collaboration with
Peter Marcuse and Eberhard Mühlich on housing
matters over the last seven years. They both
continue to be associated with the research which
this book partially reports on.
Thanks are also due to the many individuals
and organisations which were interviewed or
provided information in other ways during the
course of the research (they are listed in an
appendix), to the Library staff of the University
of Essex and to Professors David Donnison and

Acknowledgements

Della Nevitt who gave advice and encouragement
during the early stages of the work when the
project was based at the Centre for Environmental
Studies, London. Finally I owe a debt of gratitude
to my secretary Carole Allington and her colleagues
Mary Girling and Linda George who deciphered my
typing and - even worse - my handwriting with
remarkable patience at a time when the university
cuts were placing an increasingly intolerable burden
of work upon them.
     None of these people are of course
responsible for the analysis presented in this book
nor for any factual inaccuracies it contains.
The latter in particular are never entirely absent
from large scale empirically based studies, their
frequency increases when six sets of data and
information have to be absorbed.

                              Michael Harloe
                              Colchester
                              March 1984

INTRODUCTION

This book presents the first results of a research
project on the development of housing policies and
markets in the USA, Britain, France, West Germany,
Denmark and the Netherlands. It deals with the
private rented sector. Further publications will
examine social rented and owner occupied housing
and consider the overall development of housing
provision in the advanced capitalist countries.
     In recent years there have been important new
analyses of the political economy of urban
development (for reviews of these see Harloe, 1977b;
Lebas, 1982; Walton, 1982). One of the features of
such theories is that they posit the existence of
some broad cross national factors which structure
the phenomena that they analyse. But all too often
such approaches have resulted in an unconvincingly
deterministic account because of their lack of
sensitivity to the specific features of the history
and nature of the policies or developments with
which they are concerned (see Harloe, 1979; Harloe
and Martens, forthcoming). As this book will show
there are, for example, important ways in which the
housing market has been shaped by the detailed
division of powers and responsibilities between the
various levels of government, the position of
individual nations after the two world wars and
the specific timing and nature of the broader
international developments of capitalist
industrialisation and urbanisation as well as the
rise of the organised working class. Yet the
attempt to provide detailed, empirically based
comparative analysis remains essential if, for
example, the claim is to be sustained that patterns

of urban development are strongly linked to
characteristics of basic modes of production and
their associated class conflicts which to some
degree transcend national systems. This point was
put clearly by Pahl some years ago now, 'Comparative
analysis of urban and regional development in the
advanced societies is the essential foundation for
the political economy of space' (Pahl, 1977, 49).
But the range and number of such comparative studies
is little more developed today than when Pahl made
this comment.

More conventional comparative social policy
studies have provided some detailed data and
historical information. But, with a few important
exceptions (notably Rimlinger, 1971) their attempts
to develop theoretical explanations have been less
than successful (1). For example, there have been a
number of attempts by 'convergence theorists' to
explain the evolution of welfare policies in the
advanced capitalist countries which have been
heavily criticised (for example, Kerr et. al.,
1973; Wilensky and Lebeaux, 1965. For a critique
see Misra, 1977).

The inadequacy of cross national studies is
particularly evident in the field of housing. Much
of the available material is produced by governments
and international organisations for their own
purposes. Typically it will be factual rather than
analytical, confined to the briefest descriptions
of current developments and largely ignorant of the
connections between the development of housing
policy and the housing market and wider social,
economic and political changes. Unfortunately, many
academic studies repeat some or all of these
deficiencies, as well as failing to contribute much,
if at all, to a more satisfactory understanding of
the relationship between housing policies and
markets and the more general determinants of the
social structure (2).

Reviewing two such texts recently, Marcuse
(1982) described them in the following way;

> 'There is a competent if limited exposition
> of some ideas from welfare economics, less
> successful capsule expositions of "social
> theory" and "economic theory" and "political
> theory", historical sections, a chapter on
> land policy and one on urban renewal. The
> approach is descriptive and uncritical;
> decision makers try to solve housing
> problems, make mistakes, try again ...

> they adapt their polices as best they can
> to "social and economic change" ... The
> book represents what might be called tertiary
> research; neither new information nor new
> analysis, but a compendium of generally
> available information ...
>
> [The second book] ... proposes to establish a
> "framework for housing policy analysis"
> ... Yet the framework ... contributes little
> to an otherwise intelligent description of
> housing policy in the three countries (Sweden,
> the US and the UK) ... [it] turns out to be
> warmed over mainstream political science
> ... "Political actors" make decisions, which
> may be either "small scale innovations" or
> "strategic choices" resulting in
> "incremental adaptions" if successful and
> "decremental adaptions" if unsuccessful.
> The key actors are "political parties,
> bureaucracies, interest groups and public
> opinion". Just as "public opinion" somehow
> "acts", so do "policies" have objectives,
> without any person or group having to be
> named ("the objective of economic policy
> is to improve living standards") ...'

After giving some examples of how inadequate such
concepts are for understanding the evolution of
policies and the reasons why they changed, Marcuse
concludes, 'The more theoretical the discussion
tries to become, the more superficial it is. The
"framework for analysis" ends up by being little
more than a taxonomy of unreal categories'. And in
an earlier paper Marcuse (1978) has neatly
characterised much of the more policy oriented
writing thus, 'In the United States, mainstream
examinations of housing have rested on one of two
general assumptions about the role of the State.
The first is that the State is benevolent, even if
its actions are often limited, misconceived, or
ineffective in achieving their benevolent ends.
The second is that the State is neutral, and its
housing actions (and failures to act) are caused by
the interplay of conflicting groups and interests
swirling around it. If housing policy fails to
move in any unified or coherent direction, it is
because of the absence of constructive compromise
among conflicting parties and goals. The bulk of
the large US literature on housing policy is
similarly divided. One part is rich in

comprehensive and sophisticated policy analysis and programmatic recommendations with the implicit assumption that such analysis will influence the well intentioned efforts of a benevolent government. The other part is descriptive, and lays out in detail the varying fortunes of combat among diverse and plural interest groups around state housing policies; the absence of any underlying concern by a state that is neutral among these conflicting groups is postulated ... such assumptions ... clear away theoretical obstacles to the formulation of recommendations and descriptions of policy-making that more analytical approaches may raise' (3).

The research project which this book partially draws on has been conceived in reaction to the deficiencies of these conventional accounts of housing policy. But it is also intended as a contribution to overcoming some of the limitations of the new theories of the state and urban policy which have already been noted. And to do this it is necessary to develop far more detailed comparative accounts of the evolution of different housing systems than hitherto. This is the main reason why this book concentrates on a close examination of the evolution of the private rented housing market in six countries and analyses both broad trends in the fortunes of this tenure as well as particular national differences. Subsequent volumes will examine the other two main tenures and the evolution of capitalist housing provision as a whole.

However, it is hoped that this book will also be of interest to others, less concerned with the issues discussed above. As already mentioned, there have been a growing number of international housing studies which have been produced by governments and other organisations for their own purposes. There can be a number of reasons for such studies, for example a desire to see whether there are innovations in housing policies, institutions or market processes which are transferable from one country to another or, perhaps more interestingly, to try and clarify whether these are some cross national trends in the development of housing – which might therefore be relatively immune to influence by national policies – and some which are dependent on factors which could be more readily altered. Yet, as we have stated, many such accounts are insufficiently detailed (or even accurate) to provide very useful information to policy makers.

Introduction

Therefore, the account presented in this book, if
not perhaps its analytical framework, will also be
of interest to more policy oriented readers. Indeed,
the research which this book reports on was
initially conceived in a policy context, as an input
to a review of private rented housing carried out by
the last British Labour government (which
unfortunately remains unpublished). Moreover, during
the course of writing the book the research findings
have been drawn on by another official examination
of private renting, carried out by the British House
of Commons Environment Committee and published in
1982 (House of Commons Environment Committee, 1982).
     One of the reasons why many comparative housing
studies are so inadequate is that there are
considerable practical and other difficulties
inherent in such research. First, there is the
problem of organising the research. The sort of
flying visit to each country concerned which has
often formed the basis for comparative studies is
unlikely to result in more than a superficial
understanding of specific national housing
situations. Yet longer periods of study in each
country are usually impractical for financial and
other reasons. Moreover, wholly library based
studies drawing on the limited stock of
internationally available literature - language
problems apart - are inadequate. Second, there are
considerable problems concerning the availability
of information (4). For example, different countries
collect data about their housing in different ways,
at different intervals of time and so on. Yet
considerations of cost and time alone usually rule
out the large scale collection of new data and
information according to common procedures. Also
some countries have a far more developed body of
national housing data and research to draw on than
others. Third, there may be more fundamental
differences in the way in which housing markets and
policies are constituted. An important example of
this problem, which is discussed further in chapter
two, involves the definition of the private rented
sector itself. As we shall see, in the case of at
least one country the boundary between private and
social rented housing is far from clear.
     The way in which some of these problems were
tackled is described in an appendix, others are
referred to in the main text. But the reader is
warned that there are many points in a survey of
this nature when inadequacies of data and comparable

information, difficulties in arriving at a common
framework for analysis and resource limits on
further research result in analysis and description
which is partial rather than comprehensive and
conclusions which must remain tentative. But if
comparative studies are to advance such limits and
difficulties must be accepted. And, while these
problems do exist, this study should demonstrate
that they need not be an insuperable obstacle to
the development of cross national studies.
    Although this work focuses on a detailed and
empirically based examination of private rented
housing, leaving more general discussion of the
determinants of housing policy in advanced
capitalist countries to a later publication, some
further reference needs to be made to the
theoretical perspective within which this work is
conceived and to which it is intended to contribute.
It will already be clear that the most fruitful
perspective is taken to be one which seeks to relate
urban policy and development to broader social
structural factors (5). A first attempt to interpret
the development of housing in capitalist societies
from such a perspective, drawing on empirical
evidence from the early stages of the comparative
housing project, has been published elsewhere
(Harloe, 1981, see also Harloe and Martens,
forthcoming). Further development of this
interpretation depends on the outcome of the
empirical work now being carried out on the other
housing tenures. It would not be appropriate to the
present study which focusses more narrowly on
private renting. Nevertheless, a summary of some of
the major features of the tentative and schematic
analysis already published seems a necessary
introduction to this study.

1. The development of housing is characterised by
a set of processes that occur more generally in the
consumption of certain goods and services. Moreover,
there are strong links between consumption and
production processes. A central concern is the
nature of socialised and individualised consumption
and production and their consequences for capital
and the working class.
2. The main basis for a capitalist system is the
production, exchange and consumption of commodities
by firms and individuals within the market. The main
criterion of access to consumption commodities is
individual ability to pay which in turn depends

mainly on access to individual earnings. Production
involves the co-operative division of labour which
offers costs and benefits to capital and labour, the
balance of such costs and benefits depending on the
relative strengths of these two interests.
    3. This two class model is simplistic and
therefore inadequate. At the very least one can
distinguish two sections of the working class. The
first mainly works in large scale, bureaucratically
organised industry, commerce, etc. and is often,
though not always, organised in trade unions which
have close links with reformist political parties
(6). The second group has insecure and low paid
employment (if it works at all), and often shares a
position of economic and political weakness with
others such as the elderly, the physically and
mentally handicapped, lone parents and others who
have little utility for production. Political
outcomes may sometimes reflect the interests of the
more organised sector of the working class while
excluding or even disadvantaging those of the more
marginal group. Similar divisions exist among
capital, as different branches have differing
requirements and interests and varying opportunites
for obtaining these. The conflict and co-operation
which occurs is often visible in the response which
is made to specific issues.
    4. Consumption is characterised by rather
similar patterns. Some individualised consumption,
i.e. allocation of goods and services on the basis
of individual ability to pay, has been replaced by
socialised consumption, i.e. allocation on some
other basis than purely ability to pay - such as
some definition of 'need' (7). This may involve
reductions in opportunities for capitalist
accumulation but the reverse has often occurred, for
the branch of the economy supplying the goods and
services concerned is likely to profit from such
supply. Also much state expenditure has been
analysed as expenditure which indirectly assists
capital accumulation, for example to provide the
necessary skilled and healthy workforce when this
cannot be achieved out of workers' own earnings, or
to help reduce social tensions.
    5. The specific ways in which socialised
consumption is provided have frequently been
patterned by these capitalist concerns. Among the
main beneficiaries have often been key sections of
the working class, with marginal groups receiving
less benefit or receiving benefit on semi-punitive

terms. Mechanisms for excluding such groups range
from simple non-provision to defining rules of
access in ways which are exclusive, or even
ensuring that the acceptance of benefits involves
stigmatisation or labelling, so making those
eligible reluctant to claim them.
      6. Socialised consumption offers the working
class benefits which their incomes do not allow
them to purchase. Less frequently do they provide
the main basis for collective organistion, although
the socialisation of consumption (especially with
respect to health, housing and education) has often
been a key issue for reformist politics. Conflict
over socialised consumption concerns both its
nature and its availability.
      7. The outcome of consumption based conflicts
cannot be understood solely in terms of their
immediate political and economic determinants. Thus
narrowly defined conceptions of, for example, the
politics or economics of housing are inevitably
limited, for the broader state of relationships
between and within labour and capital is often a
significant key to understanding development in
housing markets and policies.
      8. In consumption as in production, one can
distinguish between the differing interests of
labour and capital. Thus some producers whc have a
general interest in a healthy, reasonably housed
etc. workforce may support the extension of
socialised consumption to the extent necessary to
achieve this end, while those who will lose
profitable opportunities as a result may object.
As already noted, among the working class,
socialised consumption may tend to benefit the
organised rather than the unorganised groups and,
more generally, variations in consumption may
engender conflict and division.
      These simple and rather abstract proportions
were then used, to provide a preliminary analysis
of the development of housing under capitalism. The
major points in this analysis were:
      1. The first major form that housing took, in
the early stages of capitalist urbanisation, was
private renting. This was a relatively well adapted
'solution', given the contemporary circumstances.
But it was not able to supply decent housing at
affordable rents for large sections of the working
class. Poor housing not only became a basis for
political agitation but also had other serious
consequences for the economic and social order.
State regulation gradually developed. The
degree and nature of this state involvement varied

according to the specific relations and
constitution of capital and labour in each country.
There was some resistance by landlords but they
often appear to have been on the defensive, given
the support for change by sections of capital as
well as the working class.

2. The social and economic upheavals which
occurred during and immediately after the first
world war resulted in significant new developments,
especially the construction of some state
subsidised housing and rent control. At this time
broader economic and political interests and other
objectives than those of property capital were
particularly influential. Their importance soon
faded in most cases, although a complete return to
the private market in housing usually proved
impossible in the inter-war years. In certain
countries and regions the growth of real incomes
provided an essential precondition for the growth
of owner occupation in this period. This
development was actively promoted by housing
development and financial interests for reasons
which, at base, concern the more attractive
investment opportunities that this tenure was seen
to offer in comparison with private rental housing.

3. Since 1945 there have been two trends.
Especially in the earlier years there was a marked
growth of social rented housing, with support from
working class organisations and, at times, sectors
of capital. Latterly, the growth of owner
occupation has become the leading trend and there
are signs that social rented housing has become
increasingly unattractive compared with this
alternative. Private rented housing, as will be
demonstrated in this book, has increasingly become
a residual tenure for those who are unable to gain
access to the other two tenures and has become
politically and economically weaker in the process.
As before, these changes have been promoted by -
and have largely benefitted   - housing
developers, landowners and financial capital. But
government policies have also played a major role
in helping to bring these changes about. The timing
and extent of these changes have varied according
to factors such as the position that each country
found itself in after the war, the level and
progress of the economy and incomes, political
history, and the changing balance of class
interests.

4. To a considerable extent (during the

period of its most rapid growth at least) social housing has aided sections of the more organised working class, various mechanisms can be described which tended to result in the exclusion of other groups. The development of owner occupation, which became increasingly possible as real incomes grew, was of course supported by conservative but also and increasingly by working class based political parties. The diminuition in enthusiasm for social rented housing can be partly related to its deficiencies. To a considerable extent these derived from the terms on which it was provided, terms which reflected an essentially capitalist concern that its impact be limited. Owner occupation has offered certain material benefits in comparison with social rented housing (and, of course, private rented housing) for those who could afford it. Once substantial numbers of the better paid working class began to enter this tenure from the other two sectors the growth of support for owner occupation by social democratic parties followed from electoral considerations, among other reasons.

5. Support for the extension of owner occupation has not been confined to those sections of capital who stood to gain directly from this development. It has been shown that this change in the housing market was linked to a more general expansion of consumption and of opportunities for profitable production. So by the end of the sixties and considerably earlier in some cases (though possibly a little later in Germany), the focus on the private market in housing in its modern and, from the point of view of capital, most effective form, owner occupation, was without significant opposition, being supported for a variety of reasons by those interests directly involved in its production, by capital as a whole and, to a very large degree, by the political representatives of the organised working class.

6. But this coalition of interests in favour of the extension of the private market in housing, with the underpinning of extensive public support, may be quite unstable in the new economic situation of the late seventies and early eighties. There are signs that the continued expansion of owner occupation and of state support for it may be in doubt and there is clear evidence that the social rented sector is under even more pressure. In these circumstances we may be about to witness a

considerable restructuring of housing provision.
These points are developed further in the last
chapter of this book which discusses the future of
private renting.

There are many questions, both of theory and
of evidence, raised by this tentative analysis of
capitalist housing. Clearly it requires further
discussion and development. But one issue needs to
be considered immediately because it relates to a
fundamental feature of the way in which the research
upon which this book draws has been organised and
presented. This concerns the decision to analyse
the three main housing tenures separately. The main
objections to such an approach are that it tends to
obscure the changing and internally differentiated
nature of the social, economic and political
relations of each tenure, imposing a false unity on
each of them, and to ignore the links between
tenures. Above all it may be argued that a tenure
based analysis is inappropriate when the real
object of enquiry is capitalist housing provision
as a whole.

Of course most conventional and even the
newer, more radical discussions of housing adopt
the division of the housing market into tenures as
a framework for analysis without much critical
attention. And often the popular and political
discussion of housing revolves around
considerations of the relative positions, advantages
and so on of the main tenures (8). But what might
be called an ideology of tenures is implicit in such
discussions and, like all ideologies, it serves to
illustrate some aspects of reality while obscuring
others. Consider, for example, the image of owner
occupation which is commonly purveyed and accepted.
According to a recent British government report
the main reason for the secular trend towards home
ownership 'is the sense of greater personal
independence that it brings. For most people owning
one's own home is a basic and natural desire ...'
(Department of the Environment, 1977b, 50). The
(Labour) cabinet minister responsible for this
report also stated that owner occupation, '...not
only makes economic sense for the individual and
the community, it also satisfies deep seated
aspirations in our people' (quoted in Harloe,
1977a).

No doubt such an image of owner occupation
would be assented to by very many people. It would
be reinforced by views of the tenure which tend to
stress, in various ways, the superiority of the

social, economic and physical characteristics of
the sector (and even its occupants) in comparison
with the other main tenures. It is indeed partly
because such a composite image of the tenure has
been constructed (although it is more strongly
developed in some countries than others) that the
expansion of owner occupation has come to dominate
housing policies.

But this is not a true image. It is not wholly
false, but it misleads because it is not an accurate
reflection of the real conditions, motivations and
satisfactions (or lack of them) of many of those in
the owner occupied sector. Nor is the implicit
claim that only one tenure - owner occupation - can
provide the most desirable housing solution
sustainable. And these 'silences' help to ensure
that fundamental problems are ignored and also that
alternative housing solutions remain unexplored
(on the latter, see Harloe, 1982; Ball, 1982).
Evidence of the problems can be found in some
academic and even (occasionally) some governmental
studies (9). For example, Karn (1979) carried out a
study of low income owner occupiers in Birmingham.
She showed that a substantial proportion of such
households were unable to sustain their mortgage
payments and so lost their homes. Many were forced
to take second mortgages at very high interest
rates in order to try and rescue their financial
position. Often low income households have been
forced to buy their own houses because of the lack
of access to adequate and reasonably priced rented
housing and they often pay dearly for poor quality
housing. The political rhetoric quoted above is
entirely misleading in such a context.

So to a considerable extent divisions within
tenures, for example, between the mass of private
rented housing and the small scale luxury rented
subsector or between poor, inner city owner
occupiers (or their rural counterparts) and middle
and upper income suburban residents, are as
significant as divisions between tenures. And class
positions which cross cut such tenurial divisions
are central determinants of individual housing
situations.

Yet there are strong arguments in favour of the
analysis of individual tenures which is being
adopted in this study. In practical terms most data
and other information is available on this basis.
Moreover, a comparative and detailed analysis of all
three tenures taken together would be far too

lengthy for one book. Also the tenure divisions
do have a reality which is significant. The politics
and ideology of tenure have important effects on the
nature and development of housing provision. The
economic position of each tenure and the legislation
affecting it - whatever the internal differentiation
- does have a degree of coherence and separateness.
As Ball has recently suggested, there are
distinctive social relations of tenure. He writes;

> 'Associated with any tenure there is a
> particular set of social relations involved
> in the provision. They are not an inevitable
> consequence of any tenure form. But their
> existence as established structures of
> provision will determine the development
> of those tenures, how much housing in them
> costs, how much is provided and of what
> type. Each category of social agent within
> those structures of provision will have
> their own economic interests, and some of
> them are in conflict ...' (Ball, 1982, 67).

Therefore, the retention of the division into
tenures in the organisation and presentation of
this study is both practically necessary and of
some empirical validity. But this can only be so if
it is recognised that the social relations within
each tenure do vary in the ways which have been
described and over time and if, in the final
analysis, it is the broader perspective of
capitalist housing provision as a whole which is
retained as the central concern.
Chapter one traces the early development of
private rented housing from the nineteenth century
to the last world war. Chapter two presents the
national background to the more recent development
of the tenure. These two chapters provide the
context for the detailed discussion of the post war
development of private renting in chapters three to
eight. These chapters outline the nature of the
private rented stock and of its tenants and landlords. There follow examinations of rents and
rent policy, subsidies and taxation, urban renewal
and improvement and landlord/tenant relations.
Chapter nine summarises the main findings of the
study and discusses the future of the tenure.

NOTES

1.   Since completing the research discussed in
this book there has been a further important
addition to the literature on comparative social
policy with the first publication in English of a
study by the Max-Planck-Institut für aüslandisches
und internationales Sozialrecht of the development
of social insurance in Germany, France, Great
Britain, Austria and Switzerland. But this study,
while it attempts to draw out explanatory factors
in each country, contains no attempt to synthesise
them (Kohler and Zacher (eds), 1982).
2.   There are, of course, exceptions to this.
Among the studies - many of them drawn upon in this
book - which go beyond this rather superficial level
are Bauer, 1934; Denby, 1938; Donnison, 1967;
Wolman, 1975; Mandelker, 1973; Fuerst (ed) 1974;
Duclaud-Williams, 1978 and Kemeny, 1981. There is
also an interesting chapter on housing in
Heidenheimer et. al., 1975. Nevertheless, to a
greater or lesser extent, when they attempt to
generalise about the determinants of housing policy
they tend to resort to abstracted and unsatisfactory
unsatisfactory generalisations. For a detailed
critique of such studies see Harloe and Martens,
forthcoming. Remarkably, the most impressive
empirical attempt to compare housing encountered
during the research dates from before the First
World War and was carried out as part of an
international survey of wages and costs of living
by the British Board of Trade (Board of Trade,
1908a, b; 1909; 1911; 1913)!
3.   The description Marcuse gives is common
to much of the literature in all six countries.
The implicit assumption that analysis will
influence governments in a 'benevolent' direction
is recognisably a part of what Marris (1982) has
recently called the 'liberal paradigm' - the set of
assumptions and ideas that has accompanied the
reformist politics of the post war era. Marris
suggests that, with the break up of the political
and economic preconditions for the post war
expansion, the limitations of this paradigm have
become increasingly apparent. The point is perhaps
illustrated by the case of the leading government-
funded urban research institution in one of the six
countries in this study. Shortly after a new
conservative government came into power it was
announced that this institute would be closed down.

Notes

A senior politician attempted to intercede with the responsible Minister, referring to the undoubted quality of much of the institute's research. The Minister readily agreed with this point but added that he could see no reason to continue to support work which was likely to be critical of the effects of his policies.

4. Of the countries discussed in this book, the two with the most developed body of existing data and research were the USA and Britain and the two where the most difficulties existed in this respect were the Netherlands and Denmark (also of course the two smallest of the six countries). However, some of the most stimulating recent research has occurred in France - especially at the Centre de Sociologie Urbaine, Paris. See Lebas, 1982 for a select bibliography.

5. At times this has been called 'the new urban sociology' (by the present writer among others), 'the political economy of space', 'Marxist urban sociology' (which may be a contradiction in terms) and so on. But, as Walton has noted, 'such labels incur the risks of reification and reaction' (1982, 278). He adds, 'if the approach has "structural" emphases they are not at the expense of process, if it stresses the economy it does not diminish the society and polity, if it alludes to Marx it does so in the same forward-looking manner that Weber would have'.

6. Most clearly, the social democratic parties in Europe and the Democratic Party in the USA. But to a considerable extent this reformism has been a powerful influence on many conservative, 'centrist' and liberal parties - at least so far as social policy is concerned - and many of the working class have looked to such parties for the satisfaction of their needs.

7. Such definitions of need often bear little or no relationship to, for example, definitions based on minimal socially acceptable standards or a poverty line. Which needs are recognised as deserving satisfaction by governments often depends as much or more on the political and economic power of those in 'need' as on any such measurement - as this study of the position of private landlords and their tenants illustrates.

8. For an illustration of the limitations of this approach (when applied to the recent British government policy of selling off social rented housing) see Harloe, 1982.

9. In this context it is interesting to note that the task force set up by President Nixon in the early seventies to review federal housing policies was highly critical of previous attempts to develop low income home ownership (especially via the subsidised section 235 programme which began in 1968 and ran into enormous difficulties with high rates of default and various scandals). The report makes the following points;

'The housing strategy embodied in existing housing statutes does not permit low cost homes to be produced or even legally to exist in many areas [the problem of low quality versus minimum legal standards] ... no clear answer emerges as to whether home ownership is a net benefit or a net burden to low-income families ... housing as an investment for low-income individuals is illiquid, risky, requires complex management and has high maintenance costs ... Low-income families, because their incomes tend to be less stable and because of high transaction costs, particularly benefit from flexible tenure ... Ownership also exposes the owner-occupant to the hazards of unexpectedly expensive repairs, especially in low cost new housing in which, too often, long-run durability has been sacrificed for low initial cost. To some extent, rental tenancy spreads such hazards over many families ... There is little empirical support for the often expressed view that a homeowner acquires a new dignity or that becoming a home owner automatically transforms a person. The evidence of the social and psychological impact of home ownership is mostly anecdotal, especially as it concerns low-income families ... no research has separated the ownership aspect from associated dimensions including ... single-family dwelling units and locations' (US Department of Housing and Urban Development, 1973, 4 - 108-9).

But the reason why a conservative President endorsed these important conclusions was not, of course, because of any intention to provide more appropriate assistance to low income households but rather was part of a general policy of cutting almost all

Notes

housing subsidies, including those for public and
private rental housing.

Chapter One

THE GROWTH OF PRIVATE RENTED HOUSING

This chapter discusses the growth of private rented
housing in the last century, the nature of the
investors in this property, the problems that arose
and early governmental responses to them; and
developments around the First World War and in the
interwar years.
    Nineteenth century housing conditions attracted
the attention of writers and social reformers, there
is no lack of contemporary writing on this topic.
But much of it is of dubious reliability, and it is
rare to find useful comparative material. However,
much early writing on housing remains to be
rediscovered and assessed. There is a good deal more
to be learnt about the early history of housing in
the modern era. However, this book is principally
concerned with private rental housing in the post
1945 period, so this chapter merely sets the scene
for what follows.

INDUSTRIALISATION, POPULATION GROWTH AND
URBANISATION

While rented housing existed in rural areas in the
nineteenth century, as Gauldie writes (about
Britain) '... the greatest part of the rural
population ... during most of the nineteenth century
... remained in the traditional country workers'
houses built by their ancestors and repaired and
extended over generations by the workers themselves'
(1974, 49). In fact rural housing existed under
various arrangements, often linked to employment.
But much rural housing consisted of low income owner
occupation (1). This has persisted into the
twentieth century in the USA, France and Denmark
where a large rural population remained.

The Growth of Private Rented Housing

Even when the spread of industry to the countryside provided new housing possibilities, there is evidence from France that these were not always taken up. Thus Zeldin writes of a mining company which built workers' housing in 1866 but only let a handful 'because the workers hated having their rent deducted from their wages, having to pay compensation for the damage they caused, and generally having the company interfere in their private lives' (1973, 266).

So rented housing was mainly located in the towns. The provision of housing as a market commodity by landlords did not originate in the nineteenth century. But with the rapid industrialisation and urbanisation occurring then such housing became the dominant tenure, housing the new working class and most of the new middle class too. Some reasons for this will be discussed later. First we examine the progress and timing of industrialisation and urbanisation in our six countries. In passing it is worth noting that, far from the growth of owner occupation being a post-1945 phenomenon, as is often assumed, the proportion of such houses fell as urbanisation progressed. This is illustrated by figures quoted by Zeldin which show that a higher proportion of the French housing stock was owner occupied in the 1880s than today (2). And in the USA the proportion of owner occupied housing declined between 1890 and 1920 (US Bureau of the Census, 1961, 395). In Germany the proportion of owner occupation in large towns fell from 42% in 1850 to 9% by 1910 and that of rented property rose from 50% to 88% (Dawson, 1914, 166) (3).

So the growth of private rented housing was linked to the rapid industrialisation and urbanisation. These processes were studied by A.F. Weber at the end of the nineteenth century (1963, 150-2). He compared the proportions of urban population in 1800, 1850 and 1890. The most rapid period of urban growth had generally been since 1850, the exceptions being England and Scotland, the USA and, to a lesser degree, a few other countries including France. More specifically, rapid growth occurred in England from 1820, in the USA from 1840, in France from 1850 but in Prussia, Denmark and the Netherlands not until 1870. In fact in the latter two countries the proportion of the population in towns diminished between 1800 and 1850.

The Growth of Private Rented Housing

As Weber concluded, 'This amounts to a
demonstration that the Industrial Revolution and
the era of railways, both of which opened earliest
in England and the United States, have been the
transforming agents in the re-distribution of
population. They are the elementary forces in the
bringing about of Modern Capitalism' (1963, 152).
Weber's conclusions are sustained and elaborated by
the following points, drawn from the work of modern
economic historians (4).

1. France was probably at a similar stage of
   economic development as Britain by 1780 but
   then, for a variety of reasons, only
   industrialised relatively slowly (except
   for a brief period after 1852) and
   continued to have a large rural sector
   throughout the century and beyond.
2. The Dutch economy was more highly developed
   than the British in the mid-eighteenth
   century because of its world trading role
   but thereafter stagnated, especially in the
   first half of the nineteenth century - hence
   the urban decline noted above. More
   extensive industrialisation occurred from
   1870 onwards but a really sharp decline in
   the rural sector did not occur until after
   the Second World War.
3. While many of the economic conditions for
   industrialisation and growth were present in
   Germany earlier in the century it was not
   until the 1870s, after unification, that the
   political conditions were appropriate. Then
   there was an extraordinarily rapid
   development.
4. Danish economic growth was set back by the
   country's participation in the Napoleonic
   wars. This seems to explain the de-
   urbanisation noted above. From the mid-
   century Britain became the major market for
   Danish agricultural produce and from the
   1870s agriculture provided the basis for
   industrialisation and urbanisation.
5. In the United States there was some growth
   in the middle of the century but it gathered
   pace after the Civil War and the United
   States economy assumed the leading world
   position by 1900.

The Growth of Private Rented Housing

In terms of proportions of the population living
in urban areas, rather than rates of urban
concentration, Weber showed that by 1890
urbanisation was most extensive in England and
Wales, where 61.7% of the population lived in towns
with over 10,000 inhabitants. In none of the other
countries was more than a third of the population
urbanised at this time (1963, 153). So, despite the
rapid growth of urbanisation, it was probably not
until later, perhaps in the interwar period - as
the United States statistics show - that the
private rented sector peaked as a proportion of the
housing stock. The later development of
industrialisation and the retention of a larger
agricultural sector resulted in a significantly
different pattern in the other five countries from
that which occurred in Britain, where by 1914 about
90% of the stock was rented (Department of the
Environment, 1977, 37).

NINETEENTH CENTURY HOUSING CONDITIONS

A classic early account of nineteenth century urban
housing is Engels' description of Manchester in the
1840s, remarkable for his analysis of the links
between capitalist industrialisation and the
spatial and social distribution of the population.
    But Engels' descriptions were echoed by many
observers elsewhere. For example here is an account
of the housing of poorer workers in Nantes in 1835.

> 'If you want to know how he lives, go ... to
> the Rue des Fumiers ... Pass through one of
> the drain like openings, below street level,
> that lead to these filthy dwellings ... Below
> street level on each side of the passage
> there is a large, gloomy cold room. Foul
> water oozes out of the walls. Air reaches
> the room through a sort of semi-circular
> window which is two feet high at its greatest
> elevation. Go in - if the fetid smell that
> assails you does not make you recoil. Take
> care, for the floor is uneven, unpaved and
> untiled - or if there are tiles, they are
> covered with so much dirt that they cannot
> be seen ...' (Pollard and Holmes, 1968, 495).

Conditions were no better in Breslau in 1845,

The Growth of Private Rented Housing

'The dwellings of the working classes mostly
face the yards and courts. The small quantity
of fresh air admitted by the surrounding
buildings is vitiated by emanations from
stables and middens...these dwellings are...
always filled with fetid air and steam,
which condenses on the walls and creates
green mould' (Pollard and Holmes, 1968, 500).

The principal causes of these conditions were, on
the one hand, the low and uncertain wages of most of
the new working class and, on the other hand,
uncontrolled speculative building. Thus Villerme
refers to the high rents that could be charged in
the rapidly expanding town of Mulhouse in 1845 -
where the demand for labour outstripped the supply
of housing - and the inevitable response of massive
overcrowding (Pollard and Holmes, 1968, 490-1). In
Breslau it was noted that often several persons or
a whole family shared a single room and bed and if
a family rented more than one room the 'surplus'
accommodation would have to be sublet. In some
cases several families shared a room and lodgers
were taken in, accommodated in stables, under the
stairs or on the floor for 'there is no question of
beds'. Newer property was only available at rents
which restricted them to the 'better classes'
(Pollard and Holmes, 1968, 500-1). Similar sub-
division of accommodation was also noted in New
York in 1853 (Still, 1974, 162).
    The form that this housing took varied. In
Germany much was in the form of Mietkasernen ('rent
barracks'), high rise, high density blocks of flats
surrounding a central courtyard in which industry
was often located (5). But in Holland and Britain
apartments were less common. The form also varied
according to the incomes of tenants. Burnett
describes the 'quality hierarchy' of housing
available to the English working class in the first
half of the century (1978, 168-73). The poorest
were in cellar dwellings. Next came lodging
houses which provided temporary accommodation
for transient workers, over-crowded and centres for
disease, crime and prostitution. Then came
tenement houses, often sub-divided into single
rooms, not much better than lodging houses but
intended for more permanent habitation. All these
forms of accommodation were adapted from their
original use as family dwellings for the better
off. Then there were terrace (row) houses, many
built 'back to back', offering more space and

5

amenity but at rents only affordable by a minority.

Burnett also illustrates the point made in every country, that decent rented accommodation was beyond the means of much of the working class, yet the rents they paid were inflated by speculation. Thus in 1866 James Hole calculated that inhabitants of the notorious London tenement 'rookery' of St. Giles paid on average £6 per year per thousand cubic feet 'as much as is paid for the most aristocratic mansions in London' (6). And there were many examples elsewhere of such speculation (see Jackson, 1976; Bauer, 1934; Dawson, 1914). So in value for money terms the working class often paid very high rents indeed. Burnett notes that a single room could not be had in London around 1850 for less than 1s. 6d. (7½p) to 2s. 6d. (12½p) a week. As this was the most that an unskilled or semi-skilled worker could afford, few workers could rent a whole house (1978, 69). Burnett states that the average proportion of working class income devoted to housing in the nineteenth century was 16%, approximately twice the proportion spent by the middle classes, but the share was inversely proportional to income, so the lowest earners might spend a third of their incomes on rent (1978, 93).

Any improvements depended first, on the growth of real incomes and second, on the growth of regulatory legislation although this alone did little positively to solve the housing problem. But such a conclusion assumes that rents only rose in line with earnings. Yet, especially as the supply of housing often lagged behind the population growth, this may not have been so. Thus Gauldie writes that rents for British workers showed an upward trend throughout the nineteenth century. They did not fall in line with other prices, for example during the last quarter of the century. In 1885 it was suggested that 60% of the wage increases of the past 50 years had been absorbed by rent increases. Moreover, there was some resistance to paying higher rents even when they could be afforded. In fact many landlords continued into the next century to offer poor accommodation at low rents - subletting and massive overcrowding ensuring that such business remained profitable. (In contrast Gauldie comments 'To make profits from property properly constructed and maintained was certainly not so easy') (1974, 167).

Although some of the worst conditions improved after the first impact of urbanisation these

6

improvements were limited. In particular, the problems of rents in relation to incomes and of overcrowding continued. A key factor was the wholly market determined supply of new housing. For Britain, Burnett notes the considerable fluctuations in house building over time and from place to place. These variations were 'determined to an important extent by local conditions such as the state of trade, the prosperity or otherwise of local industries, the level of wages and, perhaps above all, the number of "empties" on the market' (1963, 141). Chronic overcrowding persisted, exacerbated by the commercial and civic redevelopment of city centres and the demands for railway land. Rent levels put severe strain on working class budgets and, for example, the 1885 Royal Commission on the Housing of the Working Class noted with alarm that rents continued to increase in central London while wages remained static. In fact the Commission concluded that, although public health measures had improved the towns, working class housing remained wholly inadequate and overcrowding was actually increasing. Middle class houses were often converted to tenements without any expansion of sanitary arrangements and much new working class housing was jerry built (Tarn, 1973, 114).

Housing conditions elsewhere only improved slowly, if at all. In 1904 an observer noted that the working class lodgings in Paris were highly insanitary, overcrowded and inferior to their counterparts in London. Conditions were somewhat better in the blocks of working class flats, although the account makes no estimate of whether the rent levels quoted could be afforded by many working class households (Pollard and Holmes, 1972, 438). In 1911 one third to one half of the French population lived at densities above the official overcrowding level of two persons per room and in the industrial towns the situation was even worse (Zeldin, 1977, 621). In a study of Parisian housing Magri finds that overcrowding remained at a very high level from 1891 to 1914 (and only fell significantly after 1926). There was a chronic shortage of lower rented accommodation. New housing was for the better off, this was reflected in more rapidly rising rents for the cheaper accommodation. Magri shows that working class rents rose from 13.5% of incomes in 1862 to 19% by 1908 before falling slightly (1972, 83-98).

In Dusseldorf in 1900 better off workers were

paying around 15% of their incomes for a two roomed
tenement. Even the more expensive dwellings were
often defective and insanitary and rent rises were
frequent. The writer notes that the heavy demand
for accommodation enabled landlords to profit and
that building in the town was not cheap, as those
'benevolent bodies' which had built had found. But
'the difference between dwellings built by a
speculator and those by a public or benevolent body
is not that the latter are cheap, but that they are
good, whereas the former are frequently or
generally both bad and dear' (Pollard and Holmes,
1972, 441-2).

Perhaps the most reliable comparisons of rents
and incomes are those provided by the
investigations of the cost of living of the working
class carried out by the British Board of Trade
around 1910 (Board of Trade, 1908a, 1908b, 1909,
1911, 1913). The reports - on Britain, France, West
Germany and the USA - contain a great deal of
detail on working class wages, rents and
prices and were based on carefully collected
statistics in the major towns. Their findings are
worth considering in some detail.

In about half the French towns, including
Paris and many of the larger centres, the
predominant form of working class accommodation was
blocks of flats, in one third of towns small
detached and terraced houses predominated, often
subdivided. Most working class families lived in
two or three rooms and many in only one. Sanitation
was very poor and overcrowding common. Rents ranged
from about 1s. 4d. (6.7p) for one room to 4s. 4d.
(21.7p) for four rooms (about 60,000 rent
quotations were obtained on which to base these
figures). Rents in Paris were almost twice as high
as elsewhere. In comparison with Germany and
Britain, there had been few attempts by government,
housing societies or employers to improve
conditions.

In comparison with German and British towns
the French working class occupied fewer rooms and
there was a far higher incidence of single roomed
accommodation. But average rents were about 20%
lower than in either of these countries, while food
and fuel were more expensive. Hourly wage rates
were considerably lower than in Britain and
somewhat lower than in Germany.

In Germany two and three roomed tenements were
most common, these were often located on the upper
floor of large houses whose lower storeys were

8

occupied by middle class residents or in large
tenements which 'often resemble large barracks
built round small paved courtyards' (Board of Trade
1908, xii). Rents ranged from 2s. 8d. (13.3p) for
two rooms to 6s.0d. (30p) for four rooms and in
Berlin, as in Paris, rents were almost double those
elsewhere. There was considerable employer provided
housing, especially in the Ruhr, and numerous
efforts to provide housing by building societies
and semi-philanthropic organisation. In comparison
with Britain, German wages were considerably lower
and the cost of rent, food and fuel together was
higher.

In Britain most of the working class lived in
terraced or other small houses. Four and five
roomed accommodation was most common and, as
already noted, rents were similar to those paid in
Germany but higher than those in France. Taking
rents, other costs of living and wages together,
the British working class experienced rather better
conditions than its French and German counterparts.

However, the most significant differences were
between the position in the USA and in Europe.
There was a far wider range of types of
accommodation in the USA, with many single family
houses. Large tenements were only common in
Cincinnati and New York. The report noted the
socio-spatial segregation in American cities, with
blacks and recent immigrants occupying the worse
property in the worst areas (also blacks paid more
than whites for similar accommodation). Four and
five roomed accommodation was most common but many
occupied six rooms. Rents ranged from 6s. 9d.
(33.8p) for three rooms to 17s. 4d. (85p) for six
rooms. There was much less of a gap between average
rents in New York and elsewhere than in the case of
Paris or Berlin. The average quality of housing
was superior to that in the three European
countries with better sanitation, water supply and
heating arrangements. The Board of Trade concluded
that the greater prosperity of the American working
class was the reason for this difference. There was
no municipal housing provision and very little
employer provided or philanthropic accommodation.
Average rents were about twice as high in the USA
as in Britain and food cost about 40% more. In
weighted combination, food and rent was about 50%
more costly than in Britain, but this was more than
offset by wages which were about 2¼ times higher.

In all four countries many lived in appalling

conditions but it is clear that working class
housing was most adequate in the USA followed by,
in declining order of adequacy, Britain, Germany
and France. Given the relative economic strength of
these countries at this time this order is not
unexpected, although other factors, such as the
strength of the trade unions and hence their
ability to bargain up wages and the relative prices
of housing and land also have to be taken into
account (7). While comparative data for the
Netherlands and Denmark was not collected by the
Board of Trade, it seems reasonable to suppose that
their housing conditions were inferior to those in
at least the first three of the four countries
discussed above.

THE SUPPLY OF HOUSING

It is not difficult to understand why private
renting dominated the supply of housing in the new
cities. Wages were low, fluctuating and uncertain
and there was a great deal of mobility, much of it
enforced, as people moved in search of work.
Opportunities for the sort of low income, self
built housing which had arisen from the social and
economic relationships of the countryside were
inoperative in the urban market in land and
property. And the cost of owner occupation was well
beyond the means of the vast majority of the
population. Despite this, many housing reformers
suggested that working class owner occupation was
the ideal to be aimed at, not subsidised rental
housing. This was particularly the view of some
American housing reformers at the end of the
century and in the period before 1914 (Robbins,
1966, 9-11).
In Britain from the end of the eighteenth
century better off workers banded together to form
building clubs, to which they contributed their own
labour and finance to provide housing. This form of
working class organisation soon declined. Later,
permanent building societies began to grow but they
could not provide housing for the majority of the
working class. Gauldie summarises the situation,

'For the working man the payment of
membership dues, however small, over
a period of years was dependent on
steady employment and good health.
Neither could be taken for granted.

The Growth of Private Rented Housing

> The chances of avoiding unemployment became
> even slighter in the last quarter of the
> century, and ... the prevailing poor diet
> and insanitary housing ensured a level of
> health in townsmen that made them prone to
> infectious ailments of every kind ...'
> (Gauldie, 1974, 201)

Another possibility was employer provided housing.
This was not just a solution to the problem of
ensuring the availability of a labour force but a
means to industrial discipline too. Several
developments, such as those by Cadbury and Lever in
Britain and Pullman in the USA, became famous but
employer provided housing was particularly
significant in Germany (in line with the general
development in this country of paternalistic social
policies aimed at controlling the working class)
especially in the Ruhr.

> 'In 1900 12 per cent of the population of
> Essen lived in Krupp apartments, at rents
> 15 to 20 per cent below open market rates
> for similar accommodation. Despite the
> imposition of stringent directions on "how
> to live in a flat", including the right of
> Krupp housing inspectors to enter the
> dwellings at any time, married Krupp workers
> flocked to queue for these apartments ...
> Such housing schemes ... became increasingly
> popular [generally in the area]. The
> provision of housing to retain skilled
> workers, especially in isolated locations,
> was a long established custom ...'.

But the extent to which these schemes did reduce
labour turnover is arguable and, as the above quote
shows, they were mainly provided for skilled
workers (Lee, 1978, 461-2).

The most discussed alternative to private
renting was housing provided by the philanthropic
bodies which existed from about mid century onwards
in many countries (see Bauer, 1934; McKelvey, 1963,
118). In most cases housing reformers saw
philanthropic, limited dividend housing as their
main objective. Demands for direct state
intervention only arose as the failure of such an
approach became apparent (8).

Writing in the 1930's Catherine Bauer noted
that France, Britain and Holland all had 'model
housing' experiments from the 1850's. These she

refers to as a 'flurry of "model housing" and still
born legislation, directly inspired by the
activities of Prince Albert [who promoted such
experiments in Britain at the Great Exhibition of
1851], but nevertheless quite traceable to the fear
of a revolution ...'. Writing, for example, about
the French developments inspired by Napoleon III
she concludes 'The results were all too expensive
for any but the comfortable middle class, and the
tenements at least were among the worst "model"
dwellings ever constructed' (1934, 290). Tarn
(1973) has made the most detailed study of '5%
philanthropy' in Britain, and shows that for all
the housing companies' efforts, and despite some
state aid, their output was small and they did not
provide housing for the mass of the unskilled
working class.

Bauer refers with more enthusiasm to the
development of co-operative housing. In the late
eighties Germany passed the first major social
insurance scheme and also a law recognising
co-operative and limited dividend housing
societies. These developed quite rapidly under the
influence of workers' organisations and the middle
class social reform movement. By 1914 there were
about 1400 co-operatives, the basis for their
growth was cheap money supplied by the social
insurance funds. She also notes the development of
co-operative housing in Denmark. In this case it
was a relatively small part of the large scale
growth of co-operatives, especially in agriculture.

But, despite these alternatives, the private
landlord was the main provider of housing in the
larger cities, although in the USA, except in the
large industrial cities of the North and East, the
landlord was less dominant than in most European
cities. As Warner notes, from about the 1880's,
aided by the development of transport and the
plentiful supply of land, many middle and working
class Americans lived in single family suburban
houses (1972, 201). It was only in the centre of
the bigger cities that high density tenements
prevailed. Nevertheless, in 1900 63.5% of all US
non-farm housing was rented (US Bureau of the
Census, 1961, 395).

As we have seen, for all its faults, rented
housing was more congruent with the needs of the
working class than other forms of housing but this
in itself did not guarantee a supply of such
housing. Of course the essential fact here was that
profits could be made from renting and in the towns

The Growth of Private Rented Housing

there was a growing mass of small investors-
professionals, shopkeepers, builders and so on -
with capital. In all six countries it was the small
local investor who provided most rented housing. At
a time when their possibilities for investment were
limited and risky, investment in housing was
probably the main outlet for such capital. Rapid
growth meant that, even allowing for the ups and
downs of the local economy, the demand for housing
persisted. Moreover, rather than investing in some
remote and uncontrollable enterprise, becoming a
landlord enabled personal control to be maintained
over the investment. Indeed a common pattern in
Germany and other countries, with most building
in blocks of flats, was for the owner to live in
one unit and let out the rest. Local political and
other connexions were of value in ensuring, for
example, that building and public health laws did
not impinge too heavily on the profitability of
property (9).
　　There were two strategies available to
investors. The first was to build. In every country
the rents of new property meant that most new
building was for the middle class and some of the
better paid artisan or skilled working class. The
second path to profitability involved the sub-
division of housing originally built for higher
income groups into smaller spaces and/or other
methods of reducing the space and quality of
accommodation available to a level which could be
afforded by the mass of the working class.
　　A detailed comparison of building and
investment in the six countries would go beyond the
scope of this chapter but some aspects of these
processes can be illustrated with details from
specific countries. Writing about Britain, Gauldie
makes the point about the attractiveness of
housing for the small investor,

> '... the advice to put money in housing
> was based fairly soundly on the knowledge
> that housing survives periods of non-
> profitability ... for the small investor
> it compared very favourably with other
> destinations for his money which could
> seem like so many pieces of paper. Homes
> for the people remained necessary, some
> portion at least of the rents continued
> to be paid when railway manias and
> mining rushes had come and gone' (1974,
> 180).

The Growth of Private Rented Housing

And these investors were '... seldom big time
financiers' Gauldie refers to widows, spinsters
and orphans provided for by the family purchase of
houses which provided a small income and perhaps a
home and tradesmen and shopkeepers doing likewise,
living in the larger corner house and collecting
rents from the rest. Lawyers often played a key
role, advising clients where to invest. This
concentration of ownership among small investors
has recently been documented by Offer who shows
that in the United Kingdom in 1913 house and
business property formed 50% of the wealth of small
businessmen, professionals and other investors
(1981, 129). Those who had greater wealth held
proportionately less of it in this form.
    The social and economic relations which
determined the supply of rental housing in the
nineteenth century have been under-researched but
in Britain Offer's work provides new insights into
the relationships of law, politics and economics in
property development in late Victorian and
Edwardian England. And some of the earlier
developments have been examined by Ball who shows
how economic, political and ideological
considerations combined to structure the production
and ownership of rental housing. He concludes;

        'The precise relationship between each agent
        [in capitalist housing provision] evolved as
        a result of the pre-existing social relations
        in building and the desire for profit ...
        The separation between landowner, developer,
        builder and landlord was not simply as a
        a result of a specialisation in technical
        function but arose because of differences
        in their respective economic interests.
        In this, the attempt to minimise the risks
        involved in speculation were crucial. It led
        landowners to remain as rent receivers;
        estate developers to avoid as much capital
        outlay on building as possible; the actual
        housebuilders to remain as small capitals
        with little possibility of transforming
        the production process; and landlords to
        buy completed houses on the general market
        rather than having them specifically
        commissioned' (1981, 172-3).

These roles could be combined but 'The main effect
would be to enhance considerably the risk of

bankruptcy'. These middlemen added to the high cost
of building which also made existing housing very
profitable so that 'It put a very effective
constraint on the supply of housing at rents which
most workers could afford. Rents on existing houses
could rocket, and workers could be packed into
appalling conditions, in the knowledge that with
minimum state intervention little alternative
existed' (1981, 174).

New building was not always the most popular
investment and 'the ownership of old house property
was often more attractive than the building of new,
because the old property was in the central urban
areas where high rents could be extracted even when
repairs were neglected' (Gauldie, 1974, 183). These
high rents were a consequence of the factors
analysed by Ball and are explained by Burnett thus,

> 'Behind these reasons for high rents also
> lay the high profits which were being
> made from rack-renting in central area
> properties. The lease holders of most
> house-property in the poorer districts
> were not large capitalists but small
> businessmen, shopkeepers or publicans
> ... Much dealing was done by such men
> in "fag ends" of leases which had only
> a few years to run: these would be relet
> to middlemen ... who were under a fixed
> obligation to the ground landlord and
> made their own profit by overcrowding
> and charging extortionate rents. Houses
> would be broken up for subletting ...'
> (1978, 150).

The factors which determined the supply of rental
housing in Britain were not identical to those
operative elsewhere. But Jackson's account of
housing in New York echoes, with variations, many of
the same points. Thus a report in 1853 found that
'large profits were being made on slum dwellings and
that even the better newly built tenements were
'overstocked with inmates ...' (1976, 12). Most
tenements were owned by small investors and the
return was expected to be at least 10% (in New York
the aim of housing reform was 'philanthropy at 7%'
rather than the British 5%).

Regarding the means by which workers met the
high rents, 'The solution was the paying lodger'
(1976, 85). And, as in London, complex financial and
ownership relations led to high rents, although in

The Growth of Private Rented Housing

New York the details were rather different as
Lawrence Veiller, a leading reformer, noted. The
building owner, often an immigrant, was last in the
line of those who profited. The land was bought by
building loan operators who sold small plots to
builders at a 10% mark up with repayment at an
interest rate of 5½-6% and lent them cash for
materials and labour. Buildings were sold to their
landlords at a price substantially above the cost
of land and building, because of the middlemens'
profits (1976, 121).
    In New York, as in Britain, new building was
mainly for the better off and low cost building
declined in the late nineteenth century (Magri
reports similarly for Paris at this time (1972, 83-
98)). This occurred particularly after legislation
prevented new building to the lowest standards
(hence raising rents). This increased the pressure
of demand for the older housing, which was cheaper
to buy than new housing yet was easily financed,
being a good investment. Thus tenements in the Lower
East Side of New York were highly desirable
properties, 'During 1903-1905 almost every tenement
building had been sold at least once and sometimes
several times a profit' and in the areas of densest
settlement it was said that 'it is possible to
raise the rent as high as a man likes to do' (1976,
146).
    In France, Zeldin notes that in 1848 58% of
wealth was in land and houses which were considered
'the safest form of investment ... the investor
liked to know personally exactly where he was
putting his money . .. he would buy ... a house
whose tenants he would choose' (1973, 59). In the
third quarter of the century, as land prices began
to fall, housing became even more popular. Rents
tripled in value from 1850 to 1913 while house
building expanded rapidly (although there were,
as elsewhere, shorter term fluctuations in building
and in rents). The housing was usually constructed
by small builders using short term credit and
minimising risks. Property developers and banks
played important roles too (Lévy-Leboyer, 1978).
    Similar developments occurred in Germany
(Tilly, 1978, 399-410). Here speculative profits
were especially high. Thus Bauer notes that
speculation in the rapidly growing German cities led
to very high land values, so that in Berlin before
1914 values were 8-10 times higher than in London.
The result was high rents, overcrowding and
tenements 'of a grimness only surpassed in the worst

16

The Growth of Private Rented Housing

Glasgow flats and in the New York Old Law tenement'
(1934, 271).
    Writing in 1914, Dawson refers to 'wild and
often unprincipled speculation', 'unsound and
unscrupulous' building enterprise and the
'pernicious gambling of land companies' (1914, 165-
8). He continues

> '...much ... of the building is done by
> men of straw, working with money borrowed
> at high rates of interest. These speculative
> builders live from hand to mouth, they are
> provided with funds week by week to cover
> the current outlay ... by the time they
> have completed a block of dwellings the
> interest paid or accrued on advances and
> on the heavy outstanding mortgage that
> remains often represents a standing charge
> quite out of proportion to the intrinsic
> value of the property, and this charge the
> tenants have to pay. A large amount of
> house property ... is heavily mortgaged,
> thanks to the existence of an abundance
> of banks and money lenders who are prepared
> to advance readily up to a very narrow
> margin of security. The effect is to draw
> into the web of house speculation hosts
> of people without either the brains or the
> conscience necessary to the responsible
> management of property'.

Loans were so generous that the purchaser of a
property only had to meet between one fifteenth and
one twelth of the price. It could be let at rents
which brought a net return on this of 1-1½% i.e. 12%
or more on the actual investment. Moreover, as
elsewhere, middlemen's profits were not confined to
new housing for,

> 'Incidental to the practice of frivolous
> borrowing is the pernicious custom of house
> farming. A large owner of working class
> property will let a whole "book" of dwellings
> - often as many as a hundred - to a middle-
> man agent whose only capital is his capacity
> to screw out of the tenants a shilling or
> two a week beyond the amount which he agrees
> to pay the landlord in chief.'

The Growth of Private Rented Housing

EARLY LEGISLATION

Legislation concerning building existed long before
massive urbanisation occurred. For example,
Copenhagen's first building act dates from 1683
(Socialt Tidsskrift, 1947, 422). Typically, such
legislation was concerned with public safety. In
France, Germany, and the Netherlands, local mayors
had a general 'police power' to preserve hygiene,
safety and morals (Dennery, 1935, 47; Dawson, 1914,
180-1; Van der Kaa, 1935, 15). This could involve
the abatement of poor housing conditions. Similar
powers existed in Britain, Denmark and the USA
(Tarn, 1973, 1-8; Socialt Tiddskrift, 1947, 422;
Warner, 1972, 26). These laws were almost wholly
regulatory.
    This legislation made little impact on
conditions within the dwellings and rarely existed
outside the main towns, where several motives and
interests led to more effective laws in the
nineteenth century. Most obviously there was concern
for public health, given the spread of diseases
such as typhus and cholera. Also there was often a
concern with the slums as breeding grounds of
disorder and immorality (the latter often written
about as if it was a sort of political and
social contagious disease). Moreover, slum clearance
legislation was often used for financial gain by
railway companies and for commercial and civic redevelopment. Finally, there were sometimes demands
for action to improve the reproduction of the labour
force - a concern with what in Britain was called
'national efficiency'.
    The limitations of early legislation can be
illustrated by reference to Britain and the USA.
Britain encountered the new housing problem first.
But the creation of mass slums was well underway
before any national legislation occurred. The
immediate causes of action were epidemics of typhus
and cholera in the late 1830s which led to three
enquiries into the health of towns, one of which
contained the first comprehensive social and medical
survey of conditions and showed that existing
controls over building and sanitation were
ineffective (Tarn, 1973, 1-12). The reports led to
the passing of a new London building act and a
Public Health Act in 1848 establishing local and
central administrative bodies with powers over water
supply and sanitation. But these powers were weak
and permissive. Yet opposition from property owners
was strong and the arrangements by which the boards

levied local taxes and were controlled by the taxpayers had obvious limitations. The first housing
legislation came in 1851, it aimed to control
overcrowding in common lodging houses, where the
worse conditions were (Gauldie, 1974, 239-50). At
the same time local authorities were given power
to provide such housing, although very little was
built.

Conditions in the capital city, London,
gave most cause for concern, not that they were
better elsewhere. In the 1850s various reforms
provided the first reasonably effective framework of
local administration for London and powers
concerning building, sanitation and street works
(Wohl, 1977, 109-40). But most legislation failed to
get to grips with the central problem - the
inability of the mass to afford adequate housing.
Not until the late 1860s was some attempt made to
deal with poor housing, when local authorities
were given powers to enforce the repair or
demolition of insanitary houses. But local property
interests determined whether action was taken and,
as there was no compensation for demolished
property, little resulted (Gauldie, 1974, 265-81).

After 1875 housing and health legislation
began to make an impact on the freedom of private
landlords to provide housing on their own terms.
Although the Public Health Act passed in this year
still contained mainly permissive powers it did cover
sanitation, water supply, controls over cellar
dwellings, common lodging houses and other lodgings,
overcrowding and regulations governing the layout,
construction and equipment of new housing.
Increasingly, these powers were adopted locally
and some of the worst building ceased (Tarn, 1973,
74-7).

But their impact was uneven, much depended on
local politics and regulatory powers were
ineffective in getting to the root of the housing
problem (10). In London for example, the reduction of
overcrowding and demolition left the displaced
tenants to invade contiguous areas and recreate
the earlier conditions (Wohl, 1977, 117). An attempt
to deal with this problem also occurred in 1875.
Local authorities were given powers to clear areas
of insanitary housing, finding new housing for
those displaced. But the act was permissive and
involved local expenditure for rehousing and for
paying (until amended) exorbitant compensation. Soon
the rehousing obligation was weakened and, while in
Birmingham it aided the commercial and civic

redevelopment of the city, little new housing occurred and such housing was too expensive for most displacees (Hennock, 1973, 125-30; Tarn, 1973, 92-3). Increasingly, it became clear that housing the poor could not be achieved at a price which they could and would afford without reproducing the conditions which the public health acts aimed to end. But political action, while possibly informed by the activities of social reformers, was dependent on more fundamental social forces. Foster, in an analysis of these factors in London, points out that these varied from place to place, this was true internationally also (1979). In London, housing legislation tended to occur when there was a glut of property, not a shortage. Measures to, for example, abate overcrowding were supported by property interests when housebuilders were anxious to stimulate demand (11). Increasingly too, social policy was a response to the growth of the organised working class, although, as Foster shows, this was no simple relationship.

But resistance to interference with property rights and rejection of a positive state responsibility for low income housing was strong, despite concern with the political threat posed by the urban poor. The diagnosis of the problem might become more realistic, in 1885 a Royal Commission noted the prime cause as 'the relationship borne by the wages they receive to the rents they have to pav' but action was limited, although an act of 1890 gave councils power, though no subsidies, to provide working class housing (12). In fact before 1919, apart from pressure from the growing labour movement (Wohl, 1977, 317-40, but see also Foster, 1979), the main support for state provision of rented housing came from property interests, specifically from rural landowners and urban developers (13). Due to low agricultural wages, the rural provision of rented housing had collapsed so employers either had to raise wages or get the state to assume responsibility in order to maintain an adequate workforce. Also state relief was desired in order to remove the burden of rehousing those displaced by city redevelopment from those who profited from this.

The development of British legislation may be compared with that in the USA. An important difference between the two countries was that in the US federal system the national government had no role in housing and public health until much later. Constitutionally the individual states bore this responsibility, in fact the cities were usually the first to respond and developments in New York were the most significant (14).

The early development of housing in New York was as unregulated as it had been in Britain. But in 1866 a public health act was passed and a Board of Health established. This development, preceded by an investigation of slums in the city, owed a good deal of its inspiration to the British Public Health Act and the examinations which had preceded it. It was followed, in 1867, by the first act to regulate tenement design. These measures were inspired by the fear of disease but also by political fear which was perhaps an even stronger theme in nineteenth century urban America, in which mass immigration posed major problems of social integration. In New York the 1863 Draft Riots, large scale mob violence involving class and racial conflict, led to a check in the opposition of property interests to government regulation.

But as these problems faded so did the impetus to reform. The 1867 law was evaded and did little to improve living conditions. Patronage and corruption were rife and made the operation of building controls ineffective. Whereas in Britain there was a slow progression in state intervention in housing, in New York reform was a cause normally carried forward by a band of middle class enthusiasts. In this respect housing reform reflects differences in the conditions for the evolution of social policy as a whole in the two countries. As Rimlinger (1971) has shown, free market interests and ideologies were more powerful and more able to retard and mould social policy in the USA than they were in Europe, where both conservative paternalism and the rising labour movement had more impact.

In the late 1870s New York's tenement design requirements and building regulations were tightened. Interestingly, echoing the point made by Foster regarding British legislation, the reformers were supported by some property interests who wanted to eliminate the 'unfair' competition from speculators. But the gradual improvement of new housing after this time did nothing to improve the existing mass of slum housing, although demolition powers were strengthened in the 1890s. As we have noted, what probably improved standards as much as anything else was the economic growth which occurred.

As we have seen in Britain by 1890 there was legislation which, though weak, did enable some public housing to be built. In the USA housing

The Growth of Private Rented Housing

reformers looked to the regulation of private
enterprise rather than its supplementation (Robbins,
1966). The first reasonably effective tenement house
law in New York was passed in 1901 - it became a
model for a few other cities (Wendt, 1962, 144;
Friedman, 1968, 33-9). It was preceded by a
commission of inquiry controlled by the housing
reformers. Their attitude to municipal housing is
summarised by Jackson,

> '... [municipal tenements] were inconceivable.
> No large city, it was argued, could provide
> homes for all its working population. Who,
> then, would benefit other than those with
> "influence"? And even they would trade better
> housing for lack of independence. That which
> might work in Europe was unacceptable in New
> York, where reformers could envisage the
> administration stacking municipal tenements
> with voters ensuring continuing political
> support ...[so] the commission was left to
> counter existing deficiencies by modifying
> the law' (1976, 121).

Even at this time US housing reformers stressed
the moral, political and social value of encouraging
working class owner occupation - they looked to
better private market solutions rather than, as was
increasingly the case in Europe, alternative non
profit forms of rental housing.

The effects of legislation in both countries
were accompanied in the upper and middle ranges of
the rental market by rising standards due to the
growth of middle and better off working class
incomes. There was a growth of suburban housing,
aided by transport developments, and improvements in
the planning and facilities of dwellings (Warner,
1962; Dyos and Reeder, 1973). But much of the
working class remained tied to the city centres,
with the low and uncertain incomes they provided.
They continued to depend on private landlords,
supplying poor housing at rents (more or less)
within their means. Yet the growing demand for middle
income housing in the new suburbs, the impact of
regulatory legislation and the growth of more
profitable uses of city land, all helped to reduce
the likelihood that these landlords could or would
provide adequate housing for most of the working
class. And, as the work of the limited profit
companies showed, this housing could not be provided
at rents which were bearable by those in or on the

margins of poverty. Moreover, the belief
(especially strong in America) that the problem of
housing for the poor would be solved by the
'filtering' process proved false (15) (Jackson,
1976, 138-57). The alternative solutions to this
problem were higher wages or subsidised rents (16).

In Germany, as in America, there was a federal
system after 1870 and a history of strong city
government. In addition opposition to state
intervention was much less than in Britain or the
USA (Rimlinger, 1971). The German social welfare
system was an attempt to deflect rising working
class organisation. There was intervention in cities
too. Bauer summarised the situation thus,

> 'Pure Liberal individualism has never
> played an important role in Germany.
> On the one hand there was the authoritarian
> Imperial State whose interests were to be
> served above all others and which, to safe-
> guard those interests, guaranteed a minimum
> of physical security to its underlings in
> the form of social insurance. And on the
> other hand there was the much older and even
> more deeply embedded tradition of city as
> a working organism in which every citizen ...
> took an active pride' (1934, 97).

She also stated that there was little 'social
idealism' in the attitudes of ruling burghers, they
felt that, with the other citizens, they were 'a
shareholder in the town ... the quality should be
improved continually ... and that it should be
managed in an efficient and business like way as
possible' (1934, 98).

Despite this concern, however orderly German
cities might first appear, the grimness of the
housing conditions seems unlikely to have been less
than in Britain or the USA. The contrast was noted
by an observer in 1914. 'Outwardly the streets of a
German town usually give the impression of order,
cleanliness, comfort and well-being. Except in the
older quarters the streets are wide and well kept
... It is only when the high portals ... are passed
... and the interior ... inspected that the special
character and seriousness of Germany's housing
problem will be properly understood' (Dawson, 1914,
162). Dawson also refers to perverse building
regulations made to suit speculators, narrow unlit
corridors, semi-dark rooms, and neglect by the
authorities.

23

The Growth of Private Rented Housing

    Conditions were worst in the new industrial
towns, despite comparatively developed powers to
regulate land use. The towns had 'extensive
administrative areas, ... an abundance of open land,
excellent town building plans, large estates [i.e.
land] in municipal hands, wide powers to regulate
housebuilding ... unlimited opportunities of
helping building societies by the sale of public
land and the loan of public money' (Dawson, 1914,
163, see also Wendt, 1962, 113). Such powers were,
according to Bauer, the consequence of the
distinctive German attitude to urban management.
As Dawson noted, they included direct control and
ownership of land as well as powers to assist
housing co-operatives and other limited profit
housing with the funds of the social insurance
scheme (17) (1914, 176). Yet these powers were
ineffective when it came to the question of housing
supply. Indeed, as we have seen, speculation was
extensive and the working class quarters of Berlin
in particular were massively overcrowded (Dawson,
1914, 163).
    Nevertheless, state responsibility for urban
conditions was more advanced in Germany than
elsewhere by the turn of the century (Bauer, 1934,
97-101, 270-2; Dawson, 1914, 161-88). It included
some responsibility for providing of new housing to
replace slum cleared property, loans on preferential
terms for organisations to build moderate rental
housing from state insurance and other funds,,
housing for municipal employees and house
inspection and registration. Direct municipal house
building was rare, support for limited profit
builders (including co-operatives) was more common.
Low interest loans, cheap land, and, in some cases,
local tax exemptions were the main forms of subsidy.
Housing inspection was a matter for local police
powers, although by the 1900s some states were
beginning to legislate. The co-optive and
paternalistic nature of much housing (and other
social policy) is captured in this description of
Bavarian house inspection (or 'house care'),

    'The housing committees are ... composed
    of representatives of the houseowners and
    tenants [the statutory sickness funds and
    building societies being represented],
    members of the municipal authority, Poor
    Law officials, municipal doctors and women
    chosen for their interest in social work.
    Stress is laid upon friendly advice rather

than coercion; only when such advice
fails to effect does the executive intervene
with stronger measures' (Dawson 1914, 182).

Municipal house registries, an idea that was to
persist, existed in about 40 towns by 1914. They
provided a register of vacant lettings. Occasionally
landlords with working class property to let were
compelled to register it. Normally the registers
were voluntary and probably only assisted a minority
of those who applied. Efforts to improve existing
housing seem to have been fairly ineffective.

French developments were slower than those in
Germany or Britain (Board of Trade, 1909, xiv).
France's slow population growth may have been
significant (Read, 1976, 297). Bauer notes that, for
this reason, acute housing shortage was confined to
rapidly growing cities, above all Paris (1934, 290).
In addition the authorities faced the housing
problem with little interest or enthusiasm and
resistance from private property to state action
was strong (Denby, 1938, 216). Apart from Haussman's
Paris clearances (which involved no rehousing),
little action occurred and such minimal controls as
existed relied on the communal exercise of police
powers. Dennery noted this lack of progress in
comparison with Britain, Germany and the
Netherlands and listed as contributory factors the
lesser concern with housing conditions on the part
of the working class and politicians, the
fragmentation of property ownership which made
action more difficult (together with opposition to
compulsory land acquisition), the small scale of
building enterprises and the relatively slow rate
of urbanisation (1935, 7). A 1902 law reaffirmed
that mayors had responsibility for sanitary and
housing conditions in their areas, subject to
prefectorial control (1935, 47). Dennery concluded
that these powers were weak and only enforced to a
limited degree, for example, in Parisian lodging
houses and hotels. He noted that the elected mayors
had some powers 'mais le maire ... hésite parfois à
mécontenter ses administrés. Il ne désire pas se
creér, dans sa circonscription une opposition
certaine, par une application trop stricte du
règlement' (1935, 50).

The first attempt to legislate for the low
income housing problem came when the 1894 Loi
Siegfried provided for low income loans from state
pension and other funds and tax exemption for
approved housing organisations (18). But the Act

was concerned with moderate income owner occupation, not low income rental housing. Just before the First World War there were two measures to allow the establishment (where localities so resolved) of semi official Public Housing Offices, which could be involved in the provision of housing under the 1894 Act and administer housing and sanitary regulations, and the provision of some assistance to meet the housing costs of large families (Bauer, 1934, 291).

Analysing the political and economic factors behind housing policy is at this time, Magri notes that it was concerned to promote stability via working class owner occupation and to encourage private initiative (1972, 120). Both these seem to have been stronger themes in France than, for example, in Britain at the same period (19). And the rents of such limited profit housing as there was were too high for most of the working class - as elsewhere.

In the Netherlands the physical circumstances of much of the country and the growth of population density contributed to an early development of local powers to control land use but, as elsewhere, the early growth of the new cities was dominated by market processes. Denby notes that between 1870 and 1900 Amsterdam expanded rapidly with much uncontrolled speculative jerry building just outside the city's boundary. A plan by the city's architect was 'summarily rejected by the Councillors who at that time believed in private enterprise and free development' (1938, 65). By 1890 though the city was buying up undeveloped land in order to try to control development.

In comparison with Britain or the USA the Netherlands seemed, after the first phase of post 1870 uncontrolled urbanisation, to have moved rapidly towards quite comprehensive national legislation. The 1901 Housing Act required local authorities to establish minimum housing and sanitary standards, gave powers of inspection, condemnation and compulsory purchase of land and property (on the basis of existing use value), required larger and rapidly growing towns to make town expansion plans and provided loans for limited dividend and municipal rented housing. But, as elsewhere, there was still reliance on private enterprise , thus the local authorities had a duty to assess whether there was sufficient low cost housing in their area and could only build or provide loans if private enterprise refused to build. In fact the legal provisions were more impressive in theory than in practice as they resulted in only about 16,000 new units between 1905 and 1914 (Bauer, 1934, 283).

Denmark had the by now familiar early history of housing legislation, with limited and ineffective controls and some philanthropic housing from the 1850s (Socialt Tidsskrift, 1947 428-9; Bauer, 1934, 298-9). But, as in the Netherlands and Germany, municipal intervention in the land market seems to have been tolerated, perhaps because it could, by influencing land values, be of benefit to speculative builders (Socialt Tidsskirift, 1947, 426). Thus Copenhagen bought underdeveloped suburban land and controlled what, on resale, was built on it. As in Germany, assistance for local authority or limited profit housing came in the late 1880s, when second mortgages were provided advantageous terms. But these policies made little impact before 1914 (Socialt Tidsskrift, 1947, 428-9; Bauer, 1934, 298).

We have dealt in this section with the evolution of housing markets and policies and the private rented sector from the onset of industrialisation and urbanisation to 1914. In Britain this period amounted to about 100 years, in some of the other countries it amounted to barely half this period. But it was during these years that the private rented sector was established, that its inability to solve the low income housing problem became manifest and that very limited state intervention began to occur. The First World War brought about more far reaching developments.

THE FIRST WORLD WAR AND ITS AFTERMATH

In the First World War the belligerent states, France, Germany and Great Britain, suffered more profound economic, political and physical upheavals than neutral Denmark and the Netherlands. The USA, entering the war in 1917, also felt some effect but was far less severely affected than any of the five European nations (20).

In a survey of developments from 1914-23 the International Labour Office (1923) analysed the impact of these years on European housing markets. The principal changes which occurred were;

The Growth of Private Rented Housing

1. The cessation of housebuilding in the belligerent countries and a considerable contraction elsewhere in Europe. This created severe housing shortages, exacerbated by flows of refugees and war workers into major cities. Statistics collected by the ILO show that by 1918 new house building in Britain, Denmark, Germany and France was at a fraction of its pre-war level (1923, 12). Only in the Netherlands was the decline relatively short lived but still severe (see also van Weesep, 1982, 12-13).

2. The main response was to introduce rent controls, starting in France in 1914 (where for some tenants there was a rent moratorium), in Britain in 1915, in Denmark in 1916 and in Germany and the Netherlands in 1917. Security of tenure accompanied these controls. Denmark and Germany also had controls on the occupancy of housing i.e. allocation by public authorities. Also building for key industrial workers took place, on a small scale. There were political and economic reasons for the controls. Thus the ILO report refers to the need to house essential war workers and the consequent necessity to prevent shortages driving up rents to levels which the workers could not afford, the wish to control rent levels at a time of inflation in the belief that this might be only temporary and the fear that, when other prices fell, rents might not follow suit and fear of social unrest because of the housing shortage. The report concluded,

'... tenant protection legislation aimed at securing the rights of occupation of distressed tenants and preventing rent increases ... if the market had been left free, tenants would have suffered from an intolerable rises in rents and inopportune notices to quit. Against these two dangers threatening the economic and social stability of the civilian population a barrier had to be erected ...' (1923, 50).

The effects of controls were profound. The ILO report shows that by 1918 the general cost of living had approximately doubled in Denmark, France and Great Britain (no figures for Germany and the

28

Netherlands are given) but rents had stayed at
their 1914 levels (1923, 19). Moreover, the report
states 'When the Armistice was concluded it was not
for a moment possible in any country to think of
rescinding measures for the protection of tenants,
the social function of which [i.e. the political
function] now came to the fore', although some
modest increases were allowed to contribute towards
the vastly inflated landlords' costs (1923, 19-21).
These increases ranged from 35% in Denmark to 75%
in France (Paris) but on average they were
considerably less. Germany, which suffered economic
collapse and massive inflation, was an exception
having a maximum percentage increase of 58400!
But, as we shall see, this did not prevent the
collapse of its private housing market in the next
few years. Overall, by 1923, rents had fallen in
real terms by about 20% in Denmark and Great
Britain, 40% in France and 80% in Germany.

In the USA in contrast, rent controls were
introduced in a few places in 1917 and in some
others from 1918-21 to deal with the influx of
workers into major cities and profiteering (Wendt,
1962, 145). They had in most cases been soon
scrapped and rents had only fallen in real terms
by about 4% (ILO, 1923, 26-8). As the ILO pointed
out, although most new dwellings were not rent
controlled, because wage settlements took account
of the fact that the rent controls where they
existed affected most working class tenants, the
rents of new property were too high for most households. In consequence, 'no tenants for new building
can be found among the wage-earning classes. There
is therefore no incentive for private capital to
invest in building new houses' (1923, 34).

But, despite the ILO's finding that 'at the
present time there is a growing body of opinion in
most countries in favour of the abolition of rent
restrictions, in view of their economic effects',
the fear of 'dangerous results' meant that the pace
of decontrol varied from country to country
according to their particular economic and
political circumstances. In Germany and in France
(where the worst economic situations existed and
where rents had been most devalued) fear of
possible unrest led to the unchanged continuation
of controls (21) (1923, 36).

THE INTERWAR YEARS

After the War in the USA there was rapid economic

growth with rising real wages. As already noted,
rent controls soon disappeared (except in New York,
when they ended in 1929, and Massachusetts, where
they ended in 1927 (League of Nations, 1939, 145).
Suburban development and owner occupation
accelerated and, although there was a development
of local regulation (Robbins, 1966, 10; Wood, 1966,
3-4) and isolated further changes (such as limited
dividend, tax subsidised and rent controlled
housing in New York from 1926), the most
significant factor leading to improved housing was
the growing ability of sections of the working
class to buy their own homes in the suburbs or to
pay higher rents for better accommodation in the
cities. An indicator of the former change is that
the proportion of non farm owner occupied housing
increased from 40.9% to 46% between 1920 and 1930 (it
had grown by only 4% in the previous 30 years) (US
Bureau of the Census, 1961, 395). The housing
reform movement stagnated and remained, like the
broader social reform movement, without significant
support by organised capital or labour and the
problem of lower income housing was largely ignored
(Robbins, 1966, 10-11). Such government effort as
there was went into promoting owner-occupation
(Handlin, 1976, 323-4; Wendt, 1962, 147-8).
    In Europe, although the political and economic
order survived, in Germany in the form of a
republic, a simple return to the pre-war situation
was inconceivable, however much it was desired. The
situation can be illustrated by a detailed study
based on official sources, of British wartime and
early post war housing policy. Records show the
growth of working class discontent with wartime
living conditions, especially shortages of housing
and high rents (Swenarton, 1981, 81-7). They show
too that the first programme of subsidised rented
housing was initiated in 1919 above all as an
'insurance against revolution' and because, in the
inflationary conditions of the short post war boom,
there was no possibility of private enterprise
supplying the low rent housing that had been
promised to the returning troops (Swenarton, 1981,
67-87; Bowley, 1945, 2-14). At this point the
interests of the small scale capital involved in
rental housing were of little consequence compared
with those of larger scale interests and more
powerful forces.
    But soon the immediate post-war social crisis
passed, the coalition government came under pressure

for a return to orthodox economic policies and
unemployment rose as the boom ended. Trade union
resistance to wage cuts failed and, as Swenarton
concludes,

> 'Since the Armistice the pattern had been
> that while the Treasury called for the
> reduction of public expenditure the Cabinet
> was led by political imperatives towards
> generous expenditure on reconstruction,
> as an insurance against something "a great
> deal worse". Now, however, the danger was
> receding and the insurance was becoming
> superfluous' (1981, 131).

The subsidised housing programme was cut and later
ended. The main pressure for this came from
financial interests. According to Gilbert,

> '... the British government was forced to
> choose between the claims of the City of
> London as the central financial market of
> the world and the claims of domestic
> reconstruction. In this struggle the City
> prevailed and one of the important
> casualties was housing' (1970, 144).

But the small scale capital involved in rented
housing was less influential so, although rent
controls were modified, they were not abolished.
    In France similar post war shortages,
inflation, continuing rent controls and social
tensions existed (ILO, 1923, 115-28). But, although
the economy grew appreciably if patchily, there was
only a very slow rate of housebuilding and working
class pressure for reform was weak (Kemp, 1972, 70-
1). But there was considerable resistance to rent
decontrol proposals (ILO, 1923, 125). According to
Denby uncontrolled land speculation leading to very
high land prices was one reason why the authorities
were reluctant to provide much subsidised
construction (1938, 218), despite the development
of earlier legislation, notably in the 1928 Loi
Loucheur (Dennery, 1935, 33-4; ILO, 1923, 139-151).
The most significant legislation remained rent
control whose continued existence contributed to
the reluctance to build (22).
    In Germany there were more significant
developments under the Weimar republic. There was

massive inflation and the collapse of the economy,
high interest rates and a much slower development of
wages (Stolper, 1967, 74-89). Bauer estimates that
the interest rates for first mortgages rose from 4%
before the war to 10% after it and after
hyperinflation ruined many small investors few were
prepared to lend (1934, 273). The rent for a
privately financed new house in 1927 was four times
its 1914 level, yet wages only increased by 50% in
the same period. Rent controls continued and vacant
dwellings could be commandeered. In these
circumstances little new housing would have been
built without state assistance (Wendt, 1962, 114-6).
This was financed by a tax on housing (whose owners
had benefitted because inflation had wiped out the
burden of their mortgage debts and given them large
capital gains) and involved low interest second
mortgages (ILO, 1923, 317-354). Also cities often
provided land for low rent housing, sometimes
assisted by low interest first mortgages, for
example from social insurance funds (Bauer, 1934,
173-4). According to Bauer, in the five years during
which building activity was greatest (1927-31)
about 1.4 million dwellings were built, 70% with
direct government assistance and most of the rest
with indirect assistance such as cheap land, special
loans or tax exemptions (1934, 274-5). 10% of these
dwellings were built by the local authorities, 34%
by non profit housing companies (including
co-operatives and organisations allied to the labour
movement) and the rest by private enterprise (which
included many government aided limited profit landlords). Bauer estimates that only 12% of the loan
capital necessary for this building (which amounted
to 89% of its total cost) came from clearly private
sources.

Therefore, in Germany, more than elsewhere,
continuing political and economic instability led to
the virtual eclipse of unsubsidised rental
construction and a major development of state
assisted building. But Denby notes the limitations
of even this effort (1938, 143-4). Thus between 1919
and 1931 about 1.8 million new dwellings were built,
compared with the 3.4 million that would have been
built if pre-war rates of construction had
continued. Also, even with subsidies, 'the dwellings
built during the first ten years after the War were
taken by the better paid workers and the shortage of
homes for the lowest income group is still as
serious'. This point is of wider applicability

The Growth of Private Rented Housing

(League of Nations, 1939, xxvii). It was true, for example, of the new council housing in Britain (Bowley, 1945, 208-9).

In the Netherlands the pressures for a return to the private market were much more effective than in Germany. The organised working class was not strong and centre and right wing political parties dominated the interwar period, keeping the Social Democratic Party out of government until 1939, longer than any other West European socialist party (Lijphart, 1968). The response to the wartime emergency consisted of some subsidies, including for private builders, and rent control (ILO, 1923, 237-49). But these did not last after 1927 when the housing shortage was held to be over (Van der Kaa, 1935, 104-6; van Weesep, 1982, 14). Bauer estimates that 450,000 houses were built between 1919 and 1928, about 25% by limited profit bodies, 9% by local authorities and the rest by private enterprise, 20% of the latter aided by the state. 250,000 were aided and considerable numbers of these were at rents which were within the means of those that required them (1934, 284-5). She suggests that economic conditions were such that the return to the private rental market was more possible in the Netherlands than elsewhere. In the absence of effective political pressure a reversion to private enterprise is understandable but Denby (in contrast to Bauer) noted in 1938 that,

> '... there is little doubt that private
> enterprise in Holland, while meeting the
> needs of the middle and upper classes,
> is not building for families who cannot
> afford a rent above five or seven florins
> a week. This is, however, just the section
> of the community in which there is the
> greatest increase of population and the
> families are the largest. Unless, therefore,
> the State and the municipalities step in,
> the shortage will again become serious'
> (1938, 121).

In Denmark, the Social Democratic Party was an early participant in government but was the most moderate of the Scandinavian socialist parties and was involved in a political system, based on proportional representation and coalition government, in which it never had full control over policies (Berglund and Lindstrom, 1978, 37). There was high unemployment but strong pressure for a

return to the private market generally (Jorberg
and Krantz, 1976, 435; Miller, 1968, 37 62). Rent
controls were gradually repealed. Between 1917 and
1922 there were loans and subsidies for local
authority and co-operative building, half the
housing built in Copenhagen in these years was
aided, though less elsewhere. After 1922 assistance
was limited to second mortgage loans, this ceased in
1927. As elsewhere, even the aided houses were too
expensive for many and there remained a shortage of
low income housing (Socialt Tidsskrift, 1947, 432-3;
ILO, 1923, 250-66; Bauer, 1934, 298-9).

The economic depression of the thirties led to
changes in housing policy, the general trend of
which, as we have seen, was towards renewed reliance
on the private market except when and where economic
and/or political circumstances made this impossible.
In 1939 the League of Nations reported on European
housing. It noted that the economic depression
which had begun in 1929 had had a differential
impact. Countries which soon abandoned the gold
standard were able to check deflation and afterwards
adopted a cheap money policy. This stimulated
building, particularly in Britain and in Denmark.
But the Netherlands and France which remained on
the gold standard suffered rapidly rising
unemployment and falling wages, rents fell and the
private landlord faced a crisis. As a result, new
building almost ceased (23). In the USA the crisis
was so severe and rents dropped so sharply that,
despite cheap money and reflation, the building
industry only recovered slowly (League of Nations,
1939). In Germany there was a rapid movement to a
state run economy in which, at first, the building
of new urban housing for the working class was
regarded as contrary to Nazi ideology and where
there was a controlled system of prices, wages and
rents (Denby, 1938, 144-5; Stolper, 1967, 132-151).

Rent controls were one way in which European
governments responded to the situation. Controls
remained in force in France and, despite the wish to
do away with them, decontrol was limited in Britain
to higher rented and new properties. In Germany
controls remained and in the Netherlands the
government tried to force down rents (and wages) but
did not impose controls - despite protests and rent
strikes (League of Nations, 1939, 83-4; De Vries
1976, 37; van Weesep 1982, 15). In Denmark all
controls outside Copenhagen ended by 1929 but in
1936 new, rather weak, controls were introduced

The Growth of Private Rented Housing

(League of Nations, 1939, passim).

In contrast to the immediate post 1918 period, the economies of the six countries were depressed and the European socialist parties were usually in retreat (24). But in the USA organised labour was of growing political significance (25) and, when the depression led to the collapse of the housing market and the dispossession of many working class home owners, a limited programme of public housing began, not to deal with low income housing needs generally but to provide construction work and some housing for those who had to travel in search of work (26). But the most important legislation of the period aimed to promote owner occupation not rental housing (Robbins, 1966, 11-12; Warner, 1972, 232-40). But in the short run the Depression did interrupt the trend to owner occupation and the proportion of the non farm housing stock which was owner occupied fell from 46% in 1930 to 41.1% in 1940 (US Bureau of the Census, 1961, 395).

In Britain the 1929-31 minority Labour government added a new programme to the existing subsidies for rental housing (Bowley, 1945, 137). This was aimed at slum clearance and hence at lower income groups than had usually been accommodated by previous council housing. But the fall of this government resulted in the demise of these proposals and of the earlier subsidies. According to Bowley, what followed was a 'new sanitary policy' whose purpose was 'to concentrate public money and effort on the clearance and improvement of slum conditions, and to rely in the main on competitive private enterprise to provide a new supply of accommodation for the working classes' (1945, 138). She adds 'the Government had gone as near to rejecting responsibility for working class housing as it could' (1945, 140). Official recognition of the shortage of working class housing was mainly evident in a tightening of rent controls. So the private landlord rather than the government bore the major cost of assistance to low income households. In the thirties there was a boom in private building, mostly for owner occupation in the expanding suburbs of the South East where new industries had brought employment and there were increasing real incomes. Very little was located in the declining regions, even the units which were rented were only affordable by better off workers (Bowley, 1945, 175).

In France new building fell to very low levels in the thirties. Kemp notes that, in comparison

with Britain where housebuilding played a key role
in the limited economic recovery that occurred, in
France building declined from 199,000 in 1930 to
67,000 in 1938 (1972, 106-7). The stagnation of the
French economy, the lack of population growth and
the slow rate of urbanisation contributed to this,
but controls and the lack of subsidised construction
added more specific factors to the general causes of
decline. Denby commented 'the official hope was that
private enteprise would meet the need for dwellings'
(1938, 218). The 1928 Loi Loucheur was intended
to increase the supply of low and moderate income
subsidised housing by means of low interest loans
and tax exemptions (League of Nations, 1939, 80-7).
But the increase which followed was soon cut short
by the same sort of response to the economic crisis
which ended the subsidy schemes in Britain. State
loans for cheap housing rose from 837 million francs
in 1929 to 2440 million francs in 1932 but collapsed
to 47 million in 1933 and only rose to 242 million
francs by 1937 (League of Nations, 1939, 83). The
effects of these changes and the failure of the
housing market is brought out by Magri who shows
that the total output of new housing in the Paris
area fell from a peak of 41,000 in 1930 to only
5,200 in 1939 and that the output of subsidised
housing fell from 15,000 in 1933 to only 1,100 in
1939 (1972, 164). In these circumstances there was
extreme housing stress, very severe overcrowding and
the growth of 'lotissments', shanty towns on the
urban periphery (Dennery, 1935, 59-72). In the Paris
region over half the interwar increase in dwellings
took this form (Read, 1976, 304-5).

In Germany the Nazi regime ended building by
organisations connected with the labour movement.
Housing policy was wedded to the idea of moving
workers, especially the unemployed, into the
countryside. State subsidies encouraged the
construction of very low quality, owner occupied
property in rural locations. Some mortgages were
available for low rental housing but the proceeds of
the housing tax were now used for general budgetary
purposes. For ideological and economic reasons
Nazi policy was hostile to the development of large
scale urban rented housing and to the social
facilities and experiments that had accompanied such
housing in the Weimar period (Denby, 1938, 122-47;
Bauer, 1934, 176-8; Wendt, 1962, 116-9). As
elsewhere rent control was the main measure which
assisted low income households and all rents were
frozen in 1937 (Wendt, 1962, 119).

The Growth of Private Rented Housing

In the Netherlands, the early thirties saw
drastic reductions in such limited assistance as
had continued. By 1935 virtually all subsidised
construction ceased (League of Nations, 1939, 96-
100). But the shortage of low rented dwellings was,
as noted above, acute (Denby, 1938, 103). Shortages
were concentrated in the rapidly growing Randstad
area in the west of the country.
In Denmark, the return to the private market
began to be modified later in the 1930's. Miller
writes that the government, which included Social
Democrats after 1929, regarded housing as an
important issue (as the 1929-31 Labour government
in Britain did) and used construction programmes to
reduce unemployment (1968, 217). A 1933 Act again
provided subsidies for rental housing, a 1938 law
provided rent allowances for large families (League
of Nations, 1939, 54-7). The influence of the Social
Democrats seems apparent for the subsidies were
only available for non profit housing associations
(which had been brought under stricter control in
1933), local authorities and for individual owner
occupiers (there was also a small loan guarantee
programme for low cost private housing after 1938).
The rent subsidies were only available for those in
the social rented sector too, it was argued that it
would be wrong to subsidise private profit making.
But there were no new rent controls until the
reimposition of full control on the outbreak of war
(Miller, 1968, 217; Socialt Tidsskrift, 1947, 427-
8).
Two other important developments should be
listed. First, during this period increased
attention was paid to the problem of the nineteenth
and early twentieth century, mainly private rented,
city slums. As the League of Nations noted it was
gradually being realised that slum clearance could
not be left to private enterprise (1939, xviii).
First, because the new rents would be too high for
the former slum dwellers (or if affordable might
involve rearrangement of family budgets which they
would be reluctant to consider). Second, because
fragmented patterns of ownership and the necessity
to rebuild less densely reduced the profitability
of slum clearance and rebuilding. The League
concluded 'that is why, in many countries, the
conclusion has been reached that private enterprise
for profit is incapable of clearing away blighted
areas and that such work should primarily be
financed and undertaken by public authorities'
(1939, xix). In practice only in Britain was a

significant start made on publicly subsidised slum clearance and rehousing. With the war and post war housing crisis intervening, it was another 15-20 years before action became widespread. But the realisation that slum clearance needed to be subsidised and even carried out by public authorities does imply the growth of a recognition, not just by the left and housing reformers but by various other interests, that the private landlord could not wholly solve the low income housing problem.

The second major development was the growing acceptance of the need for some subsidised construction of rental housing (27). Sometimes this resulted in building by non profit organisations and local authorities. But subsidised private rental construction also became significant in the inter-war years. In Britain subsidies were provided in the twenties; in France assistance existed throughout the period and was extended in the late thirties; in the Netherlands subsidies were available after the first world war, later assistance was given via cheap second mortgages; in Germany the private sector had large scale assistance in the twenties and some support under the Nazi regime; and in the USA the Federal mortgage insurance programmes which mainly aimed at owner occupation were also available for rental construction (League of Nations, 1939, passim). Overall, what was significant was not the output from these programmes, but the fact that the idea and, to some degree, the reality of subsidised rented housing was established. It was to play a key role in housing policies after the second world war.

CONCLUSION

We have examined how and why private landlords dominated the housing markets of the expanding urban areas in the period of rapid industrialisation that commenced first in Britain and later elsewhere. The change in the housing market from the earlier forms of tenure characteristic of rural societies and their social relations to private renting, in which housing was provided as a commodity by sellers who had almost purely a pecuniary relationship with the buyers, mirrors the transformation of the economic system from pre-capitalist to capitalist forms, a transformation in which the stage of rapid industrialisation and urbanisation was predated by a longer period of less dramatic development.

38

The Growth of Private Rented Housing

The appalling living conditions in the new
cities were the product of, on the one hand, the
low and uncertain wages of the new working class
and, on the other, of uncontrolled speculation in
land and property. The situation was exacerbated
because rents tended to rise even when other prices
were stagnant or falling. There were two ways in
which the problem of low income housing was solved
by the private market, first, by cheaply
constructed or converted property and, second, by
overcrowding. The profitability of such housing was
often high and there was little incentive for
landlords to provide better quality accommodation.
Nor was there an effective demand for such housing,
outside the relatively small (but growing) middle
and upper working class. Private rented housing
provided a convenient and profitable outlet for the
funds of small investors and a complex set of
financial relationships and series of middlemen
enabled landowners and financial interests to profit
too.
Conditions slowly improved towards the end of
the century. Some sections of the working class
benefitted from rising real wages and in some cases
legislation began to be more effective, although,
in the absence of subsidised accommodation, units
provided by philanthropic or other limited profit
organisations, employers or others only made a
minor addition to supply and were usually let at
rents which limited them to skilled workers.
Early legislation was motivated by various
factors which together amount to a concern for the
preservation of the existing social order. At
first the approach was regulatory. There was an
extreme reluctance to interfere with the rights of
private property, especially in Britain and the USA
where defence of private property was most marked.
In this context the rise of the organised labour
movement and the extent to which state activity was
grounded in a more paternal or authoritarian
approach were both factors which tended to increase
the level and range of state intervention, as in the
case of other aspects of social policy. Moreover,
it was mainly small scale rather than large capital
which provided rental housing and this had its
effects too. As Friedman notes (regarding the lack
of successful opposition to tenement house reform
in the USA by landlords) it was relatively easy to
override the opposition of unorganised small
businessmen of this kind - especially at times of
economic or political crisis when more powerful

interests were at stake (1968, 39). However, it
must also be remembered that, even when government
legislated, implementation was dependent on local
administration which was open to influence by
interests hostile to change.

Demands for state subsidised housing began to
arise in Europe towards the end of the nineteenth
century. Very small amounts of subsidised housing
began to be provided in Germany, Denmark, the
Netherlands and France. In Britain local
authorities had power to supply unsubsidised
housing for general working class needs. The major
innovation of the 1914-1939 period was the
imposition of rent control during the first world
war. Controls were introduced not so much because
of high rents as such but in response to the
contribution that these made to working class
discontent and to obstructing the supply of
essential workers. The continuance of controls
after the war, together with rapid inflation in
the short post war boom and political pressures,
resulted in Europe in new or increased programmes
of subsidised rental construction. In most
countries though the easing of these pressures led
to attempts to return to the private market. In
every country this subsidised housing did not
provide accommodation at rents which could be
afforded by those living in the extensive city
slums, nor did the new private rental housing
provide affordable accommodation for them either.

The economic depression of the thirties had
varied effects. In the USA there was, for the first
time, substantial state intervention in housing
mainly to support home ownership. In Europe there
was a variety of responses which were described
in the last section. But, by 1939, while subsidised
rental housing had been tried out in all six
countries, the normal housing tenure for the
majority of the urban population remained private
renting. However, the unaided private landlord had
proved no more capable of supplying housing at
socially acceptable standards to low income workers
in the twentieth century than he or she had in the
previous century. In practice rent control was the
main means by which many governments tried to
ensure that rents stayed within the means of the
working class, even though this involved an
enforced subsidy by landlords to tenants. In many
cases severe overcrowding and poor conditions
continued to be the main ways in which the working

class housing problem was 'solved', especially in
the inner city slums, the products of the 'golden
age' of the private landlord and of industrial
capitalism.

However, the possibility of a return to this
age seemed to be less generally believed in in
1939 than it was twenty years earlier. The view that
the private landlord either had to be subsidised
or supplanted insofar as low income housing was
concerned gained ground, in Europe at least, in
these years.

The Growth of Private Rented Housing

NOTES

1. For example Zeldin notes that in France in
the 1880s 61.3% of all houses were owner occupied,
in Paris the proportion was only 29.7% whereas in
the rural communes it was 66.6% (1977, 625).
2. See note 1 above.
3. Another estimate is that in the middle of
the nineteenth century 50% of all dwellings in
large towns were rented and 42% owner occupied. By
1900 the proportions were 85% and 11% (Wells, 1932,
166).
4. For Denmark see Jorberg, 1970; Socialt
Tidsskrift, 1947; Milward and Saul, 1973; Miller,
1968; Mathias and Postan, 1978; for France see
Hinsley, 1962; Mathias and Postan, 1978; Milward
and Saul, 1973; Price, 1981; Hearder, 1966; for
Germany see Hinsley, 1962; Mathias and Postan, 1978;
Milward and Saul, 1973; Stolper, 1967; Hearder,
1966; for Britain see Hinsley, 1962; Hearder, 1966;
Mathias and Postan, 1978. For the Netherlands see
Milward and Saul, 1973; Naval Intelligence Division,
1944; for the USA see Hinsley, 1962; US Department
of Commerce, Bureau of Economic Analysis, 1973. For
a general discussion of economic growth in Europe
in the nineteenth century see Cole and Deane, 1965.
5. The German Mietkasernen were described by
many commentators (e.g. Wells,1932, 163). There is
an interesting series of discussions about building
types in the reports by the British Board of Trade
on working class living conditions in Britain,
France, Germany and the USA published between 1908
and 1913 (Board of Trade 1908a, 1908b, 1909, 1911,
1913). It has often seen suggested that these
varying national building forms were the result of
differing national propensities, for example for
apartment rather than house dwelling. Whatever the
truth of such factors, Ball points to more material
reasons why housing (usually in the form of
terraces) predominated in Britain. High density
flat construction required large sums of capital -
beyond the means of the small scale builders
operative in this country. Similarly, the maximum
number of plots - and hence profit - could be gained
by having narrow frontages so 'House size was then
varied by storey height and depth of the dwelling.
Developers and builders were able, therefore, to
adopt and adapt the traditional house form because
it suited their economic interests. Narrow frontages
became the norm for virtually every class of
dwelling, and with it the terraced house' (1981,

173). Economic considerations are likely to have played a role in determining building forms elsewhere.

6. Hole, 1866, 40 quoted in Burnett, 1978, 68. Hole's book contains one of the earliest and best examinations of the housing problem, pointing to the effects of low wages and speculation.

7. The New Cambridge Modern History notes 'Between 1876 and 1900 the average real per capita income of the population in Germany rose from £24 to £32 per annum, while that in Britain rose from £28 to £51, increases of 33 and 82 per cent respectively. The slow progress of trade unionism [in Germany] no doubt had something to do with it' (Hinsley, 1962, 62).

8. Wohl's (1977) study of housing in Victorian London discusses this in detail.

9. As Hole pointed out locally elected representatives 'are not the scientific portion of the community; but they, and those who elect them, are the lower middle class, the owners, generally speaking, of that very property which requires improvement. To ask them to close the cellar dwellings is to ask them to forfeit a portion of their income. Every pound they vote for drainage, or other sanitary improvement, is something taken out of their own pocket ...' (1866, 25).

10. Tarn (1973), Burnett (1977) have accounts of provincial developments. Hole (1866) contains a more extended contemporary study of Leeds. Hennock (1973) provides useful insights into the nature of municipal politics in Birmingham and Leeds.

11. A survey of housing in eight European countries, the USA and Canada noted (regarding house inspection) 'It has even been recommended that ... [it] ... be made more stringent, so as to encourage private initiative during a ... crisis' (League of Nations, 1939, xxxi).

12. Quoted by Gauldie (1974, 289).

13. Offer (1981) contains the most detailed and important analysis of the politics of property in this period. For the details of housing politics see Wilding (1972).

14. Jackson (1976) provides a study of low income housing in Manhattan much of which has wider geographic applicability. The following paragraphs rely heavily on his account. See also Warner, 1972; Still, 1974; Lubove, 1962; Friedman, 1968.

15. In some countries it was believed that 'model' housing, while too expensive for the poor, would enable filtering to take place. This was not

so (League of Nations, 1939, xxx).

16. As contemporary analysts realised. For example, as noted already, the British 1885 Commission on the Housing of the Working Classes wrote that the prime cause of the housing problem was 'the relationship born by the wages they receive to the rents they have to pay' (quoted Gauldie, 1974, 289). They noted that 'model' dwellings could not reach those most in need of help, but avoided the contentious issue of subsidies (Tarn, 1973, 115). Tarn comments 'Many thinking men were now prepared to accept some kind of subsidisation, but they were not prepared to recognise it as such, and in this they were only deceiving themselves' (1973, 115).

17. Bauer comments, 'Much of this new activity may be traced to the movement against Liberal individualism, which, springing from middle-class intellectuals and officials, was known as "Kathedersocialism" ' (1934, 101).

18. Magri (1972) provides an analysis of this early legislation. See also Read (1976).

19. Rimlinger notes that, despite its etatisme, France was slow to develop social rights. He relates this to the fragmented nature of the French economic and political structure and the failure of any single interest to exercise hegemony (1971, 60-1).

20. A sharp decline in residential construction in 1917 led to severe housing shortages in war affected cities.

21. In Germany there was a short revolution in 1919, followed by the establishment of the Weimar Republic in which a coalition of socialists and centrist parties ruled (Roberts, 1970, 436-8). Consequently, there was strong support for restrictions on private landlords as well as the concern with civil unrest noted in the text.

22. Certain increases in rents were allowed but despite legislation allowing for de-control of pre-1914 accommodation this was several times postponed and had not been begun by 1939 (League of Nations, 1939, 78-9).

23. In France the economy was so depressed and rents offered such a poor return that most building was for middle class owner occupation (still a small market) and 'Private enterprise has taken little apart in the erection of workers' dwellings. This has been carried out by the various cheap housing organisations in so far as was practicable with the State financial assistance

provided' (League of Nations, 1939, 72). As we
have seen this cheap housing programme soon
declined. The consequences were that housing
conditions seem to have been worse than in the
other five countries, with appalling slums and
overcrowding, the lotissments etc. (League of
Nations, 1939, 69-72).

24. In Britain the 1929-31 minority labour
government collapsed, effectively the Conservatives
took power for the rest of the decade; developments
in Germany were of course far more extreme; in
France - except for the brief period of the Popular
Front in 1936-7-conservative/centrist governments
ruled; in the Netherlands socialists only entered
the government in 1939. In Denmark the Social
Democrats formed a part of the government throughout
the thirties but its freedom of action was limited.
In many countries mass unemployment weakened the
position of organised labour too (but see note 25
below).

25. Organised labour was an important element
in the coalition that elected Roosevelt in 1932
(McCoy, 1973).

26. Roosevelt tried to delay public housing
legislation. This was strongly opposed by, among
others, labour organisations so 'The President
decided to support the bill, largely to appease
its powerful backers' (McCoy, 1973, 275).

27. This is not meant to imply that there was
a steadily growing volume of new subsidised
construction or that governments did not try to
return to the private market. But, taking interwar
developments as a whole, the growing, if grudging
acceptance that some state support was necessary
seems unmistakeable.

Chapter Two

THE NATIONAL BACKGROUND TO PRIVATE RENTING

In this chapter the six countries will be compared
in terms of size, population trends, patterns of
urbanisation, recent economic development,
administrative and political systems. In addition,
the development of their housing markets and
policies from the second world war to the late
seventies will be outlined.

POPULATION AND PATTERNS OF URBANISATION

The countries fall roughly into three size
classificiations (Eurostat, 1981, 35). First, the
United States which has a population (221 million)
and area (9.3 million sq. km) larger than the other
five countries together (all figures in this
paragraph are for 1979). Given this size, there are
substantial regional variations in physical, social
and economic circumstances. Second there are
Britain, (56 million, 0.24 million sq. km),
West Germany (61 million, 0.25 million sq. km) and
France (53 million, 0.34 million sq. km). These
countries are far smaller and more densely
populated than the USA and the variation in
conditions noted above, though still marked, is
considerably less. Third, there are the Netherlands
(14 million, 0.41 million sq. km) and Denmark
(5 million, 0.043 million sq. km). Two important
features are the high population density in the
Netherlands - about 340 persons per square
kilometre - six times the density of the USA, and
that Denmark consists of the peninsular of Jutland,
three large islands (Zealand, Funen and Bornholm)
and about 400 smaller islands. These variations in
size and density have to be borne in mind when
considering the development of the six countries'
housing situations. For example, the low density

suburbanisation of America has no counterpart in
densely populated Britain and the Netherlands or
in geographically fragmented Denmark.

The postwar rate of population growth has
varied considerably (Eurostat, 1973, pp. 66-7). In
Europe the fastest increase has been in the
Netherlands, between 1950 and 1975 its population
grew by 3.5 million (35%). But this was matched by
the USA which increased by 62 million (41%) (US
Bureau of the Census, 1979, 6). France, after
decades of stagnation and even decline, grew by 11
million (26%). West Germany, reconstituted after
the war with a population of about 46 million,
compared with 69 million in 1939 (Mitchell, 1980,
29-34), at first grew rapidly initially as a result
of migration from the east. Overall, the country
grew by 12 million between 1950 and 1975 (24%). In
the same period Denmark's population grew by 0.8
million (18%). Britain grew more slowly than the
other five countries, by 5.5 million (11%). So in
each case there was considerable new demand for
housing which was accentuated by declining
household sizes and the need to replace older
housing.

A substantial proportion of population growth
in West Germany, the USA and France was caused by
immigration, while the Netherlands and Britain had
substantial inflows and outflows of population
(Bollens and Schmandt, 1975, 73-8; Secretariat of
the Economic Commission for Europe, 1979, 128).
Immigration by ex-colonial citizens and/or 'guest
workers' and, in the USA by migrants from South and
Central America and the Caribbean has been
particularly important, especially for the private
rented sector (1). Immigration levels have been
sensitive to changing economic prospects, political
events (such as decolonisation) and policies such
as immigration control (Secretariat of the Economic
Commission for Europe, 1979, 128-31). With the onset
of more difficult economic conditions, especially
in the seventies, most governments have legislated
to stop or drastically reduce the flow of immigrants
who typically occupied less skilled occupations
which, while there was full employment, were
unattractive to the indigenous populations but which
are now sought after, or at least required, by them.
Migrant workers in lower paid jobs are one of several
disadvantaged groups in the housing market
(Poliakoff 1978, xvi, 4-5; Krane, 1979; Secretariat
of the Economic Commission for Europe, 1979, 172-
33). Given the nature of their work, they concentrate

in the larger cities which have offered service
and industrial employment.

Given the lack of comparable data, a comparison
of rates of urbanisation is difficult. But the
Secretariat of the UN Economic Commission for
Europe (1979) concludes that there were high levels
of population concentration in Denmark and the
Netherlands and that between 1950 and 1970 Denmark
and England and Wales were the only two of the five
countries in which concentration declined. On the
basis of national definitions of urban areas,
France was the least urbanised in 1975, with 71%
of the population in urban areas, and Germany, with
83%, the most (1979, 190, 237-8). In the USA in
1975 almost 73% lived in Standard Metropolitan
Statistical Areas - essentially city regions (US
Bureau of the Census, 1979, 17).

The greatest increases in the proportion of
the urban population between 1950 and 1975 were in
Denmark and the Netherlands, there were also major
increases in France and West Germany. Only Britain,
which had virtually completed its urbanisation by
the beginning of the century, had no growth and
in fact a slight decline in the urban proportion.
In Denmark, France and the Netherlands, the high
rate of rural to urban migration has been especially
significant (Secretariat of the Economic Commission
for Europe, 1979, 190). In the USA the population
in SMSAs grew substantially (US Bureau of the
Census, 1979, 17).

There have been important trends in internal
migration. In the USA 2.7 million blacks migrated
from the South into the Northern cities between
1950 and 1970, in search of jobs. Meanwhile whites
left the cities for better housing and jobs in the
suburbs and, increasingly, in the newly dynamic
Sun Belt states (the West and, ironically, the
South), as well as to escape from the new and
unwelcome migrants (Hall, 1980, 252; Sternlieb and
Hughes, 1977). The older centres developed high
concentrations of black and Hispanic populations,
many on low incomes with declining economic
opportunities as these centres lost jobs to plants
in the suburbs and the Sunbelt. In the seventies
many cities suffered a fiscal crisis and government
services were drastically reduced. These factors
combined to produce an acute inner city housing
problem. In contrast, the rapid growth of the
suburbs and the Sunbelt provided major
opportunities for the housing market, especially

for owner occupied housing but to some extent also
for rental housing (Alcaly and Mermelstein, 1977;
Perry and Watkins, 1977).

In Europe such trends were less dramatic,
partly because the social, economic and political
factors which, for example, favoured suburban and
Sunbelt locations in the USA were absent or less
powerful, although uneven regional development and
suburbanisation occurred here too. Important trends
include, as in the USA, the growth of metropolitan
regions such as those centred on London, the
Randstad (the ring of cities stretching from
Rotterdam to Utrecht), the Rhine-Ruhr area, Paris
and Copenhagen (Secretariat of the Economic
Commission for Europe, 1979, 191; Hall, 1979).
However, growth is now beginning to occur beyond
the metropolitan fringe, as housing and jobs
decentralise still further. These trends were
particularly noticeable in the USA, the Netherlands
and Britain by 1970 (Hall, 1979, 21; Kasarda,
1980). The declining population of the older and
larger cities has become increasingly evident in
Britain, accompanied by so called inner city
problems partially similar to those in the USA. And
the problem of inner city decline seems likely to
be of concern to the governments of the other four
countries before very long (Hall, 1981, 64-70).

ECONOMIC DEVELOPMENT

All six countries are within the small group of
rich, capitalist nations, without the extremes of
poverty and lack of housing which characterise
many other countries, although there are extremes
of relative poverty. Lydall has shown that income
inequality is greater in countries with high
proportions of their labour force in agriculture
and that in the fifties and early sixties the
distribution of pre-tax incomes in France, West
Germany, the Netherlands, Britain and the United
States had tended to widen, after a period in which
in some cases they had narrowed (Miller and Rein,
Lydall, 1968, 249-53). The continuing existence
of rural poverty is illustrated by data which shows
that the range of average monthly family income in
the USA in the early sixties varied from $122 in
Connecticut to $51 in largely rural Mississippi
(Hall, 1980, 245). In comparison, in Britain in the
late sixties the range was from £118 (in
Hertfordshire) to £80 (in County Tyrone, Northern

Ireland). Also local variations in income are
important. The concentration of poverty in inner
cities is of special relevance to this study,
as in the fact that there are certain population
groups in poverty. In his British study, Townsend
(1979) refers, inter alia, to the elderly, the
unemployed and sub-employed, those on low wages,
the disabled and chronic sick, one parent families,
racial minorities and large families. While we
cannot trace trends in the size of these groups in
all six countries, it is certain that some will
have grown, for example, racial minorities, one
parent families and, in the last few years, the
un- and under employed, although there has also
been a growth in state support for some of those
in poverty (Eurostat, 1977, 190-1).

By the mid seventies all six countries were
affected by the world economic crisis, with rising
unemployment and, beginning earlier, the growth of
inflation. As we shall see the latter especially
had an important impact on private rented housing.
But since 1945 there had been considerable
variation in the economic circumstances of the
countries. Broadly speaking, after 1945 the USA
resumed the economic expansion which had
characterised the 1920s and been interrupted by
the depression; Britain grew much more slowly and
continued its relative economic decline which had
begun even before the First World War; and the
other countries, several of which had suffered
greatly in the war and had yet to complete their
industrialisation had, by the sixties, outstripped the British performance and, in some
cases, were even beginning to overhaul the USA.

There are several useful indicators of these
changes. In the fifties average annual rates of
growth of GDP ranged from 1.5% in the USA (which
started from a relatively high level) to 6.7% in
West Germany (which started from a relatively low
level). In Europe, Britain (2.4%) and Denmark
(2.5%) grew rather slowly (United Nations, 1968,
567-71). In the sixties the disparity between
Britain and the rest was very clear, with an
average rate of growth in Britain of 2.9% and
elsewhere ranging from 4.3% (USA) to 3.7% (France)
(United Nations, 1981, 681-5).

But this data does not reveal the relative
progress of the six countries. This is illustrated
by Table 2.1 which shows the development of per
capita GDP and disposable incomes since 1960 (no
data for 1950 are available). In 1960 the USA

TABLE 2.1
GROWTH OF PER CAPITA GDP (US dollars)

	Year 1960	Year 1970	Year 1978
Denmark	1289	3220	10958
France	1315	2598	8851
West Germany	1301	3055	10419
Netherlands	959	2429	9383
U.K.	1358	2199	5545
U.S.A.	2804	4789	9687

Source: United Nations, 1981, Table 163, pp. 693-6

GROWTH OF PER CAPITA DISPOSABLE INCOMES (US dollars)

	Year 1960	Year 1970	Year 1978
Denmark	1191	2992	9869
France	1183	2526	7908
West Germany	1200	2748	9278
Netherlands	880	2234	8509
U.K.	1261	2037	4955
U.S.A.	2502	4285	8612

Source: United Nations, 1981, Table 164, pp. 698-703

still had far higher per capita GDP and incomes than the European countries. But Denmark, France and West Germany had achieved comparable levels to the UK. In the sixties the Netherlands caught up and the European countries surpassed British levels of GDP and income and came closer to the USA. By 1978 Denmark and West Germany had higher per capita GDP and incomes than the USA and Britain was even further behind.

The impact of inflation can be shown by trends in consumer price indices. In the fifties, prices rose by about 75% in France and Denmark, 47% in Britain, 37% in the Netherlands, 19% in West Germany and 23% in the USA (US Bureau of the Census, 1961, 125; 1965,19; Mitchell, 1980, 778-83). In the sixties this range narrowed as prices increased by around 50% in France, the Netherlands and the UK, by

about 70% in Denmark and by 30% in West Germany and
the USA (Mitchell 1980, 778-83; US Department of
Commerce, 1973, 223). From 1970-79 there was a
further acceleration with increases varying from
over 200% in Britain, 150% in Denmark, 120% in
France, 90% in USA and the Netherlands and only
about 55% in West Germany (Eurostat, 1981, 158).

To summarise, there has been a considerable
change in the relative economic positions of the
six countries. The most dramatic changes were the
new prosperity of the four mainland European
countries and the declining position of Britain.
The USA continued to enjoy a high level of average
incomes but stagnated in comparison with the four
European countries. Of these European countries,
West Germany combined high growth with low
inflation, Denmark had considerable inflation but
considerable growth too, France and the Netherlands
grew rapidly but had lower inflation than Denmark.

A detailed explanation of these patterns is
not appropriate to this chapter but there are
several aspects of national patterns which are
significant. We have already noted one, the inter-
regional and suburban shift of people in the USA.
In Europe, measures of real product per head show
that France, Germany, the Netherlands and, to a
lesser extent, Denmark lagged behind Britain in
1939 (Cole and Deane, 1965, 27). In the war the
mainland European countries suffered considerable
economic devastation. By 1945 indices of industrial
production had fallen to 75% of their 1937 level
in Denmark, 60% in Germany, 45% in France and 31%
in the Netherlands, but by only 1% in Britain
(Mitchell, 1980, 375-9).

But the four mainland European countries made
rapid progress thereafter, made substantial new
investment and underwent considerable economic
restructuring. There was a marked drop in the
proportions of GDP attributable to agriculture and
in agricultural employment (Mitchell, 1976, 75).
Urbanisation was accelerated by this trend. In the
Netherlands, governments concentrated on rapid
industrialisation and controlled wages and prices
(including rents) to improve the country's
international competitiveness (De Vries, 1976, 42).
France also embarked on a government induced
process of economic growth. Its industry was
especially backward and small scale and a
considerable restructuring and concentration of
capital occurred, leading to extensive new urban

development to provide the infrastructure for the
leading sectors of the economy (Fohlen, 1976).
Germany initially experienced allied policies of
de-industrialisation and the break-up of its large
firms. But after currency reform, decontrol and
the institution of the new Federal government,
policy was dominated by the concept of the 'social
market economy', a neo-liberal free market system
in which the state stimulated a high rate of
private savings and investment in, among other
things, housing, and in which consumption and
inflation were kept at low levels to aid economic
recovery (Hardach, 1976, 217-30; Stolper, 1967,
219-98). In Denmark there was not initially such
rapid industrialisation and there was a large,
productive and export oriented agricultural sector.
But after the mid-fifties investment occurred
elsewhere in the economy and accelerated growth
resulted. This change was in part a response to
its chronic balance of payments difficulties,
caused by having to import many of its basic
industrial requirements (Jorberg and Krantz, 1976).

POLITICAL AND ADMINISTRATIVE SYSTEMS

All six countries are representative democracies
but, importantly for this study, West Germany and
the USA are federal states. In each case there are
central government housing ministries. In addition
there are elected local governments, and, in the
USA, other special purpose organisations which
exercise housing powers. In the two federal
systems there are also state governments which
have important housing responsibilities. There have
been numerous reforms of central government
arrangements for housing policy as well as changes
in the structure and functions of local government.
In the two federal systems there is considerable
variation in policy from area to area, and central
government has had a less direct involvement in
many matters. In this study it is not possible to
discuss all these local variations. The focus will
mainly be on central government policies but the
limitations of this approach are considerable. More
generally, local government has considerable
discretion, again it is not possible to take this
fully into account, although some reference is made
to local developments. We shall now examine the
political and administrative context of housing
policy in each country.
    The French government probably bears more

responsibility centrally for housing policy than
the government of any other country in this survey,
although it often acts in partnership with private
enterprise through 'para-public' or 'mixed economy'
(public/private) companies and other means in
matters such as urban development and redevelopment
(2). The centrally responsible body is the Ministry
of Equipment (recently renamed). Local government
has been relatively weak (outside some larger
cities) and has been closely supervised by the
centre. The country is divided into ninety-five
departments with elected councils. Prefects
appointed by and answerable to central government
are the chief executives of these councils. In
addition, there are about 36,000 communes whose
population ranges from under 10 to over 2 million
(the city of Paris). They have relatively weak
councils who elect the mayor to act as chief
executive but this official also has
responsibilities to central government and is not
dismissable by the council. Local finance is
limited (mainly based on payroll and property taxes)
and many communes are highly dependent on services
and funds provided by central government. In
housing, as in other matters, much of the initiative
has come from the prefects and the external
services (i.e. locally based officials) of the
central ministries. The detailed picture is complex
due to the relationships of mayors and prefects to
local and central bodies and of the external
services to their ministries and to the prefect,
the recent development of regional government and
the great differences in the political and financial
resources of the communes. Changes have come about
in a piecemeal way with a movement towards less
detailed central supervision and attempts at more
effectively co-ordinated local action. Within the
framework of national policy, local programmes may
be determined and executed at any or all of the
levels described above. The principal sources of
social rented housing are organisations which are
normally set up with aid from the local authorities
and/or employers as well as the central government.
    French local authorities have general enabling
powers but are, in practice, greatly constrained in
what they can achieve. There is very little land in
municipal ownership, urban renewal has largely been
controlled by private enterprise and planning
control has been weak. Communes have some power to
regulate housing conditions (for example, to

prevent evictions at certain times and to order the
evacuation of dangerous structures) but they cannot
for example, effect improvement and repairs to
private property, reduce overcrowding or compel
the use of vacant units (3). They have played a
significant role in supporting the building of
social housing (for sale and for rent) but have not
become much involved in rehabilitation. Matters
such as rent control, landlord/tenant relations and
housing allowances are mainly under the control of
the central government and/or the courts.

Policies have been broadly favourable to the
private enterprise provision of housing (4).
However, governments did intervene in the housing
market and supported the construction of social
rented housing. Duclaud Williams (1978) has
suggested that there has been less of an ideological
divide between left and the right on housing
policies in France than in Britain. Whether this is
so or not, the fact is that support has been given
to all tenures in France, although more recently
support for owner occupation has taken precedence
(Magri, 1977). Since the study ended the long
domination of centre/right government has been
ended, with the election of a socialist President
and government. Whether this will alter the general
direction of French housing policies seems doubtful.

In the Netherlands the principal
responsibility for housing policy lies with the
central Ministry of Housing (5). There are
provincial governments but these are insignificant
with respect to housing. There has been
considerable discussion of local government but
only incremental changes have occurred. There are
about 850 locally elected municipalities, headed
by burgomasters, appointed by the Crown, and
assisted by aldermen, elected by councillors from
among their own number. Municipalities have the
main responsibility for implementing housing
policies, controlling building standards and the
condition of existing housing. They also have
important planning and renewal powers and duties
with respect to dwelling allocation (see chapter 4)
although not rent control. They own some social
housing which tends to accommodate poor households,
for example guest labourers and immigrants
(Williams and Colijn, 1980, 191). Their ability to
add to this stock was severely restricted in 1969.
Most social rented housing is owned by non-profit
housing associations. The municipalities are
dependent on central government for about 95% of

their expenditure. Local property taxes, their other main source of revenue, are very low. This considerably affected their scope for discretion in local housing policies, especially during the years of intense housing shortage.

Until the late seventies central government (and especially the housing ministry) was dominated by Christian Democrats governing in coalition with either conservative or social democratic parties. (The political system, based on proportional representation was fragmented, especially due to the historically important division between Protestants and Catholics). A continuing housing shortage resulted in extensive government support for all main tenures (van Weesep, 1982). In common with the other five countries, owner occupation increasingly emerged as the most dynamic sector, but this occurred later than elsewhere. Despite the general support for housebuilding there was much conflict over housing which, until the mid seventies, was the most important domestic political issue and even (in 1955 and 1977) led directly to the fall of governments. These conflicts encompassed the level of building, private rented sector policy (rents, repairs and maintenance) and the liberalisation of the system of dwelling allocation.

In Denmark too the principal responsibility for policy lies with the central Ministry of Housing (6). There are 14 counties and 275 municipalities, the product of an extensive reform in 1970. However, this reform did not alter the position in Greater Copenhagen, containing one third of Denmark's population. Here Copenhagen, Frederiksberg and the Copenhagen County Council (which includes 19 suburban municipalities) continue as separate councils, although an indirectly elected Greater Copenhagen Council now has special planning responsibilities. Councils are headed by salaried burgomasters (or chairmen) who also lead the local government administration. As in France, in theory, municipalities have many powers. In practice, they carry out many delegated responsibilities and higher level supervision has been extensive. About 30% of their revenue comes from local taxes, principally local income tax, most of the rest comes from government grants. The municipalities have responsibility for many housing matters, although often their decisions can be appealed against. Powers include the regulation of building standards

and existing housing conditions, planning and urban
renewal responsibilities, administration of rent
allowances, some aspects of rent control and,
formerly, schemes of housing allocation. They do
not have large stocks of social rented housing,
most of which is owned by non-profit housing
associations.

As in the Netherlands, the Danish system of
proportional representation tends to produce
coalition governments, but, unlike the Dutch
situation, it is the Social Democrats who have
dominated throughout much of the post war period.
The system results in a constant search for
compromise policies. Housing has been a matter of
political controversy (over, for example, rent
control, the role of private enterprise and social
housing), and there have been several 'housing
pacts',programmes which combine some of the
objectives of the major political parties.

In Britain the principal responsibility for
housing lies with the central Department of the
Environment (7). There are 39 county councils and
296 district councils, six metropolitan counties
containing 36 metropolitan districts (in the large
conurbations), the Greater London Council and 32
London Boroughs. These authorities are directly
elected, the product of a reform in London in 1963
and in the rest of the country 10 years later. The
primary housing responsibilities are exercised by
the district (plus metropolitan district and
London borough) councils. Mayors perform largely
ceremonial functions, the effective heads of the
local authorities are the leaders of the majority
parties. Local authorities have extensive powers and
considerable discretion in their exercise but are
also subject in practice to considerable central
government control. Local property taxes and
charges account for about 40-50% of local revenue,
the rest consists of government grants.
Constitutionally, in contrast to, for example, the
French situation, they are only able to exercise
powers granted in central government legislation.
Their housing powers include responsibility for
the supply and management of social rented housing
(of which they own the vast majority), planning
and building control, urban renewal and
improvement, the regulation of housing conditions
and the administration of rent allowances but not
rent controls.

The Labour and Conservative parties have

alternated in office. Historically, the former has
favoured social housing and the latter owner
occupation and, in theory at least, private rented
housing. In practice, despite sharp conflict over
specific issues such as the size of the social
housing programme and its rent levels, the sale of
social rented housing and the decontrol of private
rents, by the mid seventies both parties placed
great emphasis on the development of owner
occupation, saw social rented housing as a residual
tenure and maintained a common policy towards
private rented housing.

In Germany limited but important housing
responsibilities are exercised by the Federal
Ministry of Housing, Building and Planning (8).
But, with the exception of housing allowances
these are exercised in concert with the
states (Lander) which have the primary
responsibility for local government. There are
eleven Lander (including the city states of Hamburg
and Bremen and West Berlin which has a special
status - these exercise combined state and local
powers). Local government reform has occurred on
a state by state basis in different ways, but all
involved a reduction in the number of authorities
so that now there are about 8600 municipal units
of various forms and 425 counties. But this is an
over-simple classification of a complex system with
various intermediate tiers, for example, the
counties (landkries) form a separate layer between
the state governments (organised on a parliamentary
system with ministries) and various types of
municipalities (gemeinden), there are also some
special purpose authorities. Relations between the
layers of government are also complex and varied
but federal, state and local governments are seen as
partners in the system. In fact the states exercise
supervision over the local authorities. Leadership
arrangements vary but control by elected councils
is normal and the top officials are often selected
by the party in power and linked to it.

Housing powers are exercised by many different
bodies. With the exception already mentioned, much
housing policy is the primary responsibility of
the states, for example after federal subsidies
are allocated to them they determine the details
of programmes within their areas and may contribute
further funds. Most social rented housing is owned
by non-profit organisations although some of these
are controlled by the local authorities and the

level of indirect control by the authorities is high. The councils nominate applicants on their waiting lists to vacant social housing. The powers of local authorities include controls over building and planning, housing conditions, social housing allocations and rehabilitation and urban renewal. A wide variety of tax receipts are shared between the three levels of government and much expenditure is made by state and local, not central government. In 1974, for example, the states spent four times as much on housing as the federal government.

Until the sixties central government was dominated by the Christian Democrats and after 1969 by the Social Democrats. Under the Christian Democrats the concept of the 'social market economy' in practice involved support for all tenures but with an emphasis on encouraging private investment and home ownership. The Social Democrats traditionally supported social housing, but, as elsewhere, by the seventies both parties (and the minority Liberal Party) emphasised the development of owner-occupation. There have been several major conflicts over housing policy - for example over the decontrol of the private rented sector after 1960. But the extensive state responsibility for housing has resulted in a good deal of regional variation in policy. For example, Hamburg, a socialist stronghold, has promoted considerable social housing development.

The United States has, with the possible exception of Germany, the most complex and varied system of government (9). The states have constitutional responsibility for determining the structure of local government but in many cases local authorities exercise considerable powers. There are many special purpose authorities, often completely independent of the local governments in whose areas they operate. Two types of such bodies are of importance in housing, public housing and urban renewal authorities (sometimes these functions are combined and sometimes they are exercised by local authorities). It is not possible here to even outline the many variations in government arrangements but in 1977 there were almost 80,000 units of local government (the number has slowly declined but substantial structural reform has been rare). These include counties, municipalities, townships, school districts and special districts. Authorities have differing structures with provisions, for example, for strong and weak mayoral government, city

managers and local referenda. In many areas there
are three or even four layers of government, each
with   different and often conflicting
responsibilities. Local government is heavily
dependent on local taxes, of which, besides property
taxation, there is a wide range. Federal and state
aid to the localities has been small scale - but
has become more extensive in the last 20 years.
Housing legislation is determined at local and state
levels (except that directly concerned with
federal programmes). In fact urban housing policy
has mainly been determined and implemented by city
governments and by special purpose agencies. A
state role has only recently emerged, at first in
connection with housing finance and, latterly, as
a result of the severe problems of many cities.
      The range of local powers varies according to
local conditions (and may be federal, local or
state in origin). They can include matters such as
public housing, urban renewal, housing and building
code enforcement, rehabilitation, rent control,
development and subsidisation of low and moderate
income housing and housing for special groups and
planning. Rarely all or even most of the powers
united in one administration and conflict and
overlap between responsibilities is common. However,
despite the plethora of programmes and agencies,
financial involvement is relatively small scale,
for example, in 1972 only 1.5% of total state and
local expenditures went on housing and urban
renewal.
      Although there have been different emphases
under Republican and Democratic federal
administrations - for example, in the sixties low
and moderate income subsidised housing was expanded
under Presidents   Kennedy and Johnson - in
practice support for owner occupation is strong
and also, to a lesser extent, for private rental
housing. There is no strong constituency for public
housing. Initially, as noted already, the federal
housing policy was concerned with underpinning the
private market and the small scale provision of
public housing subsidies. In the fifties the
government began to assist urban renewal and in the
sixties subsidised private rental and owner
occupied housing for low and moderate income
households. Increasingly, the federal government
has become involved in broad programmes encompassing
many aspects of the problems of the larger older
cities - although the programmes have often not had
sufficient funding.

The National Background to Private Renting

This account has excluded much detail about
political and administrative systems in the six
countries. But some general points must be added.
First, the range of governmental housing
responsibilities has increased, so has the role of
central government. Second, there has been a growth
in the professionalisation of local administration
but ultimate responsibility usually lies in
political hands. Third, local resources have often
failed to expand in line with increasing
responsibilities. The problem of local finance is
common to all six countries (Ashord, 1980; Committee
of Enquiry into Local Government Finance, 1976a, b,
53-73). Especially in Europe there has been a growth
of attempts by central government to control local
spending and increasing difficulties with the
local tax base. In most cases significant local
resources come from property taxes but there has
been a search for other sources of revenue too. In
the USA in particular many cities have found that,
in an era of growing inflation and severe urban
problems, increased federal and state funding has
been necessary to avoid bankruptcy. The case of
New York City is well known (Alcaly and Mermelstein,
1977). Here state and federal aid has accompanied
increased controls on city budgets and severe cut-
backs in services, greatly reducing the city's
housing activities. But, more generally, the
autonomy of local government is increasingly
limited (10).

STRUCTURE OF THE HOUSING MARKET

The division of the stock into private rented,
social rented and owner occupied housing used
throughout this book appears at first sight to be
relatively clear cut. But the detailed structure of
the housing market differs in each country and, in
some cases, this classification is rather
misleading, unless carefully qualified (11).
    In the USA the main division is between owner
occupied and rented housing. In 1975 the rented
sector accounted for about 35% of all units (US
Department of Housing and Urban Development, 1977,
261). Within this sector about 9% of households
occupied public housing or private units with
direct government subsidies (there was also a small
proportion of directly subsidised owner occupied
units) (12). In addition, local and state subsidies
have been given to a small proportion of rental
housing, some of which has rent controls in

61

consequence. There has also been some growth of
co-operative housing and of condominiums and, more
significantly, in 'mobile homes' - most of which
are owner occupied. But the great majority of the
housing stock is either privately rented or owner
occupied and not in receipt of direct subsidies,
although indirect subsidies through the tax system
are provided for both tenures.

In Britain there is a fairly clear distinction
between the social housing sector (council and
housing association properties) which receive direct
subsidies, owner occupation which mainly receives
subsidy through the tax system and private rented
housing which receives no subsidy, although housing
allowances are available for private tenants. In
1977 about 13% of all dwellings in England were in
the privately rented sector, 56% were owner occupied
and 31% were in the social rented sector (Department
of the Environment, 1978a, 11) (13). Within the
private rented sector there are a number of
important sub-divisions which will be discussed
later. One important sub-sector is accommodation
let in connection with a job or business or 'by
virtue' of employment. This is often let at low
rents or rent-free and special legal provisions
apply to it. It will not be considered in detail in
this study.

In the Netherlands the principal divisions
are as in Britain. But direct subsidies have been
provided for the private rental sector and the
housing associations can build housing for sale as
well as according to the rules for subsidised
private rented construction. In 1975, 20% of all
dwellings were in the privately rented sector, 41%
were social rented, and 39% were owner-occupied.

In Denmark too the division between social,
private rented and owner occupied housing is fairly
clear. In 1970 about 30% of dwellings were privately
rented, 49% were owner occupied and 17% were in the
social rented sector (Danmarks Statistik, 1975,
48-9) (14).

In France the situation is comparable with the
Netherlands. The social housing organisations build
rental and owner occupied housing and there have
been important subsidies for private rental
construction, with some restrictions on rent and
occupancy, and for owner occupation. In 1973 about
32% of all dwellings were in the private rental
sector, 11% in the social rental sector and 45%
were owner occupied (Enquête-logement, 1973 (1),
55) (15).

The National Background to Private Renting

The German housing market fits least
comfortably into the broad classification adopted
here. Distinctions which relate tenure to subsidy
treatment and ownership are much less clear.
Governments, following the precepts of the 'social
market economy', gave direct subsidies to
individuals and commercial and non-commercial
organisations for building owner-occupied and
rented housing. So the 'social' housing sector is
not confined to rental housing or to a particular
category of builders or landlords. The position is
further complicated because much housing has also
been built with special tax subsidies. Rental
housing built with direct subsidies is restricted
to certain income groups and has cost related rents,
that built with indirect subsidies is not in
practice so restricted. A further complication is
that the arrangements for the directly subsidised
rental housing allow for the lifting of controls
after a period of years and some early post war
social rented housing is now a part of the private
rented sector.
    Therefore the rented sector consists of several
sub-sectors. First, the older (pre-1948) stock
which contains some former social housing but which
is now all privately rented, second, the post war
social rented housing and third, the rest of the
post war rental stock which has benefitted from
various tax subsidies. In this book it is the first
and third of these categories (which are not subject
to the controls on social rented housing) which is
taken to approximate to the private rented sector.
But it should be noted that some of this stock is
owned by landlords who are not principally
motivated by commercial concerns, just as some
commercially motivated landlords have built social
housing. Finally while employer provided housing
exists in all countries, it has historically
accounted for a more significant part of the stock
in Germany than in the other countries. In 1972
about 33% of the stock was privately rented (and a
further 13% rented from employers), 35% was owner
occupied and 18% was in the social rented sector
(Figures derived from Der Bundesminster für
Raumordnung etc., 1975).
    In all six countries most private rented
housing is let unfurnished. But in every country
there are small furnished sub-sectors, often rooms
within a larger property not self contained
accommodation. Usually this provides housing of

last resort or for transient households. Whatever the legal provisions, it was suggested in each country that in practice the sector was largely unregulated and offered poor accommodation to people who are often in severe housing need.

THE RECENT DEVELOPMENT OF THE HOUSING MARKET

As we have seen before 1939 there were some common developments in housing policies - limited support for construction, increasing regulation of conditions, rent controls and so on. But these, with the exception of controls and basic public health and building laws, were marginal to markets which were still based on private rented housing (and owner occupation in the USA and, to a lesser extent, in Britain).

However, in 1945 all six countries faced a large scale demand for new housing and in Germany, France and the Netherlands the wartime devastation was very substantial. In France there was the additional problem of the high average age of the stock, as there had been little building in the interwar years, and West Germany had to cope with the influx of refugees from the East. The American economy began its long post war period of expansion but in Europe the problems of reconstruction were far greater.

The USA embarked on a rapid expansion of owner occupied housing, aided by the government mortgage insurance programme started in the thirties. There was a brief period of large scale assisted rental construction but this soon ended and throughout the fifties new building for owner occupation predominated. In Britain the post war Labour government initiated a major programme of council house construction, limiting building for owner occupation and maintaining controls so that virtually no new private rental construction occurred. With the return of a Conservative government in 1951 the priorities were reversed, private building for owner occupation increased with far less emphasis on council house construction (16).

In the four mainland European countries there was much less discrimination between tenures. While at least three of these countries faced more acute housing problems than Britain or the USA other priorities sometimes came first. Thus while Germany, for various reasons (17). took early steps to stimulate housing production, France put industrial

64

development first and only later gave major
assistance to housing (18). In the Netherlands
housing production grew relatively slowly, policy
was dominated by the difficult economic situation and
by the objective of restricting prices and wages in
order to improve the country's international
competitiveness (19).

Individual governments favoured the private
market or public enterprise to varying degrees.
For instance, in Denmark the strong influence of
the Social Democrats was exerted in favour of
social housing while in Germany the Christian
Democrats favoured private enterprise, especially
owner occupation. But actual housing policies were
more uniform because of the circumstances that all
these countries were in. Facing massive housing
shortages they were in practice forced, whether they
liked it or not, to try to maximise housing output,
within severe resource constraints. As a result, all
four governments supported social and private rented
housing. Overwhelmingly, the need was for more
rented housing, rapid expansion of owner occupation
was not to occur until growth and full employment
resulted in incomes which equalled and even
exceeded US and British levels. Only in these two
countries did governments have the 'luxury' of being
able to align policies with their ideological
priorities.

All six countries imposed rent controls during
or soon after the war (see Chapter 5). Denmark,
West Germany and Holland also imposed controls on
access to housing, by the seventies these only
remained in parts of the Netherlands. Slum
clearance, urban renewal and rehabilitation only
began when mass housing shortages were reduced, from
the fifties in the USA and Britain and the sixties
elsewhere.

In 1945 about a quarter of the population of
the European countries were owner occupiers. Most
of the rest lived in private rented housing,
although there was some social housing, especially
in Britain. Owner occupation has subsequently
expanded and the position by the mid seventies was
noted in the last section. Particularly sharp
changes occurred in the fifties in Britain, the USA,
France and Denmark. In the USA the main reason was
that new building was predominantly for owner
occupation. In Britain there was new building for
owner occupation and a significant transfer of
private rented housing to the owner occupied sector.

In Denmark and France the cause is more obscure,
but some units, especially in areas of declining
rural population, were leaving the stock altogether
and others were sold off to sitting tenants, adding
to the rural low income owner occupied sector which
already existed. Denmark and France also added to
their stock of social rented housing rather slowly.
In Germany and the Netherlands the decline in the
rented sector was more gradual. Both had long
lasting absolute shortages of housing and it was
only in the seventies that they reached a closer
balance between the aggregate demand for and supply
of housing. In both these countries by the seventies
owner occupation seemed likely to take a rapidly
increasing share of the housing market, following
the trend elsewhere (20).
    Another important feature of the European
housing markets is that social rented housing has
played a major role in the provision of new rented
units and has increased its share of the rented
stock. In the USA there was, of course, from the
sixties an expansion of subsidised private rented
housing for low and moderate income households
instead of the expansion of social rented housing
which occurred in Europe. The provision of subsidies
has been an important factor in the continuance of
major private rented markets in five of the
countries. In Britain, where this has not happened,
there was an early and rapid decline in this
tenure (21). In Denmark, Holland and France, despite
the continued existence of substantial private
rental sectors, new investment never recovered to
really high levels, although a significant level of
new building was sustained until the last ten years
or so. Since then various factors have intervened.
These include a growing demand for owner occupation
and increasing difficulties in making profitable
investments in rental housing in an era of rapid
inflation and, on the whole, a less than matching
rise in rents and tenant incomes.
    In Germany, new building for private rental
stayed at a higher level, but even here it started
to decline recently. The USA shows a more complex
pattern. At first this seems paradoxical, with a
massive expansion of private rented production in
the sixties and early seventies. But it owed much
to the expansion of federally assistance already
mentioned. A further stimulus was provided by the
expansion of the Sunbelt states. In the older US
cities, the pattern has been much as elsewhere, with
declining production of 'normal' private rented

housing. In all countries where substantial
production of private rented housing continued after
the war it was adversely affected by the economic
crisis of the seventies, but behind this shorter
term trend the long term forces of decline are
evident, as will become clear in the following
chapters (22).

CONCLUSION

This chapter completes the examination of the
context within which the post war development of the
private rented sector occurred. As the main focus
of this book is on a detailed study of the recent
evolution of this tenure and its future prospects,
many important aspects of housing markets and
policies have had to be dealt with in a summary
way or ignored. Much of the rest of this book is
concerned with detailed aspects of private rental
housing, somewhat abstracted from the broader
context. But wider themes will be returned to in
the last chapter which considers the future of
private renting.

NOTES

1. This is discussed in Krane, 1979, which considers Britain, France, the Netherlands and West Germany. There is also a chapter discussing Mexican migration to the USA. See also Castles and Kosack, 1973.
2. This section draws on Ridley and Blondel, 1969; Blondel and Godfrey, 1968; Duclaud-Williams, 1978; and Chapman, 1952. For the recent history of attempts at local government reform see Gourevitch, 1981; Mény, 1980.
3. From information provided by Christian Topalov.
4. The major housing legislation of the Fourth Republic was enacted by centre coalition governments (including the Socialist Party). The Fifth Republic maintained much of what went before (Duclaud-Williams, 1978, 19).
5. This section draws on Weil, 1970; Lipjhard, 1968; Morlan, 1981a; Williams and Colijn, 1980 and information supplied by Professor Hugo Priemus.
6. This section draws on Miller, 1968; Berglund and Lindstrom, 1978; Morlan, 1981b, and Skovsgaard, 1982.
7. This section draws on McKay and Cox, 1979; Hepworth, 1980; Ashford, 1980a and Rhodes, 1981.
8. This section draws on Conradt, 1978; Chaput de Saintonge, 1961; Gunlicks, 1981a; McDermott, 1981 and Reissert, 1980.
9. This section draws on Bollens and Schmandt, 1975; Stedman, 1975; Gunlicks, 1981b; Gelfand, 1980 and McKay, 1980.
10. Ashford (1980b) contains accounts of recent developments in central-local finances and control in the USA, Britain, West Germany, France and the Netherlands. According to Ashford (219), 'local governments have almost become a part of the administrative sub-structure of most welfare states'.
11. Definitions of the private rented sector vary. For example, housing rented in connection with employment is separately enumerated in West Germany, included in the private rented sector in Britain, Denmark and the USA and, insofar as it involves agricultural or free properties, is separately enumerated in France. Care should therefore be taken when making comparisons of the size of the private rented sector as the figures given provide an approximate comparison only.

68

12. Derived from US Department of Housing and Urban Development, 1977, 53, 157, 167. Apart from public housing, the main subsidised programmes were sections 221 (Below Market Interest Rate), 236, and 8. (The programmes are named after the sections of the National Housing Act in which they appear).

13. Data is complicated because sometimes figures are available for England, sometimes for England and Wales and, occasionally, for these two and Scotland or for these three and Northern Ireland. Normally figures for England and Wales will be used. This corresponds to the area in which the housing policies discussed are operative. Northern Ireland and Scotland have somewhat different housing policies and markets. As almost 90% of the population of the United Kingdom lives in England and Wales (and 95% of these in England) the working of and prospects for the private rented sector is dominated by English developments. References throughout to 'Britain' should be taken, except where noted, to refer to the situation in England and Wales.

14. A small percentage consisted of miscellaneous tenures not elsewhere classified.

15. The balance of units consisted of free and farm housing.

16. The production of council housing continued to expand until 1954, after this date private housing construction began to overtake social rented housing construction.

17. These included the pressing political need to expand the quantity of accommodation in order to reduce social tension (in 1950 there were about 10 million housing units and over 15 million households (Zapf, 1977, 622); the need to stimulate private savings and the private capital market (Stolper, 1967, 255-6) and the belief that property ownership would help to stabilise the social order.

18. Ardagh (1977, 325) writes, 'Whereas Britain and Germany began massive rehousing right after the war, the French (perhaps wisely) gave priority to industrial recovery. In 1952 France was still producing only about 75,000 new houses a year.' When housing production did expand one important aim was to provide housing for 'key workers' in the expanding industries, such as motor car production (Magri, 1977, 98).

19. Information provided by Professor Hugo Priemus. See also de Vries, 1976, 40-4.

20. This paragraph is mainly based on information supplied by the consultants to the research project. Principal sources of data are US Department of Housing and Urban Development, 1977; Department of the Environment, 1977a; Donnison, 1967; Det Statistke Department, 1949, 1953, 1959, 1964, 1969; Danmarks Statistik, 1975; Enquêtes-logement, 1955, 1961, 1963, 1967, 1970, 1973; Recensement de population, 1954, 1962; Zapf, 1977; CBS, 1964, 1967, 1970, 1971, 1975; Central Directie van de Volkshuisinvesting, 1975.

21. See note 20. Social rented housing accounted for about 15% of all rented housing in Germany in 1948, but 36% by 1972; in Denmark 19% in 1955, and 36% in 1970; in the Netherlands 33% in 1956 and 68% in 1975; in France 5% in 1955 and 18% in 1973; in Britain 18% in 1947 and 70% in 1977. In contrast, it accounted for about 1% in 1950 and 7% in 1975 in the USA.

22. In Britain the postwar output of new rental housing has been negligible; in West Germany it has fallen from about 40% of new output in the period 1965-70 to 24% in 1981; in Denmark it fell from about 15% in the post war period up to 1970 to negligible proportions by 1981; in the Netherlands from about 15-20% in the post war period up to 1975 to under 6% in 1980; in France from 20% in 1960 to 3% in 1977-9 (Bovaird, Harloe and Whitehead, 1982b; Department of the Environment, 1977a, c; DIW, 1976; Danmarks Statistik, 1975, 1925-77; Netherlands and French data based on estimates supplied by Jan van der Schaar and Christian Topalov respectively). The pattern in the USA shows some variation, as noted in the text, with rental output falling from 9% in 1945-9, to 5% in 1950-4, rising to about 37% in 1970 before falling to 23% in 1977. (Figures derived from US Bureau of the Census, Statistical Abstract of the United States, various years 1945-77).

Chapter Three

A PROFILE OF THE PRIVATE RENTED SECTOR I - THE STOCK

The next two chapters present a contemporary
profile of the private rented sector. The
difficulties of obtaining comparable data have
already been mentioned. These problems will be
evident in what follows. In consequence
significance cannot be attached to small cross
national statistical variations. So the aim is to
highlight major similarities and differences rather
to focus on finer detail.

THE SIZE OF THE TENURE AND SOME SUBDIVISIONS

The last chapter referred to the decline in the
size of the private rental sector in the post war
period and to the size of the different tenures in
the six countries around the time at which the
research was carried out. Apart from Britain,
between a fifth and a third of the stock in the
other five countries was in the private rental
sector. The growth of owner occupation was
strong up to the late seventies and private renting
began to decline more rapidly than before in most
countries. New output fell to low levels and even
in West Germany and the Netherlands, where the
persistence of a 'crude' shortage of housing
probably contributed to maintaining the sector,
rapid decline was occurring. In addition there
was a reduction in social housing programmes - most
notably in Britain - in favour of owner occupation.
    Social rented housing had played an important
part in the provision of new rented units and had
increased its share of the stock. This was most
marked in the Netherlands and in Britain. In the
USA the public housing programme was confined to
a marginal role. However, this picture is somewhat
misleading in the sense that, rather than supply

public housing successive governments had subsidised
private landlords to house lower income households.
This sector accounted for about a quarter of what
might be called the social rented stock in 1975 (1).
Also subsidies had been available elsewhere for
private landlords and in several countries, for
example the Netherlands, the proportion of new
unsubsidised private rented units was very low by
the seventies.

As already mentioned, this book is principally
concerned with the mainstream of the privately
rented sector, unfurnished property. However, there
are also some other significant subsectors.
Unfortunately, there is very little data and other
information on these. But an indication of their
nature and importance can be provided.

Denmark had a small, declining 'residual'
housing sector, 4.6% of the stock in 1970, which
contained some 'by virtue of employment' and rent
free accommodation (Danmarks Statistik, 1975, 48-9).
Little was known about this housing. Denmark was
unique in not including data on rented rooms, i.e.
shared accommodation, among the general housing
data. In 1970 there were a little under 60,000 such
rooms, mainly owned by private landlords in the
larger towns. As elsewhere, they tended to house
young people and migrant workers, were covered by
minimal or weakly enforced legislation, and were
often, in value for money terms, very expensive
(Danmarks Statistik, 1975, 120).

In the Netherlands in 1975 it was thought
that about 0.2% of the stock was accommodation let
by virtue of employment (2). Most was let at low
rents and located in the towns of the Randstad.
There was unquantified evidence of a considerable
market in rented rooms in the pressurised housing
markets of this area.

In contrast, West Germany still had a
considerable legacy from the time when many of the
larger employers, especially the coal and steel
companies in the Ruhr, housed their workers
directly. In 1972 there were over 2½ million units
let by virtue of employment (and to foreign armed
forces) although numbers were in decline (3). This
amounted to almost one third of the private rented
sector. Many were let at low rents and their tenants
(in theory) benefitted from the general security of
tenure laws. But employers were selling out, often
with vacant possession to maximise capital gains.
Much of the Ruhr housing came into public ownership as a by product of the nationalisation of major

coal and steel interests. Rented rooms had been a
major part of the housing market   just after the war
when the extreme housing shortage resulted in much
sharing. By 1972 there were only about 1.3 million
subtenants, about 10% of all tenants (Der
Bundesminister für Raumordnung etc. 1975, 46, 102).
     In France and Britain some more detailed
information is available, in Britain by virtue of
employment and furnished accommodation has had
special legislative treatment. In France in 1962
(the latest date for which a figure is available)
1.3 million units were provided by employers, about
9% of all units. About one third of these were let
to agricultural workers, but the accommodation was
fairly evenly distributed between urban and rural
areas. A further 700,000 units were occupied free
of charge. The furnished rental sector amounted
to about 400,000 units in 1973, 5% of the rental
stock, a slowly declining proportion (4). As
elsewhere, it was concentrated in the larger cities,
especially Paris, and tended to house younger and/
or poorer small households. There were no controls
over rents or security. No information was available
on the extent of subletting in France. Although
this was probably substantial in the past, to judge
by the degree of overcrowding it likely to have
been a small scale phenomenon by the late seventies.
     In Britain as the private rented sector
declined the share of this market accounted for
by accommodation let in connection with employment
had grown. In 1976 about 700,000 units, over a
quarter of the private rental market, fell into this
category (Department of the Environment 1977c, 69).
Some of it consisted of 'tied' agricultural
cottages but much was owned by business, state
bodies, etc. The legal position of the tenants
varied but although they paid fairly low rents,
they often had little security of tenure (the
position of agricultural tenants was improved by
the duty placed on the local authority, in certain
circumstances, to rehouse them). About 10% of the
private rented sector consisted of furnished
accommodation, mainly in rooms and non self
contained flats.
     Despite the wealth of data on the US housing
market there was little information on sub-markets
but in 1976 about 1.1 million units, 5% of the
private rented sector, was occupied free of cash
rent and about 7% of the rented and 2% of the
owner occupied stock accommodated subtenants,

lodgers and resident employees (US Bureau of the
Census etc., 1978a, 5, 12).
     As we have seen, subletting and employment
linked accommodation marked the early history of
rented housing. Such submarkets remained where
alternatives were scarce, for example, in hard
pressed housing markets in the Netherlands and in
some British cities, where rented rooms provided
low quality accommodation for those who could not
gain access to better provision and when employers,
especially in service industries, such as catering,
needed low paid staff to work 'unsocial' hours.
Tied accommodation persisted in rural areas where,
again, the twin factors of low income and
accessibility to work were important. Those who
lived in this housing had been largely untouched
by the legislation controlling security and rents
which had been applied to the 'mainstream' of the
private rented sector.

LOCATION AND TYPE OF HOUSING

Given the historical development of private
rented housing, it is hardly surprising that the
sector is concentrated in urban areas. A common
pattern in the larger cities whose foundation
preceded the industrial revolution was for the
historic centre to be surrounded by a ring of high
density rented housing built for the new working
class. This pattern can still be seen in cities
such as Copenhagen or Cologne. In the new cities
there was less of a distinct core and ring
structure, the new factories and their residential
areas provided the nucleus for the settlement.
Many of these cities later developed central area
functions - but the distinctive pattern of the
industrial city can still be seen in some regions
such as the Ruhrgebeit or the North of England.
     In contrast, social rented and owner
occupied housing has often been built on the urban
periphery. There are several reasons for this, the
cost and difficulties of redeveloping central sites,
the preference, particularly by owner occupiers,
for the better suburban environment, and, especially
in the USA, the wish to avoid growing financial and
social problems. The effects of this spatial
distribution have been serious for low income
groups (such as office and retail workers) whose
jobs are located in city centres, as well as for
those who have migrated to the cities in search of
work, such as ex-colonial and other Third World

74

immigrants and 'guest workers'. The new areas of social housing often have poor services and are inaccessible from city centres. As a result, many either have to endure a long and costly journey to work in exchange for occupying reasonable accommodation or live in poor conditions in the private rented sector but have good access to jobs. This problem has only been avoided where there have been substantial programmes of urban renewal with the provision in central areas of social rented housing. Of the six countries, only Britain has had a large programme of this nature. But, for example in France, notably in Paris, the inner ring of working class housing was redeveloped for higher income business and residential uses, those displaced being rehoused in peripheral sites which are often poorly serviced and inaccessible (5).

In the USA, given the almost total lack of social housing and the power that suburbs have - by the manipulation of zoning regulations and other means - to exclude low income groups, the redevelopment of central areas has tended to push those who lived in such areas into the inner rings of the city. These areas have often been rapidly transformed, with larger owner occupied houses being subdivided for renting (6). Some elements of this pattern can also be found in British cities, such as Birmingham, where groups initially ineligible for access to local authority housing, including black newcomers, sought privately rented accommodation in areas of older and larger housing located beyond the original inner areas of working class accommodation (7).

Table 3.1 shows the concentration of private rented housing in urban areas. Because of the different definitions of such areas, direct cross national comparisons are difficult. In West Germany, Denmark, the Netherlands and France, approximately four fifths of the private rented market was in the cities. In the USA and in Britain the concentration was less. This is probably a result of the more restrictive definition of urban areas adopted in the latter two cases.

The concentration of private rented rooms and other furnished accommodation in the larger cities, has already been noted. This can be illustrated with British and French data. Thus the seven major English conurbations contained almost two fifths of all private rented unfurnished accommodation in 1971 but almost one half of all furnished accommodation. Greater London contained

TABLE 3.1
PRIVATE RENTED HOUSING BY LOCATION (Percentages)

	West Germany 1972		Denmark 1970		Netherlands 1975	
	Rented*	All dwgs.	Private rented	All dwgs.	Private rented	All dwgs.
Cities	79.5	59.0	85.5	61.4	80.8	62.0
Elsewhere	20.5	41.0	14.5	38.6	19.2	38.0

	France 1973		USA 1976		England 1971+	
	Private rented	All dwgs.	Private rented	All dwgs.	Private rented	All dwgs.
Cities	85.3	72.7	44.4	31.0	41.0	33.6
Elsewhere	14.7	27.3	55.6	69.0	59.0	66.4

* All dwellings in buildings containing three or more units.

+ Figures are for England and Wales

Cities defined as: in West Germany local authority area
with 20,000 or more inhabitants; in Denmark, Copenhagen and
all other urban areas with 10,000 or more inhabitants; in
Netherlands municipalities with 25,000 or more inhabitants;
in France 'unités urbaines' (includes Paris); in USA core
cities inside Standard Metropolitan Statistical areas (minimum
population 50,000); in England conurbations (seven largest
urban areas, including Greater London).

Sources: Der Bundesminster für Raumordnung etc. 1975;
Danmarks Statistik 1975; Enquête-logement 1973 (1);
US Bureau of the Census etc. 1978a; CBS 1975; OPCS, 1974.

TABLE 3.2
TYPE OF PROPERTY - PRIVATE RENTED SECTOR (Percentages)

	West Germany 1972		Denmark 1970		Netherlands 1975	
	Private rented	All dwgs.	Private rented	All dwgs.	Private rented	All dwgs.
Houses	N/A	47.7	21.7	57.8	40.5	66.0
Flats	N/A	52.3	78.3	42.2	59.5	34.0

	France 1973		USA 1976		England 1977	
	Private rented	All dwgs.	Private rented	All dwgs.	Private rented	All dwgs.
Houses	26.2	49.9	32.5	67.6	52.5	79.5
Flats	73.8	51.1	67.5	32.4	47.5	20.5

Houses defined as: West Germany dwellings within one or two
units; Denmark 'one and two family family houses' and farms;
Netherlands, France and USA, buildings containing one unit
only; England, detached, semi-detached and terrace houses.

Sources: Der Bundesminister für Raumordnung etc. 1975;
Danmarks Statistik 1975; Enquête-logement 1973 (1);
US Bureau of the Census etc. 1978a; Department of the
Environment 1978a; CBS 1975.

just over a fifth of all unfurnished rental housing
but over one third of the furnished stock. Overall,
the seven conurbations contained a third of the
national housing stock and Greater London one
eighth (8). In France in 1973 72% of 'other renters'
(mainly in furnished accommodation) lived in cities
of over 100,000 inhabitants, while only 44.1% of
all households lived in such areas (Enquête-
logement, 1973(1), 55).

As we have seen much privately rented housing
was constructed in areas where land prices were
high and many tenants could only afford to pay for
a small amount of space. Moreover, regulatory
legislation was weak. These factors made for high
densities but, as Table 3.2 illustrates, the type
of units built varied. In Denmark, France and West
Germany most units were flats (9). Typically these
countries still have, in the inner ring, high
density blocks of flats ringed by roads, enclosing
a courtyard occupied by small scale industries.
Of course more recent building has not normally
been at such a high density.

In Britain and the Netherlands the predominant
form of working class accommodation housing was
terrace (row) housing, again at high densities and
intermingled with local industry. In the
Netherlands the physical difficulty of building
high encouraged this form. In Britain the financial
arrangements which supported housing production
probably precluded building flats (Ball, 1977,
13-4). In the USA outside New York, high density,
high rise flats are rather rare (10). In this
country normally land has been cheaply available, so
low density housing has been common, especially for
owner occupation but also for rental. So,
especially in the smaller cities, even when flats
were built they were usually low rise. Thus in
1976, while 67.5% of tenants lived in flats, only
13% of tenants were in blocks containing 50 or
more units (US Bureau of the Census etc., 1978a,
1).

Much of the later private rental housing,
built to lower densities and higher standards than
the nineteenth and early twentieth century stock,
was for better-off tenants, many of whom were
single people, couples or small families. So much
newer rental housing has been in the form of flats.
This can be illustrated by data from the USA, the
Netherlands and France. In the USA about 3.7
million rented units were added to the stock from
1970 to 1976, 82.5% of them were located in SMASs

and 37% in central cities. Most were apartments,
38% of them in small blocks containing 5 - 19 units.
The median size of the units was 3.9 rooms and the
median size of the occupying households was 2.0
persons. Median incomes and rents were about 25%
above the level for the private rental stock as a
whole (US Bureau of the Census etc., 1978a, 10-24).
It will be recalled that the Netherlands did not
have a predominance of flats among its rented
accommodation, yet institutional investors - the
leading constructors of newer private rental units -
have built about 2½ times as many flats as houses
post war while, overall, twice as many houses as
flats were built (social housing organisations
built about equal proportions of houses and flats).
In France, in 1973 four-fifths of the post war
private rental units were flats compared with about
half the total post war stock (Enquête-logement,
1973(1), 57).

AGE, SIZE AND QUALITY OF THE STOCK

Table 3.3 indicates the age of the privately rented
sector. In most cases it shows how strongly the
sector was dominated by older housing and,
conversely, how post war private rental investment
lagged behind investment in the other two tenures.
But a comparison of the stock as a whole with the
private rented stock reveals that the countries
have had a varied history of housing development.
West Germany and the USA have relatively young
total as well as private rented stocks. The
Netherlands has a relatively young housing stock
but the post war development of private rented
housing has not been nearly as substantial as that
of the other tenures. England, Denmark and France
have considerably older housing stocks and an even
slower development of private rented housing. (But
particular attention should be paid to the varied
dates for which the data is available). More
detailed statistics add to the data in
Table 3.3. In France new housing output was, it
will be recalled, at a low level between the wars.
In 1973 21% of the total stock was built
before 1871 and 22% between 1871 and 1914, much of
this has remained in the hands of private landlords.
In contrast only 16% of the stock dated from 1915-
48 (Enquête-logement, 1973(2), 26-7). In England,
62% of the private rental stock was built before
1914, but only about 25% of the total stock. Only
13% of the sector dated from after the Second World

TABLE 3.3
AGE OF THE PRIVATELY RENTED STOCK (Percentages)

	West Germany 1972		Denmark 1970[+]		Netherlands 1975	
	Private rented	All dwgs.	Private rented	All dwgs.	Private rented	All dwgs.
Pre-war	58.6	44.2	74.0	51.3	64.4	38.0
Post-war*	41.4	55.8	22.8	43.0	35.6	62.0

	France 1973		USA 1976		England 1977	
	Private rented	All dwgs.	Private rented	All dwgs.	Private rented	All dwgs.
Pre-war	69.6	58.7	42.6	34.3	76.0	51.0
Post-war	30.4	41.3	57.4	65.7	24.0	49.0

* Post-war defined as: West Germany and France 1949 or later;
Denmark 1941 or later; Netherlands 1945 or later; United
States and Great Britain 1940 or later.

+ Small percentage - age unknown.

Sources: Der Bundesminister für Raumordnung etc. 1975;
Enquête-logement 1973 (1); Danmarks Statistik 1975; US
Bureau of the Census etc. 1978a; CBS 1975; Department
of the Environment, 1978a.

War, compared with almost half the total stock,
(Department of the Environment, 1978a, 44). In the
Netherlands in 1971, about a quarter of the private
rented sector dated from 1906 or earlier and another
quarter from 1906-30 (CBS, 1971). In Denmark, about
44% of the private rental stock was built before
1919, compared with 29% of the stock as a whole
(Danmarks Statistik, 1975, 48-9) (11).

For reasons which have already been discussed,
small units predominate in the private rented
sector. Unfortunately, wholly comparable statistics
are not available, but this characteristic was
evident in each country. The average private rented
unit in France contained about 3.0 rooms, compared
to 3.6 in the stock as a whole (Enquête-logement,
1973(1), 55). In West Germany about four fifths of
the sector contained four rooms or less, compared
with two thirds of the total stock (Der
Bundesminister für Raumordnung etc., 1975, 22).
In the Netherlands 70% of the rental stock contained
five rooms or less, compared with 64% of the total
stock (CBS, 1971). In Denmark, 77% of the stock
had three rooms or less, compared with 53% of the
stock as a whole (Danmarks Statistik, 1975, 48-9).
In England over 60% of private rented units had
four rooms or less, compared with 44% of the stock
as a whole (Department of the Environment, 1978a,
26). In the USA, 66% of the sector contained four
rooms or less, compared with 35% of the stock as a
whole (US Bureau of the Census etc., 1978, 3).

These comparisons mask the magnitude of the
disparity in the average size of private rented
accommodation compared to owner occupied housing.
For instance, in the USA only a sixth of the owner
occupied stock had four rooms or less, compared
with two thirds of the private rental units (US
Bureau of the Census etc., 1978, 3). Aggregate
statistics also mask the fact that the average size
of some rental subsectors was even smaller than that
of the whole sector. For example, in England 46% of
the private rented furnished sector consisted of
one or two rooms, compared with 3.7% of all units.
In comparison with social rented housing, the
average size of the private rented stock was
somewhat smaller in France, England and Denmark and
somewhat larger in West Germany and the Netherlands
(Enquète-logement, 1973(1), 55; Department of the
Environment, 1978a, 27; Danmarks Statistik, 1975,
48-9; Bundesminister für Raumordnung etc., 1975,
22; CBS, 1971).

The private rented sector was in poor
condition, a state consequent upon its age (and the
economic weakness of the sector, to be described
later). Table 3.4 shows one aspect of this problem,
the lack of amenities (12). This was most apparent
in West Germany, Denmark, the Netherlands and,
above all, in France, less in Britain and only to a
minor degree in the USA. The quality of the private
rented stock will be further discussed in Chapter
7. However, it is worth noting that more detailed
data for England shows that the private rental
sector was more deficient in having unshared usage
of basic facilities than the stock as a whole.
Moreover, the furnished sub-sector was even worse
off (13). In France too, the furnished sector was
markedly more deficient than the private rental
stock as a whole (Enquête-logement, 1973(1), 196).
In general the older housing is in the worst
condition, although in Germany some of the housing
built immediately after the Second World War was
less adequate than the inter war stock. Finally,
because much of the post war investment was carried
out by companies rather than by individuals, the
worst property was often owned by the latter type
of landlord.

RENTS

A longer discussion of rents is contained in Chapter
5. But in order to fill out the profile of the
sector, brief details of rent levels will be given
here.
      In France, the private rented stock was divided
into three sectors, according to the rent setting
arrangements. These were: first, pre-1949 stock
still under rent control; second, similar stock
with freely determined rents; and third, stock built
since 1948 with rents which were freely determined
or related to increases in the cost of construction.
In 1973 the average rent was lowest in the old
controlled sector, about 15% higher in the old
free rented sector and fractionally more in the
much better quality social rented (HLM) sector.
Rents in the newer private rented sector were about
75% higher than HLM rents, and yet in terms of
quality these two types of units were similar. In
fact there was only about a 15% gap between the
average rent of these newer properties and the
average financial charges paid by those who were
buying their own homes (14). Rents varied greatly

TABLE 3.4
INDICATORS OF AMENITIES IN PRIVATE RENTED HOUSING (Percentages)

	West Germany 1972			Denmark 1970		
	Private rent	Other rent	All dwgs.	Private rent	Other rent	All dwgs.
With	68.0	95.0	87.0	61.1	77.1	76.5
Lacking*	32.0	5.0	13.0	39.9	12.9	23.5

	Netherlands 1967			France 1973		
	Private rent	Other rent	All dwgs.	Private rent	Other rent	All dwgs.
With	68.3	85.0	72.4	53.6	94.9	65.0
Lacking	31.7	15.0	27.6	46.4	5.1	35.0

	England 1977			USA 1976	
	Private rent	Other rent	All dwgs.	All rent	All dwgs.
With	89.0	99.6	97.3	96.4	97.0
Lacking	11.0	0.4	2.7	3.6	3.0

'Other rent' = mainly social rented housing.

* Lacking defined as: Netherlands and West Germany, no bath;
France, no bath or sanitary installation (minimum recognised
provision, a wash-basin); USA, no complete bathroom (ie.
containing WC, bath/shower, wash-basin and piped hot water);
England and Denmark, no bath/shower.

Sources: Der Bundesminister für Raumordnung etc. 1975;
Enquête-logement, 1973 (1); Danmarks Statistik, 1975;
US Bureau of the Census etc. 1978; CBS, 1967; Department
of the Environment, 1978a.

with location, being higher in the larger cities
than elsewhere, especially in Paris. In terms of
rent paid per room occupied, HLM tenants paid
least, fairly closely followed by tenants in the
controlled stock. Households in the older free
rented stock paid a little more but those in newer
rented housing paid a lot more, almost double the
amount paid for HLM units. The worst value for money
occurred in the furnished sector where the cost
per room at over 2000f per year was about two and
a half times the cost in the HLM sector (Enquête-
logement, 1973(1), 143, 165).

In Denmark rents were lower in the privately
rented than in the social sector, but were higher in
a very small luxury sub-sector. There was a sharp
difference in rents for less well equipped and/or
older units and for the better equipped and/or newer
units. Because of subsidies, newer social rented
housing had considerably lower rents than newer
private rented units (Danmarks Statistik, 1975,
48-9, 216 and 20).

In West Germany the average rent was little
more than for social rented housing but this
conceals significant variations. In post-war private
and social rented units (of comparable size and
condition), rents in the former were about a third
higher than rents in the latter - again the effect
of subsidies is apparent (Der Bundesminister für
Raumordnung etc., 1975, 34). In Britain the same
comparisons cannot be made because there was very
little new private rented accommodation. But in 1977
the median annual rent of the social sector was
50% higher than that of the lower quality private
unfurnished sector, but the median rent for the
even less satisfactory furnished sub sector was over
50% higher than the median for the social sector
(OPCS, 1979, 22).

In the Netherlands patterns were rather similar.
The highest rents were in the pressurised markets
of the Randstad and were especially high in newer
housing on the periphery of the larger cities. Rents
for the property built in the seventies were
notably higher than those built in earlier periods,
the effects of inflation were evident. Newer
privately rented units were considerably more
expensive than newer social units, by about a third
in the case of the most recently built housing. The
association of differing rent levels within the
private sector with the two main types of ownership
was also apparent. Most of the cheaper property was
owned by individual landlords, the more expensive

units tended to be owned by companies (15).

In the USA the social rented sector was so small that comparisons between its rents and those of the private sector are of little value. Within this latter sector rents were highest in suburban locations, low in rural areas and fell between these levels in centre cities. Rents were higher in the Northeast and West and lowest in the North Central and Southern regions. Again new units were much more expensive than the existing stock (US Bureau of the Census etc., 1978, passim).

To summarise, the private rental sector offered older and poorer quality housing at rents which were often broadly comparable with the newer and far more satisfactory subsidised and non profit social rented sector. That part of the private rented sector which, in terms of quality, was comparable with the social sector was far more costly. Indeed in France, for the newer property buying was almost as cheap an option as renting and may even have been cheaper, given the availability of tax subsidies for owner occupiers. However, on the French and British evidence, furnished accommodation provided by far the worst bargain and less detailed evidence from the other countries also suggested that the market for rented rooms/ furnished accommodation was expensive. This was because of the lack of subsidies and effective regulation of the sector, which provided housing of last resort for those who were in a weak position to bargain.

PRODUCTION OF NEW PRIVATE RENTED HOUSING

Figure 3.1 gives an indication of the trend in new building in the post war years. Output declined in Denmark, the Netherlands and France to a very small fraction of all new housing by the end of the seventies. At first sight, there seems to have been a slight revival of building in England after 1960, this is wholly misleading as the post 1960 figures also include conversions. In fact it is doubtful if even 1% of new building in Britain was for private rental by the seventies and such building was largely restricted to central London plus some accommodation let in connection with employment elsewhere.

West Germany had considerable success in maintaining new private rented output, giving extensive subsidies to new investors. But even here investment was declining by the late seventies and

FIGURE 3.1   OUTPUT OF NEW PRIVATE RENTAL UNITS AS A PROPORTION OF ALL NEW UNITS
(APPROXIMATE) VARIOUS YEARS (1)

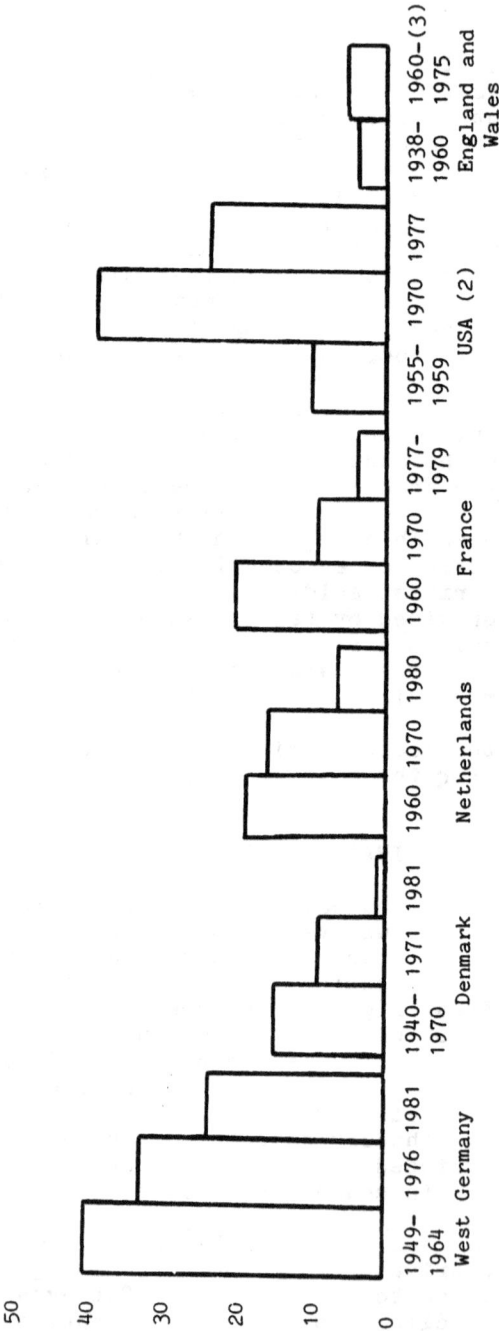

1949– 1976–1981	1940– 1971 1981	1960 1970 1980	1960 1970 1977–	1955– 1970 1977	1938– 1960–(3)
1964	1970		1979	1959	1960 1975
West Germany	Denmark	Netherlands	France	USA (2)	England and Wales

NOTES: (1) In many cases some estimation is necessary - especially for earlier years.
(2) All multi-family starts (ie building with five units or more).
(3) New building and conversions.

Sources: Der Bundesminster für Raumordnung etc. 1975; DIW, 1976; Danmarks Statistik, 1975 and 1925–77;
CBS (monthly); Christian Topalov (ex. inf. Ministere de l'Equipment); US Department of Housing
and Urban Development 1977; Bovaird, et al 1982b, Department of the Environment, 1977a.

financial institutions were becoming less and
less willing to lend for this purpose, preferring
to support building for owner occupation.

In the USA, for the reasons already discussed,
there was a recovery of output in the sixties.
There followed a decline in the mid seventies. The
relative dynamism of the rental market in the
Sunbelt states, already noted, can be illustrated
by reference to the distribution of new rented
housing for the years 1970-76. In these years about
15% of all new units were located in the north-
eastern region, which contained about 25% of the
total rental stock. In contrast, 40% of all new
units were in the south which only contained 30%
of the total rental stock (there was a closer
balance between these two proportions in the other
two regions) (US Bureau of the Census etc., 1978,
passim).

So, for a few years there was a remarkable
expansion of the rental share of new production.
But by the late seventies the rents of new units
developed rather slowly, suggesting that demand
was on the wane. It seemed likely that the output
of new units would return closer to the proportions
that it comprised in the fifties. In the older
areas, the prospects for new production (especially
when unaided by direct subsidies) have tended to
decline in the same way as they have in the
housing markets of the European countries.

Some details of production of private rental
housing in comparison with other tenures will help
to fill out the picture given above. There is
little more to discuss in Britain, because of the
lack of new private rented output since the Second
World War. Overall, new production after the War
increased to over 350,000 by 1954 and then
fluctuated around 300,000 until the early sixties.
There was a rapid increase to over 425,000 in 1968
before production dropped back to the more normal
post war levels. In the late seventies there was a
further rapid decline to about 235,000 in 1980
(McKay and Cox, 1979, 123, 127; Building Societies
Association, 1983, 14).

In France, as elsewhere, it is difficult to
obtain precise details of completions of private
rented housing. Overall, new building remained at
a low level for several years after the Second
World War. Even by 1954 only about 160,000 new
units a year were being produced. By 1959, with the
aid of new subsidies, over 320,000 completions a
year were being achieved. In the early sixties

adverse economic conditions and a reduction in
government assistance caused output to stagnate.
But the expansion of building became an important
government objective in the latter part of this
decade and by the early seventies over 500,000
units a year were being built. Later, housing was
given a lower priority and this, together with the
worsening of the economic climate, resulted in a
drop in output to about 400,000 in 1979 (Duclaud-
Williams, 1978, 148-9; Commission of the European
Communities, 1982, 126-7). No data is available
concerning how much of the early post war output
was for private rental but figures for the 'number
of dwellings authorised for construction by their
destination' exist from 1960. In 1960 about 45% of
all authorisations were for rental (social and
private), by 1971 this had fallen to 29% and by
1977 to only 19%. Within this total, private rental
output accounted for a declining share. Thus about
20% of all authoristions were for private rental
in 1960 (i.e. 45% of all rental authorisations)
but by 1971 only 9% and by 1977-9 only 3% (16).
So by this latter date HLM building dominated the
production of rental units.
      In Denmark the only way of estimating what
proportion of new output was for private rental
before 1970 is by considering the proportion of
standing stock built at various times. Overall,
output rose in the post war period, to over 55,000
by 1973, but fell to about 31,000 by 1979. From
1941-60 the non-profit housing organisations
dominated the rental market, accounting for a third
of total housing output, while private landlords
accounted for a sixth. From 1960-70 the private
rental share was maintained but social housing
construction fell away as the market for owner
occupation began to grow. By the late sixties
private rental construction began to decline too,
so that under 10% of output in 1970 was accounted
for by this tenure (Danmarks Statistik, 1975, 48-
9). Since 1970 annual figures for new output have
been available and by 1978 only 1,150 new private
rented units were produced, 3.4% of all output.
This is an over-estimate, because these statistics
also include completions of 'freehold' (i.e. owner
occupied), flats, a small but growing part of the
market (Danmarks Statistik, 1925-78; Commission
of the European Communities, 1981, 126-7).
      In West Germany total output increased to
almost 600,000 by 1966 and then fluctuated between
5-600,000 up to 1971. There was a sharp increase to

over 700,000 in 1973 and a marked decline to about
360,000 in 1979. About 11½ million new dwellings
were built between 1949 and 1974, two thirds of
these were for rental, well over half of which,
about 3.9 million, were owned by private landlords.
As elsewhere, the social sector was especially
important in the earlier years but the pattern of
development differed from that in, for example
Denmark. Thus in later years there was sustained
production for private rental. In the early post
war years about 70% of housing was directly
subsidised (including some for owner occupation),
whereas by 1971 only 21% was so assisted. But in
the seventies, although the share of new units for
private landlords had risen, the total production
of rental units had fallen. Thus about 300,000
rental units were produced in 1971, of which
230,000 were for private landlords. But by 1976
only 160,000 units were built, 130,000 for private
rental. In part this reflected generally declining
output but the trend to owner occupation was also
marked. The proportion of new output for private
landlords fell from 40% in the sixties and before
to 33% in 1976 and 24% in 1981 (Der Bundesminister
für Raumordnung, etc., 1975, 10; DIW 1976, 371;
Commission of the European Communities, 1981,
126-7; Bovaird et al, 1982, 59).
      Trends in the Netherlands show a, by now
familiar, pattern. After the war housing production
slowly rose to over 100,000 by 1964 and peaked at
over 155,000 in 1973. Then there was a sharp
contraction, down to about 87,000 in 1979. In the
late 1940s 60-80% of all output came from the
housing associations and local authorities. As in
Denmark, private renting probably accounted for no
more than 15-20% of output, then and subsequently.
From the early seventies a significant change began
to occur. For many years approximately one third
of all new building had been for owner occupation
but between 1970 and 1978 its share rose to 60%
and social renting began to provide a smaller share.
By 1980 less than 6% of new output was for private
renting (CBS, monthly; Commission of the European
Communities, 1981, 126-7; Bovaird et. al., 1982b,
59).
      In the USA post war housing starts rapidly
reached an average level of about 1.4 units per annum.
There was a substantial increase in the early 70s -
to over 2.3 units in 1972, then a rapid collapse -
to about 1.2 million in 1975. Since then there

has been another sharp rise   followed by a fall.
There was a brief period in the late forties when
private rental housing boomed, due to a generous
government subsidy. Also, as already mentioned,
there was a period in the late sixties and early
seventies when there was a further boom. But in
the following years only around a fifth of all new
production was for this sector, much of it aided by
direct and indirect subsidies (17) (US Department
of Housing and Urban Development, 1977; 1978, 29;
Le Gates and Murphy, 1981, 256).

So by the late seventies private rented housing
had a minor share of total output (which had itself
contracted sharply). New building only remained
significant in the USA and West Germany. In the
former case there were still good market
possibilities in some areas and, lacking an
effective social sector, there was a continuing
commitment to heavily subsidising some landlords
to perform this role. In West Germany government
subsidies were also significant. Even so, in both
countries new private rented building was
contracting.

CONCLUSION

The predominant role that the private rented sector
had before 1939 has not been re-established,
although it continued to be a major provider of
accommodation after 1945. But, in most cases, it
was in competition with social rented housing and,
latterly, with owner occupation.

The various attributes of the private rental
stock outlined in this chapter serve to underline
and illustrate the historical role and the
declining fortunes of this tenure. It is
concentrated in cities, areas which are often now
in economic decline. It is older than the rest of
the stock, lacks amenities and is often in poor
condition. It tends to be smaller than the average
size in the other tenures. Overall, private rents
are not much more, or even less, than rents in the
social sector - and considerably less than the
costs of owner occupation. But the social rented
sector usually offered far better value for money.

New private rented building had virtually
ceased by the late seventies in Britain, France,
Denmark and the Netherlands. In West Germany and
the USA the prospects were for no more than a
relatively minor future contribution to new

building. Moreover, during the recent collapse of housebuilding consequent on the economic depression, private rented output has suffered the sharpest decline (18). In fact, as we shall see, the economic and political climate of the last 10-15 years has been generally unfavourable to the prospects for private renting, accentuating longer term causes of decline, thus leading to the collapse of production as well as other symptoms of crisis. But in order to understand the economic weakness of this tenure it is necessary to examine who lives in and who owns the sector, as well as the relevant government policies. In the next chapter we examine the first of these matters.

NOTES

1. Information supplied by Professor Emanuel Tobier.
2. Information supplied by Jan van der Schaar.
3. Figures derived from Der Bundesminster für Raumordnung etc. 1975.
4. Figures derived from Recensement de Population, 1962 and Enquête-logement, 1973 (1).
5. A useful account of social rented housing in London is Young and Kramer, 1978. See also Harloe, Issacharoff and Minns, 1974. For Paris see Sutcliffe, 1970; Castells, 1978, 93-125 and Ardagh, 1977, 285-359.
6. The literature on urban renewal is extensive. See, for example, Abrams, 1965; Keyes, 1969; Hartman, 1974. Several useful articles and an extensive bibliography are in Pynoos, Schafer and Hartman, 1973 (new edition 1980).
7. Classic studies of this are Glass, 1960 and Rex and Moore, 1967, the former on London, the latter on Birmingham.
8. Figures derived from OPCS, 1974, passim.
9. Figures for West Germany are incomplete but flat building was important in this country. For an early description see Board of Trade, 1908.
10. The 'Old Law' tenements of New York City, built between 1867 and 1901, were comparable with the blocks to be seen in German and other cities. This is not surprising as they were produced under roughly the same market conditions. See Jackson, A. 1976; Board of Trade, 1911.
11. Unfortunately, this level of detail concerning the US stock is unavailable.
12. It is not possible to get more broadly based comparative data on amenities, the most 'standardly' available data concerns the presence or absence of a bath, even here data is not uniform.
13. Department of the Environment, 1978a, 30. The basic amenities are inside WC, fixed bath/ shower and piped hot water.
14. The data is based on the gross rent (which may include some charges, although those which can be separated out are deducted) and the gross cost of mortgage repayments less any direct subsidies but without deduction of indirect (tax) subsidies. No account is taken of housing allowances (Enquête-logement, 1973 (1), 38). All other data in this section are for gross rents, in the USA these normally include utilities costs.

15. Information supplied by Jan van der Schaar.
Based on Central Directie van de Volkshuisinvesting,
1975.

16. Information supplied by Christian Topalov
(Ministère de l'Équipement statistics).

17. About 20% of multi-family completions in
1978 were directly subsidised. At the same date
about 80% of all new multi-family housing was for
renting. So about 25% of private rental output was
subsidised. There were also extensive tax subsidies
(US Department of Housing and Urban Development,
1980a, 46 and Appendix A).

18. Although there has also been a drop in
the proportion that is directly subsidised (i.e.
mainly social rented housing). Thus from 1975-9
the share of subsidised completions dropped by
35% in Denmark (and the absolute number by about
50%); by 24% in France (and the absolute number by
41%); by 18% in the Netherlands (and the absolute
number by 37%). In West Germany there was a slight
increase in the proportion of directly subsidised
output but a 14% fall in the absolute number of
subsidised units (Commission of the European
Communities, 1981, 126-7).

Chapter Four

A PROFILE OF THE PRIVATE RENTED SECTOR II
TENANTS, LANDLORDS AND ACCESS

As the last chapter showed, the private rental
sector has suffered from declining fortunes in
comparison with the other tenures. This chapter
examines which groups were still dependent on this
sector, which types of investors still provided
such accommodation and the means of access to
private tenancies.

Housing surveys provide useful data on the
tenants of private rental housing but far less
information about landlords. Partly this is because
most surveys collect characteristics of occupiers
rather than owners. But also tracing landlords in
order to interview is often difficult as, for
example, various enquiries in Britain have
discovered (1). However some information is
available which can be supplemented with more
specific, often locally based studies. Both types of
sources are used in this chapter. Accurate
information on methods of access is even less
frequently available and only a very general outline
is attempted here, much of it is based on the views
of those interviewed in the research.

TENANTS - HOUSEHOLD TYPE, AGE AND OCCUPANCY

Table 4.1 shows details of household size in the
private rental sector, compared with owner occupiers
and the 'other' rental sector (i.e. mainly social
housing tenants). The outstanding general feature
was the high concentration of small households in
the private rental stock and the under-
representation of larger households. Data from
Britain, France and West Germany shows that this
bias was even sharper in certain parts of the rental
sector. In Britain and France approximately 80% of

TABLE 4.1
HOUSEHOLD SIZE - MAIN TENURES (Percentages)

	West Germany 1972			Denmark 1970		
	Private rent	Other rent	Owner occpr.	Private rent	Other rent	Owner occpr.
1/2 person	62.0	53.3	41.8	66.7	48.8	44.2
5 or more persons	7.8	9.3	18.3	5.2	11.8	15.8

	Netherlands 1971			France 1973		
	Private rent	Other rent	Owner occpr.	Private rent	Other rent	Owner occpr.
1/2 person	47.6	33.7	34.0	55.6	31.3	49.4
5 or more persons*	33.4	46.1	48.2	11.7	24.8	17.8

	USA 1976		England 1977		
	All rent	Owner occpr.	Private rent	Other rent	Owner occpr.
1/2 person	63.2	44.6	69.2	52.9	50.0
5 or more persons	10.4	18.7	6.7	14.5	10.8

'Other rent' = mainly social rented housing

* Data for the Netherlands for 4 or more person households.

Sources: Der Bundesminister für Raumordnung etc. 1975;
Danmarks Statistik, 1975; CBS, 1971; Enquête-logement,
1973 (1); US Bureau of the Census etc, 1978; Department
of the Environment, 1978a.

households in the furnished rental sub-sector
consisted of 1 or 2 persons only. In West Germany
two thirds of all sub-tenants were in 1 or 2 person
households (Department of the Environment, 1978a,
29; Enquête-logement, 1973(1), 101; Der
Bundesminister für Raumordnung etc. 1975, 46). In
other countries there was less direct evidence that
such a pattern also existed.

The figures in Table 4.1 suggest that the age
composition of private tenants was biased towards
the young and/or the elderly. Table 4.2 confirms
this. The clearest bias was towards the young,
although in West Germany this was obscured because
data is only available for the rented sectors as a
whole. The position with regard to the elderly
varied. In West Germany,Denmark, the Netherlands and
Britain there were higher proportions of the elderly
in private rented than in owner occupied units. In
France and the USA the reverse was true. Here the
bias to younger households was the single dominant
trend. In France the high proportion of elderly
owner occupiers was mainly accounted for by the low
income rural owner occupied sector, most of these
people were outright owners.

Data for the social rented sector is only
available for Denmark, the Netherlands, France and
Britain. In France, Denmark and the Netherlands
access appeared to be reasonable for younger
households (at least the proportions of such households in the two parts of the rental sector were
similar). In Britain access was more a consequence
of local authority allocation rules. In the other
countries the youngest households probably had less
chance of access to social housing. Only in Denmark
was there a noticeable disparity between the
proportions of the elderly in private and in social
rented housing.

The bias towards the young was considerable
in the furnished/rented rooms subsectors. In Britain
almost two fifths of those in furnished
accommodation were under 25 years old and another
third were 25 to 35 years old (Department of the
Environment, 1978a, 29). In Denmark two thirds of
those in rented rooms were under 25 years old
(Danmarks Statistik, 1975, Table 9). In France over
half of all furnished tenants and in West Germany
two fifths of all sub-tenants were under 30 years
old (Enquête-Logement, 1973(1), 95; Der
Bundesminister für Raumordnung etc., 1975, 46).

In France and Britain there were older,
controlled private rented units which new tenants

TABLE 4.2
AGE OF HEAD OF HOUSEHOLD - MAIN TENURES (Percentages)

	West Germany 1972		Denmark 1970		
	Owner occpr.	All rented	Owner occpr.	Private rent	Other rent
Under 30 years old	3.0	16.3	9.2	21.9	18.8
65 years or over	23.0	24.3	23.7	26.4	17.2

	Netherlands 1971			France 1973		
	Owner occpr.	Private rent	Other rent	Owner occpr.	Private rent	Other rent
Under 30 years old	11.0	20.0	18.0	4.1	25.2	25.2
65 years or over	17.0	22.0	20.0	28.7	11.1	21.1

	USA 1976*		Britain 1977		
	Owner occpr.	All rented	Owner occpr.	Private rent	Other rent
Under 30 years old	11.8	41.2	11.0	26.8	9.0
65 years or over	15.3	10.0	23.8	30.0	31.0

'Other rent' = mainly social rented housing

* USA - 2 or more person households, wife present, male head, no non-relatives only.

Sources: Der Bundesminister für Raumordnung etc. 1975;
Danmarks Statistik, 1975; Enquête-logement, 1973 (1);
US Bureau of the Census etc., 1978; OPCS, 1979; CBS, 1975.

were not normally eligible for. So the average age
of households in this sub-sector was high. In France
the post war rental stock housed many younger
households. In the Netherlands, although there were
similar proportions of young households in the
(newer) company owned stock and in that owned by
individual landlords, there was a concentration of
the elderly in the latter housing, the same probably
existed in Britain.

The most detailed picture of the age
composition of the private sector can be gained from
the US Census and Annual Housing Surveys (2). These
show high concentrations of single parent (mainly
female headed) younger families, single person
households and households with two or more adults
unrelated by marriage. Also of interest is the way
in which the demand for rental housing changed over
time. Between 1970-75 the number of owners grew
twice as fast as the number of tenants, except
among the 'special groups' referred to above. Among
'normal' families (i.e. husband and wife with or
without children) there was a decline in the
propensity to rent, even in age groups which had
been most liable to rent in 1970 (e.g. households
with a head under 30 years of age). In contrast,
the concentration of single parent and single households was growing. These groups were often likely
to have relatively low incomes. In Denmark the bias
of the private rented sector towards such 'non
normal' households was also evident, as well as a
bias towards households with few children (Danmarks
Statistik, 1975, 19).

National definitions and data regarding
occupancy levels vary to such an extent that
information cannot be cross tabulated. All six
countries reduced severe overcrowding very
substantially in the post war years. Immediately
after the war this was a serious problem,
especially in West Germany and the Netherlands.
In Germany too the influx of refugees from the east
exacerbated the problem. By the seventies overcrowding was minimal except in France. Thus in 1970,
between a quarter and a third of all households in
the French rental sector were overcrowded, this was
worse in the older stock than in the post-war
private rental and social sectors (Enquête-logement,
1970, 85).

In Britain occupancy levels were higher in the
private rental sector than in the stock as a whole
(though not as high as in the social sector). The

furnished sub sector contained a significant
proportion of overcrowded households (about 12.5%)
and housed very few under-occupying households. In
contrast almost 60% of unfurnished tenants had
'surplus' accommodation. This was because many of
these were elderly and were more likely than
furnished tenants to be living in houses or purpose
built flats, rather than rooms or sub-divided units
(Department of the Environment, 1978a, 29).

In Denmark overcrowding in the private rental
sector was greater than in the stock as a whole but
less than in the social sector. Again there was a
high proportion of the elderly in the private stock
(Danmarks Statistik, 1975, 48). In the USA overcrowding was generally rare (US Bureau of the Census
etc. 1978, 4). In contrast there was still
substantial overcrowding in some parts of the
Netherlands - especially in the pressurised housing
markets of the Randstad.

TENANTS -INCOMES AND SOCIO-ECONOMIC COMPOSITION

Table 4.3 shows the distribution of incomes in the
private and social rental sectors and in the whole
stock. In the USA and Denmark the data refers to all
rental housing and the whole stock. The poorest
households were usually over represented in the
rented sectors and the better off under represented.
But there were some interesting variations. A
slightly lower proportion of the poorest households
were in social housing in West Germany and the
Netherlands than in the private rental sector. In
Britain the disparity was sharper. But the
difference was greatest in France, where much
social housing had been allocated to the better off
skilled manual and 'junior' white collar workers.
In Germany a rather balanced range of incomes was
represented in the private rented sector.

The growth of social rented housing had
certainly not drained off a disproportionate number
of the least well off from the private rented
sector, leaving the latter to deal with the more
solvent demand. (Rather the reverse in fact -
compare, for example, the proportion of middle
income groups in the two tenures in Germany, France
and Great Britain). To some extent this may have
been because the allocation of social housing tended
to favour families with children. Such households
were often in what might broadly be defined as
'middle age', the peak period for earnings for many

TABLE 4.3
GROSS HOUSEHOLD INCOME DISTRIBUTION - RENTED TENURES AND ALL
HOUSING (Percentages)

West Germany / USA 1976

DM/Month	Social rent	Private rent	All	$/Annum	All rented	All
<600	12.0	12.8	11.2	<5000	30.7	19.8
600-1000	23.4	24.0	21.3	5-10000	28.9	22.0
1000-1400	26.8	23.2	23.7	10-15000	20.4	20.1
1400-1800	18.7	16.7	17.6	15-20000	10.2	14.7
1800-2200	10.7	10.7	11.9	20-25000	4.9	9.6
2200+	8.5	11.1	13.8	25000+	4.8	13.8

Netherlands 1975 / France 1973

f/Annum	Social rent	Private rent	All	F/Annum	Social rent	Private rent	All
<1200	11.0	12.0	10.0	<10000	5.9	13.8	14.7
12-18000	22.0	23.0	19.0	10-20000	17.7	23.7	21.6
18-24000	28.0	26.0	25.0	20-30000	28.9	23.6	22.2
24-30000	23.0	17.0	20.0	30-40000	25.1	18.0	17.5
30-38000	10.0	12.0	12.0	40-50000	18.0	13.8	15.2
38000+	7.0	10.0	14.0	60000+	4.4	7.1	8.5

Denmark 1970 / Great Britain 1977

K/Annum	All rented	All	£/Annum	Social rent	Private rent	All
<20000	15.2	10.0	<1000	13.0	23.0	12.0
20-40000	20.2	14.6	1-2000	32.0	32.0	22.0
40-60000	19.9	17.5	2-3000	23.0	21.0	20.0
60-80000	18.1	18.6	3-4000	22.0	15.0	22.0
80-100000	14.2	16.2	4-5000	8.0	6.0	12.0
80000+	12.4	23.0	5000+	2.0	3.0	12.0

Sources: Der Bundesminister für Raumordnung etc. 1975;
Danmarks Statistik, 1975; Enquête-logement, 1973 (1);
US Bureau of the Census etc. 1978; OPCS, 1979; CBS, 1975.

moderate and low income earners. In short, a
correlation between age and earnings may well have
been responsible for much of the variation in the
proportions of middle income groups in the two
parts of the rental sector.

In France there was a high proportion of low
income owner occupiers (mainly the rural owners
mentioned previously). Within the rented sector the
poorer families were in the pre-1949 controlled
and free rented property (although small numbers of
very high income households lived in controlled
luxury units, mainly in Paris). Post war private
rental units mainly housed those with middle and
higher incomes, whereas the furnished rental units
were mainly let to those on low incomes (Enquête-
logement,1973(1), 88).

Unfortunately more detailed data is not
available for Denmark. In West Germany the income
distribution of sub-tenants was heavily skewed, the
proportion of sub-tenants in the lowest income
group was double that of tenants (and three times
that of owner occupiers) (Der Bundesminister für
Raumordnung etc. 1975, 44). In Britain, in contrast,
furnished tenants tended to have higher incomes
than unfurnished tenants. This was because many
unfurnished tenants were elderly while many
furnished tenants were young and the middle aged
and middle income groups which existed in private
renting in, for example, West Germany, were far
less common (OPCS, 1979, 26). In the Netherlands
and the USA, as in France, there was a difference
between the incomes of those in the older part of
the private rental sector (often owned by
individual landlords) and in the newer stock (often
owned by companies) (CBS, 1971; Enquête-logement,
1973(1), 88; US Bureau of the Census, etc, 1978,
10, 23).

The US data, it will be recalled, showed that
the concentration of low income private tenants
was increasing. The effects of this can be seen
when income data is examined. Thus from 1970-76
median owner occupier incomes rose by almost 50%
whereas median renter incomes rose by only a little
over 25%. The lack of growth in the incomes of
tenants living in the centres of the older and
larger cities was even more pronounced, a
consequence of the shifts of population and
employment opportunities described in chapter 2
(US Bureau of the Census etc.,1978, 10, 65, 96).
This relatively slow growth of tenants' incomes was
also evident in Britain where average earnings

increased by over 250% between 1972 and 1977 whereas those of private tenants only increased by about 200% (OPCS, 1979).

Although the data is patchy and difficult to compare the emerging pattern is consistent with the claim that the private rental sector was losing much of the more solvent middle and upper income demand which had previously helped to sustain it. The process was furthest advanced in Britain where private renting had become a marginal sector, providing housing of a last resort for those who could not afford owner occupation or obtain social housing. But it was also evident in the USA, where private renting still provided housing for a substantial proportion of the population.

Data on the social composition of the sector illustrates the extent to which it was occupied by the economically inactive or those in lower paid occupations, although a different pattern applied to the newer units. In France the older controlled and free rented stock had a very high concentration of tenants who were retired. The newer private rented units had a concentration of better paid professional and white collar workers, this housing was too expensive for many manual workers or the retired. In contrast, social housing provided accommodation for routine office and manual workers, almost 60% of units being occupied by these groups (Enquete-logement, 1973(1), 83, 183). In Denmark the association of the private rental sector with non economically active tenants was also clear, about a third of tenants fell into this category compared with a quarter of all households. There were also above average proportions of less well paid white collar workers and skilled and unskilled manual workers. Social housing provided less accommodation for the economically inactive and was a little more biased towards those with higher status white collar occupations (Danmarks Statistik, 1975, 48).

In Britain too there was a higher proportion of economically inactive. This reflected the furnished sub-sector's role as temporary housing for better paid younger workers, and housing of last resort for those who were in a weak position in the housing market, such as single parent families and the disabled. In contrast, social housing accommodated a high proportion of manual workers

In the Netherlands the occupational classification is very broad but it shows once again that a high proportion of economically inactive (retired, students etc) were in the sector. The newer property housed many white collar workers. Again, much social housing was allocated to manual workers (CBS, 1975).

LANDLORDS

As noted in Chapter 1, the early growth of private renting was a response to the demand for housing by new migrants to the cities. This demand was not met, on the whole, by large scale industrial or finance capital but by local tradesmen, professionals and the building industry. But, except in West Germany and to some extent in the USA, the provision of new private rented units by individual landlords had declined sharply. When individual landlords entered the market in countries such as France and Britain they were often letting existing property.

The reasons for the decline in the new investment by individual landlords reflected the overall decline of the private rented sector which provides the central theme of this book. But some additional factors were important. With the development of investment media far more opportunities are now open to the small investor than fifty or a hundred years ago (e.g. lending to local authorities, unit trusts, and national savings schemes). Also a very significant development occurred within the housing market, namely the growth of owner occupation and of the agencies which financed house purchase, such as the building societies in Britain, the savings banks in the Netherlands and the savings and loan institutions in the USA. Often, assisted by government intervention, such agencies were able to operate with low margins of risk providing a safe investment medium for the small investor. In many cases these institutions had formerly financed much rental housing but the increasing economic weakness of the sector encouraged them to restrict their lending to owner occupiers. Thus the British building societies virtually ceased to lend to landlords after 1945. In France, especially after a secondary mortgage market was developed in the late sixties, the banks and other financial institutions looked to owner occuaption as the main target for their funds. In West Germany the

institutions continued to finance rental housing
until recently but increased government assistance
for owner occupiers opened up this market and by
the late seventies loans for new rental housing were
becoming harder to get (3). In the USA extensive
federal mortgage guarantees and other support had
sustained some private sector investment but
without this support new rental housing would
probably have only been constructed in the expanding
sunbelt regions. In the Netherlands from the sixties
onwards financial institutions became heavily
involved in house purchase loans.

The new rental housing that had been built in
the post war period had, with the exception of the
two countries noted above, increasingly been owned
by companies rather than individuals. Few of these
companies were large concerns, rental housing had
not been a really major area for property
investment. The development of offices, shops and
owner occupied housing was more important, although
pension and insurance funds built some rental
units. They were often less interested in short
term profits but were attracted to rental housing
let at reasonable rents because of its longer term
capital appreciation. As we have seen the main
market for such housing was middle income groups,
which had stable employment and rising incomes (i.e.
white collar and professional workers) rather than
manual workers or the less skilled and
disadvantaged. As the former groups increasingly
opted for owner occupation the scope for providing
new rental units declined and this, together with
the impact of rapid inflation on costs and rents,
made the participation of institutional and company
investors decreasingly attractive.

Apart from the new lending opportunities that
the growth of owner occupation provided for
investors, direct investment in this tenure has
also affected private renting. Especially in the
last fifteen or so years as inflation accelerated
the attractiveness of owner occupation as a hedge
against inflation grew. In each country tax and
other subsidies cushioned owner occupiers from
bearing the full impact of increases in interest
rates and house prices. In this situation one of
the best ways of maintaining and increasing wealth
was to become an owner occupier, and to 'trade up'
as incomes rose. Given the relative inelasticity
of supply, this added to house price inflation
thus further increasing the attractiveness of house

purchase. In contrast the development of the sales price of rented property was generally far weaker, as the examples noted below will show.

We now examine the detailed evidence for these trends and discuss some exceptions. In France there was still a considerable number of individual landlords entering the market in certain circumstances. The first of these occurred when people, on moving, let out rather than sold property. This practice appeared to have been common in areas where depopulation had depressed house prices so reducing the advantages of outright sales. There was also a small but profitable market in which individual landlords were letting to mobile professional workers who were unlikely to settle for long in their current locations but who required reasonable quality accommodation for a limited period. This often occurred in the provincial cities and some medium sized towns. Such landlords often evaded some of the taxes for which they were liable, thus adding to their profits (4).

Data for 1973 shows that over half of all rented property was owned by individual landlords, one eighth by companies and most of the rest by the state and the HLM organisations. But, of the newly built units completed since 1970, 60% were owned by HLMs, 15% by companies and 25% by individuals (Enquête-logement, 1973 (1), 32). The companies were particularly active in the bigger cities (above all Paris) (Enquête-logement, 1973(1), 184). Data on individual landlords shows that the socio-economic groups having the largest share of rent incomes from urban properties were professionals, other higher income earners and retired persons (INSEE, 1974, 75).

A survey of individual landlords who bought property between 1970-74 showed that, in comparison with owner occupiers, these landlords were of higher age, income and socio-economic status (CREP, 1976). The concentration of new activity in the larger cities was also evident, reflecting the significance of providing for mobile middle class demand. About 75% of the purchases were of flats, mostly just a single unit. Units were small, averaging 2.8 rooms compared with the national average of 3.6 rooms. About half were new units, few of the purchasers used the government subsidies which were, in theory at least, available for rented housing.

There was also in France, as elsewhere, investment opportunities at the bottom end of the

market, providing accommodation at 'open market'
rents, largely unrestricted by rules and
regulations, for those who had little alternative.
As earlier sections showed, the rents of such
property were high in relation to their size and
quality, and good returns were possible.

The other major feature of the market was
company investment. Full details of this were not
available, although some research was in progress.
One problem was that the financial institutions
involved in rental housing often had partial and
interlinked interests in a variety of organisations
supplying financing or directly providing housing.
This particularly applied to the banks, insurance
and pension funds, whose interests were especially
difficult to trace(5).

In 1976 pension funds put about 10% of their
investment into housing, mainly via specialist
bodies such as the SII (see below). Insurance
companies invested about 17% of their funds, most
came from a few large companies, some of these
controlled other specialist producers and owners of
housing. They were said to play a major role in the
production of new rental housing although, like
others, they were apparently finding that the growth
of owner occupation was eroding the middle class
rental demand and that inflation had reduced
profitability (a 1975 study suggested that they
were then looking for 8% return gross, 6% net).

Among the companies receiving finance from
pension funds, insurance companies and banks were
the SII (Sociétés Immobiliéres d'Investissment
formerly known as SIC - Sociétés Immobiliéres
Conventionnées). They were supposed to provide
rental housing plus a small proportion of more
profitable commercial property to enable some cross
subsidisation to take place. But - at least during
the period of the office boom in France (1969-74) -
a liberal interpretation of their statutes allowed
many of them to concentrate on commercial development. Their dividends were partially tax exempt,
holdings were not liable to death duties and they
were guaranteed against any governemnt action which
would affect their ability to freely set rents.
They had to distribute 85% of their profits. There
were 19 companies, 15 were publically quoted. They
had built about 50,000 units (60% in the Paris
region) for middle and upper income rental. In
later years the loss of some tax benefits and the
difficult economic conditions had meant that their

activities declined. In 1976 they paid 7 - 10% in dividends.

The other main group of companies backed by the financial community and the state were the Societes d'Economie Mixte (SEM). The SEM began in Paris in the late 1920's where they constructed HBM housing (Habitations à Bon Marché - the fore-runner of HLM) under the 1928 Loucheur housing programme. The companies were a partnership between private share- holders and local government and, since 1953, when reforms gave a greater stimulus to this approach, new SEMs had been established with majority public shareholdings. These companies had varied development tasks beside housing. In 1976 there were 97 SEMS, they had built about 200,000 rental units and 90,000 for sale.

An important source of funds was the 1% 'patronal', a payroll tax on all employers with more than ten employees, levied since 1953 to provide funds for workers' housing. Some of this money was used to support HLM building, and some was lent to employees for owner occupation. But it could also be used directly to provide housing or made available to SCI (Sociétés Civiles Immobilières) to build rental housing, usually with added government subsidies.

So, in France there had been developed a publically supported group of institutions investing in rental housing. Their structure was complex, containing varying degrees of public and private capital and control. In the seventies they did not appear to be adding much to the private rented stock. Often private financial interests had participated not for the direct profits to be made from rental housing but for the other benefits accruing to their activities, through construction, financing or the opportunity to carry out profitable commercial development.

Finally there was a longer established group of companies, the Sociétés Foncières Immobilières. These were founded from the 1850s onwards but had not grown in number significantly since 1945. There were 43, 17 based in Paris. They were involved in a wide range of property and other interests and their profits and dividends were subject to normal taxation. They owned some rental property, but few had added to this stock in recent years.

Little additional information existed on the nature of landlords in Denmark. Originally the pattern of small scale capital involvement was dominant. By the seventies many small landlords were

trying to get out of the sector but in Copenhagen a
few pension funds and other bodies were buying up
better quality property and retaining it as a long
term investment. Sharp rent increases (see chapter
5) had increased the attractiveness of this option
but it was only occurring on a small scale. A far
more important phenomenon was large scale sales of
rented flats to tenant co-operatives or as freehold
units. This will be discussed later.
   In Germany the role of employer provided rental
housing has been noted. But this was in sharp
decline. Further details are available concerning
the ownership of all dwellings in 1972. The data
refers to buildings containing one or two units and
those containing three or more units. The
significance of this division requires explanation.
Many landlords owned a single building containing
two units, one of which they lived in and the other
of which they rented out, often to a relative. A
further complication was that special tax
arrangements had induced many owner occupiers to
build such accommodation. But in fact in order to
qualify for tax benefits buildings only had to have
minimal additional facilities e.g. additional
points for sanitary fittings. So many of the so
called two family units were actually occupied by
a sole owner occupier household. It was estimated
that only about 30% of the 100,000 units built in
1978 and registered for two families were genuinely
so. In 1972 about 45% of the total stock consisted
of units in one and two unit dwellings, 90% of
which were owned by individuals, but further
details concerning how many were rented and what
proportion of the total rented stock they consisted
of were unavailable. Of the 55% of units in
buildings of 3 units or more, many were rented,
although the split between private and social
rented units is unclear. But about 10% of this
stock was owned by firms, some of this was by
virtue of employment accommodation; about a third
was owned by public bodies and social housing
organisations, much of this was let at non-profit
rents and was a part of the social sector, though
by no means all; and about a half was owned by
individuals, much of this was privately rented but
some was owner occupied and some social rented
(Der Bundesminister für Raumordnung etc. 1975, 12).
   These figures show the importance of individual
landlords in West Germany. There was a very strong
tradition of individual landlords constructing a
single building, living in one unit and letting

out the others. This direct involvement is thought
to have brought stability to the sector as
landlords were often concerned to retain tenants
whom they could amicably live next to rather than
to extract the highest possible rents. They also
had a good record in maintaining their properties.
But this pattern was beginning to break up under
the impact of inflation and of the growing
propensity of the better off (who formerly rented
or became small landlords) for single family unit
owner occupation.

Further details are available on the
occupational composition of these individual owners.
In 1972 30% of the 1/2 unit buildings were owned by
manual workers, 25% by retired people, 15% by
clerks. Insofar as these dwellings were rented,
many were owned by those with limited resources and
the ownership of the retired was concentrated in
the older property. The pattern of ownership of
buildings with three or more units, most of which
contained some rental units, was different. About
35% were owned by employers, 20% by pensioners and
15% by the other economically inactive persons.
There were rather few clerks, manual workers or
other employees owning such housing, as one might
expect given their likely lack of resources for
this scale of ownership (Der Bundesminister für
Raumordnung etc., 1975, 14).

Finally reference has been made to the
difficulty of disentangling which parts of the
German stock were social rented and which were
privately rented, as both individuals and
organisations had been able to build both types of
housing. But data does exist on buildings
containing three units or more newly built between
1968-75 (6). 60-70% such social housing was built
by social housing organisations or public bodies,
5-6% by firms other than property companies and a
further 10% or so by property companies, about 15%
or so was built by individual landlords. In the
case of private rented units the proportion built by
individuals dropped from 46% in 1968 to 37% in 1975.
Property companies took a larger share of this
shrinking market, up from 16% in 1968 to 26% in
1975. Most of the rest were built, in equal
proportions, by the social housing organisations and
by other firms than property companies - their
market share was fairly constant. So, despite
the historical importance of individual
ownership of private rental units,

by the seventies new investment was increasingly
being carried out, as elsewhere, by companies rather
than by individuals.

In Britain, the small investors remained the
most common form of landlord, although in a few
larger cities, especially London, property companies
and financial institutions owned substantial
holdings. A survey of the densely rented areas of
England and Wales in 1976 (defined as areas which
in 1971 contained more private renting than owner
occupying households) showed that almost 50% of the
private rented stock was owned by individual
landlords, 25% by company landlords, 6% by non
charitable trusts/executors and 22% by housing
associations/charitable trusts or public bodies
(Paley, 1978, 9). Given that this latter category
does not fall within our definition of private
renting, it may be seen that around two thirds of
the sector was owned by individual landlords. About
a quarter of these landlords lived on the same
premises as their tenants. In comparison with West
Germany far fewer English landlords lived in close
proximity to their tenants, because a far smaller
proportion of the rental' stock was in blocks of
flats.

Most resident landlords were owner occupiers
letting off a part of their premises as furnished
accommodation. They tended to be either young or
old, the young were mainly new to owner occupation,
letting - often in violation of building society
rules - in order to help out with mortgage
repayments. Sometimes, for example in inner city
areas, this pattern had been associated with the
landlord's inability to obtain conventional mortgage
finance and a recourse to fringe bank loans at high
interest rates. High rents and poor quality
accommodation often resulted. The older individual
landlords were usually owner occupiers whose
families had grown up and left home, letting surplus
rooms in order to help with general expenses.

The non resident individual landlords tended to
be middle aged or elderly. They owned much of the
older unfurnished stock. This was often bought
before the last war or inherited. Such landlords
often had few resources to carry out repairs and
modernisation and many had sold out in the post war
period or had had their property bought by local
authorities for slum clearance or, more recently,
by local authorities or housing associations for
improvement. There was a rather balanced turnover

of residential landlords' lettings, as the
circumstances which induced them to let altered and
as further individuals sought to obtain additional
income by letting. But non residential individual
landlord letting was in decline.

The company sector was also declining. A few
larger landlords had retained better quality
property especially in London where avoidance and
evasion of the rent act restrictions was widespread
and where there was a demand for short term lets at
high rents from foreign business men, tourists etc.
But many more companies had sold their properties,
either to their tenants or with vacant possession.
By the early seventies only one large company was
still retaining a large stock of unfurnished
property for middle and upper income groups, mainly
in London and the south coast resort areas. But
eventually the company abandoned this policy (7).

The 1976 survey showed that many resident
landlords had manual rather than white collar
occupations, the reverse was true for absentee
landlords. Most residential landlords had small
holdings - 36% had one letting and 42% 2-4 lettings.
Usually these lettings were of one or two rooms
only, with shared facilities in subdivided houses.
18% of non resident individual landlords had only
one letting, 60% had less than 10 lettings and only
6% had 50 or more lettings. In comparison, almost
60% of companies had over 50 lettings and 23% had
1000 or more (the median holding was 50-99
lettings). The income gained from letting was not
very substantial. 88% of resident and 73% of non
resident landlords claimed to receive less than £25
per week. 32% of companies received over £1000 per
week, but this latter figure was of course very low
by general company standards (Paley, 1978, 10-14).

In the Netherlands the pattern of individual
ownership by small landlords had continued, although
most new building had been constructed by financial
institutions. The most recent data on the size of
holdings dates from 1959, then the average holding
was six units. Detailed case studies, for example
in Amsterdam, Rotterdam and Tilburg, suggested that
by the seventies holdings of more than three units
were probably exceptional although a few larger
individual landlords existed, especially in the
areas of better quality middle class property, for
example in parts of Amsterdam (8).

Other data showed that in 1947 about 1.1 units
were owned individually and only 125,000 by

companies (9). But by 1975 the number of
individually owned units had fallen to about
575,000 whereas the company sector had grown to
about 300,000. In fact there was a continuous
decline in individually owned units. But in the
fifties and early sixties there was significant new
building by companies (increasingly aided by
subsidies). But the number of company owned units
peaked in the late sixties and then declined as new
building reduced and existing units were sold (at
a rate of 15-20000 per annum by the late
seventies). So, within a shrinking sector, the
share of the stock owned by companies grew, at first
both relatively and absolutely but in the seventies
only relatively. The contraction of the number of
individually owned units was especially rapid in
the seventies. About 80,000 units left the sector
between 1947 and 1956, 230,000 between 1956 and
1967, 100,000 between 1967 and 1971, and 150,000 in
the four years between 1971 and 1975. In this last
period the share of individually owned units as a
proportion of all the housing stock fell by about a
third (to 13%). Further,figures show that individual
landlord sales accelerated in the mid fifties,
some of these units were sold to companies, and
again in the seventies, when most sales were for
owner occupation. Between 1947 and 1975 about two
thirds of all private rental sales were to owner
occupiers and one third to municipalities and
housing associations - for clearance or for
addition to the social rented stock (10).

The bias of the company holdings towards newer
property was clear. Over 70% of this stock had
been built since 1945, compared with 20% of the
individually owned stock. The newer stock had good
facilities and was let at higher rents to the
better off. Thus 40% of the tenants of individual
landlords had incomes in the bottom third of the
income distribution, compared with 26% of those in
company owned property. Only 17% had incomes in the
top third of the distribution compared with 30% of
company tenants. Most of the higher rented property
was owned by companies and most of the cheaper
property by individuals (CBS, 1975).

Some of the same characteristics and trends
which have been noted as occurring elsewhere were
also evident in the USA. Thus for example there
were many individual landlords. In 1975 59% of all
rental units were in structures with five or less
units (buildings with five or more units are
officially known as multifamily housing), although

112

in central cities, where much of the rental market
was, only 49% of units were in such structures.
Often these properties (in fact mainly single
family houses) were owned by small businessmen,
who might deal in property as a part-time
occupation, or by owner occupiers who rented out
the 'spare' units in their buildings, as in West
Germany. But the importance of these smaller
holdings had diminished. In 1950, 79% of rental
units were in buildings containing five or less
units but virtually all the net growth in the
rental stock between 1950 and 1975 was in
multifamily housing, although 28% of all new rental
housing built between 1970 and 1975 was in smaller
holdings (11).

So there had been a shift within the rental
sector from small scale provision to a situation
where companies were frequently involved (although
mainly small companies). But in new housing
companies were often responsible for their
development and/or their management but not their
ownership. For taxation reasons (see chapter 6)
while there was no special benefit to be gained by
company ownership of rental property this was not
the case for upper income individuals. Accordingly
such individuals often joined 'syndicates', owning
rental units whose development and management was
carried out by companies.

In the older cities the stock was owned by a
mixture of businesses and individuals, including
resident landlords (often individuals formed
private companies for financial, legal or other
reasons). Larger landlords had tended to leave the
lower end of the urban rental market because of
its economic weakness and many smaller landlords
were following suit. Insofar as they were replaced,
it was often by resident landlords looking for a
home plus some income or short term operators whose
main concern was to obtain quick profits rather
than remain in the rental business in the longer
term. Common devices for achieving this included
non payment of property taxes and running down
maintenance and other services (taxes and utilities
costs were usually contained in rent payments -
for apartments at least - in the USA). Ultimately,
such landlords had often abandoned their properties,
leaving the tenants and the authorities to face
the problems which then arose. Studies of
abandonment had shown a complex and accelerating
pattern of changing ownership and mortgaging
arrangements before this final stage was reached.

Much of the abandoned property, if still inhabited
and not wholly derelict, had to be administered
by public authorities, although some small scale
success had been had - especially in New York City
- with 'co-operative conversion', the takeover of
the property by tenants. In addition some better
quality property had been sold by landlords for
middle and upper income co-operatives, again
especially in New York (12).

ACCESS TO PRIVATE LETTINGS

No simple description can be given of the means of
access to private tenancies(13). In this,as in other
respects, the variety presented by the sector was
far greater and less easily researchable than in
the case of the other two main tenures. For
example, much employer owned housing was allocated
to key personnel but other parts of the stock were
also allocated on the basis of relationships
between the landlord and the tenant which had little
to do with the housing market. Thus, it will be
recalled, many small landlords in West Germany
built property with one unit for self occupation
and one for letting. Much of this accommodation was
let to relatives or friends.
     Some subsidised units (for example, in the USA)
were limited to low or moderate income tenants.
Access could also be affected by rent controls, for
example the dwindling number of rent controlled
tenancies in France, Britain and New York could be
inherited by relatives who were living in the
premises at the time of death of the former tenant.
     Despite such factors, the main features
governing access were, first, the ability to pay
the rent and, second, the landlord's judgement about
whether someone would be a 'good' or 'suitable'
tenant. The basis for this latter decision varied
greatly. Larger landlords were more likely to
advertise vacancies, either directly or through
agencies, to have application forms and to have
standard procedures (such as taking up financial
and other references) for assessing the applicants'
suitability. Smaller landlords often used informal
procedures, advertising vacancies by word of mouth,
accepting tenants because they were known
personally or because they could be vouched for by
'good' tenants. But not all larger landlords behaved
in the way suggested above or all smaller landlords
operate less formal procedures. And there was no

evidence to show whether 'irrational' factors such
as racial prejudice and opposition to unconventional
living arrangements were more frequent with
smaller rather than larger landlords. (Such
practices certainly occurred among all types of
landlord).
        Some further details can be added for specific
countries. In France, as already noted, access to
the remaining controlled sector was open to some
relatives of previous tenants. If such a tenancy
ended by other means the letting became decontrolled
and could be offered to anyone. The most important
limitation on access to modern rented housing was
the high rents of such properties. This applied
wherever such units had been built, but was
especially evident in the larger cities, above all
in Paris. Social rented housing, as we have already
seen, was only a rather small proportion of the
stock and much of it housed those on middle rather
than low incomes, the newer private rental sector
housed the better off. The controlled sector
provided low rent. accommodation, but - for reasons
mentioned above - mainly to elderly, long term
tenants. So those who were least well off mainly
sought older, free rented housing, or, in the case
of small households, furnished lets. In both
cases, as we have seen, rents were high in relation
to quality, particularly in larger cities. Here low
income families found difficulty in gaining access
to any reasonably priced housing. The overcrowding
statistics suggested that a common way of solving
the problem was by 'doubling up' or by accepting a
unit that was smaller than was ideally required.
        Waiting lists for HLM housing, the main
opportunity for relatively low cost renting at
decent standards, were held by the communes, in some
cases these were extensive and were very long in
the biggest cities. Eligibility was determined by
incomes (there was a ceiling), household and current
housing circumstances. Applicants were often offered
accommodation at higher rents than they felt able
to pay so they frequently preferred to continue in
the older private rented stock. And many of the HLM
units were located on the urban periphery. Little
choice of unit was available, and these new estates
were often poorly serviced, especially by public
transport, so the journey to work was apt to be long,
costly and difficult.
        Where employers had donated a part of the 1%
payroll tax to HLM construction they had the right

to nominate employees to some units. Some of the housing produced by the state supported landlords was tied to the needs of expanding industry (14). In such cases the tenancy was not subsequently tied to the job, although it was in the case of the private by virtue of employment accommodation.

Various minority groups also found access to reasonable housing difficult. There were public hostels for guest workers (Cités d'Urgence), poor quality accommodation for transitory use by single workers. When the guest workers' families arrived they usually moved into poor quality HLM units or into the worst parts of the private sector. Some hostels were also provided for students but often they too were accommodated in the worst of the private sector. Some squatting, especially by students, had occurred, but even in Paris this was only on a small scale. As in many European countries homelessness seemed to be unrecognised and few people believed that it often occurred.

Denmark was one of the countries which, faced with an acute post war housing shortage, had instituted compulsory allocation. This was administered by the muncipalities. All vacancies had in theory to be notified to an allocation committee (a general register of residence provided the basis for policing the scheme). Families had to be suitable for the size of the dwelling allocated, but in practice landlords would let to such families and then obtain committee approval retrospectively. Consequently few empty dwellings became available for letting directly to those in need.

In the early days the allocation system only dealt with families, so single people had to sublet rooms. By 1970, due to progressive liberalisation of the rules, only about 40% of the units in those municipalities which still had the system were let according to its rules. In 1976 the scheme was abolished. It probably caused some immobility because people moving from one area to another often had to join a waiting list; even in the late sixties it was possible to wait 2-2½ years to get a flat in Copenhagen.

All that remained in the late seventies were municipal offices which tried to find accommodation for those in need. But they had few successes, most households had to search for accommodation in the normal way. Social housing tended, as elsewhere, to accommodate families and, as in France, there was a problem regarding the high rents of newer properties - which were what newcomers to the housing market were frequently offered. The lack of rent pooling in the social sector meant that many tenants in the older stock paid far lower rents than newer tenants, even allowing for quality differences. This reduced the supply of social sector dwellings for the worse off and there had been increasing difficulty in letting some new units. The growth of freehold flats and tenants' co-operatives also reduced the supply of rented accommodation.

Guest workers faced intense competition for housing, especially in Copenhagen. Some social housing was available but most lived in the poorer part of the private sector, including rented rooms. The government had tried to stimulate housing production for old people and students. The main agency for the production of subsidised old peoples' housing was the non profit housing associations. Non profits had also been assisted to build one room apartments for young people in the cities. There had also been a programme for private halls of residence for students and trainees assisted by government loans, but rents tended to be too high and such construction declined in the early seventies.

Despite the access difficulties for low income families, which, as in France, had been worsened by recent sharp rent rises, there was no officially recognised homelessness problem. 'Problem families' and those evicted from private or social housing were often rehoused in local authority 'barracks', old and poor units owned by the councils. Some others, particularly young people, found accommodation in unconventional ways. One of the biggest and best known of these ventures the Christiana commune, housed in old army buildings in central Copenhagen. This had been the target of much controversy, especially when the authorities had proposed to close it down.

In West Germany, as in Denmark, the grave shortage of housing at the end of the war necessitated a compulsory allocation scheme. This lasted until the sixties when rents began to be decontrolled (see chapter 5). As in Denmark, the local authorities still had offices to help those in need find housing. These offices had the right to nominate to vacancies in social housing. There was an income limit for eligibility for social housing but this was quite high and covered the majority of the population.

A general problem forcing many to remain in private housing was the lack of rent pooling in social housing, the effects of which have already been noted. In Germany the difficulties had been added to by a system of degressive subsidies. This meant that social housing subsidies were withdrawn as, it was hypothesised, incomes and therefore the 'bearable' rent rose. But the incomes of many of those who required such housing had not risen as quickly as expected, thus causing rents to rise in relation to incomes. Rent increases in modernised property had also had serious consequences for some low income households.

Although there was still a large private market, the rising rent/income ratios of the seventies meant that access was increasingly difficult for the less well off. Some households remained in poor and/or insecure conditions. The groups concerned were familiar ones, guest workers, the elderly, single people who were renting rooms (an insecure and largely unregulated market) etc. The problems of guest workers were especially noticeable. Often with menial and poorly paid jobs they frequently had little grasp of the law and customs of the host country and were subject to exploitation. In addition they often needed to send as much of their earnings as possible home, and this prevented them from seeking better accommodation. Also they only had limited civil rights and were subject to police supervision (except immigrants from other EEC countries). They could be sent home if the authorities decided that they were living in inadequate conditions. Many had bought their families into Germany illegally and resisted involvement with officials for fear of such action. They often lived in older housing in the inner cities, along with other poor families, young people etc. Their landlords often charged high rents for poor accommodation, benefitting from the lack of regulation of much of this stock and the need of their tenants for rental housing conveniently located in relation to inner city job markets.

In addition some elderly and young households, low income and low income/large families had poor housing conditions in the older private sector. As elsewhere single parent families were especially likely to have restricted access to reasonable and affordable housing. Homelessness was just beginning to be recognised as a problem. One estimate was that, including those in very poor and insecure

housing, there was, in the mid-seventies, about
800,000 people in this situation. The origins and
composition of this population was poorly understood
but the two major components were probably former
refugees from the East who had found it difficult
to settle and find steady employment and also
'problem families' and individuals, including those
who had been evicted from rented housing and who,
as a result, were unable to find new accommodation.
These people often stayed in the centres of the
bigger cities. They might squat in empty property
and some even lived for a large part of their time
time in the concourses of major railway stations.
     As elsewhere, the local authorities had a legal
duty to rehouse those who were evicted from
conventional accommodation. Often they used older
housing which they owned and kept in a minimal state
of repair. Such housing tended to be heavily
stigmatised and it was said that the mention of an
occupant's address to a prospective employer might
be enough to prevent employment being gained. There
was also increasing stigmatisation caused by the
segregation of some poorer families in sections of
the private rented and social stock, in the former
case this was caused by market processes and in the
latter by housing management practices.
     The number of those who were rehoused in this
way was unknown but in 1978 there were somewhere
between 1-5000 such people in Hamburg alone. The
upper figure seemed more likely as the city
authorities, in trying to reduce homelessness, had
established 15 areas in which these people were
rehoused. In 1977 these accommodated 4000 formerly
homeless people. One area visited during the
research consisted of old public housing which was
surrounded by light industry and was rather
isolated. Inhabitants paid 60 - 120 DM per month as
an accommodation fee, this was usually paid from
welfare funds. They did not have the usual tenants'
rights and were closely supervised. But, despite the
official explanation of the causes of homelessness
given above, many inhabitants were not 'problem
families' or ex refugees but had been evicted from
rental housing because they could not afford rents
which had risen steeply in recent years (they could
not obtain social housing until rent arrears had been
paid off). Standards of accommodation were poor,
for example toilets and bathrooms were shared. A
school and kindergarten were provided on the site,
this reinforced its social isolation.

A Profile of the Private Rented Sector   II

Access to private rented accommodation was
more difficult in England than elsewhere, although,
in contrast with these countries, there was a
growing number of local authority and voluntary
housing advice centres which tried to help households find accommodation. Where there were
relatively high incomes and a high level of owner
occupancy and/or a good supply of social housing,
the lack of private rented housing was perhaps a
minor problem. Some furnished rooms were usually
available as a result of owner occupier subletting.
But in the tighter housing markets of big cities
(especially London), in expanding areas and in other
special situations, for example resort and
university towns, severe difficulties often
occurred. Official figures underestimated the number
of homeless families (there were no data on the
single homeless), but homelessness had risen as the
role of the private sector had declined (15). In
the late sixties and seventies, squatting, some of
it officially sanctioned, had re-emerged as a
significant phenomenon. There was also pressure on
councils to use the substantial number of vacant
properties they sometimes held (awaiting demolition
or rehabilitation) for 'short life' housing and for
measures to force or induce landlords to let vacant
property.
This shortage, combined with the effects of
controls on rents and security, resulted in
landlords pursuing various techniques to restrict
access. For example, many would not let to a wide
variety of supposedly undesirable tenants who
might cause trouble and be difficult to evict.
Blacks, single parent families, large families,
people with pets and many others were discriminated
against (racial or sexual discrimination was illegal
but was hard to prove). Some landlords only provided
'holiday lets' or let to those who would not stay
long - in inner London many flats were only let to
foreigners. Others let their property on a sharing
basis (and thus mainly to young single people) in
order to avoid creating secure tenancies (16).
Rented accommodation was rarely advertised, in
sharp contrast to the situation in the other
countries. Often accommodation was obtained through
personal contacts. Thus new tenants might be
friends or relatives of satisfactory outgoing
tenants. The luxury end of the market was often
more formally organised though. An increasing
proportion of units were controlled by employers

120

and let with jobs. A few tenants were the
successors of deceased controlled tenants who were
living with them at the time of their death. But
this provision was finally abolished in 1980.

The problems of access to private housing were
most serious for the following groups; first, those
in housing stress areas who had a low priority for
social housing (even though they might have been
housed in this sector in other areas where the
housing market was not so tight); second, people
who needed quick access to temporary housing on
moving to a new area or on forming a new family but
who intended to move on again, to buy, or to gain
access to social housing before too long; third,
small households who required permanent private
rental housing because they were ineligible for
social housing and could not afford to buy; finally,
households who, preferred to rent privately (this
was a small minority, hardly surprising considering
the subsidies and better conditions available in
the other tenures) (Bovaird et. al., 1982c, 31).

The Netherlands was, as already mentioned,
the only country which still had an allocation
system. The acute shortage of housing which lasted
until the early seventies (and began to re-emerge
in 1978-9) led to the institution of an allocation
system in 1947 similar to the Danish system.
Gradually this had been relaxed, so that eventually
it only applied to areas where rent was controlled
and only to property in a broadly defined middle
range of rents. Local authorities had discretion in
the way in which they operated the scheme. Thus,
Rotterdam had very restrictive rules in housing
improvement areas to prevent an influx of families
hoping to obtain better housing. Also the percentage
of vacancies to be notified to the councils varied,
Rotterdam nominated to 50% of all vacancies (in
theory) whereas Amsterdam tried to nominate to 100%
of all vacancies in the most popular part of the
market and 50% of the rest.

Each municipality established housing waiting
lists. In Amsterdam households had to be resident
for a year before qualifying and for many years had
had to be at least 25 years old (in the seventies
this was reduced to 18, which had greatly lengthened
the list). In Rotterdam applicants had to be over
18 and work locally, for the housing in greatest
demand they had to be at least 28 and married.
People on the waiting list could obtain an occupancy
permit but usually had to find accommodation
themselves. If in severe need they went on to an

emergency list, it was from this that the local
authority nominations were made. But, as elsewhere,
it could be a long time before even these
households got an offer. (Interestingly there were
also weak controls, on who could occupy less costly
owner occupied housing).

The system was massively evaded. The reaction
(in an interview) of a major and highly respectable
Amsterdam landlord to allocation was apparently
typical (and confirmed by information from
Rotterdam). 80-90% of his property was controlled
but he complained that the system was bogged down
by a mass of frequently changing regulations. He
said that many landlords tended to offer the worst
property to nominees, feeling that families on
the waiting list might have social or financial
problems. The non profit landlords also did this
and it resulted in social segregation and 'sink'
estates. Discrimination against guest workers and
ex-colonial immigrants, especially blacks, was
common. Landlords could object to nominees on
certain grounds, for example by suggesting that
they had a bad tenancy record. In this case the
rent committee arbitrated, if it decided against
the landlord the city could requisition the unit.
But this was rare and landlords were often
successful in refusing to take a tenant even when
their case was weak.

The landlord suggested that racial
discrimination had occurred partly because landlords
were worried that the council did not operate the
scheme to ensure dispersal. This, he said, was
important if social tensions were not to increase.
Another problem was that the system, because of
the size of the stock allocated, did little to
help large families who had to wait up to ten years
for decent accommodation. He also felt that it was
undesirable to have a system which only allowed
low income households to settle in large areas of
the city (he suggested that the system was mainly
aiding such people).

Many landlords had improved properties to take
them beyond the upper limit of the allocation
system, although a change in this had made such
action more difficult. However, even if the improved
unit stayed in the system, the landlord then had
the right to select the first tenant and negotiate
a rent. But the landlord admitted that most landlords tended to ignore the allocation rules; indeed
he regarded this as a reasonable form of 'civil

disobedience' in response to a system which should
be scrapped. Various loopholes could be exploited
but, above all, the system was cumbersome and could
not be enforced without many more staff to operate
it. Local officials confirmed this. Often, for
example, landlords let to people with occupancy
permits who were in housing need knowing that, if
the authority objected, it would then have a
rehousing duty (illegally housed families could in
theory be removed). Often landlords were presented
with a fait accompli, when tenants leaving a
property told friends or relatives who then moved
in. Empty property in Amsterdam tended to be
squatted and one of the problems was that the
allocation system was so long winded that property
was often empty for some time (a new anti-squatting
law was under discussion).

The allocation system was under heavy pressure
and the number of units covered by it was
declining. Sales, improvement and demolition all
reduced the number theoretically available and
evasion further reduced this total. New non-profit
housing was often too expensive for needy
households, even when they were assisted by housing
allowances, also, as elsewhere, it was often
located on the urban periphery. Reaction to these
problems varied. For example, several decontrolled
suburban localities had requested new controls.
They saw allocation (and rent controls) as ways of
ensuring that access to housing was not monopolised
by newcomers who could outbid needy local residents.
In Amsterdam some argued for a reduction in the
proportion of dwellings which had to be notified
to the authorities. In Rotterdam, some argued for
more control - but even the non profit
organisations opposed this. Here there was a demand
also for more staff to run the system. It was
pointed out that, for example, in one housing
stress area, about 750 vacancies occurred every
year, 50% of these should have been available for
allocation but only about 20% were - the rest
being squatted with or without the landlord's
collusion (here 'squatted' meant occupied without
council approval, most of these tenants paid rent).

In 1978 new proposals were being discussed for
rent control (later enacted - see chapter 5) and
allocation. Broadly speaking, allocation was to be
extended to any area of housing stress at the
request of a municipality. In such areas landlords
would have to notify the local authority of all

vacant property. After a year, such property could be requisitioned for letting.

The allocation system excluded many who were in housing need. More generally, the decline of the private sector and the high cost of new social housing had severely limited access to adequate rental housing by the young, low income/large families, guest workers and blacks especially in the big cities. There were close similarities with, for example, London and Paris in these respects. The rental sector was gradually becoming polarised between the young and the old as those who could not afford to buy preferred eventually to transfer to social housing. Government help for the provision of new accommodation for some of the excluded groups had proved unattractive to private investors, although some non profit building had occurred.

The situation in Amsterdam illustrates the difficulties which existed in the Randstad cities. About 30,000 people were on the waiting list in the mid seventies, this had reached 80,000 by 1979. Some people found accommodation in substandard units whose low rents took them out of the allocation system, others, as we have seen, simply took over units. Many, especially foreign workers, had to rent rooms. In theory rents for sublet rooms were controlled, in practice exploitation was common. Squatting was on the increase, in 1978 there were about 5-8000 squatters in Amsterdam and about 10,000 in the whole country. In many cases such squatting was in opposition to the growth of commercial redevelopment which was reducing the low cost housing stock, or to middle class 'gentrification'. Some squats were highly organised and had resisted attempts at eviction by the authorities and developers (17).

In Rotterdam housing pressure was concentrated in the inner ring of older properties and especially where the city was carrying out a 'municipalisation' policy (see chapter 7). Here some landlords were involved in speculation, offering their property to people who could not gain access to more satisfactory units on payment of illegal key money or on other onerous terms. Many, especially guest workers and ex-colonial immigrants, had to rent rooms for which they paid a great deal. The housing associations were reluctant to help. Some companies exploited the fact that guest workers needed to have adequate accommodation before their families were allowed to join them by arranging the families' travel and accommodation, charging high fees. Sometimes they waited until the family was in transit and then demanded more money, knowing that the household was committed to the move.

In the USA few organisations existed to assist people to find housing, although there had been some compulsory allocation in the second world war. Access to some sort of rental property was not usually difficult, even in tight housing markets there was a high rate of mobility and so a considerable volume of vacancies available for reletting. But, in a more fundamental sense, there were severe access problems, the main difficulty being the price which tenants had to pay (although widespread discrimination in letting, especially against blacks and welfare recipients, existed). Declining ability to pay and increasing operating costs had resulted in many tenants, especially the poor, the old, single parent and large families and minorities, paying very high proportions of income in rent. Recent changes had intensified this problem.

In 1973 it was estimated that 13 million households did not have access to decent housing, i.e. housing in reasonable condition costing not more than 25% of their income (House Committee on Banking, Currency and Housing, 1975, 195). Only about 2.8 million households were in public and other subsidised housing (US Department of Housing and Urban Development, 1973, 4-15). Very few had access to social housing and, although there was some owner occupation especially among poor white elderly households, most of the poor were dependent on the private landlord. The only help (for some) was via welfare payments but these varied widely from state to state and studies of so called 'welfare housing' (certain landlords specialised in letting to such families) showed that it was extremely poor quality and was, in value for money terms, very expensive (Lowry, et. al., 1972; Gordon, 1973, 25). The new section 8 housing subsidy (to be described in chapter 6) provided the main possibility for low income households to obtain decent private housing at a reasonable rent. Monitoring of this still relatively small programme showed that it reached many of those in the most disadvantaged groups.

Another serious constraint on access to rental

housing was the reluctance of the suburbs to allow
rental projects to be built in their areas. In part
they wished to exclude lower income, especially
black, tenants (considerable civil rights
litigation had occurred on this issue). But there
was also a general wish to prevent any rental
development, except perhaps for the highest income
groups (Poliakoff, 1978; Clawson and Hall, 1973).

CONCLUSION

The picture of a sector with severe difficulties
and in decline is reinforced by this chapter's
examination of the characteristics of tenants and
landlords and the problems of access. Increasingly,
the sector seemed to be housing the young and, in
some countries, the elderly. Both these groups
tended to be relatively disadvantaged in the
housing market, yet many were unable to gain access
to the two tenures which received most government
assistance, owner occupation and social renting.
So the rental sector was becoming increasingly
polarised in terms of age and incomes, housing many
on low incomes plus a small but significant section
of better off households. Many poor tenants had
incomes which were rising rather slowly. This was
a serious situation in an era when landlords' costs
were rising very rapidly.
      The provision of new private accommodation was
historically the business of small local
entrepreneurs but their role had declined, except
in West Germany and in the USA for special
reasons. But in some countries, for example, France,
the small landlord was still bringing existing
property on to the market for middle income letting
and, more generally, owner occupiers continued to
let out rooms when they required extra income.
Also in cities such as New York, Amsterdam, Paris
and London some landlords were entering the market
when they could let at high rents to those who had
little alternative choice.
      In several countries much of the new private
rental property had been built by companies and by
financial institutions. But this property had been
for the middle and upper income market and was
often little cheaper than the costs of owner
occupation. In recent years even these agencies were
ending their investment in new private rental
property.
      Individual landlords tended to own the older,

less desirable property. Many did not have the
resources to upgrade their property (and many
tenants could not afford the increased rents which
would be required). This housing formed the hard
core of the improvement problem to be discussed in
chapter 7.

Access was usually by normal market processes.
Compulsory allocation still existed in the
Netherlands but was ineffective. The means of access
were many and varied, for example via employers,
by recommendation from an outgoing tenant, by
squatting, by answering an advertisement, or
through an agent. Discrimination on grounds of
colour, family situation etc. was common.

In all six countries, the same types of
disadvantaged household found access to decent
housing at a reasonable rent difficult, these
included minorities (especially blacks), guest
workers, large/low income families, single parent
families, the young and the elderly. They often
paid high rents for poor accommodation and, because
the bottom end of the market was largely
unregulated, they often had little security of
tenure. In some cities, squatting had revived in
reaction to these conditions. Most governments
accepted some residual responsibility for housing
homeless families, but usually the 'welfare'
accommodation provided was of poor quality and in
some countries was provided in ways which
deliberately stigmatised and punished those who
lived in it.

NOTES

1. See, for example, the discussion in Committee on the Rent Acts, 1971, 321-5.

2. I am indebted to Professor Emanuel Tobier for the analysis in this paragraph. It is based on US Bureau of the Census etc. 1977, Table A-1.

3. For example, in interviews in 1978 officials and others in Darmstadt referred to the growing reluctance of the banks to support new rental construction. But finance was available for new owner occupied apartments.

4. Based on interviews with landlords and others in 1978.

5. The following paragraphs are based on interviews, information supplied by Christian Topalov, and Ibanez, 1975; CNRC, 1978; Cofimeg, 1977; Sefimeg, 1977 and Ufimeg, 1977.

6. Data supplied by Dr. Rudi Ulbrich, Deutches Institut fur Wirtschaftsforschung, Berlin.

7. See Harloe, Issacharoff and Minns, 1974, 98-132 for an analysis of landlords in London in the early seventies.

8. Based on information supplied by Jan van der Schaar.

9. Data derived from Dutch housing censuses by Jan van der Schaar.

10. Information derived from Jan van der Schaar, 1979.

11. Data provided by Emanuel Tobier. Based on Census and Annual Housing Survey reports.

12. Based on interviews with officials and landlords' representatives in New York City, 1978.

13. This section is based on interview material. Other sources are noted in the text.

14. See Magri, 1977 for a discussion of this.

15. The 1977 Housing (Homeless Persons Act) required local authorities to rehouse certain priority groups of the homeless (mainly families with dependent children). This was a limited measure, hedged around with restrictions, for example, those who were judged 'intentionally homeless' even if in priority need could be refused accommodation. Many local authorities applied this rule in a very stringent manner.

16. The growth of this is discussed in House of Commons Environment Committee, 1982.

17. The situation in Amsterdam in the seventies is described in Anderiesen, 1981.

Chapter Five

RENTS AND RENT POLICY

This is the first of four chapters which review
the main policies affecting the private rented
sector. Subsequent chapters consider subsidies and
taxation, renewal and improvement and landlord/
tenant relations. This chapter examines rents,
rent controls and the general financial situation.
All these themes have already been touched on but
here they are bought together with an account of
policies. As we have seen, the European countries
have all had rent controls. In the USA, only New
York has a long history of controls, so much of the
United States material in this chapter will concern
this city.

RENT CONTROLS FROM 1939

Information about controls in the interwar period
is scanty, clearly they remained strong in Germany
and had, at the other extreme, ended soon after 1918
in the USA and later in Denmark (1). In France, in
1939 controlled rents (only on pre 1919 property)
were at about 200% of their 1914 levels after
various increases had been granted. Vacancy
decontrol was operative but subsequent rent rises
were also limited (2). But there is no good data of
rents in relation to costs and incomes and hence
of the effect of controls on profitability.
     But some more information is available for
England and Denmark. In England, as already
mentioned, new building was not controlled after
the war and from 1923 vacancy decontrol began
(measures were taken to prevent evictions solely
to gain rent rises). These 1923 measures continued
until 1933. The effects of the 1923 Act on the
landlord's profits may not have been too severe.
The law allowed rents to rise by 15 - 40% of

pre-war levels. At this time earnings were falling
and the immediate post war inflation had ceased
(compare this situation with Germany which suffered
hyper-inflation and where those who depended on
income from rents were disastrously affected). From
1933 vacancy decontrol, which created much hardship
at the bottom end of the market, ceased for such
property; it was continued for a middle range of
property and more expensive units were decontrolled
immediately. A proposal to abolish all controls
within five years was not accepted as there was
still a considerable housing shortage and political
pressure for the retention of controls. From 1933
to 1939, as the economy revived in some areas,
rents grew slower than incomes but returns based on
1914 values were probably still not grossly
inadequate. Furthermore, landlords obtained via
vacancies the decontrol of some 3% of their
property per annum. Nevertheless rents were not
based on the principle of providing competitive
returns on vacant possession values so there was an
incentive to sell out and, as opportunities for
owner occupation increased for those with stable
employment, this began to occur. But by 1938 the
number sold was only about 1.1 million out of the
estimated 3.6 million pre-1919 decontrolled
properties. At this date approximately 2.1 million
dwellings remained controlled. There were also
about 900,000 free rented properties built since
1919. So many landlords could charge what the
market would bear (Bowley,1945; Nevitt, 1966;
Department of the Environment, 1977a, 38).

There was substantial new building in Denmark,
even before complete decontrol in 1931. This was
partly because some increases occurred in
controlled rents. From 1916-24 rents rose by about
56% and new dwellings were let at considerably
higher rents - in 1924 rents for post 1916 housing
were 40% above the average in the older stock.
Between 1924 and 1940 there were further rent
increases (35-40%) which outstripped wage increases
(about 14% throughout the period).

The second world war led to the reintroduction
or strengthening of controls in all six coountries.
In 1939 control was reintroduced in Denmark and in
England was extended to almost all rented property.
In both countries rents were frozen and security
extended. In the Netherlands a similar policy was
introduced after the Germans occupation in 1940.
There had been a rent freeze in Germany since 1936

(as already noted). In the USA federal rent control
began in 1942 and in 1943 all rents were frozen in
France.

After the war the US controls continued in
order to deal with the great pressure on the
housing market after demobilisation. They were
extended during the Korean emergency, but all
controls ended in 1954 (they were already being
phased out) (House Committee on Banking, Currency
and Housing, 1975, passim; Lett, 1976, 2-5).
Between 1954 and 1969 only New York City had
continuing controls. But, as we have seen, the
housing shortage was far more severe in Europe
and its economy was much weaker. Governments wanted
to expand production, especially of rental
accommodation, but they were also anxious to ensure
that landlords did not exploit the housing
shortage and generate political and social unrest
(as had sometimes occurred in and after the first
world war). In order to rapidly expand production,
given the economic circumstances, most governments
looked to the private landlord to make a
contribution, yet if strict controls remained this
was unlikely. Only in England, where the Labour
government had been elected on a programme which
included major expansion of council housing and
the nationalisation of land, was there little
concern about the fate of private landlords. In the
other European countries, private rental building
was subsidised (see chapter 6) and, by the late
forties and early fifties, all of these countries
had eased some controls.

France was the first country to take action
(3). From 1948 new dwellings not controlled
(although special rules applied to those erected
with subsidies) and an elaborate scheme was
introduced for pre-1949 property. This scheme only
applied in some communes - in the larger cities and
their surroundings, areas of poor housing and
growth areas. The rest of the older stock was decontrolled. Communes could enter or leave the
control system if they so requested. The system
attempted to relate rents to the quality of the
property, taking into account factors such as
building costs. The new rents were to be phased in
between 1949 and 1954. Despite the reference to
'taking into account' costs, the main basis for
computing 'reasonable' rents was the base salary
for the calculation of family allowance
entitlement, i.e. the intention was to link rents

to incomes not costs. Two other rent setting
systems were available, but neither made much
difference to the actual pattern of evolution of
rents and neither was greatly used. In fact,
despite this reform controlled rents remained
fairly low and tenants more commonly complained
about rising charges for services and utilities,
which were not controlled. In Paris in 1951, these
charges amounted to 25 - 35% of the rent and the
problem of uncontrolled charges has remained a
cause of complaint.

No other countries attempted as elaborate a
reform as France. In Denmark the freeze lasted
until 1951, when rent control boards were re-
established in every locality. A small general rent
rise was allowed ($3\frac{1}{2}$-6%) and further increases
followed, so that by 1957 rents could be 24% above
their 1939 levels. An attempt was made to encourage
maintenance by requiring that a proportion of the
rent increases set aside for this purpose. In West
Germany the effects of the post war freeze on
landlords may have been rather limited because of
the low inflation rate and the effects of the 1948
currency reform. From 1950 private rental
accommodation built only with the aid of income
tax reliefs was freed from control. In 1953
decontrol was extended to all new indirectly
subsidised rented housing sectors (see chapter 6,
in fact very weak controls continued - rents had to
be related to costs in the first five years,
afterwards the units were treated as normal private
rented units). For controlled units there were
regular rent increases based on a combination of
officially tabulated and cost related rents.
Between 1955-1960 increases of 10-20% occurred
(before 1955 there had been a series of ad hoc
rises). In 1960 there was a rise of 15% and in 1963
of 20%. Over the next few years increases totalling
about 70% occurred.

In the Netherlands pre-1940 units had a 15%
increase in 1951. Landlords demanded 25%, arguing
that maintenance costs alone had risen by 200% from
1940-1951 (equivalent to a rent rise of 24%). But
rents were restricted, as the government wished
to keep wage costs low in order to increase the
country's international competitiveness. However,
rents of post 1940 unsubsidised construction were
freed. As elsewhere, rent policy was politically
controversial. Landlords and the more conservative
parties pressed for large rent increases and the

132

tenants' organisations and the Socialist Party
pressed for smaller increases and for some rent to
be earmarked for maintenance (as in Denmark). A
complex series of increases resulted, the percentage
increase allowed varied according to the age,
location and level of maintenance of the stock (4).
In 1957 an unsuccessful attempt was made to ensure
that a part of the increase was placed in a
renovation fund. Increases continued until 1971
(being then replaced by a new system - see later)
and new procedures were adopted which required rent
advice committees in each locality to certify that
low rented pre-war dwellings were reasonable in
quality and maintenance before they could receive
the prescribed rent increase.

In England there was little possibility of a
reform until the Conservative Party took office in
1951. From 1954 new units were freed from controls,
although - unlike elsewhere - this did not lead
to significant new construction (probably because
no subsidies were available, a large programme of
social rented housing continued and owner
occupation was increasing). In addition the 1954
Act permitted small rent increases subject to proof
of expenditure on repairs. But there were
restrictive provisions to protect tenants and the
change was of little benefit to landlords.

THE MOVEMENT TOWARDS LIBERALISATION AND
HARMONISATION

As the European economies recovered and post war
housing shortages began to ease (although they
remained serious, especially in the Netherlands and
West Germany), pressure for decontrol grew.
Political battles took place between landlords (and
conservative parties) and tenants (and socialist
parties), the former arguing for an diminuition of
social rented housing and the extension of the role
of the private landlord, the latter arguing the
reverse. In fact the effects of rent controls were
increasingly serious, at least in the form which
they often took. The first effect, more noticeable,
for example, in the Netherlands and England than in
Germany was that, as costs rose faster than rents,
maintenance was reduced in order to maintain
profitability. There is less evidence of this in
Germany, partly because of its low inflation rate
but also perhaps because of the close relations
between many small landlords and their tenants

which may have reduced the former's willingness to disinvest.

The second problem was that rents were poorly related to quality. Different principles applied to rent setting in the newer and the older stock. The social sector was subject to yet another set of rules, usually having historic cost rents. Consequently there were great differences in the rents of newer and older property (even those of comparable quality). Often there was a concern that the older established tenants, in social and private housing, were paying low rents in relation to their incomes, whereas newcomers (who often had low incomes) were having to pay much more for newer housing. So attempts to liberalise (i.e. raise) and harmonise (i.e. relate to quality) rents occurred from the mid fifties onwards.

In France though the main emphasis was on liberalisation. In 1953 the government announced that controls would be ended by 1958 but there was strong opposition and this did not occur. Subsequent attempts to link rent increases to increases in salary or construction costs were also unacceptable. So the increases allowed under the 1948 Act simply continued beyond 1954 and in 1959 gradual decontrol began.

First some small communes were decontrolled and no more were allowed to join the system. Later more areas were decontrolled and later still higher quality properties were decontrolled. From 1962 all new lettings in some areas were decontrolled and by 1970 vacancy decontrol was general. The series of regular increases in controlled rents continued, eventually based not on the assumed 1948 value of the property but on a simple increment on the last rent payable, varied according to the type of dwelling and, sometimes, the level of maintenance. After the better quality properties were decontrolled, landlords could obtain decontrol by improvement (Duclaud-Williams, 1978, 17-63).

In Denmark attention was paid to harmonising and loosening controls. In 1958, later than in the other countries, the rents of new property were freed. Regulation was abolished, (unless the locality objected) in the smallest municipalities and some larger areas could o t for decontrol. In 1962 this scheme was extended and landlords were allowed to raise rents by 25% of their 1939 values on reletting. High rents for new property led to the reintroduction of controls for new rents in

Rents and Rent Policy

controlled areas in 1963. But decontrol was
extended, on the same basis as before, to further
areas in 1964. In fact the continued shortage of
housing and political opposition to decontrol
ensured that few localities did become decontrolled
in this year. Instead most units continued to
receive differentiated rent increases, so that by
1966 overall rent levels were about 90% above their
1939 levels (and up to 125% in dwellings which had
been relet since that date) (Boligminsteriet, 1965).
    At this point the simple process of decontrol
was replaced by measures to harmonise and
liberalise rent setting. In 1966 the main political
parties agreed to a housing pact to run for eight
years. An important goal was to ensure that rents
reflected the size, quality, location etc. of
individual dwellings and not their age. This
involved measures lowering the rents of new
property and raising those of the older stock. The
basis for rents in the controlled zones (excluding
property built before 1900 and after 1962, unless
the landlord so desired) was the 'reasonable and
real' value of the dwellings. This was determined
on the assumption that the market was free, that
there was an adequate vacancy reserve and that the
price of construction would remain stable as
interest rates and land costs fell. The increases
were to be phased over eight years and three
quarters of the increase had to be devoted to
maintenance and put in a special fund to pay for
future modernisation.
    From 1966-74 rents rose by about 40% nationally
and 60% in the housing stress area of Copenhagen
(Det Økonomiske Råd, 1970, 44). The rent
differentials between new and older dwellings were
reduced. But the policy failed. First, the increase
helped to inflate the price of rental properties,
although landlords could only retain 25% of the
increase there was evidence that the whole sum was
being capitalised; second, the assumptions about
future levels of building costs were wrong, interest
rates and land costs rose rapidly and, as before,
it was the newer, more expensive property which was
hard to let while the older units were still in
heavy demand (5). Overall, the gap between the
rents of newer and older units (allowing for
quality) remained and even widened.
    West Germany also found it difficult to adopt
policies to improve landlords' returns and achieve
harmonisation without creating social and political
problems. As we have seen, the Christian Democratic

government adopted a 'new liberalism' in economic
and social policy, the so called 'social market
economy' - reliance on the private market with
state support where necessary. Also it regarded the
spread of property ownership as of the utmost
importance in reconstructing a democratic society
whose inhabitants had a tangible stake in its
continuing prosperity and stability. This ideology
strongly influenced the country's approach to
housing involving support for non profit rental
housing but also direct subsidies for private landlords and owner occupiers (as well as subsidies for
private individuals to build non profit units - the
benefit being that such units would revert to free
private renting some years after subsidies ceased
being paid for them) (Hallett, 1977) (6).
        The general wish was to abolish controls but,
given the continuing housing shortage, this was
not easy. It was not until the sixties that a rapid
decontrol began. The 1960 Rent Act provided for
the decontrol of pre-1948 housing. Vacancy
decontrol was to occur in areas in which the crude
housing deficit had fallen below 3%. If allowance
is made for vacancies etc, it may be seen that
decontrol occurred in areas in which there was
still a considerable housing shortage. It was first
thought that the decontrol would be complete by
1965 but some controls remained in large cities
such as Hamburg, Munich and West Berlin until 1977.
As we shall see, rents rose rapidly in the later
sixties and decontrol led to much tenant protest
and political opposition. One of the worst aspects
of the legislation was that it encouraged landlords
to issue notices to quit in order to relet at
higher rents or to force tenants to pay more. This
was ended in 1971 by a protection from eviction act
(see chapter 8) and a new rent setting system which
will be discussed below.
        In England the government elected in 1951 also
wished to return the housing market to private
enterprise and in 1957 passed one of the most
contentious and bitterly opposed pieces of postwar
social legislation. The act provided for immediate
decontrol of better quality property (about 10% of
the rental stock). After a short period landlords
were to be free to recover possession and/or
increase the rent to whatever the market would
bear. Other properties were to be subject to
vacancy decontrol. An attempt was made to harmonise
the remaining controlled rents by relating them to

the 1956 housing valuation (carried out for local taxation purposes) by a multiplier which varied according to landlords' repairing and decorating obligations (as this 'rateable value' was supposed to be based on the rent which could be obtained from the property the process was circular and depended on the valuer's 'art' rather than an objective yardstick) (Short, 1982, 177-8; Nevitt, 1966).

Because of the political storm which it raised the Act was amended in 1958 to virtually prevent landlords gaining possession of decontrolled dwellings before 1961. The average increases permitted under the 1957 Rent Act were one half to two thirds the rents previously paid. The Act aimed to restore a healthy rental market but it failed. In fact sales to owner occupation increased as landlords gained possession of their property (many were also sold to sitting tenants), few new units were provided and there was a growth of symptoms of acute housing stress such as homelessness and the harassment of tenants, especially in London and other major centres. In 1963 the government held an enquiry into housing conditions in London. Its recommendations led to the introduction of a new system of rent setting in 1965 (Committee on Housing in Greater London, 1965).

In the Netherlands the pressure for harmonisation and liberalisation had some effect from the early sixties onwards (7). From 1964 increases were differentiated according to the age and condition of the property. For example in 1966 increases of up to 15% were allowed. Less was allowed for poorer property and more for better quality units but increments also varied according to the age of the property. So higher rented interwar dwellings received the largest increases, whereas property built before 1921 with very low rents (and usually in poor condition) received no increase.

Decontrol began in 1967. In contrast to Germany, decontrol only occurred in areas where there was a crude housing surplus of 1.5% or more. Directly subsidised private dwellings continued to have government determined rents though. Between 1967 and 1973 a large area of the country was freed, but not the Randstad and some municipalities elsewhere. But the latter areas contained the bulk of the private rental stock so in 1973 when

liberalisation ceased about 60% of the stock was
still controlled.

In 1971 more changes were made with the aim of
harmonising all rents. A points index of housing
quality, based on the standards and rents of social
housing built in the last five years in the region
concerned, was developed. Initial rents in the
social sector were to be based on the index. Rent
increases in the social sector and in the
controlled private rented sector were decided
annually by the government and were to be linked to
cost increases in the social sector. The points
system could be appealed to by private landlords of
controlled property who felt that the rent being
charged was too low, tenants could also appeal to
rent advice committees if they felt that the rent
was too high in relation to dwelling quality. In
1974 changes were made in the basis on which the
'quality points' were calculated and arrangements
to phase in rent increases which were above the
annual 'trend' rate.

To summarise, up to 1979 (when further changes
occurred - see below) the situation was complex.
Private housing in the liberalised zones, and post
war property in the controlled zones, had freely
set rents; all private subsidised property could
obtain the anual trend rate increase plus any
further increase determined   the points system
(phased if necessary); older controlled property
was subject to the same rules. In both these
latter cases tenants could argue that the rent
should be frozen if it seemed to be too high.
Finally, another system operated for newly built
private property aided by 'dynamic cost price'
subsidies. But very little such building was
occurring (see chapter 6).

In the USA most rents were freely set. Only
in New York City, as already mentioned, were there
continuing controls (8). Here landlords were
allowed a 6% return on their investment plus 2% for
depreciation. Increases could be granted if the
landlord was not getting this 'fair return' or on
a few special grounds such as the provision of
substantially improved services and major
rehabilitation. If the city's rental vacancy rate
rose above 5% there was a provision allowing the
ending of controls, this had not yet occurred at
the time of the research. Any increases were phased
and in 1953 a general increase was allowed for
units which still were at wartime rent levels.
Landlords could also increase the rent by 15% when

new tenants moved in. Landlords who claimed
increases had to have their properties in good
order and tenants of poor property could obtain
rent decreases. New property and some luxury units
were not controlled nor, later, were units in one
and two family homes. Vacancy decontrol occurred
from 1962 in owner occupied buildings which had six
units or less.

This system set rents in a way which was not
at all closely related to quality. As inflation
rose in the sixties there were demands from landlords and their supporters for decontrol or for
more flexible rent setting. In 1969 the first major
change occurred. A new system (rent stabilisation)
regulated rents, the provision of services and
evictions in all property in buildings of six or
more units built between 1947 and 1969 plus most of
the few units which had already been decontrolled.
The legislation covered about 350,000 newer units
which mainly housed the better off. At the same
time account was taken of the pressure to increase
controlled rents which, it was claimed, were too
low to provide a reasonable return (subsequent
evidence threw doubt on this). In 1970 all
controlled units became subject to the Maximum Base
Rent programme (MBR). It introduced a cost plus
profit basis (profit set at 8% of market value)
for rents. Using a complex and slow procedure, MBRs
were established for every unit and progression
to this level was allowed via $7\frac{1}{2}$% per annum rent
increases. Units had to be in sound condition, 1
million properties were eligible in 1970.

But the state government felt that this was
far too elaborate and slow and in 1971 followed the
example of other governments (e.g. England and
Germany) in allowing vacancy decontrol for all
stabilised and controlled units. Large rent
increases occurred (figures of 30-50% have been
suggested) and pressure grew for a further reform.
Between 240-325000 controlled units and about
88,000 stabilised units were decontrolled before a
new state law ended vacancy control in 1974 (Real
Estate Research Corporation, 1975a; Kristof, 1976;
Sternlieb and Hughes, 1976, 225-9).

THE SITUATION IN THE LATE SEVENTIES AND THE
OPERATION OF CONTROLS

We have seen how there was a movement away from
rigid controls towards more flexible systems of rent

setting. These, to a greater or lesser extent,
tried to relate rents to some notion of costs or a
'fair' return and/or reduce the wide differences in
rent levels between properties of similar quality,
the consequence of fragmented systems of rent
setting. Some countries tried more drastic
decontrol when there was still a substantial
shortage of housing. But housing stress increased
and the resulting opposition forced policy
modifications.

At the beginning of the seventies there was, in
several countries, a brief reversion to more general
rent controls. This had little to do with housing
policy being part of the effort to control
inflation which many Western governments were then
pursuing via prices and incomes policies. Even in
the USA a federal freeze on rents was briefly
enforced, followed by a rather weak control on rent
increases (1971-3). In France the measures were
more limited but longer lasting. At the beginning
of 1974 all rents of new housing and all controlled
rents were frozen for six months. At the end of
1976 a further short freeze occurred followed by a
limitation on rises in 1977. In 1978 there were
some further restrictions. In Britain rent increases
were phased over 1-3 years from the late sixties
onwards, but in the mid seventies there was also a
short rent freeze. In the Netherlands extra controls
were imposed on rent increases in 1974-75 when
inflation increased after the oil price rises.

By the late seventies there was still very
complex rent setting arrangements in most countries
and few governments had been able to proceed as
fast as they desired with total decontrol. Indeed,
as we shall see, in one country there was a
tightening of controls. A common constraint was the
limited capacity of tenants to pay increased rents,
as already shown many of those who by then lived in
the sector had low incomes.

In France, at the time of the research only a
few elderly tenants plus some 'inheriting' relatives
remained in the controlled sector which accounted
for 60% of private rented units in 1955, but only
about 12% by 1973 (Enquête-logement, 1955, 42-3;
Enquête-logement, 1973 (1), 31). However, post war
directly subsidised private units had
administratively set rents. Normally, their initial
rents had been a fixed percentage of construction
costs and were indexed to the official construction
cost index. For example, in 1972 initial rents of

such property were set at 8.75% of total building
costs plus an allowance for management. Increases
were calculated by a formula which regarded 40% of
the initial rent as fixed and allowed the other 60%
to be increased by the same percentage as the annual
rise in the construction cost index (CNL, 1974). In
the free rented stock there were often lease
provisions for six or twelve monthly increases
indexed to construction costs. In most countries
controls were enforced by local
government. But as already noted, in France there
were only rather limited local housing powers so
here aggrieved parties had to rely on the courts.
Yet complex regulations still governed the
controlled sector and there was a good deal of
evasion. And in many cases the incorrect rents were
charged from a failure to take account of all the
circumstances affecting the unit concerned.

In Denmark after the failure of the 1966-74
system negotiations began to find a new arrangement
(interestingly both the landlords' and the tenants'
organisations played a role in these). In 1974 a
new pact was concluded between six parties,
including the biggest, the Social Democrats. Among
other things it introduced cost determined rents to
the private rental sector. All areas with over
20,000 population continued with controls unless
the council decided otherwise, all smaller
municipalities were decontrolled unless they opted
into the new system. In mid 1975 there were about
360,000 private rented units in the former areas and
200,000 in the latter, so most units remained
controlled. Controlled rents were based on costs
plus a return on capital. In most cases this was 7%
of the tenanted value as assessed in 1973 (on
average eight times the annual rental) and from
this debt servicing had to be paid. In the case of
units built since 1963 the allowable amount
consisted of debt service on normal mortgages plus
a variable return on invested capital (note, not on
the assessed value). 8% was allowed if the house was
built in 1964, more for newer property. Rents also
included an amount indexed to building costs (in
1979 17 Kr per square metre) which was put into a
special fund for improvements and external
maintenance. More could be claimed if the landlord
was also responsible for internal maintenance.

This system did not apply to rented rooms. For
these there were no controls (except under rarely
used general provisions of the Landlord and Tenant
Act, which prohibited any 'unreasonable' rent). By

virtue of employment, accommodation was also
uncontrolled but these rents were usually low. The
main enforcement agency was the Rent Board, which
existed in every locality in the controlled zones.
It consisted of a neutral chairman (usually a lawyer
or a civil servant) plus one member nominated by the
landlords' organisation and one by the tenants'
organisation. By the late seventies Rent Boards
dealt with all landlord/tenant matters, formerly
some matters were dealt with by Housing Courts, but
these were later restricted to being courts of
appeal against Rent Board decisions (they were
constituted in the same manner as Rent Boards) and
courts for all housing matters in the free zones.

The new legislation, especially the calculation
of rents, was complex and both landlords and tenants
had had some difficulty in operating it. So one of
the Board's main functions was to act as a source
of information. In principle, landlords could claim
increases whenever costs rose. In practice they
went to the Boards annually. They had to prepare a
written budget plus supporting documentation, the
Boards could impose a daily fine if these were not
made available when requested. Boards also obtained
information from municipal and taxation authorities.
The tenants could inspect landlords' budgets and
challenge them. While cases were proceeding tenants
had to pay the increased rents demanded (subject to
an upper limit) with a rebate later if appropriate.
Even if the budgets were reasonable in relation to
costs the Boards could reduce the requested increase
if the resulting rent would be substantially out of
line with comparable local rents. Officials said
that this was rare except in buildings which were
being sold off as freehold flats. The point was
that the legal conversion involved before sales
were possible increased assessed values, thus
raising rents. This was regarded by some as
unjustifiable, although landlords objected to the
'comparability clause' being used to limit such
increases.

No studies had been made of evasion, but the
main devices used were the submission of incorrect
budgets and failure to carry out budgeted works or
maintenance (9). A considerable responsibility was
placed on tenants to police the system by
complaining to the Boards if necessary, but, as
mentioned above, they did then have quite strong
powers. Complete evasion seemed difficult. Landlords
were normally required to relet property within

four weeks, and the Boards policed this. A check
was possible because they had access to the
'register of movement'. In Denmark everyone had to
register with the local authority where they resided.
But the Boards had sometimes been reluctant to act
and community groups had campaigned on this issue.
    The system seemed to have a fair amount of
acceptance. The national tenants' organisation
(established in 1917 covering social and private
renting, with close links to the Social Democrats
and the trade unions, representing about 70,000
private tenants) when interviewed pointed out that
many of the big rent increases had occurred in older
properties with exceptionally low rents. It felt
that Boards often favoured the tenants and that the
nomination of tenant representatives to the Boards
worked well. The landlords' federation (representing
about 50% of the private landlords and a greater
proportion of the stock) disliked the complexity of
the scheme but felt that the rents were now far
more realistic than before. They too felt that the
Boards had worked well but criticised the growing
use of 'comparables' and were appealing in a number
of cases against Rent Board decisions.
    The new controls introduced in West Germany in
1971 had a mixed approach (10). The rents of newly
tenanted units were freely set (as already noted
tenants could not be evicted simply to increase the
rent). For the rest increases could be obtained by
application to local courts (as in France no special
agency existed) first, when increases occurred in
operating costs,interest charges or land taxes -
the full amount could then be passed on to the
tenant; second, after rehabilitation or
modernisation (for details see chapter 7); third,
when the landlord could show that locally comparable
units had higher rents. In this latter case the
landlord had to provide three examples of
comparables. Three methods could be used to
establish this. First, the landlord could search
out comparables, second the landlord could pay for
expert advice to provide the evidence, such experts
had to be licensed by local courts; the third
method, which was growing in popularity but which
still only covered about 20% of units and 150
localities, was for the local authority to establish
a 'rent mirror'. This was a table of rents for
different qualities and locations of housing,
determined on the basis of a local survey. The
authorities could not impose this on landlords and

143

tenants, the agreement of their local organisations
was required and considerable argument sometimes
occurred about the validity of the surveys.

Landlords could use either of the first two
methods even where a rent mirror existed, but in
these cases the judge would usually insist on using
the mirror. Landlords had a legal right to
increased rents, this was only abrogated if a
tenant objected. The acceptance of a new rent had
to be in writing, if tenants failed to respond to
landlords' requests they were deemed to have
objected. Judges could confirm, deny or alter
proposed increases and were not bound to accept
the validity of any evidence but they normally did,
especially where a rent mirror existed.

The only restraint on the rents for new lets
were contained in the criminal law on economic
exchange which stated that they could not be set
at levels 'substantially higher' than levels fixed
by the rent mirror or by comparables. Prosecutions
had to be initiated by local authorities and were
rare, both because few councils monitored rent
increases and for political reasons. Tenants'
organisations pressed for greater use of this law
whereas the landlords wanted to see it repealed.
It had been used to stop increases of as little as
20% but was mainly used when extreme exploitation
came to light. Rent controls were weak at the
bottom end of the market and poorer groups, such as
guest workers, often paid high rents.

Reaction to the provisions varied. One problem
was the lack of consistency in the decisions of
different judges. Although landlords and tenants
could appeal against their decisions they could
only go to the state courts, so there was no
national review of decisions. The tenants'
association (founded in 1900, organised on a federal
basis and having about 1 million members and a
long history of protest over rent issues) when
interviewed was concerned about the lack of
assistance for tenants and their ignorance of their
rights. But it had campaigned for the 1971 law and
was fairly satisfied to defend it. The landlords'
association (established for about 100 years,
organised on a federal basis with about 80,000
members, representing landlords and owner
occupiers) was far less happy. Officials explained
that in the sixties landlords expected within ten
to fifteen years to be able to charge cost
covering rents and begin to make profits thereafter
(this did seem to have been a fairly common
assumption on which rental housing investment was

based). By the late seventies building and other
costs had risen steeply but the comparability
provisions prevented rent increases in line with
indices of, for example, the cost of living or of
earnings so,decreasing the profit prospects. The
landlords also wanted to see the criminal law
provisions repealed and changes made in the rent
mirror to base it on recent rent agreements and
ensure that it reflected the full range of
properties being let (apparently many towns based
it on the rents paid by those receiving housing
allowances, this excluded much higher value
property). The government's view was that there was
no strong political support for such changes, anyway
a survey had shown that 90% of all rent increases
were amicably agreed between landlords and tenants
and that most landlords were able to increase rents
without having to look for comparables and go to
court. The real problems occurred in a minority of
cases, for these it was doubtful whether the
existing laws were very effective.

In England the abandonment of vacancy control
in the mid sixties was followed in 1965 by a new
system of rent regulation. This was preceded by a
Protection from Eviction Act which gave back
security to most unfurnished tenants. The new law
established a system of rent fixing consisting of
publically appointed Rent Officers backed up, as
a court of appeal, by Rent Assessment Panels. These
were to fix 'fair' rents. In setting rents, regard
was to be had to all the circumstances of the
property (excluding the personal circumstances of
the tenant) especially its age, character, locality
and state of repair. But 'scarcity' was to be
disregarded, as rents were to be set on the
assumption that 'the number of people seeking to
become tenants of similar dwelling houses in the
locality on the terms (other than those relating to
rent) of the regulated tenancy is not substantially
greater than the number of such dwelling houses in
the locality which are available for letting on
such terms' (the formula was taken from an
earlier legal precedent relating to long leased
premises) (Committee on the Rent Acts, 1971, 3-7).
These provisions did not apply to the remaining
controlled tenancies but other rents remained
frozen at their 1965 levels until a 'fair' rent was
determined. Application to the Rent Officer, and
appeals to the Panel, could be made by the landlord
or the tenant or jointly. 'Fair' rents could only be

reassessed every three years, failing a major
change of circumstances such as the improvement of
the property.

Thus from 1965 rent regulation began to replace
control. Apart from its immediate application to
previously decontrolled property, controlled
property which had been 'inherited' for a second
time became regulated and other controlled property
became regulated when vacated. Moreover a 1969 act
which dealt with improvement (see chapter 7) enabled
controlled properties with adequate amenities and
in reasonable repair to become regulated. In the
early seventies further measures were taken to
transfer controlled property which was in good
condition to regulation and to begin the transfer of
other controlled property en bloc. This latter
process was stopped by the new Labour government in
1974 but by this time the controlled sector was
very much reduced (11).

In England there had been little control on
rents in furnished property until after the last
war when Rent Tribunals were established to fix
'reasonable rents' for furnished dwellings, those
let at a rent which included payment for services
and unfurnished property in which living
accommodation was shared with the landlord. But in
1974 the legal distinction between furnished and
unfurnished accommodation regarding rent setting
and security was replaced by a distinction between
property with absentee and with resident landlords
(i.e. landlords sharing living accommodation with
the tenant). The former property (protected
tenancies) was subject to regulation and the
latter to Rent Tribunals (tenancies with restricted
contracts).

There was opposition from the two main
landlords' organisations (one of which represented
larger property interests and the other the small
landlords, neither with as large a membership or
influence as some of their counterparts in the other
countries) who wanted regulation to be abolished
or, failing this, the concept of a reasonable return
for the landlord made the basis for rent setting.
But there was a considerable measure of political
agreement about at least the basic principles of
the 'fair' rents system. In fact, apart from the
remaining controlled sector and a small amount of
luxury property, most private tenancies should have
been covered by the legislation although, as will be
discussed below, many rents were set by agreement
rather than by recourse to its provisions, as in

West Germany. This had been assisted by the fact
that, since 1972, if a property had never had a
registered rent the rent applicable was whatever
the tenant and the landlord agreed although either
could go to the Rent Officer at any time if they
wished to. Landlords and tenants could apply
jointly, three years after a fair rent had been
fixed, for it to be cancelled so that they could
set a new rent by agreement. The Rent Officer might
agree to do this. Local authorities had the power
to refer any property in their area to the Rent
Officer, this was intended for use when the tenant
was reluctant to act but it rarely happened (12).
    For tenants with resident landlords there
was a considerable disincentive to use the
Tribunals as these ('restricted') tenancies only
had limited security of tenure and landlords were
likely to give a tenant notice to quit if this
occurred (if a tenant applied to a Tribunal
regarding security it also considered the rent
level). Local authorities also had the power to
refer cases to the Tribunal.
    The Rent Officers were independent of central
and local government as were the Panels and the
Tribunals (in most cases these two services were
eventually combined). Usually these bodies consisted
of a lawyer, a valuer and a lay member. There was
no appeal from their decisions except on a point of
law. The arrangements were examined by an official
committee in the early seventies. There were
criticisms from some landlords of the slowness of
the procedures and the lack of uniformity in
decisions between differing areas. There was much
argument about how the concept of a 'fair' rent was
operationalised and some evidence from London that
'fair' rents did reflect the scarcity of
accommodation there. It was also claimed that the
Panels were biased towards professional, pro-
landlord interests (13).
    In fact the concept of 'fair' rent was hard to
operationalise. In practice, the officials tended
to take some account of landlords' returns. They
also used comparables or sometimes referred to the
freely set rents of luxury property. Tribunals had
even less legal guidance on how to set rents but,
in practice, followed similar procedures, although
20-30% could be added for furniture, based on its
value and likely life.
    As elsewhere, there was widespread evasion of
these legal requirements, especially at the bottom

of the market. Some landlords had developed types of
tenancy which avoided the rent (and security)
provisions of the Rent Acts (see chapter 8). But, in
a very tight rental market, many tenants were in too
weak a position to refuse the landlord's terms,
even if they were aware of the legislation, which
was fairly rare.

In the Netherlands the arrangements for rent
setting were changed in 1979(14). Interestingly,
these seemed to mark a turning away from simple
decontrol in favour of an extension of
administratively set rents to the whole country.
One reason was that the decline of private rental
housing led to growing shortages outside the
controlled zones. Consequently some towns in the
liberalised zones were experiencing very high rent
levels because of the imbalance between supply and
demand. The new law placed all private rented
property under rent control via the points system
and the annual 'trend rate' increase (computed by
the government in relation to the cost of living,
wages and building costs and higher in the Randstad
than elsewhere). The system was operated by the
Rent Committees. New subsidised building was still
subject to the special arrangements for rent fixing
already mentioned. The rents of new tenancies could
be freely agreed by landlords and tenants but if
either was dissatisfied they could go to a Rent
Committee when the points system was applied, except
in the case of the very best quality, newer property
whose rents (as before) were set by reference to
comparables. But some check on excessive rents
existed because if a landlord relet for more than
the previous rent plus any applicable trend increase
the Rent Committee had to be informed and could
reduce the rent if it seemed unreasonable. The
power that controlled tenants already had to obtain
a rent freeze if maintenance or repairs were not
done was extended so if the rent was higher than
the property quality merited, a freeze could
continue until this was adjusted.

The system of annual increases had, according
to the Amsterdam landlord previously mentioned,
been largely accepted as preferable to the previous
series of irregular increases, although the reaction
of landlords who could, since 1979, no longer
freely set rents was likely to have been less
favourable. This informant suggested that, despite
early opposition, landlords felt that, taking one
year with another, they were receiving reasonable

treatment. In fact in the late seventies rent
increases in the liberalised and in the controlled
zones had stayed more or less in line with each
other (despite the problems in some towns already
noted).

But in the Netherlands, as elsewhere, in some
cities and for some categories of tenant, high rents
were being extracted, despite the existence of
controls. For example, although sub-tenants in the
controlled zones were legally entitled to
controlled rents, there was general agreement that
they actually received little protection. As in
England, few sub-tenants were in a position to
refuse accommodation at the rent that the landlord
chose to demand (and tenants had to appeal to the
Committee before they accepted) and some very high
rents, in relation to the size and quality of the
accommodation, were paid.

The Rent Committees consisted, as in Denmark,
of landlords' and tenants' representatives and a
neutral chairman who had to have legal training.
They had full time secretariats and their decisions
could be appealed to the municipal courts. The
system was funded by the national government but
the selection of committee members was the duty of
provincial deputies - in order apparently to
demonstrate the system's independence.

By the late seventies the controls which had
developed in some localities in the USA in the
late sixties and early seventies (15), were on the
wane (16). In many cases they had been abolished
or were greatly weakened. However, they still
existed in Washington D.C. This city had had an
influx of well paid employees as a result of the
expansion of the federal government and associated
organisations. It had developed a highly pressurised
housing market, with upper income groups competing
for property, either for rental or for conversion
to owner occupation (in these respects this city
contrasted with most older US cities, including New
York, where inner city decline has accompanied the
departure of middle and upper income groups)
(Richards and Rowe, 1977; Committee on Finance and
Revenue, 1976). In response the city introduced
controls in 1974 (following a brief period of federal
controls) and an anti-eviction law (17). A Housing
Commission was established to ensure that rents were
kept no higher or were reduced to 10% above their
early 1973 levels. The rents of new property could
be freely set but were then frozen. The Commission

could also make some adjustments in cases of tenant
or landlord hardship but was required to maintain
levels which would ensure 'reasonable' returns.

A new system began in 1975. A Commission was to
establish fresh rules and procedures and hear
appeals from decisions made by a new Office of Rent
Control. A formula set maximum rents at levels
which allowed an 8% return on assessed (i.e. current
market) values plus a maximum of 2% for
depreciation. Rents could be increased by 5% per
annum to reach this level, but were reduced if the
return was above the ceiling. Rents could be
reviewed in cases of hardship and the same rules
as before governed the initial rents of new units.
In calculating the rate of return certain operating
expenses were deductable, including losses through
arrears and vacancies, a management fee that was
normally 6% of the maximum annual rental income,
the depreciation allowance and the amortised cost
of capital improvements. Interest payments were not
deductable and the rent payable was based on the
past year's situation without any adjustment for
expected inflation.

In New York the measures taken in 1974 in
response to the problems caused by vacancy
decontrol placed all units completed between 1969
and 1974 under rent stabilisation, as were all
units which had been decontrolled by the former
state law. Rent controlled units vacated after 1974
could also be transferred to stabilisation, thus
allowing a gradual run down of the controlled
sector to occur. These changes added another 400,000
units to the stabilised sector immediately (Real
Estate Research Corporation, 1975a).

Rent control was administered by a city council
department (18). This office approved rent
alterations, set maximum rents, regulated decontrol,
granted or denied certificates of eviction and
settled legal disputes. Rent increases were still
based on the MBRs established in 1971 but the
process of reviewing every rent was too cumbersome
so across the board increases were adopted (they
occurred every two years and were 8½% in 1974/75
and 22% in 1976/77, i.e. quite substantial).
Tenants were supposed to be given information by
their landlords on how their rent was fixed and how
to appeal. Increases were not supposed to occur if
the building was seriously in violation of the
city's housing code or if all the normally provided
services were not supplied (lengthy and complex

statutes and procedures existed to define and decide what, for example, 'normal services' were). Some opportunities existed for landlords to claim increased rents, for example if they were not receiving the minimum return on their investment or if there were major improvements.

Rent stabilisation partly relied on landlords' self regulation. All landlords who wished to charge such rents had to join the Rent Stabilisation Association (RSA), a policing body financed by the landlords. Otherwise in theory their rents remained controlled, although landlords could join the RSA retrospectively. Landlords had to adhere to a rent stabilisation code which provided for a Conciliation and Appeals Board. The CAB determined the proper rent for apartments, granted rent increases and decided what services a landlord had to supply. (In some cases its jurisdiction overlapped with that of the city's Housing Court, see chapter 8). Its members were appointed by the Mayor and were supposed to be neutral. Landlords who infringed the code could be fined or suspended from the RSA. Their apartments then reverted to control. The other important body was the Rent Guidelines Board (RGB), again independent and appointed by the mayor. Its role will be discussed below.

When tenants moved into a stablised apartment they freely negotiated the length of the lease but afterwards they had to be offered a choice of 1, 2 or 3 year renewals. Landlords could not vary the terms of this new lease, except the rent. The basis for rent setting was the amount payable when a unit first became stabilised but the CAB could decide that this was too high (these provisions applied to units which had been decontrolled under the former state law as well as those units which were moving, on vacancy, from control to stabilisation, in the latter case landlords could, in principle, seek whatever initial rent the market would bear). Once this base rent was known a simple but cumbrous calculation determined the rent currently payable. Every year the RGB set levels of permissable rent increases, based on estimates of changes in costs etc. It issued separate figures for vacancy and renewal leases. In each case figures were given for 1, 2 and 3 year leases. Substantial increases had occurred, for example in 1977 the percentages ranged from 11.5% - 16.5% for vacancy leases and 6.5 - 11.5% for renewal leases (of the previous year's rent). In the early years there were rather large

increases especially for vacancy leases, presumably
for 'catching up' purposes.

THE EFFECTS OF CONTROLS AND THE PROFITABILITY OF RENTAL HOUSING

In this section we consider the impact of controls
and their liberalisation or removal on rents, and
analyse the economic situation of the sector in the
late seventies. We have outlined the great variety
of controls on private rents and the tendency for
these to be made more flexible and responsive to
rising costs. But steeply rising costs in recent
years have often resulted in a reduced profitability
even though rents have been allowed to increase more
rapidly than in the forties and fifties.
Paradoxically, the stricter controls of this earlier
period accompanied a relatively slow decline in the
fortunes of the sector (masked to some extent by
disinvestment via undermaintenance), whereas in
latter years the loosening of controls has been
unable to prevent many landlords from facing severe
economic difficulties. Yet when governments have
taken the ultimate step of abolishing controls
considerable tenant hardship has resulted and there
have been pressures for a return to some degree of
regulation. The reason for this is that many of
those who now live in the sector have low incomes
which do not necessarily increase in line with
average incomes (or rents). The evidence for these
conclusions varies in its coverage and quality but,
taken together and in broad terms, justifies the
conclusion that the main obstacle to a more
satisfactory economic situation for private
landlords is the inability of many tenants to pay
rents which allow profits to be made from the
letting of decent accommodation. Rent controls are
a reaction to this situation rather than the root
cause of the difficulties which have arisen. Details
of the situation in each country will now be
outlined.
     A French study shows that from 1961-73 the
percentage of income spent on rent rose (Ansidei,
Carassus and Strobel, 1978). The increases were
especially large in the older free rented sector.
Generally, higher charges added a great deal to
housing costs. Between 1962 and 1976 rents rose
about three times faster than the cost of living
index and in 1975-76 there was an especially rapid
rise (which led to the imposition of temporary

controls at about this time) (Massu; 1977, 18). Also
new entrants to rental housing paid appreciably
higher proportions of their incomes in rent than
tenants as a whole (Ansidei, Carrassus and Strobel,
1978, 144-5). Longer term movements in Fench rents
in relation to incomes and prices are harder to
assess, partly because of the inadequacies of the
various official and unofficial price indices.
However one source does suggest that controlled
rents had increased by about 35 times their 1950
level by 1977, in comparison HLM rents rose by about
19 times their 1950 level (Massu, 1977, 24).

As already noted, the different rent setting
systems used resulted in much variation, with the
HLM stock offering the best value for money and the
older part of the private sector offering poorer
quality accommodation at lower rents (except in
Paris and other hard pressed urban housing markets
where even this property was rather expensive in
relation to many tenants' incomes) (19). The overall
result of decontrol was to raise the rents paid by
many of those at the bottom of the market to far
higher levels in relation to incomes than in the
early post war period. This was in fact an explicit
aim of government policy and must be viewed in the
light of developments in the provision of rent
allowances (see chapter 6). Not long before the
research was carried out a Paris landlords'
association suggested that rents should amount to
18-25% of household income. But there was much
political opposition to such levels, so complete
abolition of the remaining controls seemed unlikely.
But by the late seventies the government wanted to
press ahead with further block decontrol, raising
rents in the remaining controlled stock and
facilitating decontrol by improvement. But perhaps,
given the small size of the controlled sector, a
more important problem was the rapidly escalating
levels of charges and the lack of controls over
them. Certainly the main tenants organisation was
particularly concerned with this (Massu, 1977).
Much of the increase which had occurred was a
direct result of inflation (especially of energy
costs). But unjustifiable increases had occurred in
some parts of the stock where rent rises were
controlled.

Good evidence on the rates of return being
obtained by French landlords was unavailable. The
main landlords' association claimed that the
controlled rents were too low even to ensure proper
maintenance but elsewhere the situation did not

seem to be so severe. Thus the rents of newer units
in areas such as central Paris were very high, and
even though the returns might not be comparable with
those available from other investments the benefits
of appreciating capital values must be taken into
account. And in some sections of the market lettings
were very profitable, for example when making poor
property available at high rents to those who were
not able to gain access elsewhere and when providing
accommodation for mobile professionals in the larger
provincial cities. Thus one estimate made in the mid
seventies suggested that landlords in this latter
submarket could gain a 9% return after all costs
were met (plus capital appreciation) (20).

In Denmark a 1976 survey examined the effects
of the most recent rent setting provisions
(Boligministeriet, 1977). The average rent increase
amounted to as much as 42%, far more than had been
predicted. In fact, although no statistics of rents
in the free market areas existed, it was believed
that the increase would be unlikely to have been
much greater if all controls had been abolished. In
some cases the administratively set rents might
even have been higher than those that would have
been set in a free market. This reversal of the
normal relationship between controlled and free
rents was not confined to Denmark, as we shall see.
It was a measure of the extent to which the problem
of the private sector derived from the lack of
purchasing power of its tenants and not just the
existence of controls. As in France, in Denmark the
older property had had the largest rent rises,
for example, excluding Copenhagen, pre-war dwellings
without a bath or central heating had their rents
increased by an average of 49%, whereas the rents
of post war property only rose by about half this
percentage. Given the association of poorer
households with older property, the burden of rent
increases had fallen more heavily on them than on
the better off.

The view of the Landlords' Federation that the
current system of rent setting was preferable to
the previous system will be recalled. But at the
time of the research interest rates were at around
16% and the Federation suggested that few landlords
made more than 1-2% net return unless they had
rather old loans outstanding on their property.
Certainly many landlords were seeking to take
advantage of rising capital values by selling out
to tenants' co-operatives or to owner occupiers.

Rents and Rent Policy

The changing proportion of income paid in rent and
charges was not known but there seemed little doubt
that for many households the trend had been in an
upward direction.

More detail was available for West Germany,
including calculations which illustrate the
declining profitability of new investment (even
though new investment had been supported and there
had been a rather low rate of inflation). Again, the
impact of changes in rents was particularly
significant for those on low incomes. But there had
also been a general rise in the proportion of income
paid in rent (the data covers all rented housing).
Thus the proportion of income paid in rent by a four
person household of average income rose from about
9% in the early fifties to over 15% by the mid
seventies. The effects of the changes in rent
setting legislation were evident, for the proportion
remained around 9-10% until the early sixties,
then rising to over 15% by 1968 - the period of
decontrol. But in the seventies, with the new
controls, the figure then stabilised (Statistisches
Jahrbuch, vs. years). However the impact on
pensioner households of the new controls seems to
have been weaker, thus such households paid 12-13%
of their incomes throughout the fifties, rising to
over 20% by 1960 and continuing to rise, albeit more
slowly, to stand at 22.6% by 1976 (Statistisches
Jahrbuch, vs.years). The overall impact of changes
in rent policy was also made clear by figures which
show the proportion of households paying over 20%
of their net household income in rent at various
dates. Only 6% of households fell into this category
in 1956, the proportion rose to 8.5% in 1960, 13%
in 1965 and 20.6% in 1972 (Zapf, 1977, 640). In fact
incomes stagnated in the late sixties (due to a
mild recession), while rents rose rapidly under the
impact of decontrol. It was the combination of these
two facts which provided the economic basis for
the pressure for new controls at this time.

Further data shows that increases had fallen
heavily on lower income groups, such as the
pensioners already mentioned and - as elsewhere -
tenants in the older stock. Increases in the older
stock in the post 1960 period had partly resulted
from improvement but the extent of this influence
was unknown. In fact between 1962 and 1976 rents had
risen most rapidly in the pre-1948 stock, a little
less rapidly in the social rented stock and
considerably slower in the more recently built
private housing (21).

Rents and Rent Policy

Recent research has analysed the varying
returns to owners of new privately rented housing
from 1965-76 (22). It illustrates several points
which have already been discussed including the
declining profitability of recent years. Because
the main subsidies available to private landlords
were via the tax system (see chapter 6), the exact
position depended on landlords' individual tax
positions and the age of the buildings concerned. A
further complication is that construction was
usually financed from several sources. Four are
included in the calculations, first, a mortgage
loan from a financial institution such as a savings
bank; second, a building loan from a Bausparkassen
(housing savings bank); third, own savings and,
finally, other borrowed capital. Different
combinations of loans lead to different financial
outcomes because of the variation in interest
payable and in tax relief (23).
        Calculations have been carried out for
profits/losses etc. incurred at tax rates varying
from 0-50% for property built between 1965 and
1976 (24). Taking account of the net income received
and the appreciation of capital values involved
(estimated from price data), a positive return
should have been earned by landlords in all tax
brackets in most years from the first year after
completion, but sometimes (when estimates showed
that building costs were slightly above market
values - as occurred in 1965, 1967 and 1975-6)
after one or two years more. Higher tax payers
benefitted more than those who paid less (presumably
the relatively poorer landlords). Also those who had
greatest recourse to ordinary commercial loans,
more expensive than other sources, did least well.
Because of the complex interaction of tax and other
considerations profits peaked after about six
years, then declined for another five years before
recovering. Significantly the first year deficits
of housing built in 1976 were four to ten times
higher than they had been for property built in
1965. This was partly a result of rising interest
rates but also because depreciation allowances were
reduced in 1973 and this partially affected higher
tax payers. Overall, the change which occurred
between 1965 and 1976 is a measure of the
increasing unattractiveness of private rental
investment over this period.
        Disregarding the appreciation of capital
values, the net income obtained for property built

during the period reviewed was low and even negative
for some tax payers. Again, the position of those
who paid more tax and those who had least recourse
to the commercial capital market was better. The
declining fortunes of those who paid relatively
little tax was especially evident. In fact further
data shows that, as already mentioned, landlords in
Germany did not obtain quick profits from building
rental property. Disregarding capital appreciation,
about six to eleven years of losses could be
expected, losses were greatest for those who paid
least tax. After this period profits could be
expected.

Unfortunately this analysis does not cover
property constructed before 1965. But clearly long
term profits have been possible in rental housing.
Their extent must have varied enormously, so any
one figure is bound to be misleading. However a
landlords' representative suggested that a return
of 4% exclusive of capital appreciation would be
the least that would be expected. But the
profitability had declined in recent years and had
mainly been obtained by better off landlords and
those who had not borrowed much commercial capital
(i.e. the wealthier, individual small landlords who
had, as we shall see, been assisted by subsidies).
However, it must again be emphasised that many
German landlords only owned one or two properties.
As already noted, the motive for landlordism in
their case was often not a highly commercial one,
or if it was it was more likely to be concerned
with capital appreciation than with current profits.
Moreover, many small landlords spent time looking
after their own properties and the use of this
unpaid labour probably disguised the fact that, on
strictly economic grounds, the current returns on
the investment were minimal. It seems that one must
look to factors such as these, rather than the
persistence of large scale commercial investment
opportunities when considering why the supply of
rental housing had continued at so high a level in
Germany, in contrast with several of the other
countries in this survey.

In England there is also some data on changes
in rent levels and incomes although there is less
information on investment returns. But data on the
relationship of 'fair' rents to costs and on house
prices, suggests that, as elsewhere, the position
of landlords had worsened in an era of rapid
inflation. Thus between 1970 and 1976 rents
increased on re-registration with the Rent Officer

by considerably less than housing repair costs and
general prices. In 1970 the average return on
private rented units with 'fair' rents was probably
about 3% net of amortisation; but by 1975 only a
little over 1%. Clearly in such circumstances few
landlords were on purely economic grounds likely
to continue to let property, at least if it was
subject to 'fair' rents (25).

More detailed data for 1966 and 1970-78
shows that from the start of the new legislation up
to 1970, 'fair' rents increased in line with house
prices, repair/maintenance costs, retail prices
and earnings(26). But since 1970 rents had lagged
behind the other indicators and counter inflation
policies which froze or restricted rents
(apparently more successfully than prices and
incomes) had had a noticeable impact in the mid
seventies. (Interestingly, despite also being
affected by counter inflation policies, social
housing rents rose faster from 1966-1978 than
private rents, although from a lower base.) These
results suggest that the trend of declining returns
in the seventies noted above was correct and also
suggest that since 1975 many landlords actually
began to lose money on 'fair' rented property.
In this situation disinvestment via declining
maintenance and repair was likely to occur. In fact
rental income on such property rose noticeably
slower than the decline in the average purchasing
power of the pound while increases in average
earnings had more than compensated for this decline.
There had also been a very rapid growth in house
prices, making the option of selling off property
for owner occupation ever more attractive.

But the comparison of 'fair' rents and overall
average earnings is a limited one, because only a
minority of unfurnished property was regulated and
because tenants' incomes did not increase in line
with average earnings. Data exists by which
comparisons of median tenant incomes for all
unfurnished and furnished tenancies (separately)
and rents may be made for the period 1972-7 (27).
Comparisons may also be made with levels of 'fair'
rents and average earnings. This shows that the
average level of unfurnished rents was much lower
than the average of 'fair' rents alone. In fact the
'fair' rent system was mainly being applied to the
more expensive and, possibly, better quality units
(many of them owned by the larger and more organised
landlords). But also in 1972 the average level of
unfurnished rents was depressed by the inclusion of

many controlled units with very low rents. However,
by 1977 this latter section was very small, yet the
differential between all unfurnished rents and
'fair' rents remained, although the gap had narrowed
considerably. Thus all unfurnished rents increased
twice as fast as regulated rents during this period
- in fact at roughly the same pace as overall
earnings. This suggests that, despite the existence
of the legislation, by the seventies market forces
had a considerable influence in determining rent
increases. But, while unfurnished tenants' incomes
increased faster than 'fair' rents, they lagged
behind the increase in all unfurnished rents and
the rent/income ratio grew steadily from 8.3% in
1972 to 11.9% in 1977. So, although overall rent
levels were not very high, even the increases which
occurred could not be matched by a similar increase
in the ability to pay of unfurnished tenants. Rent
regulation alleviated this problem but
significantly reduced profitability. So beyond
the effects of rent regulation there lay the more
fundamental problem of the lack of profitability
of the private provision of rental housing for those
on low incomes - the major role of the sector today.
        Furnished rents were far higher than
unfurnished rents, although the differential
narrowed between 1972-7 as, especially after 1974,
furnished rents increased more slowly than
unfurnished rents (possibly an effect of the 1974
Rent Act). Furnished tenants, not surprisingly
given their composition, had higher incomes than
unfurnished tenants and these had increased more
rapidly than those of unfurnished tenants (although
again not as fast as overall earnings). But the
income differential between the two sectors was not
as great as the rent differential. So the rent/
income ratio for furnished tenants was much higher,
varying between about 21% in 1972 and 19% in 1977
with no clearly visible trend. This was very high
in comparison with other tenures and points to one
of the main forms of housing stress in this part of
the privately rented sector. Essentially it
illustrates the outcome of a situation where
alternative, better quality and cheaper
accommodation was not available to certain
disadvantaged groups who therefore had to accept
less satisfactory accommodation, supplied by
landlords at whatever price the market would bear.
From the evidence already provided, it seems likely
that a similar situation existed at the bottom of
the market in most of the other countries surveyed.

Rents and Rent Policy

    Data for the Netherlands illustrates the slow
development of contractual rents under rent control
compared with the costs of construction and
salaries (van der Schaar, 1982). These figures were
obtained by applying the various increases legally
available throughout the period to the relevant
stock. In practice rents did not develop in quite
this way, as will be shown below. Thus, between
1950 and 1980 earnings rose by 965% and
construction costs by 776%. In contrast contractural
rents rose by 710% but this was much faster than
the cost of living index which rose by 420%.
However, in 1950 rents were still at their 1939
levels whereas the cost of living and earnings
doubled over this period and building costs rose
by 350%. Overall, rents rose faster than the cost
of living up to 1968, rather more slowly up to the
mid seventies and rather faster since then. But
over the whole period rents increased their share
of the cost of living.
    Comparison of the various indices suggests
that the cost of maintenance and repair increased
while average rent/income ratios fell. In fact
before 1939 about 15-25% of income was spent on
rent (28). By 1951 the figure was 10% and this was
only exceeded again in the early seventies (but, as
already noted, such aggregate comparisons may
obscure the position for poorer tenants). By the
seventies as much as 45% of the calculated level of
contractural rents might have been spent on
maintenance, compared with 12% in 1940. Whether
this still left room for any profits depended on
the situation of the individual landlord and
property; landlords with long established holdings
or speculators might still have done well in these
circumstances.
    From 1967 onwards data for the actual
development of rents is available (CBS monthly, a,
b). The real increase between 1967 and 1976 was
greater than that resulting from the contractural
rent calculations. After correcting for the effects
of newly built units entering the stock, the index
of actual rents stood at 181 in 1976 (1967 = 100)
and the contractural index at 167. Interestingly,
the increase in the index in the liberalised areas
hardly differed from this overall figure (a point
suggested earlier) thus showing that increases in
controlled rents had kept in line with market
determined increases in areas where, in the
aggregate at least, the market was more or less 'in

balance'. Of course if the same freedom had existed
in controlled areas there would have been a more
rapid increase there because of scarcity.

These data show that the rents of existing
housing increased in line with increases in the cost
of living but lagged behind increases in building
costs and the rents of new subsidised housing
(built by private landlords or by the social sector).
In contrast with elsewhere, rents in the older
stock had increased more slowly than those in the
newer part of the sector.

Also, unlike elsewhere, rent/income ratios (for
all rental property) had not shown any significant
increase over the years. But the rent/income ratio
of first year occupants of new private rental
housing had increased sharply - from 15.5% in 1950
to 23.6% in 1970 (as occupancy continued the ratio
then declined) (van der Schaar, 1982). Despite the
increase in this ratio, increases in incomes had
tempered its effects. Also older households, those
living in older property and those who had occupied
the longest paid lower proportions of their income
in rent than others. Pensioners paid rather more
than average, although, in comparison with Germany,
the situation had improved (CBS, 1975; van der
Schaar, 1982), due to improvements in pensions
(the ratio fell from 15% in 1967 to 12.7% in 1975).
Information is also available on rent/income ratios
in different sectors of the rental market for 1964,
1967 and 1970 (but not for 1975 unfortunately)
(CBS, 1964, 1967, 1970). This shows that the ratio
was rather high in the social sector because many
occupants had low incomes and much of the stock was
fairly new and expensive. The ratio increased in
the mid sixties, but between 1967 and 1970 there
was little change. In the private sector there was
a similar increase in the mid sixties followed by a
small decline.

The evidence from the Netherlands suggests
that landlords had not been able to gain as much
from changing rent policy as in some other
countries. Nor had those who owned the older
property (with rents depressed by the wartime
freeze) been able to catch up as much as those in,
for example, Germany. It is a pity that detailed
data for the seventies was not available. Since
1974 rent/income ratios had been affected by the
provision of housing allowances which, according
to a 1975 survey, reached 75% of those who were
eligible (see chapter 6).

In such circumstances it is not surprising

that the Netherlands had a rapidly declining private
rental sector. One consequence was that the market
in tenanted properties became less attractive. So
landlords faced not just a lack of current income
but capital losses, or at least less capital growth
than obtainable from other types of asset. The
pressure to sell with vacant possession for owner
occupation (benefitting from the rising capital
values in this part of the property market) was
evident. Thus the price index for single family
housing sold with vacant possession rose by 400%
between 1965 and 1977 whereas that for sales of
similar tenanted housing only rose by about half as
much (CBS, monthly b). A smaller but still
considerable disparity existed in the case of multi-
family housing. The highest prices for tenanted
flats were in the commuter suburbs of the larger
cities (where much of the newer rented property
was built, for occupation by better off tenants)
and the lowest prices in Amsterdam (with controls
on rents and occupancy, older stock and many lower
income tenants). On the other hand, vacant property
was most expensive in the big cities, including
Amsterdam, and their suburbs. The advantages of
selling off rented property were evident, especially
in Amsterdam where the price of tenanted apartments
actually declined by about 20% between 1965 and
1976.
     Between 1965 and 1977 the price of rental
property lagged behind increases in the cost of
living and construction, but the index for owner
occupied property outstripped both these indices
and in the mid seventies inflation in the owner
occupier market was acute (in common with many other
countries). Considering the period from 1953 to
1976, until 1965 there was little difference in
the rate of price rises in the rental and in the
owner occupied markets. Both indices increased
faster than those for building costs and general
prices. The collapse of the rental property market
occurred after 1965 when an era of rapid inflation
and more limited opportunities to increase rents,
together with the growing demand for ownership by
the better off, had taken its toll.
     Until 1965 there was considerable new
investment in rental property by institutional
investors seeking long term capital gains. (They
often bought from individual landlords). But by the
mid sixties it was clear that rent controls would
persist and costs began to rise rapidly. So the

institutions began to dispose of their investments
and the rented property market slackened. By the
1970s the growing demand for owner occupation
revived the market, but only for sales with vacant
possession. Hence the 'break up' of blocks of
rented flats became common (as in Britain).

The effects of rent controls in the USA
were minimal when considering the market as a whole.
It is nevertheless useful to consider overall
movements in rents and incomes a little further as
well as focusing of what occurred in New York and
Washington D.C. - the two cases of rent control
which were described earlier.

In New York, as already mentioned, the rent
control law set a vacancy rate of 5% as the level
for decontrol. In order to check whether this limit
has been reached, regular surveys are made. These
provide a wealth of detail about the city's housing
market and the impact of controls. The 1975 survey
(Bloomberg, 1976) found that the city had a far
tighter rental market (as measured by vacancy rates)
than most other central cities. Yet, despite the
strong demand, there had been a decline of just
under 10% in the number of units between 1970 and
1975. Mainly because of vacancy decontrol, the
controlled sub-sector had shrunk by about 50% - to
about 640,000 units. The dominant element in the
rental market was now the stabilised sector
(777,000 units). There were also about 250,000
decontrolled units in which rents were freely set
and 150,000 free market and regulated units
(including post war buildings with six or less
units, all post 1974 building and units with
subsidised and regulated rents). There were also
some public housing units and a few very old one and
two roomed units without full facilities. Both came
under special regulations regarding rents and other
matters.

The decontrolled, free market, regulated and
public sectors generally offered better quality and
rather larger units than the other sectors. But for
reasons of cost and/or lack of availability, this
housing was rarely available to the mass of poorer,
larger families who relied on access to controlled
or stabilised property - mainly the latter. The
movement from control to stabilisation had increased
rents considerably. Thus the median gross monthly
rent per room for the controlled sector was $39,
whereas for the stabilised sector it was $65.
Controlling for age and quality, rents for the pre-

1947 stabilised units - most of which were formerly
controlled - were $56 per room, over 40% above the
controlled rents. The worst housing conditions were
to be found in the controlled sector and in this
older part of the stabilised sector equally, thus
much of the older stock in the latter section was
indistinguishable in quality, though not in costs,
from the former.

35% of tenants were black or Puerto Rican.
They were overrepresented in the older stabilised
sector and underrepresented in the controlled
sector. Many of them were relative newcomers to the
city and the legislation had pushed them into the
older stabilised sector where they paid higher rents
than those in the controlled sector paid for
similar housing. Few could afford the better
quality, newer stabilised housing. Data on incomes
completes the picture of a stabilised sector which
consisted of two very different parts. The newer
housing, the stock originally stabilised in 1969
plus some later additions, was in good condition,
had high rents and housed tenants who had much
higher incomes than the majority of renters. The
older stabilised sector housed a low income
population, younger than the low income population
in the controlled sector, but even worse off because
of the levels of rents resulting from stabilisation.
In the controlled units it had been argued that many
tenants, despite the low median income in the
sector, were rather well off, i.e. that there was a
wide dispersion of incomes. But, according to the
1975 survey, this was not so and higher income
tenants appeared to have left this stock just as
rapidly as lower income tenants.

The problems of providing privately rented
property for a low income population is illustrated
by calculations based on the 1975 Survey and other
data which relate family budgets for different types
of household, (including a calculation of how much
they could 'afford' to pay in rent) to actual rents.
About a third of all tenants did not even have
sufficient income to meet the costs of a lower
standard budget (based on Federal government
estimates of living costs and budget levels for the
area) and a further 18% could only afford the low to
moderate standard budgets. When the actual rent/
income ratios of all tenants whose incomes were
sufficient to meet the lower, moderate and higher
income budgets were examined, at the lower standard
33% of income was being spent on gross rent compared
with an 'affordable' 21% and at the higher standard

17% compared with an 'affordable' 19%. So in many
cases the limits of tenants' rent paying ability
had been reached or surpassed - despite the various
rent controls.

Inflation had worsened the situation. The slow
development of tenant incomes in the USA has already
been noted. In New York tenants' real incomes
declined by about 10% between 1967 and 1974 and by
far more in certain areas and among certain groups.
For example, the decline in the Bronx was 18% but
in Manhattan only 4% and in surburban Richmond there
was a rise of 4%. Five person families had a
decline of 21% and Puerto Rican families a similar
amount. These figures refer to pre-tax incomes,
allowing for tax increases the decline was even
greater. Between 1970-78 the median gross rent rose
by 93%. Median gross rent/income ratios, having
been stable at around 18-20% from 1950-70 rose
sharply to about 28% by 1978 and were much higher
for the poorer groups (Marcuse, 1979, 196-203). The
effect of inflation and lagging incomes was that
more and more households were falling into poverty.
Rents were one of the main costs which were
increasing far more rapidly than incomes for a large
part of the population. The situation was a
consequence of the changes which have occurred
recently in the centres of the older, larger US
cities. So, even with controls, rents in New York
were so high that many tenants could hardly afford
them. Rent stabilisation had increased landlords'
incomes but had also increased the burden on many
households. The purchasing power was simply not
available to pay greatly increased rents in future.
In these respects the situation was similar to that
in most of the other countries which we have
examined.

But, even though rents had risen sharply and
were often as high as the market seemed likely to
bear, many landlords had found that their returns
were still inadequate. In fact the problem had
worsened due to rising labour, building materials,
loan charges and, especially, utilities costs. Also,
because of the fiscal crisis of the city, property
taxes had increased sharply (in common with many US
cities). In large parts of the city conventional
mortgage lending had ceased, sometimes being
replaced by high interest loans from 'fringe'
lenders which were utilised by landlords who then
had to 'sweat' their properties in order to make
profits.

A detailed survey of a sample of rented

housing illustrated some of the problems (Real
Estate Research Corporation, 1975a). By 1974 30%
of the rent controlled buildings had a negative cash
flow, 15% seriously so. These proportions had
doubled since 1967. In fact rents had kept in line
with costs until the rapid increase in energy costs
in the early seventies. Owners adapted to inflation
by cutting maintenance and obtaining reductions in
tax assessments because of the declining value of
their properties, or simply stopping paying taxes
altogether (often as a prelude to abandonment). The
position was worse in the stabilised sector. About
50% of properties had negative cash flow in 1974
compared with 17% in 1967 and about 25% had severe
negative cash flow compared with almost none in
1967. These developments were, as in the
Netherlands, resulting in a serious decline in
capital values. The market value of the controlled
properties fell from 3.8 times gross annual income
in 1967 to 1.9 times in 1974 and of stabilised
units from 5.4 to 2.8. Previously landlords had
resorted to frequent remortgaging to realise capital
gains but with the fall in values refinancing, let
alone capital gains, was becoming ever more
problematic.
    Thus, despite claims that rent control had
been the main reason for declining profitability and
had led to disinvestment and abandonment, the
evidence suggests that reality was more complex. The
root of the problem, as has been emphasised before,
was the stagnant or declining real incomes of the
rental population, combined with a sharp increase
in costs. The New York evidence shows that, at least
since the introduction of MBRs and stabilisation,
rent increases had kept up with and even exceeded
the levels which many sections of the population
could reasonably afford. So, even if the market had
been freed, rents could probably not have risen
much faster because of the lack of purchasing power
(and given building costs etc. it is unlikely that
much new construction which, in theory, could
increase supply and reduce the rents, would have
resulted). Free rents would probably have led to
increased numbers of tenants paying excessive rents
and/or an increase in sharing and overcrowding.
    An interesting small scale survey produced
results which underline parts of this argument (29)
(Womens City Club of New York, 1977). Unlike the
property included in the survey referred to above,
the property in this survey was representative of
many of the older units in the poorer areas. In 1970

eleven of the buildings (out of 38 surveyed) were
abandoned, by 1976 another eleven were vacant. There
was no single cause for this and no correlation
between the maximum controlled rents chargeable and
abandonment, nor did the landlords ascribe their
decision to abandon to control. In fact in several
of the blocks rents were below the legal maxima.
The main problem was that the type of tenants who
wanted such units could not afford to pay more,
indeed controls may have kept some rents higher than
they would otherwise have been.

In the fifties the area had been occupied by
reasonably paid whites of German, Jewish and Irish
descent but by 1960 blacks and Puerto Ricans
accounted for 50% of the population and by 1970 for
95%. Only 10% of the 1970 population had lived in
the area for more than ten years and 25% for more
than five years. Only 47% of household heads were
employed and their median income was a little below
the median for all households in the city. The other
53% had a far lower median income, most were on
public assistance or other welfare payments. The
median income for the area as a whole was about a
third lower than the city wide median. There were
many dependent children, female headed households and
social and other problems which added to the forces
of decline in the area.

Most of the landlords, who were all white, were
small operators. Few thought that if controls were
lifted they would be able to raise rents
significantly. In fact the building which in 1965
had had the highest rents per room was eventually
abandoned. Studies of the abandoned buildings
showed how they had moved out of stable management
to a more unstable pattern marked by recourse to
unconventional high interest finance, to frequent
changes in ownership and failure to maintain
property tax payments, all symptomatic of a
situation where profits could not be obtained by
normal letting practices and management or by sales
to owner occupiers or to other landlords, so
recouping the original investment plus capital
appreciation.

Fewer details were available on the impact of
controls in Washington DC. But it will be recalled
that the problem here was not an absolute decline
in purchasing power but the influx of tenants who
could outbid and hence expel a longer established
and poorer population. This was like the situation
in some European cities such as Amsterdam where
'gentrification' was occurring.

Rents and Rent Policy

According to a report published by a real
estate research organisation in 1976, controls were
having a deleterious effect on new investment
(Black, 1976). The report, based on interviews with
informed sources, concluded that very little new
investment would now occur. A hypothetical example
is presented for a 100 unit rental block erected in
1976 which, according to the regulations, could
have its initial rents freely set but subsequently
controlled. The rate of return on the equity
invested after the first year, based on some
reasonable assumptions, would be about 11% pre-tax
and 14.6% post-tax. This was an attractive initial
return but, due to control, it was estimated that
the return would then decline to 6.3% before tax
and 9.3% after tax - an unattractive proposition.
Also, because of the declining return, capital
values would decline and even the cash flow might
become precarious, thus dissuading lenders from
granting mortgages. The report suggested that this
had happened in New York and Boston because of
controls, although, as we have seen, even without
controls investment prospects in such cities were
unlikely to have been good.
    But Washington's controls did appear to have
reduced investment in the type of upper income
rental development which harmed many lower income
tenants. In fact the report stated that the demand
which was being stifled was 'in the upper end of
the rental market' (it argued that the influx of
higher income residents could have been encouraged
so that city revenues would rise, the authorities
could pay subsidies to less well off tenants, and
they could then pay the higher rents that would be
charged in a free market).
    Data collected by the city council shows just
how difficult the market had become, especially for
the less well off, and why there had been so
much pressure for controls (Committee on Finance
and Revenue, 1976). The overall vacancy rate in
the area fell from 2.7% in 1971 to 1.8% in 1976 and
was below 1% in some areas of the city. This was
extraordinarily low especially for the USA where
mobility is high. Median rents rose by 34% between
1970 and 1974 (incentives to sell off are
demonstrated by the fact that median owner occupied
house prices rose by 72% in the same period). In
these years median civil servant salaries (and many
tenants were civil servants) rose by only 16% and
the cost of living index by 25-30%. Further figures
show that shelter costs (i.e. rent or other housing

payments excluding services and utilities) were
especially high for low income groups. Based on
complete housing costs, almost 40% of tenants
spent over 25% of their income on housing in 1970
and very low income tenants spent 35% on average.
One indicator of the degree of housing stress was
that in 1970 almost 15% of city units had an
occupancy rate of more than one person per room
compared with only 5% in the suburbs.

This pattern of an increasing burden of rent
payments can also be seen when examining national
data, in this case of course most rents were freely
set (30). Some reference to this has already been
made in chapter 3. But further details show the
increasing problem of low tenant incomes and rising
rents. Thus, between 1970 and 1976, median owner
occupier incomes rose by 59% whereas median tenant
incomes rose by less than 30%. The differential
resulted from the increasing concentration of those
with slower growing incomes in the sector and the
high losses of the better off from the sector. The
weakening income position was especially noticeable
in the central cities. These tenants had incomes
somewhat lower than the national median renter
income in 1970 but by 1976 the gap had increased
considerably. Such areas had particularly high
levels of costs, so the additional decline in
tenant purchasing power was especially serious.

Rent/income ratios had changed quite sharply,
in line with the evidence from New York already
mentioned. The median ratio increased from 20% in
1970 to 24% in 1976. By this latter date 45% of
tenant households paid over 25% of their incomes
in rent (25% was usually regarded as a reasonable
proportion to have to pay), 15% paid over half
their incomes in rent - of course most of these
were very poor households. Many of the poor were
blacks and other minority groups, these groups
tended to rent more frequently than whites and pay
more of their incomes in rent. More of them lived
in the central cities where the sector faced its
greatest difficulties. Thus 60% of all black
households were in centre cities in 1976 compared
with 31% of all households and, despite paying
lower rents than whites, because of their low
incomes their median rent/income ratio was 27%
higher than that of white tenants. The situation
of the other main minority group, the Hispanics,
was broadly similar.

CONCLUSION

This chapter has dealt with the area of policy
which is most vitally connected with the state of
the private rented sector, given that the main
motive for investment in it is to make a profit.
But it is not at all clear that the direct and
fundamental connections that many have claimed
between the economic decline of the sector and rent
controls can be demonstrated, as a summary of the
discussion will highlight.
        Controls began around the time of the first
world war, although the shortage of low income
rental housing predated this era. The institution
of controls was a response to the political and
economic pressures generated by wartime conditions.
In the interwar period controls were gradually
lifted and, in most cases, continued building of
rental units occurred. The second world war led to
the reintroduction or the strengthening of controls
in all six countries. After the war there was pent
up demand for housing and difficult economic
conditions, especially in Europe. As a result
controls remained, only gradually being liberalised
– although they were finally abolished throughout
most of the USA by 1954. Most European governments
looked to private landlords to contribute to the
post war housing effort, whether they were
ideologically predisposed towards the sector or not,
the exceptional case being Britain. So some effort
had to be made to encourage new production and to
compensate landlords for rising costs.
        The first problem was dealt with by exempting
new building from controls and the second by
granting a series of across the board rent
increases. In France some limited decontrol also
occurred. Later, in the fifties and in the sixties,
decontrol and/or rent setting procedures which were
more sensitive to cost increases began to be
implemented. Problems of lack of maintenance and of
fragmented and inconsistent rent structures were
two of the main difficulties which these reforms
hoped to alleviate. But there was often strong
political opposition to decontrol, especially where
there was still national or local housing shortages.
Countries which attempted radical decontrol were
often forced to backtrack. Rent harmonisation also
proved difficult to achieve.
        In the sixties and early seventies all six
countries began to be affected by high levels of
wage and price inflation. This had serious

consequences for private rental housing especially
because increasing proportions of tenants only had
a limited ability to pay greatly increased rents.
For a short period several governments instituted
additional controls as part of their counter
inflation strategies. These had severe effects on
landlords' returns and the prospects for new
investment at a time when costs were rising sharply.
Throughout the period the rising demand for owner
occupation and rapid growth in house prices
increasingly encouraged landlords to sell out.

Countries had not managed to establish simple
or coherent rent setting arrangements covering the
whole of the rental sector and many at the bottom
of the housing market, with limited access to more
satisfactory forms of rented housing were forced
to pay high prices for inferior accommodation (or
if they were in social housing more than they could
afford for better quality units). But the new
arrangements for rent setting usually reflected,
to some degree, the impact of rising costs and
the concept of a 'fair' return to the landlord. In
consequence, rents had risen faster than under
previous control systems, indeed in a few instances
administratively set rents were probably above free
market levels. But, as the example of New York
City illustrated, even these rents had not
necessarily solved the problem of maintaining
positive returns in an inflationary era.
Paradoxically the stricter controls of the forties
and fifties were accompanied by a relatively slow
decline in the fortunes of the sector whereas,
despite the liberalising and/or lifting of controls
in later years, the prospects for private landlords
had worsened.

In most countries it was the poorer tenants,
living in the older housing stock, who had had the
largest percentage rent increases as a result of
the changes in policy which had occurred. Of course
the older property was most likely to have had very
low rents as a result of the earlier controls. But
many of these people had slowly growing incomes and
the rent increases had often had a serious impact
on the proportion of their incomes which they were
forced to spend on housing.

Data from West Germany, England and the USA
illustrated the declining fortunes of landlords and
the reduced prospects for continued investment.
Some sections of the market were better off, for
example when catering for those with restricted
access to other housing in a situation where free

market rents could be charged or when providing
newer housing for a more affluent, mobile middle
class clinetele. But in several countries landlords
also faced a reduction in the capital values of
their stock. This could eventually lead to a
collapse of the sales market in private rental
properties, as in parts of New York City where
widespread abandonment had occurred.

The situation faced governments with a dilemma
which could not be resolved within the terms of
the history and current context of housing policy.
On the one hand, rent controls added to the
problems that landlords had regarding rising costs;
on the other hand, the abolition of all restraint
would have increased the already heavy burden of
housing payments on many less well off tenants, and
probably generate considerable political conflict.
Even if governments had thought that this was an
acceptable price to pay there was reason to believe
that many landlords would still not be able to make
what they would regard as a reasonable return. In
fact as security of tenure is usually removed or
reduced when controls are ended, total decontrol in
these circumstances might simply have accelerated
the movement of property out of the rental market.
Certainly this was one of the main consequences of
the vacancy decontrol attempted in England after
1957.

Rents and Rent Policy

NOTES

1. Except where noted the details on the
development of rent controls derive from interviews
and the project consultants.
2. From 1926 tenants of furnished
accommodation and sub-tenants also benefitted from
controlled rents (if the property was built before
1919 and they had been the tenants since then). In
1935 all rents were reduced by 10%, but this was
repealed at the end of 1937 (Information supplied
by Christian Topalov).
3. A useful account of post war French
controls is provided by Duclaud-Williams, 1978,
27-63.
4. The details of these increases are in
Priemus, 1981, 303.
5. Instead of the expected interest rate of
6.5%, it rose to 10-11% in 1970 and 15-16% in 1974.
Building costs did not stabilise, they increased by
80% between 1968-74, and the price of building
plots rose by 245% - these had been expected to
decline.
6. According to Professor Hellmut Wollmann,
'There were Christian Democrat initiatives already
in 1953 to make the publicly subsidised housing
policy the vehicle of an ambitious "property and
family policy" with the underlying (partly
ideological) rationale that, vis-a-vis the Cold War
situation of the fities, "sound families" dwelling
in their own property would prove to be adamant
adherents to the Western (capitalist) cause'
(Wollmann, forthcoming).
7. Developments are reviewed in Priemus, 1981.
8. Lett, 1976, 13-19 contains a detailed
summary of the New York rent control laws.
9. According to interviews with Rent Board
officials in Copenhagen.
10. A very brief account is to be found in
Brenner and Franklin, 1977, 17-8. See also Hallett,
1977, 27-33 (a very opinionated account).
11. As already noted, it was abolished (after
the research had ended) in 1980.
12. According to a survey in 1976, 60% of landlords preferred to agree rents rather than have them
registered. Almost 40% of these stated that the
reason was that they could get a higher rent this
way (Paley, 1978, 19-21).
13. Many of these points are discussed in
Committee on the Rent Acts, 1971. See also House of
Commons Environment Committee, 1982.

14. The developments are briefly reviewed in
Priemus, 1981.
15. Lett, 1976, 6 and Ch. 3, discusses
developments in the sixties and seventies. Briefly,
apart from the period of federal controls, there
were eight states with legislation allowing the
local adoption of controls.
16. Later still the demand for controls again
increased, notably in some areas of California in
the aftermath of 'proposition 13' (which cut
property taxes, a benefit which many landlords
refused to hand on to tenants in the form of reduced
rents).
17. These developments are reviewed in Black,
1976. See also Committee on Finance and Revenue,
1976, and Richards and Rowe, 1977.
18. Detailed accounts of the rent control
administration and laws are to be found in Striker
and Shapiro, 1978 and City of New York, Office of
the Mayor, 1974.
19. These comments are based on the analysis
in Nora and Eveno, 1975, 179-90.
20. According to an article in La Revenue
Francais in March 1978 (quoted in an interview at
the Ministry of Equipment, 1978).
21. The figures were 147% in pre 1924 private
rented housing, 149% in private rented housing
built between 1924 and 1948, 130% in social rented
housing and only 106% in post war private rented
housing (Figures derived from Schneider and
Kornemann, 1977, 41).
22. The research was carried out by Rudi
Ulbrich at the Deutches Institut für
Wirtschaftsforschung, Berlin. I am indebted to Dr.
Ulbrich for access to his preliminary, pre-
publication calculations.
23. Dr. Ulbrich carried out his calculations
on the basis of three reasonable variants of
combinations of loans from the four sources. The
first involved maximum reliance on the commercial
mortgage market, the last maximum allowance on
cheaper money from a Bausparkassen and own capital
resources. The second combination was mid way
between the first and the last.
24. The results reported are based on the
second financing alternative. The landlord's
position was rather less favourable in the case of
the first alternative and better in the case of the
last.

25. Data available for the first time in 1982 shows that the gross ratio (ratio of registered rents to vacant possession values) was 6.9% in 1970, falling to 4.4% in 1976. By 1981 the range was 3.6-4% (medians, England and Wales). Net returns were about 2-3% less (Bovaird et. al., 1982, 33,41).

26. The figures are derived from Department of the Environment, 1977d, updated.

27. The data were derived from OPCS, 1979, 21-54; CSO, various years; Department of the Environment, various years.

28. Estimates in this paragraph provided by Jan van der Schaar.

29. A detailed analysis of abandonment in New York is contained in Home Front, 1977.

30. The data in this paragraph and the next are derived from US Bureau of the Census etc. 1978.

Chapter Six

SUBSIDIES AND TAXATION

As we have seen in a situation in which private
rented housing is increasingly confined to housing
those on the lowest incomes, the claim that
landlords would necessarily gain higher rents if
controls were abolished is not sustainable.
Nonetheless in most cases rent controls have served
to reduce rents to a sub free market level. But
such legislation is only one aspect of state
intervention in the economics of private renting.
No final assessment of the impact of policy on the
sector can be made without considering the extent
to which it has been subsidised, either directly
or via the taxation system. Furthermore the relative
subsidy treatment of the main tenures has had a
crucial impact on private renting.
    In this chapter we shall consider construction
subsidies, allowances and the taxation of rental
property and income. Finally, the position of the
private rental sector will be compared with the
other two main housing tenures.

CONSTRUCTION SUBSIDIES

As already mentioned only in Britain was no attempt
made after the war to stimulate the production of
private rental housing with subsidies. In contrast
the Netherlands, the USA, France and Denmark have
all, at one time or another, subsidised
construction by methods which, in effect, made low
cost loans available. Indirect (tax) subsidies have
been the main source of support in West Germany,
they have also been important in the USA. It has
been normal to have some controls on rent levels,
the levels of incomes of those accommodated, and the
cost and quality of construction. But these

subsidies have declined in more recent years. We
shall now examine these schemes in detail.
In France there has been a shift away from
direct government loans for construction to far
greater reliance on private landlords. In this
connection it is important to note that no well
developed mortgage market, able to offer long-term
loans at reasonable interest rates, existed after
the war. It was not until 1967-8 that the government
took the decisive steps to stimulate such a market.
It authorised lenders to extend the minimum term to
20 years (from 14 years) and to issue bonds which
could be taken up by the larger financial
institutions. Even so most refinancing institutions
were of a para-public nature and closely linked
to the general money market. This was probably one
of the causes of the instability of interest rates
which subsequently occurred (1).

TABLE 6.1

SOURCES OF NEW LOANS FOR HOUSING: FRANCE 1964-1976
(INDICES)

Year	1964	1965	1966	1967	1968	1969	1970
Public lenders	100	119	130	160	178	198	210
Crédit Foncier	100	102	118	105	101	109	108
Banks	100	130	173	252	355	421	371
TOTAL	100	118	138	166	197	229	224

Year	1971	1972	1973	1974	1975	1976	1977
Public lenders	236	264	310	379	493	627	738
Crédit Foncier	109	115	131	139	179	249	279
Banks	584	875	870	773	860	1071	967
TOTAL	294	399	411	413	491	615	626

Source: Ansidei, Carassus and Stroebel, 1978.

Subsidies and Taxation

The first important development occurred in 1950
when the Crédit Foncier (a para-public body, dating
from 1852 which had previously mainly granted
shorter term loans for improvements) was reformed.
Annual subsidies were provided plus cheap Crédit
Foncier loans. In most cases this assistance was
available for owner occupied and for private rental
units, arrangements for HLM building were separate.
The Crédit Foncier refinanced its loans via the
Banque de France and the Caisse des Depôts et
Consignations, the latter held the funds of savings
banks and social security organisations. In rural
areas the Crédit Agricole performed a similar
function. Later the Banque's role was phased out and
there was a reduction of direct Treasury
financing (2).

The evolution of new housing credit between
1964 and 1976 is shown in Table 6.1. Note the sharp
decline in the Crédit Foncier's share and the growth
of bank lending. The rapid acceleration of the
latter in the early seventies was the product of a
'property boom'. The state sector also grew
relatively slowly until the mid seventies and here
there was, as noted above, a shift away from direct
Treasury funding. But at this time the effects of
inflation and unsettled economic conditions and the
collapse of the property boom led to increased
resort to state linked funds to finance the rapidly
rising mortgage debt. But the general trend towards
bank finance remained.

During this period there was also a tendency
for mortgage terms to lengthen. This latter helped
those on moderate incomes to invest in housing but,
as was intended, this was mainly for owner
occupation, not for letting (the establishment of a
subsidised saving scheme in the early seventies also
mainly aided owner occupiers). Also the movement
towards bank financing meant that construction was
more directly exposed to economic fluctuations and,
crucially, to the high interest rates of the
seventies. This discouraged rental construction for
other than an affluent minority of tenants.

The various subsidy schemes were complex, only
a brief outline can be given here (3). The 1950
legislation provided for loans with a subsidy
(primes) of 6 francs per annum per square metre for
twenty years to reduce the loan repayments. Units
were limited in size and cost (though not as
severely as state aided HLM units) but there was no
limit on the incomes of the tenants and owner-

occupiers inhabiting them. Typically, the loans were for 10-20 years, covering 70% of the cost with an interest rate reduced from 6.8% to 4% by means of the prime. The government was trying to involve more private finance in housing and stimulate owner occupation. In the latter case the size of the deposit required and other factors meant that success was limited.

In 1954 because of these limited results a new scheme was added. The principles were as before, but the terms were more generous. The size and price restrictions were closer to those operating in the HLM sector and the regulations were designed to encourage small and medium builders. Some rental housing was produced by small investors. But more significantly large scale developers began to build for sale, aided with the substantial subsidies provided by this 'Logecos' programme. There was also a growth of professional developers who bought together small scale investors to build such schemes.

Another important aspect of policy was the development of para-public rental housing developers and the 1% levy on employers, already noted in chapter 4. These developments were linked to policies encouraging economic modernisation and developments by the new organisations were often built specifically for the workers of the growing companies which were central to this strategy. (The institutions providing HLM housing were not thought to be sufficiently flexible and subject to central direction to carry out such a task). In fact between 1954 and 1958 most new rental housing in the Paris region was produced by these bodies (including, for example, developments to house the Simca, Renault and Peugeot workforces). In the fifties most units were for renting, later more were for owner occupation.

Between 1958 and 1963 important changes occurred in the subsidy and loan schemes. Loans were at fixed interest rates but the rate for new loans increased as general interest rates rose. This led to considerable political protest. After 1958 it became possible to convert the primes into a reduced interest rate, and primes were also provided for use with private loans. The cash amount of the maximum loan obtainable was now fixed (varying only according to unit size) so, as costs rose, the proportion of them covered by the loan fell. In 1963 the Logécos scheme ended and

different terms were applied to rental and owner
occupied housing. In the former case loans were
available at 4.25% over 30 years with deferred
amortisation for the first 4½ years. There were no
income limits on eligibility and rents were fixed
at a maximum of 8.72% of the costs of construction.
Owner occupied housing was treated less generously,
limits were put on the incomes of their occupants
and they were prohibited from being let out.

Other measures were also taken to alleviate
the problems caused by cash limited loans - but
only for owner occupiers. The priorities - owner
occupation and private finance - which the general
development of policy showed from this time onwards
left the HLM sector as the only important source of
low and moderate income rental construction. The
rental housing produced with Crédit Foncier loans
was for the better off. The proportion of new
assisted units which were for sale topped 50% by
1960 and was almost 65% by 1964. For many it became
cheaper to buy, with the aid of subsidies, than to
rent. So the supply of new private rented housing
contracted. It should be noted too that the
government controlled the annual number of Crédit
Foncier loans and their use. This provided another
means by which owner occupation was favoured.

In 1965 a further attempt to encourage private
finance occurred. New loans enabled the refinancing
of private construction loans to take place. These
loans were in practice mainly used for owner
occupied units targeted at those whose incomes
were a little above the limit for fully aided house
purchase. But the subsequent movements of costs,
incomes and interest rates meant that fewer and
fewer were able to benefit sufficiently from state
assistance to enter the sector and subsidised
private rental building also declined.

In 1971-72 more changes occurred, partly to
further limit state expenditure on housing so that
aid to industry could be increased (4). At the
same time the Crédit Foncier was increasingly
restricted to refinancing private capital. There
was a new ceiling for tenant incomes and the new
loans covered an increased proportion of costs but
the subsidy was made degressive (for owner
occupation too). Rents were not to exceed 8.75% of
the cost price. The new arrangements were intended
to encourage the SIIs and others to build
accommodation for middle income workers, especially
younger skilled manual and white collar workers and

technicians who could not yet afford to buy but
whose incomes made them ineligible for HLM rental.
Degressive subsidies were thought appropriate,
because such peoples' salaries were likely to
inflate fairly rapidly, and because their real
incomes were also likely to rise. Henceforth much
of the 1% patronal was to be used as supplementary
finance for this sector (rather than for HLM units,
as hitherto).

Data showing annual completions and the share
of non-HLM renting have been given in chapter 3.
More detail is available from the sixties onwards.
Between 1965 and 1972, 80 to 100,000 units per
annum were built with state aided loans,
approximately two thirds were for ownership (5).
The rental units were far smaller in size than the
units for sale, the former tended to house younger
and smaller households, as already noted. Moreover,
this difference became more pronounced over time
(reflecting the growing difficulty of producing new
housing at reasonable rents). From 1972 the new loan
arrangements biased the system even more firmly in
favour of ownership, thus in 1975 of the 94,000
units built only 18,000 were for renting.

We now consider who built these units. Data
are only available from 1960 (Topalov, 1974, 48-50).
These show that building by companies fluctuated
from around 54% in 1960 to over 60% in 1963, falling
to a little over 45% in 1968. The share of building
by individuals, not surprisingly, moved in the
opposite direction. But this division is not very
useful, for the company sector contained both very
small and large scale companies. In fact in the
sixties there was a growth (although not a stable
growth) in the proportion of all new building by
commercial developers for sale (Topalov, 1974,
285-308). Policy, as already stated, supported this
tendency, with the reduction of direct public loans
and, since 1965, special tax advantages for owner
occupation. Up to the early sixties much new
building had been done by smaller builders or by
families for their own use. The larger companies
concentrated on producing blocks of flats. But in
the late sixties, aided by the state, there was a
property boom and commercial developers greatly
increased their share of the market, often working
closely with banks and other financial institutions.
Housing became a major field of activity for finance
capital and the lack of effective planning controls
and the widespread speculation in land and property
were both a cause and a consequence of this shift

in the nature of housing production. But, as
elsewhere, this boom soon collapsed and from the
early seventies the operations of the large
developers diminished, as did the role of financial
capital in directly promoting development, though
it continued to provide extensive construction
finance.

As we have seen, state assistance for private
rental investment was a declining priority. After
the late fifties there was a desire to shift much
of the middle income demand away from rented housing
into owner occupation and, despite some set-backs,
the policy succeeded. So by the late seventies new
private rental building had become a very small
proportion of total output. There was, however, a
persistent effort to create a limited rental sector
for those whose incomes made them ineligible for
HLM units but who could not yet afford, or did not
want, to buy. The para-public organisations were
expected to build this accommodation. An interview
with one such body in Paris gave a good idea of
what was being provided. Flats contained, on
average, three rooms and rents were about 2000f per
month plus another 20% for service charges. Tenants
paid up to 30% of their incomes in rent and charges.
Such rents only appealed to a small minority, most
preferred (or were forced) to move to cheaper
suburban housing which they could buy, often
commuting for long periods every day to centrally
located jobs.

The waning of state support for private rental
housing construction has been a virtually universal
process. Thus, in Denmark, one of the earliest
attempts to aid privately rented units was made
after the First World War (6). State loans and
grants were made available for private rental
building and, cheaply, for social housing. There
were some limited controls on rents and controls on
standards. This was a temporary response to high
commercial interest rates. In the thirties private
financing again became difficult and a new system of
state loans began. Again these were more generous
for social rented units (and for owner occupation).
Later state assistance was restricted to the social
sector (as were the housing allowances then
introduced). The arguments for excluding private
renting are interesting. It was felt that there was
no way, short of comprehensive rent control - which
was felt to be too difficult to implement, of
ensuring that state aid was reflected in lowered
rents, and also that private rents were so great in

comparison with social rents that the amount of assistance needed would be unjustifiably high.

Private renting would probably not have been state aided again without the exigencies of the second world war. After the occupation unemployment rose and assistance for private renting was reintroduced, especially for building in slum clearance areas. Loans for up to 90% of costs were made available and amortisation was deferred for ten years, during which period a low interest rate was also charged. After the war, as elsewhere, private rental subsidies were provided to stimulate production. But the concern with limiting expenditure and ensuring that it did not simply inflate profits remained. Direct cash payments were rejected, it was thought that these would inflate prices. Loans on favourable terms were continued but this was seen as a temporary measure during a transitional period. A 1946 act provided for loans at 3½% with repayment over about 43 years. This was below the commercial interest rate and provided for a far longer repayment term. Moreover, the repayments were reduced still further for the first 20 years. But this assistance was only in the longer run to be provided in areas where the private sector had a special role to play, such as in slum clearance schemes and the loan terms were differentiated to favour social housing.

Most of the private rental housing built in these years was subsidised, rents were set to cover costs and provide a small return. But, as owner occupiers and social rental organisations received even cheaper loans (and were less highly taxed), the system only favoured private renting to a limited degree. From 1954 loans were at market rates, but loan repayments were subsidised with annual allowances. In 1958 private rental construction subsidies (though not those for social renting) were ended. Henceforth, only allowances were available, these will be discussed in the next section.

In West Germany the post war government also decided to encourage private building. There was much less concern about the principle of aided private landlords and the commitment to the 'social market economy' meant that social rented housing, while supported, was never seen as playing the leading role. In Germany the aim was to return to the private market in housing as soon as possible (Marcuse, 1981, 112; Wollmann, forthcoming). Owner occupation was favoured but, in the

contemporary circumstances, support for private
landlords was the key element in the stimulation
of the private market. Direct subsidies and tax
benefits were made available for the private rental
and owner occupied units. In addition, as discussed
below, subsidised savings schemes helped builders
to accumulate the required capital (Marcuse, 1981;
Hallett, 1978). The planned withdrawal of direct
government assistance for housebuilding soon began.
In 1950 public sources contributed 43.9% of the
total cost of housebuilding but by 1975 only about
7.5%. Over the same period the share financed by
the capital market rose from 41.9% to 76.6%
(Schneider and Kornemann, 1977, 21-2).

Although there were detailed changes in the
schemes of assistance the principles were
established in the First Federal Housing Act in
1950 and a second measure in 1956 (7). The basic
policy instruments were low or zero interest
government loans, subsidies covering part of the
operating and/or interest costs or mortgage
repayments, tax exemptions and savings premia (with
the option of an alternative scheme allowing tax
deductions). Until 1974 the loans, subsidies and
tax exemptions were only available for new units (a
legacy of the earlier need to concentrate on
expanding the size of the stock). After 1974 they
were also available for rehabilitation and since
1977 for second hand housing as well. In part this
latter change reflected the (Social Democratic/
Liberal) government's desire to stimulate owner
occupation, an aim shared with the Conservative
parties.

As already noted, the provisions for loans
and for annual payments to meet operating costs were
only available for social housing (but note that
social housing could be owner occupied or rented).
From the mid fifties governments moved away from
providing low or zero interest loans to reducing
repayments via annual allowances. This subsidy was
made degressive, reducing as - it was assumed -
incomes and ability to pay increased.

The main subsidies for private rental
construction were via tax reliefs and the savings
premia. There were two tax relief schemes. Housing
(for sale or letting) which did not exceed the size
limits established for the most heavily subsidised
social housing by more than 20% was exempted from
property tax for ten years and from the land
acquisition tax (normally 7% of the purchase
price). All private rented housing benefitted from

a 2% per annum depreciation allowance (up to 1973
the rate was a preferential 3.5%). But all owner
occupiers including those building two units, one
for their own use and one for renting, could deduct
5% of the cost for eight years and 2.5% thereafter.
Individuals could only do this once and there were
cost ceilings on the allowance. (As noted above,
after 1977 tax reliefs were available for second-
hand as well as new housing).

So, despite the reduction in direct public
lending for building, there was extensive indirect
support. It is difficult to assess the total impact
of these measures but three important points can be
made. First, many of the benefits applied to owner
occupiers as well as landlords and increasingly the
former had preferential treatment. Second, there
was a strong emphasis on aiding the small investor
who might only build two units, one for self
occupancy and one for letting. Finally, the tax
concessions were regressive, giving most aid to
those on higher incomes (8). Such people often
found it advantageous to use some of their rapidly
rising real incomes to become small scale landlords,
thus sustaining a tradition which was in decline
in most of the other countries in this survey.

As already noted, private rental construction
in Britain was not assisted in the post war period,
although subsidies had been available in the 1920's.
After the second world war the acute Dutch housing
shortage led to the adoption of a policy which was,
in a sense, midway between those adopted in Britain
and in Germany. The main responsibility for new
building rested with the social housing
organisations but a minor role was also envisaged
for private investors. In 1947/48 new subsidy
schemes began (9). The rents of new units were set
according to what it was reasonable to expect
tenants to pay. On the basis of an assumption about
what would be a reasonable return for the landlord,
his/her appropriate capital investment was
calculated and the government promised to make a
capital grant to meet the difference between this
hypothetical capital investment and the actual
building cost. But payment was deferred for ten
years, during which time the interest charges on
the state's share of the investment were paid as a
subsidy (premiums). As in Denmark, there was a
concern to limit landlord subsidies. The theory
was that rents would increase over the ten year
period thus reducing the capital sum which would

eventually need to be paid. The uncertainties in
this approach resulted in relatively little new
housing being produced.

From 1950 the government paid a lump sum on
completion. This was less than the 'unprofitable'
capital expenditure calculated with respect to rent
levels, thus taking some account of future rent
increases. The scheme was more popular as its terms
were quite generous. In 1953 the government began
to revert to the earlier approach (and moved
towards harmonising subsidy arrangements in the
social and private rented sectors). Investors could
choose between the lump sum or annual premiums for
ten years. In 1960 the availability of the former
was reduced and from 1966 the premiums became the
only form of support. (In the mid fifties a
separate scheme provided shallower subsidies for
free rented housing for some years. It proved
popular with investors). The premium system remained
until the mid seventies, although their value and
hence the incentives to invest varied considerably.
In the mid-sixties the government tried to expand
output very rapidly in order to end the continuing
housing shortage, at this time the payments were
very generous (10).

In 1968 the subsidies for the two parts of the
rental sector were brought into line. Social
housing loans were now only available from the
market at market rates and the scheme of decreasing
annual subsidies was applied across the board. One
problem which these changes did not remove was the
gap between the cost related rents of newer and old
units (even in the social sector this was not
alleviated by rent pooling). As inflation increased
in the seventies, the scale of the problem grew.
Many entrants to the housing market could only find
accommodation in new units with high rents which
were not easily affordable.

In 1971 the concept of dynamic cost rents was
advocated as a solution to this problem (11). The
basic principle was that the intital rate of
interest on housing loans is higher than it
otherwise might be because it contains a premium to
compensate the lender against future losses in the
real value of the loan, due to inflation. The system
provided for the lender to be compensated for
inflationary losses by additions to the amount of
the loan in the early period after construction
which would, it was planned, be eventually repaid
by increases in rents occurring in line with rising

incomes. At the time the current subsidy was
reducing the initial annual rents of publicly
financed units from about 10% of costs to 5%. But
by the introduction of dynamic cost rents, initial
rents could be reduced to about 6% of costs and the
total subsidy bill reduced at the same time.

The new scheme began in 1975. Initial rents
were supposed to be affordable in relation to the
modal income of those whom the housing was expected
to accommodate, improved rent allowances were
available for the less well off. At the time of the
research subsidies were available for 50 years,
allowable returns were calculated on the basis of
the average yield on five medium term state bonds
(a figure revised monthly and applicable to
dwellings started within the subsequent month) plus
half a percent for private investors. On the basis
of projections of the future development of rents
and costs, given the yield, the initial rent which
had to be charged to discharge the debt by means of
rising annuities could be calculated. Because no
one could forecast rents and costs over 50 years
this was done for a ten year period, the initial
yield was only operative for the same period. If
after ten years actual developments were less
favourable than expected the government would
compensate landlords. If a surplus was made it could
be retained. The various calculations were to be
revised every ten years. If deficits were
subsequently incurred they were to be offset against
any previous surpluses. Since the start of this
scheme rents had fluctuated around 6% of building
costs, equivalent to a starting rent of 10-11% of
the modal incomes used in the calculation. Because
this was felt to be too high an additional subsidy
of 1% of costs had been given in most cases.

The scheme was not very attractive to private
investors. It required commercial loans with rising
repayments (in the social sector these were
provided by the state). But private landlords had
found commercial lenders reluctant to make such
advances. So, as an inducement to them, the
government agreed to provide 100% guarantees. A more
important disincentive was the level of the yield
and the rule that surpluses would be offset against
losses. At the time of the research the scheme was
still very new, it was possible that in time it
might become more widely used but most informed
opinion felt that the era of substantial private
rental building was over.

Subsidies and Taxation

The arrangements for housing finance in the USA were
complex and the means for supporting privately
rented construction will be better understood if
this system is outlined (12). Various lenders
financed new multi family housing (i.e. the bulk of
all new rental building). In comparison with the
originators of finance for owner occupied units,
federal credit agencies played a larger role in
rental construction. But, as with construction for
owner occupation, the most important multifamily
lenders were the Savings and Loans Associations
(S and Ls), which operated under federal or state
regulation rather like British building societies.
For many years S and Ls were restricted to operating
in their own localities but latterly they had been
much criticised for channelling savings out of inner
city areas and investing them in suburban home
ownership.
     Other significant institutions included mutual
savings banks, commercial banks, insurance and
pension funds and various forms of mortgage
companies and trusts. All were subject to some form
of federal or state regulation and all invested to
varying degrees in housing. There was an important
system of federal institutions which supported the
mortgage market. This originated in the thirties
Depression as a response to the collapse of the
housing market. The Federal Home Loan Bank Board
(FHLBB) acted as a central bank for its members,
mainly the S and Ls. The Federal Savings and Loan
Insurance Corporation (FSLIC) insured deposits in
members of the FHLBB and was controlled by the Bank
(the Federal Deposit Insurance Corporation (FDIC)
insured deposits in institutions which were
not covered by FSLIC). The Federal National Mortgage
Association (FNMA) provided secondary market support
for government insured mortgages although more
recently it had also bought conventional mortgages
and another body, the Government National Mortgage
Association (GNMA) had taken over the more risky end
of the business formerly done by FNMA, leaving the
latter to deal with more conventional risks. Under
special guarantees many of these more risky
mortgages were sold on to private lenders and at
the time of the research much rental housing was
financed in this way (the so called Tandem Plan).
Finally, the Federal Home Loan Mortgage Corporation
had recently been created to serve as a central
credit facility and secondary market for non
governmentally insured conventional mortgages.

Subsidies and Taxation

So far as rental housing was concerned the central institution was the Federal Housing Administration (FHA), a part of the Federal Department of Housing and Urban Development (HUD). It was created in 1934 to provide government support for the market and to develop mortgage loans on easier terms than hitherto, prior to this time 50% deposits and five year terms were commonplace. As already explained, FHLBB provided the main lenders with protection against sudden withdrawals by a mass of investors and in general acted like a central bank. FSLIC and FDIC insured deposits and FNMA provided a secondary mortgage facility, thus making residential mortgage lending more liquid. FHA's role was to insure mortgages advanced on approved terms by private lenders to approved types of property, both new and second hand (in fact mainly the former). Fees were paid for the scheme which was to be self supporting. FHA intervention via a specially tailored mortgage insurance programmes - in some cases with a subsidy as well - had been the main means of governmental support for owner occupied and rental housing. Such arrangements fitted well into a system in which the private market had supremacy and the state's role was mainly limited to supporting it.

Originally FHA only insured 1-4 family housing but very soon, under the Section 207 programme, it was also able to insure multifamily mortgages. But FHA standards were quite strict and this was only a small programme. After the war it insured a large proportion of all new housing but, as confidence returned to the housing market, commercial bodies began to offer insurance on better terms than the FHA, so by 1976 only 10% of all new mortgages had FHA cover. The proportion of its business which was concerned with rental housing had grown, although by 1976 it had only insured about 2½ million rental units compared with 12 million owner occupier units since 1934 (US Department of Housing and Urban Development, 1977, 50-8).

Of these rental units, the Section 207 programme had only accounted for about an eighth. During and especially after the war a new programme (Section 608) proved much more attractive to investors. It involved lower and cheaper design standards than Section 207 and these became the norm for later FHA rental programmes. But the most attractive feature was a loophole by which the FHA insured mortgage could cover the full cost of

189

TABLE 6:2
COMPARISON OF s207 AND s236 FHA/HUD PROGRAMMES 1972

<u>s207</u>

1. ELIGIBLE MORTGAGORS   Private profit motivated corporations, trusts, partnerships and individuals.

2. TYPE OF HOUSING   New/rehabilitated rented housing of eight or more units.

3. MORTGAGE LIMITS   For private mortgages $20 million. For public mortgages $50 million. Per unit limits from $9,900 - $28,050 depending on number of bedrooms and presence/absence of lifts. More in high cost areas.

4. MAXIMUM TERM   40 years or three-quarters of remaining economic life.

5. MAXIMUM % LOAN   90% of estimated value for new building, some variation for rehabilitation.

6. OCCUPANT ELIGIBILITY   All families subject to selection by owner, who must agree not to discriminate against families with children.

7. INTEREST RATE   7%

8. SUBSIDY   No direct subsidy. Indirect subsidy through accelerated depreciation and GNMA Tandem Plan where applicable.

9. MISCELLANEOUS   Mortgages covering five or more units or mortgages covering property in older declining urban areas eligible with certain requirements.

Source: National Centre for Housing Management, 1972.

190

Subsidies and Taxation

s236

Private, non profit corporations, co-ops and invester-sponsor mortgagors selling to a co-op within two years, limited dividend entities, mortgagors intending to sell to a non profit.

New or substantially rehabilitated housing of five or more units. Basic rent to be not more than 25% of maximum income limits for the locality.

$12.5 million.
Per unit limits from $9,200 - $26,262 depending on numbers of bedrooms and presence/absence of lifts.

40 years or three-quarters of remaining economic life.

100% of estimated replacement cost for private non profts and co-ops, all others 90% of estimated replacement cost.

Low and moderate income families, elderly, displaced, handicapped, military personnel. Income limits generally not to exceed 135% of local public housing limits. 20% of units can be allocated for those with incomes not exceeding 90% of area median. 10% of units can be occupied by single people under 62 years old; 20% - 40% can be occupied by rent supplement tenants; units may be occupied by non subsidised tenants paying market rents. Income includes gross income of all adult earners, less 5%, less $300 for each minor. Tenants pay greater of 25% of income or basic monthly rent based on 1% mortgage.

Can be reduced to 1%

Direct subsidy paid to mortgagee not to exceed difference between payment on 1% mortgage and payments of insurance premium on a mortgage at the FHA rate. Indirect subsidy - accelerated depreciation and favourable recapture and roll over provision for limited dividend mortgagors.

Some provision for commercial, community etc. facilities eligible.

schemes or even more (loans were based on estimated
replacement value and not building costs). In these
circumstances developers incurred no risks and might
profit even if a scheme failed. The programme was
ended by the mid-fifties because of the scandals
that occurred, but Section 608 accounted for about
80% of all multifamily starts between 1946 and 1950.

In the fifties there were few new developments
in FHA assistance (13). But in 1959 the Section 202
programme began to provide below market interest
loans for non profit developers building for the
elderly. This was the first step towards direct
subsidies for low income private rental housing.
The Kennedy and Johnson administrations went
further. In the early sixties a new programme
attempted to apply the principles of Section 202
more widely (the Section 221 (d) (3) Below Market
Interest Rate programme). But this never really
took off and when ended by President Nixon had only
supported about 175,000 units. One problem was that
it was restricted to use by non and limited profit
developers.

Given this failure, the Johnson administration
proposed to pay rent supplements to households in
the private sector whose incomes were just above
the very low levels set for entry to public housing.
The aim was that no more than 25% of income should
be paid for rent, and that these supplements should
be combined with the provision of new FHA housing.
Congress greatly restricted the programme but
supplements were used in this way thus enabling
conventional commercial developers to construct low
income housing. By 1976 about 365,000 units had
been built, the supplements were however being ended
by the Nixon administration.

By far the most important and interesting
development, at least until the seventies was the
Section 236 programme launched in 1968 (with a
similar programme for owner occupation). This was
an insurance cum subsidy programme which provided
about 400,000 units by 1976 (it was ended in all
but a minor form by Nixon). The main details of
Section 236 are shown in Table 6.2 along with those
of the conventional Section 207 programme. It may
readily be seen that the 236 Programme aimed at a
low and moderate income population whereas Section
207 did not provide the subsidies that were
required to induce private developers to build for
the less well off.

The basic advantage of the 236 Programme was
that the interest rate could be lowered to as

little as 1% in order that not more than 25% of
income was paid in rent (very poor tenants only
paid 15% and also got rent supplements). 100% loans
were available over a term of 40 years and the
accelerated depreciation provided large tax benefits
for investors. (In fact the main motive for   the
investment that occurred was these benefits, which,
as we shall see, were not without their problems).
The loans were issued at market rates by private
institutions with FHA guarantees but normally
mortgages could be resold to GNMA. Annual subsidies
were paid, in theory these were to be degressive -
reducing as tenants' incomes rose. But the
financial prospects for 236 projects depended not
on future debt repayments which would fall in real
terms but on future levels of operating and
maintenance costs, which could only be kept in
check by efficient management. However, the way the
scheme was structured gave owners little incentive
to ensure that this happened. The tax benefits were
mainly obtained in the early years of a project
and were received whatever happened to the housing,
provided that it was not foreclosed. As costs
rapidly inflated and projects got into difficulties
most tenants were eventually required to pay 30%
of their income as the government attempted to
improve project revenues.

In broader perspective the Section 236
programme was adversely affected by the increase in
inflation and the decline in economic growth and
in the growth of incomes in the late sixties and
early seventies. In 1973 President Nixon suspended
most subsidised housing programmes and subjected
them to a review (US Department of Housing and
Urban Development, 1973). It concluded that they
were complex, inefficient, helped very few of those
in need, were often excessively costly and so on.
A move to housing allowances, enabling poor
households to rent privately, was advocated.
Congress criticised these conclusions, suggesting
that supply side subsidies were still necessary
and that the faults of previous programmes had been
exaggerated (House Committee on Banking, Currency
and Housing, 1975, 198-9; Senate Committee on
Banking, Housing and Urban Affairs, 1976).
Interestingly, it was also pointed out that Section
236 was never intended for those at the very
bottom of the market but for the slightly better
off. This was supposed to eventually lead to better
housing for the poorest via the filtering process

Subsidies and Taxation

(actually an unlikely result).
     Eventually, pending the development of housing
allowances (which will be discussed later) the
Nixon administration introduced what became the
major programme (section 8) for the provision of
new and rehabilitated low and moderate income
rental housing. This enabled local housing agencies
(public authorities or other organisations) to
contract with private landlords to let to households which had not more than 80% of their
localities' median income (this figure could be
adjusted up or down according to circumstances).
Subsidy payments were available to owners of
existing and new/rehabilitated housing. Section 8
therefore combined elements of personal and of
construction/rehabilitation subsidies (14).
     The maximum rent charged could not normally be
more than 110% of a federally calculated 'fair
market rent' (FMR) for the type of housing
concerned, based on estimates of the housing
element in the cost of living in each locality.
Families who participated were free to seek out the
unit they required on the private market provided
that it met minimum standards. Tenants paid between
15-25% of their gross incomes in rent, depending
on the number of children, their income, and medical
and child care costs. The 'rent gap' was met by the
federal subsidies. Further details of the arrangements for existing units will be mentioned later..
Any developer could apply for contracts for
new and rehabilitated units. These could be for 20
and in some cases 40 years, the idea being that
they could be pledged as security for obtaining
commercial finance.
     Section 8 soon became, in comparison with
previous subsidised programmes, a large scale
scheme, although its impact on new construction was
more modest. By the end of 1976 contract authority
was available for about 470,000 units, about 25% of
them were for new or rehabilitated property (US
Department of Housing and Urban Development, 1977,
167). Much of the new housing was for the elderly,
because developers expected them to be easy to
manage and there was less suburban political
resistance to such projects (few developers built
for families in troubled central city areas). Also
the FMRs for elderly housing were higher than
those for family housing although, given the
differential risks involved, the reverse would have
been more rational.
     In response to these problems family FMRs were

194

eventually increased. But, despite the hope that
much of the new housing could be conventionally
financed, in practice most was financed by the FHA
or by state housing finance agencies. Another
development in the late seventies was the creation
of non profit building agencies by the local
authorities. These were able, like the state
agencies, to raise finance by selling bonds whose
interest was tax exempt. In mid 1978 bonds bore an
interest rate of about $6\frac{1}{2}$% - 3% below the market
level. So this provided a considerable indirect
subsidy for housing. Section 8 also benefitted from
the availability of tax shelters for rental housing.
    A government survey of newly built Section 8
projects found that 90% of the projects sampled
were completely subsidised (Blankespoor and Jaffee,
1978). The aim had been to create a 'social mix'
via the provision in each project of subsidised and
unsubsidised housing. Two thirds of the units were
for the elderly and relatively few for families.
About 70% of the developers were private investors,
the rest were government or government backed
agencies. The scheme was administratively complex
and some rather dubious adjustments had been made
to the allowable building costs which might
eventually make the projects rather costly. Finally,
only 15% of the projects were conventionally
financed. It seemed likely that substantial
subsidies would continue to be needed to keep the
production of new low income rental housing going.
    As already mentioned a key aspect of support
for private rental building was the availability of
tax shelters via depreciation allowances. First
we shall consider the federal tax arrangements and
then those concerning local property taxes (which
had a substantial impact because much governmental
activity was locally funded). Although this section
concentrates on subsidies for new building and
other tax matters are discussed in section 4, here
it is necessary to consider tax arrangements for
rental housing as a whole (15).
    Before a 1969 reform the tax codes did not
contain special incentives for investment in
residential property, although incentives for
investment in new property were greater than those
for investment in second hand property. This
neutrality discouraged investment in the more risky
field of housing, especially low income housing.
Moreover commercial property developments which did
not need subsidies were being marketed for the tax

195

shelter that they offered for high income investors
(as the tax allowances could not be passed on to
individuals via corporation dividends, firms
marketed developments to 'syndicates' of individual
investors).

The 1969 changes aimed, in part, to increase
the production of low income housing. As already
mentioned the 221(d)(3) BMIR programme was not a
great success, because the rate of return to
investors was limited to 6% of what was called their
'recognised equity'. For various reasons in reality
investors often had to find more than this amount,
so making less than a 6% return. Legislation in
1968 and 1969 set out to deal with this problem.
Thus the Section 236 programme allowed investors to
benefit from larger tax deductions than the BMIR
programme, the latter had an interest rate of 3%
compared with the market rate applicable to 236
projects (even though investors had to declare as
income the 236 subsidies, they could deduct in full
market interest payments, this increased the
proportion of tax deductible debt repayment in the
early years of 236 projects in comparison with BMIR
projects).

Of more permanent importance was a change
which continued to allow the deduction of
accelerated depreciation for new housing while
restricting its availability for commercial
projects. Also sales of HUD insured property were
exempted from capital gains tax if the proceeds
were reinvested in low and moderate income housing.
Finally, favourable changes were made in rules
concerning the 'recapture' of gains on the sales of
rental property. Before 1969 most property could be
depreciated over 40 years according to a straight
line or an accelerated method, but second hand
property could only be depreciated at 150% of the
straight line method whereas new property could be
depreciated at 200%. Part of the capital gain on
the sale of property was recaptured and taxed as
ordinary income rather than at the, normally lower,
capital gains rate. The amount subject to ordinary
tax was equal to the capital gain or the amount of
depreciation claimed in excess of the straight line
multiplied by a varying percentage - 100% if the
asset had only been held a short time reducing to
zero after ten years - whichever was the smaller
sum.

After 1969 new residential property could still
be depreciated at 200% but other new property only
at 150%. Used property, non-residential property

and rental property with less than 20 years useful
life could only be depreciated according to the
straight line method, used rental property with a
longer life could be depreciated at 125%. Further
assistance was given to certain low and moderate
income units (including Sections 221(d)(3) and 236
and later Section 8 and certain state and local
subsidised programmes) because only this property
was now eligible for the ten year phase out
recapture rule. In all other residential cases all
the accelerated depreciation was liable for income
tax if the property was sold within 8½ years of
acquisition, reducing to zero after 16⅔ years. In
the case of non-residential property all accelerated
depreciation was recaptured wheneover the property
was sold.

These arrangements were explicitly designed to
encourage higher income individuals to form
partnerships for investment in low income rental
property. A 1972 estimate suggested that individuals
needed to have an income of over $65,000 per annum
in order to benefit appreciably. Those paying less
than an aggregate federal and state income tax rate
of 50% (a high rate in the US) would not benefit by
the tax shelter which, in effect, was a shelter
from both types of tax. As explained already such
wealthy investors linked up with developers who
sold the tax losses on projects to the partners.
The reason for the need to involve individuals
via partnerships has already been explained, the
advantage of involving companies was that they (but
not individuals) had limited liability.

These measures did divert substantial resources
from non residential to residential building. It
was estimated that by 1972 this amounted to
60-80000 units. Also the ending of favourable tax
treatment for producers' durable equipment in 1969
was thought, in the years that followed, to have
diverted resources into the production of another
140-180,000 units (US Department of Housing and
Urban Development, 1973, 2-17). So the changes were
significant for private rental housing. Section
236 also had additional tax benefits. For example
the mortgages were over 40 years, thus providing a
very high proportion of interest to capital
repayment in the early years. Also all rental
projects benefitted from the fact that certain
expenses incurred during the construction period,
such as interest and property taxes, could be set
against taxable income other than that arising from

the operation of the housing itself, rather than
being capitalised and included in the project cost
to be depreciated.

The major problem was that the main concern of
the partners was not the profits to be made from the
rents but the ability that tax loss housing gave
them to shelter part of their other income (16).
This proved to be particularly so for 236 projects.
Generally such a project would produce losses for
the first 15-18 years because of, on the one hand,
the high level of mortgage interest payments which
could be deducted and the accelerated depreciation
and, on the other, the gross rental income which
was limited to a level which covered expenses plus
a 6% return on the partners' equity. But by about
the 20th year the partners would actually be out
of pocket because cash flow would be insufficient
to cover amortisation (non-deductable) plus tax on
the limited net rental income. Partners only had an
interest in keeping projects sufficiently well
managed to avoid foreclosure, especially while
there would be a liability to pay income rather
than capital gains tax on disposition (10 years for
236 etc, projects, 16⅔ years in other cases). This
frequently resulted in minimal attention being paid
to management and maintenance, often the management
companies had no interest in the equity. Also the
system did not encourage investors and developers
to take undue risks, a preference for suburban
sites and building for the elderly was often noted
(as with the later Section 8 projects). The
developers had no interest in the projects that they
initiated, following their syndication. In fact,
the whole process led to housing which had no real
landlord, in the sense of someone whose profit was
closely linked to the quality of the housing
services offered. Ironically a project which was
marginal, incurring high expenses and a small
surplus, was more beneficial in tax terms, as long
as it did not actually collapse financially.
Moreover, these schemes involved various costly
middlemen-tax lawyers, accountants and securities
salesmen - whose talents added little to the
quality or success of the housing produced. Also,
because the tax benefit was based on depreciation,
there was little incentive to economise on building
costs.

The tax subsidy was substantial. For example,
it was calculated on the basis of reasonable
assumptions, that the benefit gained from a section
236 project costing about $3.9 million (in which

198

the partnership's equity would be 10%) over 20 years
would range from $400,000 (for a 'well run' project)
to $534,000 (for a 'marginally run' project) in the
case of investors on the minimally beneficial tax
rate of 50% (National Center for Housing Management,
1973, 331). Apart from the cost of this method of
attracting capital into rental housing and the other
problems already mentioned, the approach was also
criticised because of what might happen after the
20 year period ended. Then the partnerships would
have little positive reason for keeping the housing,
at best there would be the negative reason that if
it was sold there could be a substantial tax
liability. It has been suggested that the
'caretaking' operation which the project's running
would then have become would be unlikely to produce
good management. The project could of course be
sold, but as second hand property (even though a
new tax allowance could be claimed) the tax shelter
would be not nearly so attractive and, as
amortisation would be continually rising (the
mortgages transfer with the sale), the project's
new owners would soon be in the position of the old
owners, with cash flow insufficient to cover
repayments plus expenses and tax liabilities. Many
commentators suggested that much of the rental
housing produced under these regulations would
eventually find its way into liquidation.

As already mentioned states and localities
could issue bonds, the interest on which was tax
exempt. This was because of the general provision
for intergovernmental tax immunity in the USA. Such
bonds had been used by state housing finance
agencies to provide cheap money for rental housing.
At first they were used for middle and moderate
income housing (for example in New York via state
and city 'Mitchell - Lama' housing, which also
received property tax exemptions), later section
236 mortgage subsidies and insurance were often
linked to cheap state money to provide low income
rental housing. Later still this source was used
for Section 8 construction. The role of tax exempt
bonds grew in the sixties and seventies as the
number and scope of state housing finance agencies
increased (17).

The last important source of tax assistance for
rental housing were the many and varied local
property tax exemptions for new and in some cases
for rehabilitated units. For example, in 1971 New
York exempted some new and rehabilitated rental
housing from all property tax on the enhanced value

of the site for two years followed by a partial
exemption for ten years. Rents were subject to
stabilisation and some other controls and there were
construction cost yardsticks. The programme had a
substantial impact, between 1971-5 about 29,000
units were completed or under construction aided by
these benefits. This was about 90% of all New York's
multifamily starts in these years. Critics suggested
that, because of the relatively shallow subsidy
that it gave, it tended to assist middle and upper
income housing and that much of this development
would have occurred anyway (18). If this was so, it
meant that others, who might be worse off, were
paying, via increased property taxes, for a subsidy
to the better off. As high property taxes were one
of the factors putting pressure on the economics of
rental housing in the city this point was
significant. But, if the developments would not have
occurred otherwise and if they were occupied by
people who would not otherwise have lived in the
city, it has been suggested that the effects were
positive, after allowing for all the tax effects
including the local sales tax on the new purchasing
power brought into the city.

Another major New York programme, already
mentioned, was Mitchell-Lama housing which began
in 1955. Development could be by commercial
investors, co-operative associations, or non-profit
membership corporations. Commercial projects were
limited profit (in the sense that Section 236 was
'limited profit'). Below market loans, on terms of up
to fifty years were available from the state and the
city. Commercial developers were required to put up
10% of the equity, the other bodies had to find
less. Non profit developments were wholly exempt
from property taxes, commercial developments had
up to 30 years exemption on up to 50% of the
assessed value of the project or on up to 100% of
the enhanced value created by the project. Together
the city and the state programmes resulted in about
100,000 new units in New York City. Despite the
subsidies and the fact that many tenants had higher
than average New York tenant incomes, there had been
many financial difficulties - most notoriously in
the vast Co-op City, a large state aided project
where there was a prolonged struggle between the
tenants, the state and the project management. Apart
from the profits to be made via tax shelters, it
was clear that the provision of sub-standard
management for excessive fees had become an important

source of income for some organisations and that
the lack of tenant control over such matters, even
in so-called co-operatives, was a major problem.

In 1973 HUD published a study of the effects
of property tax incentives on new construction,
based on an examination of the situation in nine
cities, including New York, Boston, St. Louis and
Newark (Price, Waterhouse and Co., 1973). It found
that, when tax incentives had been used in
conjunction with urban renewal programmes, they had
not usually resulted in much new low and moderate
income housing because developers preferred to use
the tax abatements to subsidise 'safer' middle
income housing or even, when allowed, non
residential development. Often these subsidies were
simply treated as a windfall rather than as clear
incentives to build, especially for the less well
off, and they shifted the burden of taxation
towards other taxpayers who could not take
advantage of the subsidy.

HOUSING ALLOWANCES

As we have seen Denmark introduced social rented
housing allowances in the later thirties. More
frequently this was a development which occurred
after 1945. In several cases rent allowances were
introduced, or greatly extended, from the sixties
onwards as a part of the movement away from support
for new construction and low rents towards cost
covering rents and the restriction of subsidies to
households in the greatest financial need. In the
private rented sector the extension of rent
allowances tended to accompany the movement towards
a free or more loosely regulated rent system. It is
important to note that many general income
maintenance schemes, such as the US system of
welfare payments and the British system of
Supplementary Benefits, incorporated housing
payments, although the focus here is more narrowly
on housing allowances per se. Allowance schemes had
certain common deficiencies which will be referred
to later. But first some details of their
development will be noted.

France had various allowances, available to
tenants and owner occupiers (19). The longest
established formed a part of the system of family
allowances. This 'allocation de logement familiale'
(AL),   financed from employers contributions,

was revised annually. Since 1974 the scales had
been linked to the retail price and construction
cost indices. The amount of aid was related to
household income and the number of dependents, with
an upper limit for allowable housing payments. AL
was only payable to those in units with at least
basic facilities and a minimum surface area
graduated according to family size. By 1975 about
1½ million households benefitted, about two-thirds
were tenants,mostly in newer housing
(unsurprisingly, as this was more expensive than
the older stock).

The second scheme, 'allocation de logement
familiale' (ALS) began in 1971, replacing an earlier
scheme. ALS was only available for the handicapped,
the elderly and young workers. In other respects
its regulations were similar to those for AL. By
1975 it was benefitting about half a million
households, 85-90% of whom were pensioners,
although the number of young beneficiaries was
growing. This reflected the rapidly rising cost of
housing for newcomers   to the housing market noted
in Chapter 5.

Some details about the beneficiaries of these
schemes were collected in the 1973 Enquête-logement.
18% of all tenants and mortgagors were in receipt
of allowances (10% of mortgagors, 31% of those
renting HLM units, under 10% of those in the mainly
cheap pre-1949 privately rented units, and about
24% of those in post-1948 rented units). The
allowances reduced housing payments as a proportion
of income to the same level, in the case of
mortgagors, or to about 25% less, in the case of
tenants, as those paid by non-beneficiaries in the
respective tenures. They did not alter the
differences in the proportions of income spent on
housing which existed between the various sectors
as a whole, i.e. mortgagors and those in newer
private housing still paid rather higher proportions
than those in the older rented stock and in HLM
housing. Payments to tenants of newer privately
rented housing were as high as those to mortgagors,
nor surprisingly given the very high rents of much
of this stock. But other tenants, especially those
in the controlled stock, received far less. The
schemes assisted rather few in the lowest income
group compared with those in the next three
divisions (septiles). Because of the linkage of
AL to family allowances and of ALS to age, very few
households without children benefitted except when
the head was over 65 years old. And the proportion

of beneficiaries among families with children
increased steadily with size, so that 65-70% of
families with more than five children got help.
Finally, although the schemes reduced the proportion
of income spent on housing they did not seem to
alter the overall relationship of housing costs to
income, i.e. those who were poorest still paid
proportionately more for housing than those who
were better off (Enquête-logement, 1973(1), 157,
161).

So these schemes were limited in coverage and,
as a part of a wide ranging reform of housing
subsidies in the late seventies, which aimed to
align rents more closely to economic costs, a new
'Aide Personnalisée au Logement'(APL) was being
introduced. It was linked to new rehabilitation
policies and so it will be referred to again in
Chapter 7 but, in common with the general trend in
government policies towards the rental sector, the
aim was to concentrate assistance on those who
needed it most, while raising housing costs for
others. APL was being introduced slowly because it
was feared that a sudden increase in the purchasing
power of poorer consumers might simply inflate
housing costs. It was eventually to replace the
older allowances and would give more help to those
on very low incomes, especially when they lived
in expensive housing (mainly new and rehabilitated
units). It had some similarities with Section 8 as
it was intended to act as a stimulus to production.
In the first instance APL was made available when
social housing organisations were acquiring and
rehabilitating property, when they carried out
improvements in areas of mixed ownership especially
in inner cities and when they were rehabilitating
properties for owner occupancy at controlled
standards and prices. Generally it was being used
in the HLM sector in conjunction with a move towards
market level rents and was also available in
property owned by the larger landlords, such as the
para-public organisations. Eventually it was hoped
to extend it to all rented property but this was a
rather distant aim.

Minimum conditions were set for eligible
dwellings. Increases in APL were linked to the
retail price and construction cost indices. The
benefit was based on household income, with
deductions for childcare, according to a complex
formula which included set proportions of income
which households of different types had to pay

towards their rent. There were maximum rents (with some areal variation) which could be taken into account and also limits on the charges met by APL. Comparisons with AL are difficult, particularly as the introduction of APL was accompanied by higher gross rents for most properties, but the main French tenants' association suggested that the new system would be more beneficial for the very worst off, leave the slightly better off in an unaltered situation and require all others to pay considerably more (Massu, 1977, 46-7). Certainly such a conclusion seemed in line with the general strategy of the French government towards rental subsidies.

Danish allowances were extended to the private rented sector in 1955. The scheme's coverage was increased in 1961. Minimum size standards were set and the allowance was only available to families with children (aged persons in social housing and some owner occupiers also benefitted). Most beneficiaries were in social or private rented housing but the scheme was limited to households on very low incomes.

As elsewhere the scheme was expanded along with the reforms in rent policy and the move to higher rents which occurred from 1966 onwards (Ministry of Housing, 1974, 25-6). A system of graded rents was established for tenants in all rented housing. Minimum dwelling standards and minimum and maximum standards for occupancy were set. Three factors determined the level of the allowance, household income adjusted for the number of children, the number of children and the rent. The formula which was used was complex but, broadly speaking, the rent which the household itself paid was a function of the level of household income, taking into account the presence of children. In addition the subsidy could not exceed two thirds of the difference between the rent charged and that which was regarded as reasonable for a household to pay. Moreover the subsidy could not exceed a certain percentage of the former figure, varying according to the number of children. There was a separate scheme for pensioners. This exceedingly complex scheme required frequent amendments to take account of income growth. So in 1976 indexation was introduced. Since 1973 there had also been a special scheme for those rehoused from slum clearance areas (see Chapter 7).

Despite its complexity and the inability of many tenants to calculate whether they were eligible,

the Ministry of Housing believed that the take up
rate was around 90%. It was suggested that most
tenants were prepared to apply in the hope that
they could benefit and that there was no stigma
attached to such benefits in Denmark. But hard
evidence for such conclusions was lacking. Up to
the mid seventies about 225,000 households a year
benefitted, the proportion of pensioners had
increased from about half in the late sixties to
two-thirds. About a quarter of all households in
rented property benefitted and about the same
proportion of pensioner households. Among the non-
pensioner households it was mainly those with
children, especially large families, that
benefitted, but also increasing proportions of one
parent households. The scheme seemed to have become
decreasingly available to 'normal' familes, partly
because in the period reviewed here, their incomes
were increasing rather rapidly as more married
women went to work (Danmarks Statistik, 1925-77,
1975, 48, 192).

Nevertheless the graded rents scheme was
considerably more widely available than the earlier
housing allowances. In 1978 the upper income limit
for eligibility fell between the average earnings
levels for skilled and unskilled manual workers
and 50% above the level of the minimum welfare
benefit. The costs of the scheme had increased
rapidly, the average subsidy per household had more
than doubled between 1969/70 and 1977/78 but the
share of subsidy as a proportion of gross rents
remained almost constant in the first part of this
period (Danmarks Statistik, 1925-77). But it
probably fell quite sharply in the later seventies
because rents were then increasing very rapidly as
a result of the cost rent principle while the
average subsidy payment rose more slowly. The
scheme was the responsibility of the central
government but was administered by the local
authorities who had to fund 40% of its costs (but
only 25% of the separate pensioner scheme). The
division of the subsidy between the two parts of
the rental sector was unknown.

The evolution of housing allowances in West
Germany follows the, by now familiar, pattern. A
limited system was introduced in 1956 and extended
in the sixties when, it will be recalled, the
decontrol of rents began. These early schemes were
inadequate and, in some cases, were supplemented
by funds from the Lander. The scheme operating
at the time of the research (for tenants and owner

occupiers) dated from 1970 and, unlike the earlier
schemes, was open to all (20). It was governed by
Federal laws and administered by the local
authorities. The costs were split between the
Federal government and the Lander. These costs had
increased greatly since 1970 due to inflation and
increased take up. But by the late seventies take
up had stabilised at about 7-9% of all households,
10% of all tenants and 1% of owner occupiers.
About 90% of the recipients were tenants and 10%
owner occupiers. Take up was about 70% (21).
    The original idea was to formulate 'bearable'
housing costs as a fraction of disposable income,
varying with income and family size, all costs
above this being subsidised. But it was felt to be
wrong that this would allow families with similar
needs and income to occupy housing of varying
standards at similar personal costs. It was also
thought that this would encourage the over-
consumption of housing, inflate prices for better
quality units and depress those for older units. So
the original principle was supplemented by a rule
that renters or owners of units at above average
rents or prices had to bear a higher fraction of
costs. Conversely, those in cheaper units got
relatively greater relief.
    The basic rules of this complicated scheme
were that a maximum floor area was set, varying with
the size of the family, and a maximum admissable
rent per square metre. For this latter purpose
housing was divided into twelve categories on the
basis of age, quality and the population size of
its locality. These rents were supposed to be based
on comparable market rents. Eligibility depended on
household income with deductions for dependents, on
this basis the proportion that families could
'afford' to spend on rent was calculated and applied
to the administratively determined ceiling rent.
The difference between the 'affordable' and the
ceiling rent was payable as an allowance. Those who
actually paid more than the ceiling rent had to
bear the extra burden themselves but those in
cheaper than standard property were better off. A
maximum of 90% of the payable rent might be met by
the allowance. In practice about 35% on average was
covered by the allowance.
    Some data was available on the scheme. The pre-
1970 scheme was limited to tenants and was on a
very small scale. Only 0.8% of tenants were covered
by it in 1964, this rose to 4% by 1970. By 1974

Subsidies and Taxation

there had been a rapid growth in recipients, to
over 1½ million, over 90% of whom were tenants.
About 70% were in post-1948 housing, two-thirds
were in social housing and two-thirds were
pensioners (Der Bundesminister für Raumordnung etc.,
1975, 118; Ballerstedt and Glatzer, 1975, 163).
The scheme was still limited to rather low income
households and had mainly been used by the elderly
and/or those living in the expensive newer social
rented housing. There was often a considerable gap
between the ceiling rents and the actual rents,
leaving a heavy burden still to be met by tenants.
The Federal Ministry accepted that this had
reduced the access of poorer household living in
the worst housing conditions to the new social
rented units which were often their only source of
improved housing. In 1978 changes were made which,
it was claimed, would enable more families with
economically active heads to benefit.
    British rent allowances were confined to the
social rented sector until the early seventies and
were a matter for local discretion (22). The
establishment in 1972 of a national scheme in the
social sector accompanied increases in public
housing rents. At the same time, allowances were
made available for tenants of unfurnished private
accommodation and, a little later, for tenants of
furnished accommodation. The allowance was related
to the rent and to the husband (and wife's, where
applicable) income, adjusted for the number of
dependants and certain other expenses. There was a
ceiling on the amount payable, more in London
than elsewhere, and a minimum payment by the tenant
of 40% of the rent (unless the income was very low
in relation to needs).
    Problems included the low take up, about
35-40% in 1976 (Cullingworth, 1979, 134). Ignorance
of the scheme, fear of the consequences of
applying (in case the landlord objected to official
attention being drawn to the rents being charged)
and stigma were all thought to contribute to this
situation (Wicks, 1975). Also the allowance was
based on registered 'fair' rents, when these were
available, or on the local authority   estimate of
what such a rent would be, exclusive of payments
for furniture or services. Often this figure was
much less than the rent actually paid and so the
relief was inadequate. The scheme was nationally
determined with some room for local discretion, it
was operated by the local authorities and the costs
were shared but mostly met by central government.

Data for 1977 showed that very few tenants of
furnished accommodation were receiving allowances
and under 10% of all unfurnished tenants. The
scheme mainly aided the elderly and on average
approximately one half of recipients rents were met
by the allowance (OPCS, 1979, 49-50).

In the Netherlands allowances began in 1970.
This scheme was introduced to alleviate high rent
levels in new social housing. An expanded scheme
began in 1974 when dynamic cost rents were
introduced. There were two schemes, the first was
for families, single people over 30 years old and
other well established households (23). The second
was for single people under 30. The eligibility
limits were based on the earnings of the highest
earner in the household adjusted for the number of
dependents, but the allowances was reduced if there
were other incomes. The allowable rent was the
controlled rent in the controlled zones and was
administratively determined elsewhere. The subsidy
reduced rents as a percentage of income for those
on the legal minimum wage to about 11% on average
and to about 17% for those on the highest
qualifying incomes (the proportions were higher in
the second scheme).

The scheme was financed by central government
but administered by the municipalities. According
to a 1975 survey there was a 75% take up rate.
About half the recipients were elderly and many of
the others were under 25 years old (24). The scheme
was still principally used to reduce the rents of
newer social housing. In interviews, it was
suggested that the allowances were still not
effectively aiding many of those who were paying
high rents for newer property and for some improved
property.

There was no general system of rent allowances
in the USA. Most low income households were
dependent on welfare payments for assistance with
housing costs and the details of these schemes
varied widely from state to state (25). But, it
will be recalled, the section 8 programme could be
seen as a type of housing allowance scheme.
According to a 1978 survey most recipients were
elderly women living alone or female headed
families (Drury, 1978; Drury et. al., 1978). Most of
the male headed households were very large minority
group families. Most recipients had very low
incomes, i.e. income below 50% of the area's median,
and were dependent on state and other benefits.

Most wanted help with existing housing costs rather
than to use the allowance to move to better quality
units, although some had to move because there were
minimum property standards laid down for
eligibility. The effect of the allowances was
dramatic. Comparing those certified as eligible but
who, for various reasons, did not find a suitable
unit with those who did, the former were paying on
average 48% of their income in rent, the latter
24%.

Section 8, as already noted, was supposed to
be a temporary expedient pending the introduction
of housing allowances. At the time it began a large
scale Experimental Housing Allowance Programme
(EHAP) was already underway. This pilot scheme was
never expanded into a full scale programme but it
is nonetheless of interest (26). EHAP began in
twelve localities in 1973, by 1977 about 21,500
households had benefitted. There were three
different sub programmes, carried out at different
sites. The first tested administrative procedures,
the second tested demand effects and the third
tested supply effects. About 60% of eligible tenants
and 30% of eligible homeowners enrolled in the
schemes. Some did not apply because of stigma and
others because their incomes were sufficiently high
to ensure that they would have received little
benefit. Families had to be living in or move to
sound property - it was hoped that EHAP would help
to upgrade housing conditions. But many families
did not want to move, ties to locality were
important, especially for minority households (who
were also impeded by racially segregated housing
markets) and the few elderly households. Welfare
families were more likely to apply than working
families and female headed households more often
than male headed ones, as with section 8.
Households living in lower quality housing were
less likely to apply than those in better quality
property. The allowance did not seem to have any
inflationary effects on the local housing markets
in which it operated. It only had a modest effect
on inducing landlords, tenants and owners to remedy
housing defects.

EHAP, which cost $180 million, had been
criticised for being too small scale, and for being
operated in an unrepresentative selection of local
housing markets. It was suggested that few
conclusions could be drawn from this experiment
concerning the effects of a larger scheme
(Comptroller General of the United States, 1974,

209

1978). But HUD officials argued that EHAP provided evidence about individual households' reactions to allowances which were likely to be generally applicable (US Department of Housing and Urban Development, Office of Policy Development and Research, 1978, 24-5; Comptroller General of the United States, 1978, 90-125). In fact proposals to establish housing allowances have been debated in the US since the thirties and the introduction of measures such as rent supplements and section 8, had already contained elements of this approach. But, apart from the cost of a large scale scheme, EHAP demonstrated that it was difficult to change the situation of the poorest families, at least if they had to move in order to benefit. Even when offered quite substantial financial incentives people had ties to their locality which appeared to outweigh their desire for better/cheaper housing. Many eligible families did not even try to find acceptable accommodation and the conclusion was drawn that providing financial incentives via allowances alone was not the most promising means of improving housing for the poorest. This is one reason why section 8, combining elements of demand and supply assistance, eventually seemed preferable. Another important consideration was that it was easier to restrict access to this subsidy, in line with budgetary constraints, than it would have been to restrict access to a housing allowance.

The common problems of the various schemes which have been outlined include (1) the limited extent to which those eligible take advantage of them, whether through ignorance or because of the actual or assumed stigma they engender; (2) their complexity which is confusing for potential applicants and administratively expensive; (3) their inadequacy, for example the gap between 'admissable' and actual rents, and provisions which limit the proportion of the difference between 'bearable' and 'admissable' rents which is met by subsidy; (4) the assumptions about what is a 'bearable' rent which ignore the fact that this amount may be far more than households have previously devoted to housing. In the USA, for example, the common assumption that even quite poor households could afford to pay 25% of their incomes for housing without reducing other essential expenditure was quite arbitrary; (5) the limited coverage of schemes, in many cases they mainly assisted the elderly and/or supported the continued production of costly social housing. In general, the development of allowances was part of

a wider strategy of limiting rental housing
subsidies to the very poorest and sharply increasing
in housing costs for other tenants, a principle
which was notably absent from owner occupation
subsidy policy; (6) the limitations of demand side
subsidies when there is still an inadequate supply
of decent rental housing for low income households,
a point illustrated by EHAP.

TAXATION

The regulations and laws governing the taxation of
income and capital gains from rental property are
always complex and difficult to evaluate (27).
All that could be attempted within the broader
perspective of the work on which this book is based
was an overview of the arrangements in each country.
   In France the social sector was not subject to
most of the taxes which private landlords were
liable to pay. Owner occupiers were somewhat
beneficially treated too, thus since 1965 some
mortgage interest had been tax deductable. As
elsewhere owner occupiers had been given this
advantage as part of a general strategy of
encouraging this tenure. But local taxes and
registration duties were still payable by private
landlords and owner occupiers. There was no capital
gains tax on a principal home but there might be on
a second home (if it was bought to make financial
gains) or an investment property, though there was
widespread evasion of this duty by those owning
second homes and by small landlords.
   Rental income was taxed via income or company
tax depending on the status of the landlord but
there were several different ways in which tax was
incurred, for example profits from letting furnished
accommoddation came under the rules for commercial
enterprises not those governing property income.
Before 1963 companies and institutional landlords
were exempted from tax on profits which related to
buildings constructed since 1950, including sales
profits. These measures were a part of the early
post-war policy of encouraging rental production,
their abolition was an indication of a shift away
from this rather favourable attitude to rental
investment. A further indicator of this shift was
that from 1950 to 1973 new units were exempted from
local property taxes for 25 years but after 1973
for only two years. (HLMs had a 15 year exemption
continuously from 1950). Landlords could deduct a

wide variety of expenses from rental income,
including the costs of maintenance, repair and
improvement, local taxes and mortgage interest.
There was also a fixed deduction which was intended
to allow for other more intangible expenses such as
bad debts. This was set at 25% of the net revenue
but before 1970 was 35%.

The para-public SIIs were subject to a
favourable tax regime. Their income from rental
housing was not liable to company taxation (they
also had other development income), nor the interest
earned on short term deposits of operating funds.
Tax on profits from the sales of residential
property and registration taxes were limited.
Dividends were liable for tax but 20% was tax free
as was that part of the dividend which related to
government subsidies. Subscriptions to the share
capital of SIIs and share transfers also benefitted
from preferential provisions up to 1973.

In comparison with many other countries the
tax advantages of French owner occupiers did not
seem much greater than those available to the
private rental sector especially as, in the case of
small landlords at least, tax evasion was common.
But there were greater tax advantages in investing
in new rental property between 1950 and 1963,
though the 1963 changes adversely affected all
property owners. The ability of owner occupiers to
obtain some interest relief, which began in the mid
sixties, helped to make this sector more attractive.
The HLM sector also had substantial advantages.
But there were still generous provisions governing
the expenses which could be set against gross
income in comparison with elsewhere.

In Denmark all sectors paid property tax, but
only owner occupiers could deduct this tax from
income for income tax purposes. However, as local
taxes were low this was a relatively minor benefit.
Owner occupiers could also deduct interest
payments and a maintenance allowance but they paid
an imputed income tax, in 1979 this was a little
over 2% of the assessed (1977) value of their
properties. Landlords could deduct interest,
management and maintenance costs but not
depreciation, except for certain major items of
equipment such as lifts. Owner occupiers were not
taxed on the capital gains from the sale of a single
house, landlords were taxed on all capital gains
and those whom the tax authorities decided were
property dealers seeking short term gains were

taxed at a higher rate. One purpose of this was to
discourage the speculative selling of rented
property for owner occupation.

In West Germany there had of course been
generous tax arrangements for small private
landlords. The provisions for depreciation
allowances which discriminated in favour of those
building for owner occupation and building two
units, one for themselves and one for letting, have
already been noted. In addition, all landlords and
owner occupiers deducted debt charges, maintenance
and other expenses plus property taxes from gross
income up to certain limits. There was no capital
gains tax.

The taxation regime in Britain was less
generous towards landlords than in any of the other
countries surveyed. Although all sectors paid local
property taxes with no facility to deduct these
from income tax and landlords as well as owner
occupiers could deduct mortgage interest, landlords
were then liable for tax whereas the provisions
which made owner occupiers liable for a tax on
imputed income (albeit a very low one) were
abolished in 1963. Moreover, most owner occupiers
were exempt from capital gains tax, unlike
landlords. But the disadvantage of the landlord was
also manifest vis a vis other businessmen because
landlords could not deduct depreciation whereas
other businesses often benefitted from generous
provisions. One anomalous consequence was that the
capital cost of an improvement in the amenities
of a property was not deductable, whereas if it was
provided as a replacement for an existing amenity
it was deductable (28). Apart from property taxes,
social housing was tax exempt.

Dutch landlords could deduct all expenses
including interest payments from gross rental
income. Depreciation was included, private owners
could deduct a sum equivalent to 15% of their
annual rents and companies 1-2% of the historic
costs of their properties. The assumption was that
these deductions would allow landlords to save
enough to cover major replacements. Other major
expenses could be deducted from income in the year
in which they occurred, in some cases this could be
spread over several years. Owner occupiers could
deduct interest but not expenses or depreciation.
They also paid a tax on imputed income, in the late
seventies this was approximately 1.3% of the
assessed value of the property (equivalent to 60-
70% of the market value). The assessments were

based on the occupants' own estimates which, not surprisingly, tended to be rather low! Before 1971 the imputed income was a higher proportion of the value but costs could be deducted, the system was abandoned because it was cumbrous and difficult to operate. Both owners and landlords paid property taxes (but as already mentioned these were rather low), a 5% sales tax and a tax on capital. Non-profit housing associations were tax exempt.

These provisions were not altogether unfavourable for the private landlord in comparison with the owner occupier. But there were no special incentives for rental investment, companies in particular were not affected in their choice of investments by reason of the tax provisions. One increasingly important factor was the lack of a capital gains tax. As the demand for ownership had grown, large capital gains had been made by some of the break-up companies and speculators who had bought and sold desirable property in localities such as inner Amsterdam. Some of the more spectacular results of these operations were publicised in 1978, they refer to housing in the historic New Market area of Amsterdam (Bijlsma and Salverda, 1978). Thus, one property was bought for 115,000 guilders and sold for 200,000 guilders the same day and another for 150,000 guilders and sold for 350,000 guilders - again the same day. These are extreme examples but many less spectacular but very profitable deals had occurred. But the largest net gains were probably made by individual landlords selling off longer held properties for, despite the absence of capital gains tax, other individuals and companies who had been more actively dealing in property were subject to income or corporation tax.

The role played by tax shelters in stimulating the construction of rental property in the USA has already been described. More generally, landlords and owner occupiers paid local property taxes but these taxes and interest payments could be deducted from income for the purpose of federal taxation (29). Owner occupiers benefitted differentially from the absence of a tax on imputed income. In addition they were able to avoid paying much capital gains tax. Landlords normally paid this, although in some cases it was deferred if they reinvested in low income housing. Landlords could deduct all normal management and maintenance expenses and depreciation.

CONCLUSION

The general theme of the declining fortunes of the
private rented sector which has characterised the
earlier findings of this book has also been present
in this chapter on subsidies and taxation. With the
exception of Britain, despite varying attitudes
towards the desirability of assisting private
landlords, the immediate post war housing shortages
led the other five countries to provide some
very substantial encouragements to private investors.
However, these benefits were gradually reduced. In
some countries, such as Denmark, there were always
reservations about subsidies for private landlords
and they were seen as a purely temporary expedient.
In other cases, such as France, the emphasis
switched away from the rental sector as the
objective of encouraging owner occupation
became the main aim of housing policy. West Germany
provides an interesting variant. Here support for
property ownership was explicitly linked to a
concern with political stabilisation. Owner
occupation was thought to be desirable but was, in
the circumstances of the late forties and fifties,
a rather theoretical option. But even in Germany,
while incentives for small landlords still existed,
support for owner occupation, especially via tax
benefits, had been growing. The country which had
the most interesting, and from the investor's point
of view, most positive developments in incentives
for construction was the USA. But the tax shelters
were of very questionable value in providing sound,
well managed housing.
     One of the most significant developments which
had accompanied the shift away from supply side
subsidies had been the growth of housing allowances.
Factors which underly this development included
the continued acceptance, despite the withdrawal of
building subsidies, of governmental responsibility
for housing costs assistance, especially when the
withdrawal of these subsidies had been accompanied
by movement towards market rents. Such developments
can be seen as marking a shift away from
'institutional' to 'residual' welfare in housing
(Mishra, 1977, 90-1). But this ideological shift has
been almost entirely confined to the rental sectors.
Owner occupiers have continued to benefit from
extensive (and regressive) subsidies. The faults of
housing allowances have already been outlined but
the US experience in particular highlights two key

issues. First, the limited usefulness of demand side subsidies when there is an urgent need to increase lower income housing supply. Second, the failure of such subsidies to bring about more than minimal improvements in housing quality. Yet, without this, governments would be subsidising substandard housing - a course which many (though not Britain) found unacceptable.

The relatively more beneficial treatment of owner occupiers also occurred, though sometimes less clearly, in the case of taxation. (Note that social housing was still the least burdened by taxes, though it had been losing some of its other earlier financial benefits in more recent years). The taxation of property presents the researcher with a complex mass of detail and in this section it was not possible to do more than skim the surface of this topic. It must be added that the extent to which tax benefits are to count as subsidies could be the subject of a whole book on its own - as recent debates on this issue in Britain have shown (30).

Despite the lack of adequate data on the tenurial distribution of and trends in tax benefits, some information was available for certain countries. Thus it has been estimated that in the UK in 1973 social rented (local authority) housing received £1680 million in subsidies, compared with £2,856 million in the case of owner occupation and only £193 million in the case of private renting (Odling-Smee, 1975, 34). Data for the Netherlands is not disaggregated by tenure but it was estimated that in 1975 owner occupiers received about 2,420 million guilders. In contrast rented housing received about 1,100 million guilders, an increasing proportion going to social rented housing (Van Weesep, 1982, 33). In Germany it has been estimated that in 1975 the subsidies per square metre for new social rented housing were about two and a half times as great as those for new private rented housing (and this gap had widened markedly since 1965) (31). In the USA the estimated cost in 1975 of the main federal tax reliefs for owner occupiers was about 8.3 billion dollars compared with 0.65 billion dollars for rented housing. At this date the cost of all direct subsidies for low and moderate income housing (which included units in all main tenures) was 2.1 billion dollars (President of the United States, 1976). By 1978 the cost of home owner deductions and capital gains relief was estimated at 14.3 billion dollars, compared with

reliefs of about 0.8 billion for rental housing and
direct Federal subsidies of 3.6 billion dollars
(US Department of Housing and Urban Development,
1980a, 2-8, 18). A more complete assessment was made
in 1972 when it was estimated that total federal
housing subsidies amounted to 14.3 - 15.3 billion
dollars, of which 6.2 billion dollars related to
home owner tax allowances, 2.5 billion dollars to
federally subsidised housing programmes (which, as
above, did not just involve rented housing), 2.6
billion dollars was accounted for by the housing
element of welfare payments (some of which went to
low income owner occupiers) and 3 - 4 billion
dollars to other tax benefits such as the home
owner capital gains arrangements, accelerated
depreciation for rented housing and so on (US
Department of Housing and Urban Development, 1973,
2-2).

Clearly, this data suffers from a number of
inadequacies. Moreover, to obtain a true picture
the aggregate figures quoted above would need to be
related to the proportion of units or households in
each tenure and the distribution of subsidies by
household income. But such data as there is does
support the conclusion that social rented and, above
all, owner occupied housing has been more heavily
subsidised than private rental housing and that
this characteristic has become more marked over
time.

NOTES

1. The following details are derived from
Magri, 1972; Duclaud-Williams, 1978; Ansidei,
Carassus and Strobel, 1978; Welfeld, 1972 and
Whitbread, 1975; interview material and information
provided by Christian Topalov.
2. From 1963 the Banque's role was limited, it
ceased to have one in 1971. Longer term refinancing
arrangements varied. From 1950 there were two
sources: funds from the Crédit Foncier (funded by
the issue of medium term bonds and longer term
borrowing) and the Treasury. Since 1963 the latter
source has been replaced by a public body financed
by initial capital from the Treasury, a levy on the
commission paid to lenders of medium term finance
and from loan repayments. The aim of disengaging
the state from direct funding of housing is evident.
3. Derived from Magri, 1972.
4. The interest rate was 4.75% for 15 years,
then 6% for 4 years, and 9% for the last 10 years,
(Magri, 1972, 180).
5. Based on statistics from the Crédit Foncier.
6. This section is derived from Socialt
Tidsskrift, 1947; Whitbread, 1975; Ministry of
Housing, 1974, and information provided by Lars
Østergaard.
7. The subsidy details were obtained from
project interviews and in earlier visits to Germany
in the company of Professor Peter Marcuse (who is
preparing a major work on post-war German housing
policy). I am grateful for his assistance with
clarifying the details of the subsidies and also to
Herr Pfeiffer (formerly Ministerial Direktor,
Federal Ministry of Housing, Building and Planning)
for his help over several years on this and many
other issues, as well as Dr. Eberhard Mühlich.
See also Hallett, 1978; Whitbread, 1975; Marcuse,
1981.
8. See the discussion of the calculations
made by Dr. Ulbrich in Chapter 5.
9. The following information is based on
interview material, information supplied by Jan van
der Schaar and Professor Hugo Priemus also van
Weesep, 1982 and Priemus, 1981.
10. In 1967 the share of total subsidies going
to the private rental sector peaked at 30% (from a
low point of 15% in 1965). The share stabilised at
around 10% until the late seventies when there was a
new subsidy (see below) (CBS, monthly, b).

11. The details were complex. Full accounts
are in Priemus, 1981; Floor, 1972 and Emmerich,
1976.
12. Aaron, 1972 provides a useful overview. See
also Harloe, 1978, (part I) and US Department of
Housing and Urban Development, 1973.
13. Post-war developments are reviewed in
National Center for Housing Management, 1973.
14. For the details of this programme see House
Committee on Banking, Currency and Housing, 1975,
205-6; Edson, 1974, 3-6, 31-2; US Department of
Housing and Urban Development, 1976b. For an
overview of rental subsidies in the late seventies
see Striech and Clarke, 1980.
15. For developments in tax subsidies see US
Department of Housing and Urban Development, 1973;
Heinberg, 1971 and National Center for Housing
Management, 1973.
16. For a detailed discussion of this see
National Center for Housing Management, 1973, Ch.
VI, and passim.
17. Developments are reviewed in US Department
of Housing and Urban Development, 1973, chapter 5.
18. For a critical examination of the New York
programmes see Sternlieb, Roistacher and Hughes,
1976 from which the following details are taken.
19. For a detailed account of the various
allowances see Schaufelberger, 1980, 69-100.
20. The details of the scheme are taken from
Der Bundesminister für Raumordnung etc., 1976.
21. These details were provided by Herr Ulrich
Pfeiffer.
22. The development of these allowances is
described in Cullingworth 1977 and 1979, 132-142.
23. The details are taken from Ministerie van
Volkshuisinvesting en Ruimtelijke Ordening, 1977.
24. Information provided by Jan van der Schaar.
25. The magnitude of this assistance can be
seen from an estimate which suggested that in 1972
4.2 billion dollars of welfare payments were used
for housing, 2.6 billion of this was provided by
the Federal government. In comparison the Federal
government spent 2.5 billion dollars on direct
housing subsidies. The range of housing welfare
payments in 1972 was from 16 dollars a month in
the Virgin Islands and 19 dollars a month in
Alabama to 162 dollars per month in Connecticut
(US Department of Housing and Urban Development,
1973, 2-25/7). Other countries also provided
assistance with the housing costs of welfare
claimants but only in the USA, given the lack of a

a general housing allowance, were welfare payments the main means of provision. There is controversy about whether these should be viewed as housing subsidies or as a part of general income maintenance - often they are not included in estimates of the total or distribution of housing subsidies. Nevertheless, they are relevant to questions concerning the effective demand for housing. Lack of time and resources prevented the research project examining the role of welfare benefits.

26. The programme was extensively evaluated, the details here derive from US Department of Housing and Urban Development: Office of Policy Development and Research, 1975, 1976, 1978, and 1980. See also Glatt, 1978; Trutko et. al., 1978; and Carlson and Heinberg, 1978.

27. It was not possible within the scope of the research to adequately explore this topic which has a specialised literature and which few 'housing experts' have a detailed knowledge of. The following account leans heavily on information provided by the project consultants and interviews.

28. The tax position of landlords is reviewed in Nevitt, 1966; House of Commons Environment Committee, 1982, I, xxvii and II, 272-4.

29. For a discussion of the tax benefits for rental and owner occupied housing see Aaron, 1972, 53-72 and US Department of Housing and Urban Development, 1973, chapter 2.

30. See, for example, the discussion in McLennan 1982, 198-9; Kilroy, 1978; and Shelter, 1982, 9-11.

31. The figures derived from the calculations made by Herr Rudi Ulbrich (see chapter 5). It will be recalled that these were based on a series of reasonable assumptions regarding the tax position of landlords, the combination of loan sources etc. The figures referred to here are based on profit making landlords paying a medium tax rate of 40% and on the assumption that there were 35% of profit making landlords in the social rented sector and 85% in the indirectly subsidised sector (non-profit organisations did not pay taxes on their surplus).

Chapter Seven

URBAN RENEWAL AND IMPROVEMENT

For several years after 1945 the problems of the
older housing stock, especially concentrated in the
larger urban centres, took second place to the need
to increase the stock to meet the acute shortage of
accommodation. But from the fifties onwards
attention began to turn to this older stock. At
first governments supported urban renewal - whole-
sale demolition and rebuilding. Particularly in
Europe this often involved the provision of new
social rented housing. In the United States downtown renewal became notorious for its replacement
of low income housing by commercial development and
higher income housing, despite the hope of some
early advocates that it would result in more and
better quality low income accommodation.
    Latterly, in all countries the emphasis
switched to improvement. Many reasons have been
given for this change, including the high costs of
redevelopment and the physical and social
disruption that it often caused, but the
availability of   relatively cheap older housing
suitable or improvement, and conversion to owner
occupation in the process, has also been
significant. Whether this policy has been cheaper
or, in the long run, more effective in producing
satisfactory housing is questionable. Certainly
the switch from redevelopment linked to social
house building to improvement involving
conversion to owner occupation cannot have improved
the position of many of those at the bottom of the
housing market.
    In the rural areas of, for example, the USA
and France there was, as we have noted, a
considerable stock of old, poor quality owner
occupied housing. In most of the six countries the
quality of some of the social rented stock was

giving rise to increasing concern. Nevertheless,
most housing which has been subject to urban
renewal/improvement has been owned by private
landlords. Therefore, the effects on this sector
of such policies have been especially significant.
In this chapter we shall add to the details about
the condition of the private rented stock which
were given in chapter 3, examine the development of
clearance and improvement policies and consider
their impact.

POST WAR TRENDS IN THE QUALITY OF THE PRIVATE
RENTED STOCK

In chapter 3, Table 3.3 showed that most private
rented housing was built before the last war. Only
in West Germany and the USA were there considerable
proportions of newer stock. In France and Britain
much of the stock dated from before the first
world war. Lack of amenities, as Table 3.4 showed,
characterised the sector in all the European
countries. In the USA much of this housing was
located in deteriorating inner city neighbourhoods
and suffered from disrepair.
     Unfortunately, further comparable information
on the condition of the stock and trends in its
quality is not available. In Britain and the USA
relatively detailed surveys of condition and
amenities have been available for some years,
elsewhere additional data is only available on a
more fragmentary basis. This information is often
not available for the private rented sector alone.
     The main French source is an official report
compiled in 1975 (Nora and Eveno, 1975). This
provided policy recommendations which were
incorporated in the subsequent wide ranging reform
of housing policy (which included the moves towards
market level rents and APL discussed previously).
The report showed that, in 1973, 39% of the total
stock lacked basic sanitary facilities-down from
90% in 1954. Most of the change had resulted from
demolition and additions to the stock, not
improvement. 63% of the pre-1949 stock was still
inadequate. About 16 million people lived in this
inadequate housing, 40% of which was in rural areas,
25% in small and medium towns and 35% in the big
cities. 70% of the pre-1949 rural housing was
inadequate and the other main concentration of
poorer property was in the heart of the big cities.
Thus, in central Paris 83% of the stock was built

before 1949 and 59% of this was inadequate. Overall, 72% of the controlled stock was inadequate, in central Paris there were over 300,000 controlled units and about 200,000 were inadequate. The position of the pre-1949 free rental stock was little better, except in the larger cities and even here over 50% was unsatisfactory.

The report linked the poor quality of this housing with the financial position of the dwellings and their occupants. The worst housing was often occupied by aged households, and most old people lived in such housing, together with many young workers. The average per capita income of those in the poorer stock was 20% below the average in the sound stock (after allowing for the preponderance of low income elderly in poor housing compared to the proportion in the better housing).

Stock changes are difficult to trace as data is only available for net losses from the permanent stock (i.e. demolitions, changes to non-residential and holiday use, vacant property and amalgamations of units minus additions). Stock losses had risen, from an annual rate of 104,000 from 1954-62, to 147,000 per annum from 1962-8, and to 195,000 per annum from 1968-73 (Enquête-logement, 1973 (2), 54). In the latter period 23% of the net loss was accounted for by demolition, 23% by changes to non-residential use, 11% by conversion to holiday homes and 43% were left vacant. In the country abandonment had been widespread and was linked to depopulation. At the other extreme in the big cities far more losses resulted from demolition. The increase in vacant housing did not always involve a permanent loss of units from the stock in the towns where many vacancies were caused by the general loosening up of the housing market as new construction had increased supply (Enquête-logement, 1973 (2), 57-58).

Estimates are also available of stock improvements between 1968-73 (permanent dwellings only). Of housing which remained in use throughout this period, about 370,000 units per annum (2.5%) had had some significant improvement. But less progress had been made in the full provision of three 'basic facilities' (running water, a w.c., and a bath or shower). Between 1963-67 about 170,000 units per annum were brought up to full standard (1.2% of the stock and 1.7% of the then defective stock), 200,000 per annum were dealt with between 1967-70 (1.3% of the stock and 2.3% of the then defective stock) but from 1968-72 progress had slowed slightly (195,000 units per annum, 1.2% of the stock and 2.4% of the defective stock) (1).

Danish data is especially sparse. But the number of private rented units remained almost constant between 1960-70. Stock losses almost balanced out new dwellings, the latter being estimated at 50,000 for the decade (a little over 10% of the sector) (2). In the seventies the stock had probably declined more rapidly due to the reduction in new building. So much stock improvement took place simply as a result of the loss of older housing and its replacement by new units - as in France. However, improvement in the older stock had taken place but very slowly, so that, in 1970, about half the privately rented stock still lacked central heating and the sole use of a toilet and bath. The gap between conditions in the privately rented sector and the other two tenures was very marked.

Further information is available as the result of a 1969 act which required larger municipalities to survey the need for slum clearance (Boligministeriet, 1975, 24). Surveys occurred in twenty-four provincial towns and three municipalities in Copenhagen. They showed that 156,000 properties were only suitable for demolition, half of them in Copenhagen. A quarter were in a state which made them liable for closure within five years and half were improvable but not at economic cost. This survey probably over-estimated the need for demolition in the smaller towns and underestimated it in Copenhagen (Boligministeriet, 1975, 25). Allowing for the rural areas and the smaller towns it was suggested that in fact about 200,000 units were ripe for clearance, about 40,000 within five years, 60,000 later and 100,000 because of their lack of improvability at reasonable cost. As most social housing was relatively new, even allowing for rural low income owner occupation, a considerable proportion of the private rental stock of just under half a million dwellings must have been unfit.

Up to the late seventies progress was slow, though accelerating. About 700 dwellings per annum were affected by urban renewal schemes in the late sixties, rising to about 2,300 units per annum by 1972/3. Taking one year with another this rate was maintained up to 1977. More than 90% of these units were in Copenhagen (Boligministeriet, 1977, 22).

Urban Renewal and Improvement

In addition there were about 10,000 demolitions per
year by 1977. The overall rate of improvement was
not known, although about 1500-2000 rented dwellings
were being renovated by urban renewal companies
every year. Only about 500 of these were privately
rented (3).

In 1972 about 17% of the West German stock
dated from 1900 or earlier, this housing was
concentrated in the mediaeval centres of smaller
cities (Der Bundesminister für Raumordnung etc.
1975, 16) (4). There was a higher concentration of
1901-48 property in larger towns, much of it
consisting of high density flats - seen also, for
example, in Copenhagen. A good deal of this stock
required modernisation or demolition but a
considerable part of the 1945-60 stock was also
substandard. This was partly a legacy of the need
to build cheaply during the immediate post war
emergency. Overall only 42% of the stock (8.7
million units) were adequate i.e. had a bath, inside
w.c. and central heating. 11.9 million units needed
improvement, 36% only lacked central heating, 7%
had no bath but an internal w.c., 6% had no bath
and only an outside w.c. and 3% lacked a kitchen.
Lack of facilities was slightly more common in the
largest towns. Most serious deficiencies were in
the private rented sector. Over one million of
these units lacked a bath but had an internal w.c.
and another million had no bath and an external
w.c. In all it was estimated that 7 million
defective units could be modernised, the rest should
be demolished. Demolitions had risen from about
0.1% of the stock in 1953, understandably low
because of the severe shortage of housing, to over
0.2% in 1963-7 but declined again in the late
sixties (Ballerstedt and Glatzer, 1975, 163). So
even by this time progress with the problem was
slow.

More recent statistics were not available at
the time of the research but a 1972 survey did ask
whether improvement had occurred or was likely to
begin in the next three years (Der Bundesminister
für Raumordnung etc., 1975, 18-19). About 10% of
the stock fell into this category. Over 40% of
actual and proposed improvements were in post war
housing, almost three quarters of these involved
the installation of central heating, alone or with
other facilities. The best estimates suggested that
by the late seventies 250-300,000 units were being
improved per year. Most of these were probably
owner occupied, improvement of the older stock,

especially that owned by individual landlords, was
much slower. Moreover, losses by demolition were
still very low. In 1965 there were 4.51 million pre
1948 privately rented units, this had only reduced
to 4.31 million by 1976, an average loss of about
20,000 per annum (and some of these were sold off
to owner occupiers) (DIW, 1976, 371). Interestingly,
there was a far faster reduction in an 'other
rented' category (including by virtue of employment,
charitable and rent free housing). A substantial
part of this reduction was probably due to tenure
change, mainly the transfer of employer provided
units.

Britain started mass demolition in the mid-
fifties and then moved to improvement, in the mid-
sixties, more rapidly than the other European
countries. There was relatively good data on stock
changes and condition. In England and Wales from
1914 to 1975 approximately 1.5 million units were
lost from the private rented sector via demolitions
and change of use, over half this total was lost
between 1960 and 1975, the product of the active
slum clearance policy (Department of the
Environment, 1977a, 39). Since 1967 successive house
condition surveys had measured changes in the
quality of the private rented sector in England
(Department of the Environment, 1977c, 87-157;
1978b). They assessed disrepair, unfitness and lack
of amenities. In 1967 a total of 1.8 million
dwellings were unfit - far more than had been
expected. Of these 60% were the residual category
'other tenures' (mainly private rented). This
amounted to about a third of the private rented
stock. About half this sector lacked one or more of
four basic amenities (internal w.c., fixed bath,
wash basin and hot and cold water at three points).
This was almost one half the total number of
properties lacking amenities. While most defective
housing in the other tenures only required minor
repairs, almost one third of the private rented
stock needed major work costing £500 or over at 1967
prices. This amounted to three fifths of all stock
needing such extensive repairs. So the problem of
defective housing was heavily concentrated in
the private rented sector, although this tenure only
comprised about a fifth of the total stock.

The 1971 survey showed that fitness had
improved considerably. Yet about half the unfit units
were still privately rented, this amounted to about
a quarter of the stock in this tenure. There had
also been an improvement in facilities, but 40% of

the sector was still deficient and a third still
required major repair. Thus poor housing was still
highly concentrated in the private rented sector,
which now only accounted for about a sixth of the
total stock. The 1976 survey showed a further large
fall in unfit properties, to about 800,000. About
40% of these were privately rented, of all the
dwellings in this sector 15% were unfit. A quarter
of the private rented stock lacked one or more of
the basic amenities and about a third required
major repair (a little more than in 1971). The
private rented sector now accounted for about an
eighth of the whole housing stock.

The 1976 survey was accompanied by a social
survey of occupants (Department of the Environment,
1979). It concluded that about 2.6 million households, 16% of the total, lived in housing which
required repairs, improvements or both. Over half
of these units were rented, one million from
private landlords and half a million in the social
sector (which was beginning to develop a significant
proportion of poorer housing). 12% of owner
occupied units but 41% of privately rented dwellings
were in need of rehabilitation and, even allowing
for the differential age of properties in the two
sectors, the latter were in poorer condition than
the former and were more costly to put right.

As in France, there was a concentration of
low income households in the poorer housing, about
half were elderly and retired. Rehabilitation
activity was low (probably lower than before due to
the economic crisis). Even in the owner occupied
sector only 10% of properties which required major
repair or improvement were dealt with in the
previous year. In the private rented sector the
percentage was even less. Given the low incomes of
those in poorer housing, many simply could not
afford the costs involved, even with the aid of
government grants. Also many did not realise the
need for repairs and improvement. About 560,000
privately rented dwellings needed work done and
appeared to be eligible for government assistance
but few landlords had taken up this opportunity.
Also many tenants (especially the elderly) were
unwilling to tolerate the disturbance which would
be caused by major works.

According to the 1976 survey, the decline in
unfit property in the private rented sector mainly
resulted from demolition (75% of all units
demolished between 1971-76 were in the private
rented sector) and transfers to other sectors

(mainly owner occupation and sales to local
authorities and housing associations, for
improvement and reletting as social housing). These
factors had also affected the rate of reduction in
the other two indices of inadequacy.

As elsewhere, only a very few houses had
been demolished immediately ai er 1945. In the
fifties an average of 50,000 units a year were
demolished, but numbers rose towards the end of
the decade, as new policy made an impact. In the
sixties the rate of demolitions rose sharply to
average about 94,000 per annum and in 1971 it peaked
at almost 100,000. Later, partly due to the
reduction in the 'backlog' of slums but also
because of the growth of improvement, the rate
fell back to the level of the fifties (Department
of the Environment, 1977a, 23, quarterly). No good
statistics existed on improvement trends in the
private rented stock but an indicator which suggests
that landlords' willingness to improve might have
declined as the economics of the sector worsened
is contained in the figures for take up of the main
government improvement grant scheme. These show
that the proportion of grants utilised by private
landlords fell from about 25% in 1966 to about 15%
in 1974, though, given the declining size of the
sector, this is hardly conclusive evidence
(Department of the Environment, quarterly).

In 1975 a house condition survey was carried
out in the Netherlands (Central Directie van de
Volkshuisinvesting, 1975). This showed that
16.5% of all rented property was in a poor state
of maintenance compared with 7% of the owner
occupied stock. Poorer property was highly
concentrated in larger cities and, naturally,
among older units. As elsewhere, the main problem
was in the areas of older working class property
near the centres of these cities. Since 1945 stock
losses had been at low levels, they increased
slowly up to 1971, then declined again (CBS,
monthly, b) (5). Given the continuing housing
shortage and the need to increase the stock these
figures are not surprising recalling what happened
elsewhere, e.g. in Germany. Houses leaving the
stock averaged over 70 years old although only
about one third of the more recent years' losses
were of dilapidated properties. But many more must
have been nearing the end of their useful life
(without major rehabilitation) as 85-90% of all
houses withdrawn in the mid seventies were built
before 1925. Most of these were privately rented.

Urban Renewal and Improvement

There was little information on the extent of recent improvement activity. But some figures suggested that, starting in the late sixties, about 90% of all pre-war social rented units had been improved by 1977 and that, from 1974, modernisation of the post war part of this stock had begun (6). But far less had been done by private landlords and 85-95% of government improvement grants had gone to owner occupiers. In 1977, 22,000 social rented units were improved (10,000 built pre-war). 50,000 privately owned units were improved, of these privately rented units only accounted for 1000-1500, although many more landlords carried out some work without government assistance and in a piecemeal way. (In 1966 research showed that only 13% of the costs of improvement were officially known about through various records. However, few landlords of the older and most deficient properties spent much.)

As we have said, the physical condition of the private rental sector in the USA seemed similar to that of the owner occupied sector. But disaggregated data showed a rather different picture (US Bureau of the Census etc., 1978). First, despite the low percentage of inadequate housing, there were in 1976 still nearly six million households in such units. Second, although the percentage of inadequate housing was higher in rural than in urban areas, the majority of such units were in the cities. Third, between 1974 and 1976 inadequacy declined in rural areas but increased in urban areas. Fourth, while only one third of all metropolitan housing was in the centre cities, nearly half of all the inadequate urban housing was in these areas. These urban conditions were a consequence of the declining purchasing power and declining public resources in such areas available to deal with the situation. But the most important development was the accelerating neighbourhood dereliction which had occurred in many centre cities. This was on a scale and of a severity unlike anything experienced in the other five countries. Large areas contained block after block of abandoned burnt out and wrecked buildings, interspersed with a few inhabited buildings whose occupants' physical safety, in such a neighbourhood, was often extremely precarious.

The Annual Housing Survey collected details of residents' evaluation of their localities and this decline is clearly documented. For example, in 1974, 11.8% of tenant households in centre cities

reported that abandonment was a problem, by 1977
13.5% reported this problem (US Bureau of Census
etc., 1976, 1979b). Things were far worse for those
in the most vulnerable position. For example, in
1977 24.2% of black tenant households in central
cities reported that there were abandoned buildings
in their neighbourhood. Other important deficiencies
which were especially marked in urban areas
included high levels of crime, disruption and noise
from traffic and lack of neighbourhood services -
especially police, public transport, shops and
health facilities. This was reflected in the fact
that in 1977 almost 90% of owner occupiers, but
only 70% of tenants, felt that they lived in 'good'
or 'excellent' neighbourhoods. Overall, about twice
the percentage of tenants compared with owner
occupiers wanted to move because of neighbourhood
conditions. But the clearest indicator of worsening
conditions was that between 1974 and 1977 there was
a two-fold increase in the numbers of households
who wished to move because of adverse neighbourhood
conditions.

As noted in chapter 3 there was an accelerating
loss of rental housing in the sixties and seventies,
especially in the central cities. Partly this was
caused by urban renewal, particularly in the sixties,
but latterly the collapse of the lower income
rental market, as manifested by abandonment, became
important. The 1976 Annual Housing Survey found that
about two and a half million units had left the
stock since 1973, 60% of these were in the rented
sector (in the SMSAs about 70% and in the centre
cities about 80%). About 70% of the losses were in
pre-1939 housing, so substantial numbers of more
recently built units were lost. Much of this stock
housed low income households, the 1973 median
income of the tenant households that had occupied
the lost units was only $ 5200 compared with the
median for all tenants of $ 7200 (US Bureau of the
Census etc., 1978).

Although the Annual Housing Surveys collected
data on past and proposed improvements in the owner
occupied stock, the same questions could obviously
not be asked of tenants. But data on expenditure
on maintenance, repairs and improvements for 1969
and 1976 is roughly divisible into expenditure by
owner occupiers and by landlords (US Department of
Housing and Urban Development, 1977, 289). These
show that the rates of increase in such expenditure
were rather similar for the two tenures. But most
expenditure on rental housing (63% in 1976) was for

230

maintenance and repair while in the case of the
owner occupied housing it was mainly for
improvement (73% in 1976). This data has several
deficiencies, for example it does not report on
maintenance done by owners themselves, rented
property - because of its tenure and building type
- probably needed more maintenance, and units in
the two sectors had different age profiles. But
clearly improvement, as elsewhere, was far more
common in the owner occupied stock. And the data
suggests that the economic difficulties of the
seventies might have been having an especially
severe effect on the rented sector. Between 1975
and 1976 total expenditure on owner occupied
housing increased by about $ 3.2 billion but in
rental housing under $ 0.3 billion. Moreover,
improvement expenditure fell by $0.4 billion in
this tenure, compared with a rise of $ 2.5 billion
in the owner occupied sector.

URBAN RENEWAL AND IMPROVEMENT POLICIES

So the heart of the problem of the older stock lay
in the private rented sector, or, to put it another
way, one of the most serious problems for tenants
and landlords was the condition of the property in
which they both had an interest. Moreover, progress
in dealing with this problem had, in most countries,
been slow and had often been as a result of
demolition rather than improvement and repairs. A
principal reason for this was the lack of resources
- although resistance to disruption, especially by
the elderly, was also probably significant. The
economic decline in the seventies may have been
reducing the progress, slow though it was, that had
begun to be made in the previous decade. Yet during
these years governments had 'discovered' the
problem of older housing and, in some cases, made
considerable policy innovations in an effort to
deal with it. We now examine the nature and
limitations of these policies.
     As we saw in chapter one, the assumption in the
nineteenth century of responsibility for ensuring
minimum standards of safety and sanitation, marked
the first tentative step towards the adoption of
wider housing policies. But these powers had a very
limited impact, usually only providing means for
enforcing the closure and/or demolition of unfit
properties.
     In France this tradition was still evident.
Local authorities had powers to control bad housing

but until the seventies there had been little
official concern for improvement. The state had
encouraged some privately financed renewal, with
controversial political, economic and social
consequences, especially in Paris where in 1963 a
policy of employment dispersal was reversed and a
decision taken to build up the city as a tertiary
centre. This resulted in large scale urban renewal
and the demolition of working class housing in the
city centre (Castells, 1978, 93-125). Those
displaced were mainly relocated at the periphery,
often on unpopular large estates of HLM housing.
Many were forced to find a new job or to commute
long distances to work. The redevelopment of central
Paris greatly enhanced land values and excluded a
wide range of income groups from living there. The
local authorities had insufficient resources to
play a major role in renewal, which - insofar as it
involved new housing - had normally been for upper
income groups. Ineffective controls on land use and
speculation had accentuated these problems. Very
little land was owned by the local authorities and
they had had little control over the density of new
building. Prices of new property were very high
and land costs rose sharply in the later sixties
and seventies. In 1976 an average sized unit with
an área of 100 square metres had cost from about
580,000 francs in Paris to about 315,000 francs in
the provinces (Ansidei, Carassus and Stroebel, 1978,
21-3) (7).
There had been little government aid for
improvement and the 1948 act had only had a limited
impact. As already pointed out, AL had gone mainly
to occupants of newer housing rather than helping
tenants to afford the rents of improved units. The
main government initiative had been the
establishment of the Agence Nationale pour
l'Amélioration de l'Habitat (ANAH) which replaced
an agency set up immediately after the war (8).
The earlier agency's funds came from a 5% tax on
controlled rents, paid by the landlord. This was a
very limited source of money and the agency was only
able to provide cheap loans for repairs and
improvement to the controlled stock at a rate of
about 10-20,000 units a year. In the late fifties
the incentives to improve and so obtain higher rents
were introduced and a tax deduction for improvement
expenditure began in 1966. At this time some
experiments in area improvement also occurred.
ANAH was set up in 1970. It benefitted from a

3.5% on the rents of all pre-1949 property. This
allowed operations to expand a little. As the 1975
report pointed out, there were no controls on the
rents of these improved units and no account taken
of the social and financial position of tenants.
Generally improvement had been carried out with
the landlords' own capital or with commercial loans.
These were usually of 3-5 years duration, except
in the case of major reconstruction. Longer term
loans were used by developers who brought up blocks
of property, removed the tenants and sold off
modernised units to owner occupiers. Many of the
tenants had suffered in the course of such
improvement. Except in the controlled stock,
security of tenure was normally limited to the
length of the existing contract. So possession could
eventually be gained. Moreover, even when tenants
were protected, there had been harrassment and
illegal eviction. Anyway, the new rents were often
beyond the means of the original tenants. In the
larger cities some poorer tenants were pushed out
into unimproved property. This 'gentrification' had
had far reaching effects on the social composition
of inner city areas. Moreover, there was an absence
of organisations (especially local authorities)
able to control these changes. (9)

Uncertainties also surrounded the rules for
compensation for acquired property and there had
often been insufficient funds for matters such as
relocation. Techniques and procedures more suitable
for greenfield development had often been applied
in the very different circumstances of inner city
areas and the social consequences were ignored.
The tax deductions for landlords (see chapter 6)
had several disadvantages. First, the costs of
changes in the shape and size of rooms were not
deductible, but these were often required. Second,
the 25% fixed deduction gave least help to owners
of the worst property with the lowest rents and
gave most to those who owned the better units.
Third, the receipt of this benefit was not linked
to a requirement that improvement be carried out.
Subsidies had simply added to speculative profits,
it had been easy to obtain tax and other benefits
and then sell off the improved property shortly
afterwards.

Few loans had been available for improvement
from the public lending bodies which had
concentrated on new housing. Banks were reluctant
to lend on older property and landlords' own means
- especially of those owning the poorest property -

had been too limited. Much of the improvement
funded by ANAH or other sources benefitted the less
inadequate post war property. Even in 1973 three
times as much was spent on new building as on
improvement. In 1975 only about 4% of improvement
expenditure (700 million francs) came from public
funds. The 1975 report listed eight sources of
official aid, most of them very small scale.

The 1975 report aimed to change all this. Its
proposals were a part of the government's strategy
of concentrating public assistance on the older
stock and on those in the greatest need while
moving to market level rents and limiting public
expenditure on housing. The report stated that
French housing policy was centralised and
inflexible. It focused on new building and was
insensitive to the social and economic patterns in
inner city areas. Policy should be more coherent
and flexible and local authorities needed new
powers. Detailed proposals covered these points,
proposing new roles for the regions, departments
and communes. Programmes for the treatment of older
areas were to be drawn up and there was to be
smaller scale, better co-ordinated and more flexible
action which was more sensitive to local residents'
needs than hitherto. Contractual agreements were
to be made with owners enabling assisted improvement
to occur under controlled conditions. Properties
could also be taken over for a limited period and
improved by publicly based improvement agencies.
This might be especially useful for the poorer
landlords. In some cases compulsory takeover might
be necessary and when costs were so high that they
could not be regained from rents during the period
of a limited takeover compulsory acquisition might
occur.

The improved units were to be let at market
rents, APL providing assistance when required.
'Aide à la pierre' might also be needed when the
prospect of increased rents did not induce landlords to co-operate, for some of the badly run down
controlled property and in areas where market
rents were depressed. In cases where APL was not
yet available, funds from ANAH would be supplied
according to revised rules. Similar procedures
would operate in rural areas. Standards and
allowable costs would be set locally but guided by
national rules. Allocation of funds to the regions
would be centrally determined but detailed
allocation would be dealt with by lower levels of
government.

State aid, including APL, would be made
available on the basis of contracts between the
central agencies and the localities. These would
specify the objectives, means and intended results
of improvement. To finance this a tax on all non-
public housing was suggested. The 25% deduction
would be cut to 20%, thus further increasing funds,
and other changes would be made to re-
distribute subsidies, including changes in the
deductability of owner occupiers' interest charges.
     These proposals, together with contemporaneous
ones on housing finance, were wide ranging and
politically controversial(10). But many of them
were adopted in the late seventies. (The policy
should also be seen in the context of the strategy
contained in the Seventh National Plan to shift
resources from housing to industry). In the first
place higher rents plus APL were being introduced
to the HLM sector, later these were to be extended
to the para-public sector and then to other larger
landlords.
     But, according to experts interviewed in 1978,
it was doubtful whether the new system would ever
appeal to smaller, especially elderly, landlords.
In fact 'pure' privately rented units were only to
join the new system when their improvement was
required. The proposal that rents would be freely
set, only being controlled during the relatively
short period of the contract between the authorities
and landlords, led the tenants' associations to see
the whole policy as a landlords' charter, without
any obvious benefits to tenants who, while they
might have improved housing, would pay far higher
rents. Important matters such as how to control
levels of charges in the modernised property had
been ignored.
     In general it must be doubted whether the new
schemes would ever be effectively extended to the
pre-1949 units most in need of improvement. The
large scale improvements envisaged (covering perhaps
150 units) using modern, technological solutions,
are most appropriate for blocks of company owned
flats rather than for the more fragmented,
individual holdings which predominated in the older
housing. The higher rents might simply push
better off tenants into owner occupation while
excluding those at the bottom end of the market
from better housing because, even with APL, the
percentage of income they would be expected to pay
would be too high (assuming that there would be an
upper limit on the proportion of the new rents

covered by APL).

The first Danish slum clearance legislation
dates from 1939 (11). Local authority health
committees were were established with powers to
inspect dwellings and make closure orders. At the
time of the research these committees, who did
little before the 1950s, had powers to abate overcrowding and could set future dates for closure of
between six months and twenty years. If closure was
delayed more than six years landlords could be
compelled to right defects but not if the cost was
more than 20% of the annual rent, this was a very
limiting condition. The 1939 law provided cheap
loans covering 75% of the cost to the localities
of acquisition and demolition and central
government met 20% of any loss that they incurred.
In 1941 favourable state loans were introduced for
building new rental housing in clearance areas,
100% acquisition loans became available and the
deficit grant was raised to 50%.

Immediately after the war it was estimated
that 100-125,000 dwellings needed clearance, about
65,000 in Copenhagen (Indenrigsministeriet, 1945).
However, little action occurred. A 1959 law
allowed guilds of landlords to carry out improvement
in conjunction with local authority redevelopment.
Losses were met by the central and local government.
But no help was given to individual landlords.
Again little happened, so in 1969 three slum
clearance companies were established, two for
social housing and one, a private company, run,
like the Landlords' Investment Fund, in conjunction
with the Landlords' Federation.

The 1969 Act increased the availability of
state loans. These were further increased in 1971,
and about a quarter of the available funds were
given as grants. Much of the older rented stock in
the cities consisted of the type of high density
late nineteenth and early twentieth century workers
flats found in several European countries, such
as Germany. The flats surrounded courtyards
containing commercial premises, these had to be
removed if improvement was to occur. The 1969 Act
provided special loans for this purpose. If the cost
of works was greater than the enhanced value of
the properties concerned a deficit grant was
available. However, progress was slow and, as in
France, the greatest obstacle was the cost of
works which often neither the tenants nor the
landlord could afford. One reason why subsidies had
been restricted was the political objection to

subsidies for private landlords. In fact only the
social rented renewal company (there was only one by
1978) could afford to redevelop, the landlords'
company was limited to small scale improvement
schemes.

Some improvement loans had been available for
many years from the mortgage credit institutions.
The normal loan was 75% of the costs, repayable
over 20 years (provided that the value of the
property was increased by at least 15%, if this was
not so less was available for a shorter period).
As an added incentive, for a short period up to the
end of 1980, more generous terms were available.
A less significant source of funds has been the
Landlords' Investment Fund. It accumulated about
a billion kroner during the life of the 1966
housing pact from the compulsory payments to it of
half the rent rises during this period (a low rate
of interest was paid on these 'deposits'). Loans
of up to 90% of the costs of major improvements at
the advantageous rate of 6.5% were available.
After 15 years the money in the Fund was to be
repaid (over a 20 year period). In fact relatively
few loans were made. The main reason for this was
thought to be the fact that rent rises were
limited to 6.5%. Given the lack of an immediate
financial benefit, the prospect of enhanced capital
values evidently did not attract much interest.
In the late seventies new fire regulations for
older properties faced many landlords with heavy
capital costs and the Fund devoted all its resources
to assisting them. It was then agreed that the Fund
should be repaid more quickly.

A combination of reasons lay behind the
introduction of improvement grants in the second
world war but, with the rejection of direct subsidies
for private renting after the war and the stress on
new building, a new grant scheme was not introduced
until 1975 and then only as a temporary measure to
ease unemployment. 25% grants were available
for the repair and maintenance of pre-1963 property
and could be obtained by tenants or landlords (and
owner occupiers). Tenants did not have to pay a
higher rent for their own improvements but the rent
could be raised on re-letting. Grants could not
exceed 2000 kr per unit for landlords and 3000 kr
for tenants. Tenants had to be compensated when
leaving on a ten year write off basis.

In 1976 grants were restricted to energy
saving measures, and later to use by landlords. By
the late seventies this was the only form of

improvement grant and had been little used. A 1977 study showed that 70% of grant money had been used for energy saving, 72% had gone to owner occupiers and only 28% to landlords, including the social sector. The schemes were centrally funded but administered by the localities who had considerable discretion to set costs and distribute aid.

There were of course also the normal tax reliefs and, in the controlled areas, provisions relating to the repair and improvement of property. As elsewhere, the failure of landlords to repair their properties was one of the main complaints of tenants' representatives, the evasion of regulations setting out the proportion of rent to be spent on this was a major problem for the Rent Boards. Much of the responsibility for ensuring compliance rested with the tenants through their scrutiny of budgets. Rent Boards could reduce rents until repairs were done and local authorities had enforcement powers. But local authorities carried out few systematic and regular inspections, and both bodies usually only reacted to tenant complaints.

Rent increases after works had been carried out were largely a matter for negotiation between landlords and tenants except in the controlled areas. In these areas rents could not be increased after repairs. In principle landlords could recover improvement costs (less any grant received). tenants often asked landlords to carry out improvements. If so the tenants had to propose how they would be financed, i.e. agree to rent increases. In other cases tenants could object to the proposed new rents and ask for a Rent Board decision. If the proposed increase was over 25% landlords had to go to the Boards anyway, unless they had the tenants' acquiescence. A representative of the Copenhagen Rent Board pointed out that these rules did not provide much incentive to landlords who wished to increase current income but were more attractive to those who wanted to improve capital values. According to the Landlords' Association and others, private rented sector improvement was at a very low level. Only the institutional investors, who took a longer view, were involved on any scale in upgrading their property.

The activities of the landlords' improvement company, faced several difficulties, apart from limited finance (in the late seventies 90 m kr was available annually to the two companies (50 million kr in interest free loans, the rest as grants). The loans were used during building, they then had to be refinanced at market rates (about 16% at this time). The new rents were determined by the government and did not cover costs, the gap was filled by an income related tenants' subsidy. In the first year the entire difference between the old and the new rents payable could be subsidised, provided that the former was 2000 kr or more per month. The subsidy was progressively withdrawn over 5-10 years. But low income tenants might still be pushed out as the withdrawal took place, so the control of improvement costs was vital. In some Copenhagen blocks being rehabilitated in 1978 rents were expected to increase by 3-700%. The company reckoned that the tenants formerly paid 7-10% of their incomes in rents, after improvement, even with the subsidy, they would pay 15-20%. Increases were especially large in some of the city's eighteenth century buildings where rehabilitation costs could exceed rebuilding costs by 50%.

Tenants often preferred to be rehoused. The companies had to offer rehousing which was suited to tenants' incomes and family sizes. Non-profit organisations had to make 20% of their vacancies and some new units available for rehousing from property affected by works. The landlords were not so obliged but their Federation had suggested that they should agree to make a contribution to avoid possible legislation. In some cases, the landlords' company and the municipalities were carrying out minimal works, hoping that later tenants would carry out further improvements.

In Germany there was an early history of controls on urban development (by the extension of police powers) and in 1875 Prussia passed a building bye-law to regulate the rapid urban growth then occurring. Similar measures were later adopted throughout most of the country. But there was no unified system of urban development controls until the 1960 Federal Building Law (12). This limited measure included provisions governing compulsory purchase but left the formulation of detailed building ordinances to the Lander. The Law covered the control of development via building permits, the appropriation of property at market value in certain cases and so on. But these measures were inadequate in areas where large scale works were needed. So the 1971 Urban Development Act provided powers for the local authorities to draw up plans which had to be discussed with the inhabitants of the areas concerned. Normally, the authorities carried out basic and infrastructural works but the treatment of individual properties was the responsibility of their owners, although compulsory powers could sometimes be used. There were powers to recoup the betterment caused by public expenditure and price controls prevented this being recouped via private sales before the government benefitted. Other provisions dealt with matters such as demolition. Finally, the authorities had to resell acquired properties unless they were definitely required for public purposes.

Assistance for modernisation was first made nationally available in 1974, previously the Lander provided cheap loans on a small scale (13). The various measures noted above had been used for some inner city redevelopment but had been rather unattractive to private owners because of the time and money involved in their application. From 1974-1978 300 million Dm per annum were spent by the Federal and state governments on improvement The aim was to concentrate funds in 'key modernisation areas' which had to contain a preponderance of defective units, have a lack of modernisation activity, and be, to a great extent, inhabited by people 'who are generally unable to obtain adequate living space of a suitable quality'. So the measures were initially aimed at improving conditions for low income tenants.

Assistance was available to landlords (and low income owner occupiers) provided that they carried out essential repairs (which could sometimes qualify for subsidy), that the improvements were 'essential', and that the new rents did not exceed by more than 20% the limits for comparable social units. Normally grant aided costs could not exceed 25.000 Dm. A grant equivalent to 7.2% of costs was paid for three years, then 4.8% for the next three years and 2.4% for the last three years. This is equivalent to 43.2% of costs. Landlords normally had to meet 15% of costs themselves.

Tenants could formerly object to modernisation on grounds of 'undue hardship' (disputes being settled by the courts) but the 1974 legislation reduced these rights. They could not apply for grants. During the period of grant payments land-lords had to subtract the sums received from the legally payable rent. Until 1978 landlords could increase rents by up to 14% of modernisation costs

(less the subsidy). But then the figure was reduced
to 11% (a quid pro quo for new tax concessions
on energy saving improvements, a subsidy which was
not passed on in reduced rents). If landlords
thought that an 11% increase was too low they could
have the rent determined through the normal rent
fixing procedure. By the late seventies it was
thought that 60-70,000 assisted improvements per
annum were occurring.

In addition Land programmes for subsidising
modernisation (and maintenance) still existed.
These usually took the form of cheap loans,
eligibility was restricted to those with low
incomes. Modernisation was also financed by the
saving for building scheme and tax concessions. As
already mentioned in chapter 6 maintenance
expenditure could be deducted from annual income
and deductions for large expenditures could be
spread over 2-5 years. Modernisation costs could be
written off over 10 years (but landlords could
still only depreciate the building's original cost
at 2% per annum, while, since 1977, owner occupiers
who acquired an old property could depreciate it
much faster). The tax reliefs were most helpful to
higher income landlords. But much of older property
was owned by low to moderate income landlords who
paid little tax. Also the owner occupier tax
benefits were probably stimulating the
gentrification which was beginning to occur in the
more attractive inner city areas.

Earlier urban redevelopment had proved costly,
slow and was often politically controversial and
socially disruptive (Konukiewitz and Wollman, 1982,
101-3). Extensive protests had occurred in some of
the big cities such as Frankfurt. The growing
emphasis on rehabilitation was a response to these
problems and an attempt to improve conditions in
inner cities at a time when the output of new
housing was beginning to decline. The aim was to
focus resources on the selected areas in order to
achieve results within five years, but without
forcing the original population out. Improvement of
private rented units was a key objective as this
sector contained some of the worst property which
was beginning to be unlettable because of its
condition.

The difficulties encountered included the low
income of landlords and the complexities of ownership (15% of pre-1919 multi-family houses were, in
1972, owned by 'communities of heirs' (Der
Bundesminister für Raumordnung etc., 1975, 12)).

Also elderly landlords were often not willing or
able to get involved in complex works. Often as
elsewhere, improvement was privately agreed between
tenants and landlords and carried out to their own
unofficial standards. Because of a failure to make
a major impression on the living conditions of
poorer tenants and other reasons, the government
soon began to stress the objective of improving
the physical nature of the areas. Even this proved
difficult, so from 1977 half the funds were made
available for scattered improvement. Tenants
objected to their lack of control over improvement
and the very steep rises which occurred in some,
previously low, rents. Some modernisation resulted
in increased rents without the unit being promoted
to a higher quality category so becoming eligible
for an increased rent allowance. Other problems
included the lack of assistance to the local
authorities for environmental improvements.
      In consequence private landlords had not used
as much of the funds as hoped. So the social housing
organisations had used the surplus on their own
older stock (but not apparently to buy up private
rented property and renovate it). Research (by the
Institut für Wohnen und Umwelt at Darmstadt) had
shown that there were several types of older
housing areas (14). First, areas of poor mainly
inner city housing whose landlords were 'sweating'
the stock by letting it at high rents to those
who had little alternative, such as newcomers and
foreign workers. Second, areas of property owned by
elderly, poorer landlords and inhabited by low
income tenants. Neither type of landlords was
interested in the government scheme, for obvious
reasons. Third, areas where gentrification was
occurring, here little assistance was required to
bring about improvement. Landlords here did not
want subsidies because of the restrictions that
were involved. Fourth, areas of property in good
repair needing little work. Landlords made modest
profits, had been in business for many years and
had settled tenants. They might only own one or
two houses and often regarded their ownership as
a hobby or as a capital asset for old age. There
were large areas like this and some of these owners
might well be attracted by government aid. Finally
there were areas with good environment and
architecture. Tenants were well off and often
carried out their own modernisation, the landlords
only increasing the rents when they left (although
there were some problems because tenants were not

entitled to compensation). The research concluded
that policy needed to recognise these differing
situations but that the existing policy only
appealed to some landlords in the fourth type of
area and not to those in the second type at which
it was originally aimed.

A federal official broadly agreed with this
conclusion but stated that the grants were only
intended for use in less difficult cases. The urban
renewal laws were for use in the harder areas but
it had been difficult to get the states and
localities to move from rebuilding to
rehabilitation, except in a few places such as
Berlin and Hamburg. Landlords' representatives
thought that the modernisation subsidies were
inadequate. They should be concentrated on the
poorer landlords, others should get more help
through the tax system. It was clear that, despite
the increasing funds for improvement, the poorest
property in the poorest areas was hardly being
touched and other options, such as takeover by the
social housing organisations, were not considered
feasible, and were certainly not favoured by most
of these bodies.

In Britain the first national attempt at the
slum clearance programme began in the 1930s when
subsidies were made available for building local
authority housing for people from slum clearance
areas. This programme ended in 1939 (15).

In 1949 the first steps were taken to
encourage improvement with grants of up to 50% of
the cost of bringing properties up to a standard
which provided for 30 years of life (subject to a
maximum amount) (16). In 1959 a lower grant also
became available for installing five standard
amenities where these were lacking. For various
reasons, such as their complexity and low value,
these schemes were little used. But slum clearance
restarted in the fifties. In 1956 council housing
subsidies were almost entirely restricted to
building in conjunction with slum clearance. This
was partly responsible for an upsurge in
clearance in the sixties. Other factors included
the growth of commercial and civic redevelopment of
town centres, urban road construction and other
public works. Not all demolished housing was unfit
and/or privately rented but the impact on both
these categories was considerable. As elsewhere,
the social and physical effects and the costs of
this clearance were often criticised. In the mid

sixties the first official and comprehensive
examination of the older housing stock concluded
that much of this housing should be improved not
demolished.

The 1969 Housing Act introduced the new policy.
It attempted to obtain concentrated, area based
improvement. This idea had been tried since 1964
but the powers available to the local authorities
were weak. Now 'general improvement areas' (GIAs)
were to be declared. The authorities had some
powers to acquire land and carry out works but their
main role was to plan and provide grants. A small
sum was also available for environmental works.
More generous grants were provided but it was hoped
that the declaration of GIAs, and hence their
protection from demolition, would increase owners'
confidence and encourage them to improve their
properties. Other powers in the act enabled local
authorities to regulate and improve conditions in
the many rented houses in multiple occupation in
large cities such as Birmingham and London which
accommodated, among others, newly arrived black and
Irish immigrants. An important part of the act,
mentioned in chapter 5, enabled controlled
properties to be converted to regulated lettings
by improving them. But low income tenants could
object and the courts were bound to uphold this.

Grant levels were increased in 1971 and in
areas with high umemployment 75% of costs rather
than 50% could be met. This, together with the
scrapping of some of the more restrictive controls
on the grants, led to an upsurge in activity. At
the same time the housing associations, with strong
government support, were beginning to expand, many
of them specialising in improving older, ex-private
rented property in the inner cities. After 1974,
when they were given a very generous subsidy, their
activities expanded still faster. Their units were
let at 'fair' rents. This was only possible because
of their non-profit nature and the subsidy. Local
authorities also began to 'municipalise' housing
in the mid seventies, encouraged by the Labour
government who for a time saw this as the long
term answer to the problems of the private rented
stock. 25,000 units were bought in 1974/5, 60% in
London, but the total had fallen to less than 10,000
by 1977/8, a consequence of successive public
expenditure cuts (Department of the Environment,
quarterly).

As elsewhere, landlords were supposed to keep

their properties in good repair and tenants could
take them to court for disrepair, although direct
action, such as the withholding of rent, was
illegal. Also various housing and public health
powers gave the local authorities rights to
intervene. But these powers had certain
deficiencies. They often required limited repairs,
rather than the more fundamental alleviation of
defects and the stronger powers (which could,
for example, allow a council to take
over and manage a property) were hedged around with
safeguards for the owners and made heavy demands on
scarce local authority manpower. So, although some
local authorities had tried to use these powers,
the main hope for substantial rehabilitation,
especially in the dilapidated private rental
sector, was the area improvement policy.

Despite the upsurge in improvement the policy
was often criticised. The main complaint was that
it focussed on physical improvement without any
concern for the social consequences. Also it only
had a very limited effect on the private rental
sector, which contained the hard core of the
problem of older housing. In some areas, such as
parts of inner London, where there was
intrinsically attractive property, the ready
availability of grants helped to fuel the process
of gentrification. Older rented properties were
bought up and improved by relatively affluent
owner occupiers and low cost housing opportunities
disappeared. In some cases property companies and
others used financial inducements or harrassment to
'persuade' tenants to leave so that improvement
could occur. Estate agents and property speculators
were heavily involved and, as for example in
Amsterdam, they often realised large capital gains.
This phenomenon was a minor part of the improvement
effort of these years but its impact on low income
tenants was considerable and gave rise to much
concern.

The 1974 Housing Act initiated a new approach.
GIAs continued much as before but it was now
recognised that they were only likely to succeed in
areas where owner occupier improvement was
possible. Areas of older housing with many low
income tenants were to be dealt with by Housing
Action Areas (HAAs). Before declaring HAAs the
authorities had to consider the condition of the
housing and social conditions. The aim was to
complete improvement within five years without

displacing the existing residents. The housing
associations were to play a major role and
residents and owners were to be involved in the
planning of schemes. Councils were given powers to
acquire houses and/or land, by compulsion if
necessary, and to carry out works. Modest grants
were now available to private owners for
environmental works. All notices to quit to tenants
and sales of non-owner occupied property had to
be reported to the local authorities, this was
intended to inhibit gentrification. For the first
time, grants could be made available solely for
repairs (before only half the grant could be spent
on this purpose). But grant conditions were
changed. In most cases, owner occupiers had to
declare that they would live in the house and
landlords that the property would continue to be
let for five years after improvement. Local
authorities could demand grant repayments if these
conditions were breached. But in HAAs landlords
who carried out improvement had to promise to let
for seven years. The cash value of the grants was
increased and in HAAs up to 90% of costs (up to
the ceiling grant of £3,200) was available in
hardship cases. Most of the costs were, as before,
paid by central government. Local authorities were
now able to compel landlords to improve property.
In this case help with rehousing tenants, either
temporarily or permanently, had to be provided.
Tenants could also initiate compulsory improvement.
Such improvements could be carried out by the
local authorities and recovered from the landlords
later. Owners who did not want to improve could
compel the authorities to buy their properties.
        These new powers were attempted to focus the
improvement effort on low income housing. But
another clause in the act enabled central government
to control local authority spending on improvement,
formerly this had been a matter for local
discretion. This was soon used to limit local
authority action as the economic crisis caused the
Labour government to reduce expenditure. So
progress was far slower than had been expected.
Levels of improvement grants after peaking in the
early seventies soon fell back again. There were
also defects in the working of the legislation.
Shortage of skilled local authority staff was an
important constraint. In 1977 a departmental report
found that even in the earliest declared HAAs only
a third of improvable properties had been touched.
Moreover, grants still went disproportionately

246

to owner occupiers and there was still a low take-
up by landlords (17). It will be recalled that the
1976 House Condition Social Survey found that many
could not afford improvement, this was borne out by
the findings of the 1977 study. Also more money was
needed for repairs, grant ceilings were too low and
the main source of loans, the building societies,
were still reluctant to invest in the low income
inner city areas (where most HAAs were located).
The compulsory improvement powers were cumbersome
and slow. Good progress had usually only been made
when local authorities or housing associations
had brought up much of the housing. Overall, it
was becoming clear that the 1974 act was not coming
to grips with the problem of the older, often
privately rented housing (much of which was anyway
not concentrated in areas suitable for the HAA
approach but distributed more diffusely).

Additional evidence on improvement and the
private rented sector is contained in the survey of
densely rented areas which was referred to earlier
(Paley, 1978). This found that about half of the
resident landlords and four fifths of other
landlords felt that the rents they received were
insufficient to cover all the necessary repairs to
their property and given them a reasonable return.
About half the non-resident landlords and a fifth
of the resident landlords had carried out some
improvements in the past five years. Few had used
grants, though about 60% of the larger company
landlords had done so. As in France, government
sponsored improvement worked best with larger, more
businesslike and better off landlords. About a
third of all landlords thought that bigger grants
would encourage more improvement, one half thought
that higher rent levels would also be required but
almost a half thought that neither of these changes,
nor both, would persuade them to improve their
housing. In fact almost 70% of landlords thought
that their properties did not need major repairs
or improvement. Interestingly, almost 60% of
tenants agreed with them - possibly such a finding
relates to the tenant resistance to improvement
which has already been mentioned. About two thirds
of tenants who thought that major work was needed
were prepared to pay 'a bit more rent', though it
seems unlikely that this implied an acceptance of
substantial rent increases.

In the Netherlands at the time of the research
if a house was declared unfit its rent was reduced
to its 1950 level and it had to be demolished

within 2-3 years. Alternatively, the owner could be
compelled to repair or improve it but the
improvement had to be profitable, though not the
repair. As in Denmark, the authorities reacted to
complaints and rarely used their powers. Improvement
subsidies were first made available for the cities
in 1938 and for the whole country in 1948 (18).
But these measures were mainly intended to assist
owners in meeting maintenance costs. In the fifties,
as described previously, the question of tying
rent increases to adequate maintenance was an
important political issue.

Large scale urban renewal began in the sixties,
aided by 80% grants for acquisition and demolition.
This period of large scale clearance was relatively
short, giving way to more emphasis on
rehabilitation. Developments in Rotterdam illustrate
this transition (City of Rotterdam Development
Department n.d.). In 1953 the city
earmarked twenty-three areas for renewal over the
following twenty-five years. By 1961 little had been
done because of the housing shortage, a lack of
finance (especially for replacement low income
housing) and the lack of effective compulsory
purchase powers. Much more was done in the sixties
but by 1970 the cost of large scale redevelopment
and opposition from neighbourhood groups forced
the city to adopt a mixed strategy of rehabilitation
and renewal. This too was hampered by the lack of
finance and also by the inability of the local
authority to force improvement or sale on an area
basis.

By the late seventies the government had
developed a range of improvement policies (19).
There were separate schemes for social and owner
occupied housing. Landlords were eligible for grants
which met 40% of improvement costs, paid in a lump
sum if the costs were low but in twenty annual
payments, declining over time, for more expensive
works (over 15,000 guilders). The allowable rent
increase was linked to the cost of the works, from
2% of costs, rising to 5.7% if the costs were over
95,000 guilders. As the annual subsidies declined
rents could be increased so that a positive return
might be made. But if a unit was loss making before
improvement these arrangements would not alter the
position. If a subsidised unit was sold off for
owner occupation the subsidies ceased. Owners who
applied for subsidies had to provide professional
plans and cost estimates. Standards were set by the
municipalities who had discretion in distributing

assistance. Repairs were not subsidised.

There was also a standard grant scheme, like the British one. In 1977 80% of all grants took this form. It also involved controls over rent increases. Also there were thermal insulation grants and rent readjustment grants, payable for three years on a dimishing basis to enable tenants to meet the increased rent on relocation and/or improvement. Special schemes covered historic buildings and temporary improvement of short life housing. Grants for environmental improvements were available for use by local authorities who were trying to bring about concentrated improvement.

Municipalities were required to select areas of older housing which with improvement would have a life of at least 25 years. Owners and tenants had to be consulted. Some of the problems which arose will be noted below, in response to them the government experimented with some pilot schemes based on a more simple financial approach in which the government met any net deficit incurred by the local authority after improvement/renewal had been completed. It remained to be seen whether this would overcome the principal difficulty of the lack of finance.

As already noted, landlords had often avoided improvement subsidies and the accompanying rent controls (this meant in practice that in the controlled zones rents could be increased by 12-15% and elsewhere be negotiated more freely) (20). Landlords had often carried out improvements in response to tenant requests with prior agreement about rent increases. Others had waited until the unit was vacant. Sometimes the tenants had carried out improvements, often these were sold to incoming tenants but in other cases the landlord benefitted by being able to raise the rent on re-letting. In some cases tenants paid money and higher rents. Tenants had no legal right to compensation for their improvements.

The tenant's position with respect to improvement was complicated, depending on the Civil Code and on the laws dealing with control and protection from eviction. But in all areas landlords could eventually get tenants who resisted improvement removed by the courts. However, after reforms in the late seventies the law governing tenants' rights was clarified and strengthened - as well as being uniformly applied throughout the

249

country. Courts were given stronger powers to
decide whether the proposed new rent was reasonable,
given the landlord's investment, and whether the
improved dwelling was still suitable for the sitting
tenant. If the tenant still refused to pay a
reasonable rent the court had discretion to decide
how much longer the tenant could stay on. Landlords
could also free units for improvement by
offering suitable alternative accommodation (again
the courts could arbitrate). Some local authorities,
for example Amsterdam, assisted landlords by
providing alternative accommodation.

Some of the problems which the improvement
policy encountered can be illustrated by examining
developments in the two largest cities, Amsterdam
and Rotterdam (21). The historic central area of
Amsterdam had provided a great deal of low income
housing in a city where there had been a continuing
shortage of accommodation. In the seventies this
stock came under great pressure because of
extensive conversion to high income owner
occupation and commercial and infrastructural
development (including an underground railway which
required large scale clearance). Landlords used
various means to gain vacant possession and sell
off in an improved or unimproved state. The local
authority had not been able to control this, apart
from its lack of effective powers, resources were
simply not available on the scale required. Also
there had been political resistance to improvement,
many local politicians continued to prefer
redevelopment. But demographic pressures and vocal
protests over schemes such as the new underground,
plus the changes in national policy, eventually
forced their hand.

But even in the late seventies the social and
tenurial conversion of the inner city was
continuing. More effective work was being done in
the areas of late nineteenth century high density
workers' flats surrounding this core. Here the
city was implementing a policy of selective
demolition and improvement for a mainly low income
population. Earlier redevelopment plans had been
scrapped after protests. Area planning and action
teams were established, operating in response to
pressure from residents. But lengthy and complex
procedures and a lack of finance were hampering
these efforts. Little money was available beyond
the normal budgetary allocations to city
departments. A good deal depended on the receipt

of central government money given the financial
weakness of local government (in the seventies
Amsterdam faced a fiscal crisis similar to that
experienced by New York City). Another problem was
the lack of co-ordination between central
government agencies. Also it could take up to
eight years to compulsorily acquire the property
of an owner who refused to improve. Finally, the
speculators who had been active in the
gentrification of the inner city were beginning to
move in to some of these buildings, buying them up
and selling off the units to the sitting tenants
(usually being able to remove those who refused to
buy).

In contrast, Rotterdam had attempted a more
direct approach to the problem of older housing.
In 1975 it became the first municipality to initiate
a policy of large scale municipal purchase. It
identified eleven inner city areas for priority
action and gave the landlords six months to decide
whether they would accept an offer to buy their
properties at 125% of its assessed value. The
city made it clear that if they refused it would
vigorously exercise its rights to compel adequate
repair and maintenance. Eventually about 40% of
the privately owned stock was bought by the city.
There was strong opposition from some speculator
landlords who thought that capital gains could be
made and who made counter offers to the owners.

The city hoped to persuade the government to
provide financial assistance for the purchases and
to obtain the preferential improvement subsidies
available for social housing. But this was resisted,
probably because it was thought that massive
financial demands would then be made by other
cities, following Rotterdam's example. The city
faced a huge financial burden as a result, mainly
because of the need to carry out extensive repairs
to the acquired units. Other problems included
the limited extent to which rents could be raised
after improvement, given the tenant's low incomes,
and the limited availability of relocation housing.
Many of the areas contained communities of guest
workers who wished to stay together and did not
want to pay increased rents (in German cities such
as Hamburg this problem had also been encountered).
Management was a problem too, although it was
eventually taken over by a new management agency
and by some of the social housing organisations.

Planning for areas was largely in the hands of

local committees of residents and officials (the
former had fought to have landlords excluded, and
had won). Similar problems to those encountered in
Amsterdam had occurred, lack of money, slow and
cumbersome powers against speculative landlords or
those who would not do repairs, lack of central
government co-ordination etc. By the late seventies
the policy was beset with difficulties and seemed
unlikely to be repeated in Rotterdam or elsewhere.
In fact, apart from Amsterdam, Rotterdam and
Groningen, few cities had active and large scale
improvement/renewal policies. Various proposals
were being debated to improve matters, for example
by enacting stronger compulsory improvement powers
but these were still controversial and new measures
had not yet been approved.

In the United States the basic tool for
maintaining housing standards was local housing
code enforcement. But more recently the availability
of federal assistance for urban renewal and
rehabilitation had often been linked to active
local code enforcement. However, these efforts had
been patchy and had had equivocal results. On the
one hand, in large cities such as New York the
volume of deficiencies and of tenant complaints
about them was so extensive that the available
inspectorate could not deal with them (corruption
had also played a role here). On the other hand,
when effective enforcement did occur, it could have
a serious impact on low income tenants. There had
been a very rapid growth of municipal housing codes
(National Commission on Urban Problems,1968, pt
III, Ch. 4) (in 1956 under 100 of the largest
cities had one, by 1968 over 4,900 localities had
one) but they had the effect of increasing rents
and, in some cases, forcing out poorer tenants.
Another source of difficulty was the rehousing of
tenants displaced from units which had to be
abandoned or demolished. There was no general duty
on local authorities to rehouse although there was
a federal relocation scheme. The scale of such
displacements was unknown but a survey of one
hundred cities, carried out in 1964, had suggested
that it was substantial. Usually when large scale
code enforcement had been carried out far more
people were displaced than were reaccommodated in
new low income rental units (Hartman, Kessler and
Legates, 1974).

Federal involvement in urban renewal dated
from the 1949 Housing Act which authorised large
scale slum clearance and redevelopment

subsidies (22). Areas had to be mainly residential
before or after redevelopment or both. Special
purpose renewal authorities were established in
many areas. Renewal progressed slowly at first, the
first project was not completed until 1956. But
activity accelerated in the sixties and early
seventies. By then some policy changes had occurred.
These weakened the requirement that redevelopment
be linked with new housing and opened up the
programme to commercial development. In the fifties
there had been increased emphasis on mixed renewal/
improvement and some rather ineffective mortgage
insurance programmes were developed in an attempt
to provide relocation and other housing. But
renewal mainly benefitted business interests,
indeed many localities saw it as a means of
removing older housing and their low income
inhabitants and creating an enhanced tax base (the
latter policy was somewhat vitiated because cities
competed for commercial development by offering
property tax abatements).

In 1956 federal relocation grants became
available though the payments were small (up to
$100 for a household and up to $2000 for a
business). A revised scheme first introduced in
1970, had (by 1978) the following provisions which
applied to all federally assisted projects (23).

1.   No-one should be forced to move unless
reasonable (in physical, financial and accessibility
terms) alternative housing was available;

2.   Adequate information and assistance should
be provided;

3.   Payments for moving and related expenses
of up to $500 and for the cost of replacement
housing were provided. Home owners could get up
to $15,000 to bridge the gap between the price
which they got for their house and replacement
housing plus certain other costs; tenants could
get help with the downpayment on a house or up to
$4,000 over four years to reduce rents. But the
scheme was very limited, for example in 1976 only
about 13,000 tenants received help, many of them
black households.

'Title I' home improvement loan insurance had
been available since 1934 but was mainly used by
home owners for purchasing consumer durables,
adding garages, etc. In 1964 section 312 low
interest loans became available to owners and
tenants of buildings in renewal areas if they could
not obtain other finance. Its applicability was
later broadened. One hundred per cent of the costs

253

could be covered up to $10,000 per unit. This was
the first direct subsidy for rental housing
rehabilitation, but only about 60,000 units had
benefitted by the end of 1974 (US Department of
Housing and Urban Development, 1977, 51) (a similar
programme for low income owner occupiers started a
little later). At the same time a new type of urban
renewal programme started which mainly consisted
of federally subsidised concentrated, area based
code enforcement. It was rarely used but after
1968 the insitutiton of more flexible,
incrementally planned renewal projects
(Neighbourhood Development Projects) proved rather
more popular.
        Throughout the sixties several general
programmes to assist rental housing had provisions
which encouraged their use in renewal areas and
more generally for rehabilitation. For example, the
rent supplement programme could assist those
displaced by government action and section 236 was
used for substantially rehabilitated housing as
well as for new units. The impact of these
programmes was quite small. For example, by 1976
only about 90,000 units had been supported by the
various mortgage programmes available for
rehabilitation (US Department of Housing and Urban
Development, 1977, 51). In addition other
initiatives such as the Model Cities programme,
started in 1966, produced some rehabilitated units.
From 1968 the FHA was given more freedom to use
any of its programmes in declining areas for new
and rehabilitated low income housing, provided
that the areas were 'reasonably viable'. With this
step the conversion of the FHA from its earlier
rather conservative role to a significant supporter
of inner city housing was completed.
        But some of the effects of this shift were
controversial. For example, the 221(d)(2) scheme
had allowed many owners of housing which was
difficult to dispose of with conventional finance
to sell at inflated prices to newcomers to the
cities concerned - often these were low income
blacks (24). Speculators moved in and by various
dubious means induced white residents to sell out
to them cheaply. This 'blockbusting' then resulted
in sales, at the inflated prices with the aid of
FHA programmes, to low income households. The
liberalisation of FHA terms often allowed inflated
assessments of values to be made and little regard
being paid to households' ability to support a
mortgage. Corruption also played a part. From this

time the rate of default on FHA mortgages began to
rise and by the seventies the federal government
was becoming the owner of much vacant, foreclosed
property, especially in the centres of the large
cities (Stegman, 1978). This added to the
dereliction of such areas. Small scale programmes,
such as urban homesteading, were started to put
some of this housing to use and to secure its
rehabilitation (25).

The 1969 tax reform contained an important
provision regarding rental housing rehabilitation.
Landlords of property occupied by low and moderate
income tenants could depreciate rehabilitation
costs over five years. The 'recapture' rule was that
if the property was sold within 100 months (8½
years) of rehabilitation that part of any capital
gain attributable to the 'excess' depreciation was
taxable as ordinary income. The amount recaptured
reduced so that after 16⅔ years none of it was
repayable. It is unclear how successful this was
but a theoretical study carried out in 1971
concluded that it would be of marginal value to low
income tenants and would not be widely used
(Heinberg, 1971). A disadvantage, as with all tax
shelters, was that it only helped landlords in
high tax brackets, hardly the first to need help.
Moreover the disadvantage of tax shelters with
respect to the long term delivery of housing
services also applied. In 1973, as already
mentioned, the Nixon administration suspended or
terminated many of the HUD low and moderate
income programmes including most of the urban
renewal and renewal related programmes. A new block
grant system was established, this will be
discussed below. Overall, the impression is that
the mass of previous legislation had had relatively
little impact on modernising the housing stock,
although urban renewal had had a considerable
effect in removing older housing altogether in some
cities (it was often called 'negro removal').

Many studies of renewal had been carried out,
some of the best known focussed on its operation
in Boston in the late sixties (the city had a very
active programme) (26). In 1967-8 HUD had carried
out an experiment in rapid urban renewal in Boston's
black ghetto area of Roxbury. In one year two
thousand units were brought up and rehabilitated
for low income occupancy. This involved the far
more flexible approach to renewal already
mentioned, rules were simplified, standards lowered
and corners cut. In some cases economic realities

were ignored. For example, buildings with 20 year
lives were given 40 year mortgages. The problems
that this inevitably caused were postponed to the
future, the long mortgages providing the immediate
benefit of lower rents. The developers who were
used often boosted their profits by ignoring the
worst properties, concentrating on those only
needing minor works. There was inadequate rehousing
for the 1700 displaced households, despite prior
assurances to the contrary.

A local advocacy planning organisation examined
the scheme. It found that 97.6% of the buildings
in the programme had all basic facilities in 1960;
that the developers were selected without local
participation and that some were well known as
slum landlords in the area; that many tenants were
evicted and that many could not afford the new
rents as the subsidy was insufficient - anyway the
developers exercised strong control, only
readmitting tenants whom they considered 'desirable'
(after community protest this aspect of matters
was improved); that services were discontinued
during rehabilitation, yet tenants were forced to
continue paying full rents or risk eviction; that
the developers did not finish the work on many
apartments once they had been sold; and that the
FHA and the developers formed a powerful coalition
in opposition to the interests of the tenants.

One of these developers explained just how
lucrative the renewal process could be. The typical
unit was bought for about $4,000 and cost about
$8,000 to rehabilitate. So eighty units could be
dealt with for $1 million. Under the federal
programme involved (in this case 221(d)(3)) the
developers could claim a sum equal to 10% of the
rehabilitation costs as a 'profit and risk
allowance' (27). In the case mentioned this amounted
to $62,000. The allowance could be left in the
project as the developers' equity. With a 90% FHA
mortgage, the developer then only had to add
$38,000 of his own money to have a $1 million
development fully funded. Given the low income,
low rent nature of the development and the rule
that dividends be limited to 6% of equity, the
developer pointed out that the project's tax
benefits were the main attraction to the partners
to whom it was syndicated. On the basis of
reasonable assumptions, about $80,000 of expenses
could be claimed in the first year (accelerated
depreciation plus interest payments) and the net
income from rents would be about $50,000 making a

'loss' for tax purposes of $30,000, worth $15,000
at the minimally beneficial tax rate (plus the
dividend of course). On this basis the initial
$38,000 investment was recovered after the second
year and the net gain over ten years would be about
$100,000. Of course capital gains would be payable
on any sale; if this occurred in year eleven, when
tax benefits were beginning to run down, the net
gain would still be about $70,000. Even if the
project became marginal, due to a rise in expenses
or a fall in rental income, the FHA could waive
the repayment of principal, so preserving the
developer's profits.

Overall, the impact on housing quality of most
of the policies discussed seems to have been small,
although opportunities for profit were certainly
present. Summarising progress in 1976, the President
noted that between 1969 and 1977 it was estimated
that about 350,000 units would have been
rehabilitated with the aid of federal subsidies, of
these only about 140,000 would be rented property.
He noted 'rehabilitation of deteriorated older
structures in marginal neighbourhoods has proved a
most difficult programme to administer, and one
marked by some disappointing experiences. As a
result, the number of rehabilitations has declined'
(President of the United States, 1976, 58).

Even before the introduction of a new approach
in 1974, there were many small scale experiments in
housing rehabilitation and 'neighbourhood
preservation' (See Real Estate Research
Corporation, 1975b; Ahlbrandt and Brophy, 1976).
These cannot be described here, but many of them
aimed to encourage low income inner city home ownership, and some were adopted and subsidised by the
federal government and expanded in scale. When
successful they often led to a further contraction
of the rental sector with the displacement of low
income tenants (there were exceptions, for example,
low income tenant co-operatives in formerly rented
buildings in New York City).

The new federal approach already referred to
involved a system of block grants, introduced in
1974 and usable by localities for a wide variety
of urban programmes, including housing (28). In
the second year of the new system nearly two thirds
of all assistance was supposed to be spent in areas
which had been using rehabilitation as an
important aspect of their locally determined
schemes, about 90,000 units were programmed for
some type of action in this year (US Department of

Housing and Urban Development, 1976b). The main
mechanism for achieving rehabilitation was that
part of the section 8 programme which assisted new
and substantially rehabilitated housing (section
312 loans were also expanded). In addition block
grant money was used for rehabilitation, for
example, by providing commercial loan guarantees,
to reduce interest on such loans or as a grant to
lower costs.

These techniques were usually combined with
other aid, for example from the section 312
programme. Interesting though such techniques were,
in most cities they were aimed mainly or even
exclusively at home owners. And attempts to use
block grant funds to 'lever' private money had been
far more successful in smaller and suburban
communities than in the central cities. So far as
area improvement was concerned, the most popular
approaches involved intensive rehabilitation
throughout the area or more modest rehabilitation
coupled with considerable environmental
improvements. Problems included a lack of skilled
staff, organisational complexities and a shortage
of firms willing to do the work, especially in the
inner cities. Only a minor part of the section 8
programme actually provided substantially improved
units (24,000 units programmed for 1977 for
example, although 70,000 units were programmed for
1979) and it seemed unlikely to involve many of
the worst units. A new scheme, Neighbourhood
Strategy Areas, rather similar in conception to
British HAAs, with a variety of federal aids, was
also to be tried out.

According to an authoritative review of
rehabilitation programmes carried out in 1976, 'To
a tremendous extent local rehabilitation programmes
have not supplied financing to investor-owners
although more programmes are now beginning to
develop investor-owner components, recognising that
a neighbourhood preservation programme cannot be
effective without one. The reluctance of local
programmes to deal with the investor-owner is based
on the inevitable consequence of rehabilitation:
rent increases to tenants. There is often great
political pressure from within the community to
exclude investor-owners, even from low income
tenants of properties in need of rehabilitation'
(Gressel, 1976, 30). Despite the hope expressed by
Gressel the situation did not change. Most
assistance continued to go to owner occupation,
sometimes being used to convert rental housing

or other property into owner occupied units (for
example, in New York a local programme - the J51
scheme - originally for low and moderate income
groups, was used to convert non-residential property
into housing for the better off) (Sternleib,
Roistacher, and Hughes, 1976). Section 8 mainly
aided units which required little if any work to
bring them up to reasonable standards and, to a
lesser extent, new building. Anyway its complex
procedures were mainly suited to larger, more
organised landlords and developers and not to the
small scale, often rather poor owners who held much
of the worst property (cf. France).

CONCLUSION

In each country the private rental sector contained
much old and dilapidated property. This was
concentrated in city centres because of the
historical conditions under which the sector
developed. Very little was done about this situation
until the sixties because of the earlier pressing
need to expand the supply of accommodation. When
positive policies were adopted the initial focus
was on redevelopment but this was heavily
criticised for several reasons. First, it was found
to be expensive, complex and slow, although
subsequent experience has shown that the suggested
alternative, area based rehabilitation, may be no
less problematic in these respects. Second, it was
physically and socially disruptive. A particular
concern, expressed by academic studies and more
directly by local inhabitants, were the problems
that arose when these inhabitants had to be rehoused
in scattered locations, for example in Paris where
many were moved to the periphery. In most countries,
some or even many tenants were simply evicted and
left to fend for themselves. Third, much renewal
benefitted business interests and upper income
residents at the expense of the poor. The
development of central Paris and many downtown
renewal schemes in the USA had clearly had this
effect, for example. Finally, these schemes reduced
the stock of private rental housing, although in
some countries such as Britain programmes of new
social housing were explicitly geared to providing
rehousing from clearance schemes.
     What evidence is there that the switch to
rehabilitation had solved these problems? Very
little, although the aesthetic results were

259

arguably better. Area based rehabilitation proved about as difficult to operate as earlier policies and, given the limited life of the improved property, might be no less expensive than rebuilding (in some cases for example, in Amsterdam and Copenhagen, the preservation of old buildings actually cost more immediately). Moreover, although there were some successes in retaining the original inhabitants in improved housing, for example, in Britain's HAAs, in Denmark and in Rotterdam, there was evidence from all countries that improvement often involved the removal of low income tenants and their replacement by higher income tenants or owners (see for example, Kuttner, 1976). Indeed, in the USA many federally supported neighbourhood preservation programmes had this as an explicit aim. Evidence concerning the take-up of improvement grants shows that they had mainly benefitted owner occupiers. In some countries tenants (or some tenants) had statutory rights to object to improvement if they could not afford the new rent levels or did not want their housing improved (as many elderly, for example, did not) but many more had little or no control over the process.

Above all in each country there is clear evidence that for all the (sometimes remarkable) mass of policies and legislation it had only made a marginal impact on improving property and retaining it within the private rented sector. Indeed improvement aids had often enabled developers and landlords to provide a saleable product for owner occupiers, thus reducing the rented stock still further. A major problem was the financial weakness of the sector and the stronger position of the other major tenures, especially owner occupation. Many landlords were catering for a population which could not afford to pay for accommodation provided to modern standards and many of these landlords themselves did not have the resources or the skills required to carry through extensive improvements.

However, this conclusion is too general for it ignores the distinctive situations of different types of landlords and tenants. A more satisfactory account was given by the German research mentioned earlier, which, with some modifications, would be applicable in whole or in part more widely (29). It will be recalled that this work suggested that there were five types of older housing areas with substantial proportions of rented housing. First,

there were areas of inner city housing where poor
people were being exploited by landlords who knew
that these tenants had no alternative housing
available. Such properties existed in most of the
larger cities in the six countries. They were often
very profitable and their owners had little to gain
from improvement which would probably reduce
occupancy levels, increase costs and reduce total
rents, thus reducing profitability. Second, there
were areas of older housing, owned by small
landlords with few resources, housing poor tenants.
These were discussed in the last paragraph. Third,
there were areas where gentrification was taking
place, here government aid simply seems to have
added to profits. Fourth, there were areas
(especially in Germany but also elsewhere) with
small landlords letting better quality property.
These had probably been helped by the types of
policies which were adopted - although even their
response may have been rather limited. Finally,
at the upper end of the market, there were areas
of housing whose landlords improved property in
response to tenant suggestions or where the tenants
might do the work themselves.

Improvement polies had hardly begun to
recognise that these distinctively different
situations existed. Governments had usually relied
on a voluntary approach, making grants available
for those who wanted to use them. Yet this probably
only suited a minority of landlords. In some cases
more elaborate approaches were being attempted,
for example in France, but large scale programmes
could not easily cope with the individual needs and
circumstances of the many small landlords. So the
French effort, for example, concentrated on the
holdings of the larger landlords - but these were
often not the owners of the worst property. (In
the USA rather similar problems surrounded the
section 8 rehabilitation programme). The USA
provided the main example of tax subsidised
improvement. We saw that this suffered from all the
disadvantages that the stimulation of new building
by tax benefits involved, including the fact that
it benefitted the better off owners rather than
those who most urgently needed assistance.

Some governments had tried to ensure that
subsidies were not simply a source of quick profits
for owners, yet there was evidence that in practice
this is just what they had often turned out to be.
The switch to improvement must be seen in the
context of other changes in housing policy, such

as increasing rents in the private and social
sectors and switching from the production of new
rented social housing to the encouragement of owner
occupation. From such a perspective it seems clear
that those at the bottom of the housing market
had had their chances of obtaining adequate and
affordable rented housing reduced in recent years.
No government had a very effective means of
improving the rented stock which also retained it
in this tenure. Neither the political nor the
economic circumstances of the times had normally
allowed the more radical alternative of the
incorporation of this stock in the social sector
to be implemented or even considered seriously (30).

NOTES

1.   Some figures are estimates (from Enquête-
logement, 1973 (2) 60-1). They derive from more
than one survey, hence the inclusion of data for
1967-70 and 1968-73. More adequate data is
unavailable.

2.   Figures and estimates provided by Lars
Østergaard, derived from Danmarks Statistik, 1975.

3.   Officials of these companies were
interviewed, the figures were supplied by them.

4.   The details in this section were supplied
by Ilona Mühlich-Klinger (who, with colleagues
at the Institute für Wohnen and Umwelt, Darmstadt,
was carrying out research into the rehabilitation
of older housing).

5.   Withdrawals averaged 2/3000 per annum in
the late 40s and early 50s, they then rose
gradually to average about 18,000 per annum by the
late 60s and early 70s before falling back to
average about 14,000 in the late 70s. Withdrawals
in 1975 amounted to 0.35% of the total stock.

6.   Figures supplied by the Ministry of
Housing and Jan van der Schaar.

7.   In an interview in 1978 current prices for
an average four roomed unit of 100 square metres
were estimated to range from 1.6 million francs in
central Paris to 350,000 francs in the cheapest
provincial area.

8.   The details in this section are taken from
Nora and Eveno, 1975.

9.   Various types of intervention were
possible, including urban renewal with special
powers of pre-emption and some control on land
values inside a Zone d'Aménagement Concerté (ZAC),
private or publicly sponsored rehabilitation, and
powers over unfit properties. Planning and building
regulations and transport, social, educational and
other policies could also affect areas of older
housing. Many problems arose from different, limited
and sometimes conflicting requirements and
processes. Legal ambiguities and administrative
complexities abounded. In many cases large scale
urban renewal and improvement had been carried out
by private enterprise at the request of the local
authorities. An appendix to the 1975 report
noted 'il est difficule de concilier les aspects
politiques d'une intervention importante en tissus
anciens avec les intérêts privés d'un operateur'.
Often neither elected representatives nor the
affected population had had much knowledge about or

control over what happened.

10. The proposals on finance (contained in the Barre Report) are discussed in Duclaud-Williams, 1978.

11. The details of policy and developments in Denmark are derived from Socialt Tidsskraft, 1947, information supplied by Lars Østergaard and interviews and visits to housing projects in Copenhagen made in 1978.

12. The history and contemporary situation discussed here is described in Federal Minister for Regional Planning etc. (ed), n.d. and Wollmann and Konukiewitz, 1982.

13. Information on policy development supplied by Ilona Mühlich-Klinger (see note 4) and Herr Ulrich Pfeiffer.

14. See note 4.

15. The period is reviewed in Bowley, 1945, and Burnett, 1978, 215-43.

16. The post war history of slum clearance and improvement is reviewed in Cullingworth, 1979, 74-97 and, in inner city areas, in Lansley, 1979, 220-41; Paris and Blackaby, 1979; SHAC, 1981; English and Norman, 1974.

17. Interestingly, the report was suppressed by the Ministry, but leaked to and published in the journal of the main housing pressure group, Shelter (Roof, Vol. 5, No. 4, September, 1979, 151-3).

18. Information supplied by Jan van der Schaar and from interviews carried out in 1978.

19. Information on current policies and their impact supplied by the Ministry of Housing in 1978.

20. The changes in rent setting policy (noted in chapter 5) which occurred in the late seventies ended the basis for this distinction.

21. The following material is based on visits to the two cities and interviews with local officials and others in 1978.

22. The early history is outlined in Abrams, 1965. There is an enormous literature on virtually every aspect of this topic. The policy developments traced in the next paragraphs are taken from House Committee on Banking, Currency and Housing, 1975, passim.

23. Details taken from information leaflet published by US Department of Housing and Urban Development.

24. Essentially a scheme that enabled housing to be purchased by low and moderate income families for virtually no down payment (US Department of

Housing and Urban Development, 1973, 1-20). For a
case study of its use by inner city speculators see
Harvey, 1977.

25. This programme, which involved the transfer
of derelict property for a nominal sum to
households who then undertook to carry out
rehabilitation, is described in Harloe, 1978.

26. The account below is derived from Keyes,
1969, 1970; Urban Planning Aid Inc., 1973; and
Goldston, 1973.

27. Similar to 221(d)(2) (see note 23 above)
but for rental housing and aided with rent
supplements.

28. The legislation is set out and explained
in Edson, 1974. For a review of area improvement
policies as a whole see Carlson, 1978.

29. See note 4.

30. Since this chapter was completed the
results of a comparative study of urban renewal in
Britain, the Netherlands, Sweden and West Germany
has been published (Fassbinder and Kalle, 1982).
It stresses the extent to which even the newer
rehabilitation based renewal often has adverse
consequences for poorer residents.

Chapter Eight

LANDLORD/TENANT RELATIONS

This chapter is limited in content due to the
nature of the subject and to the limitations of
the research method adopted. Each country had
complex legal provisions which aimed to regulate
landlord/tenant relations. These laws could, in
principle, be analysed without too much difficulty.
But in so personal a matter as the relationship
between a landlord and a tenant, the ability of
the law to govern actual conduct was severely
limited. These limitations were probably most often
experienced at the bottom end of the market. The
private rental sector was contracting yet it still
provided the main source of housing to many who
were effectively barred from access to
owner occupation or social rented housing.
In these circumstances landlords were often able to
pick and choose tenants and to control the terms of
their tenancies in ways which had little regard to
the law. Tenants who might protest at the unfair
burdens which this placed on them knew that it
could cost them their tenancy. In some cases
disregard for the law was also the product of the
widespread ignorance of its provisions which both
landlords and tenants frequently displayed.
     Given the widespread realisation that the
gap between officially sanctioned behaviour and
actual practices was often a wide one, it might be
thought that a substantial amount of research
would have been carried out into this problem. In
fact little information, was available, certainly
not from governments (who probably had a vested
interest in assuming that the legislation that
they passed was effective). Given the lack of
existing information the research could only
examine landlord/tenant relations in one of two
ways. The first was to mount a substantial

266

'primary' research effort in each county. This was
not possible, given the time and resources
available. The second approach, which was the one
adopted, was to collect information on the legal
framework and significant changes in policy, to
draw on such research findings as existed, patchy
and inadequate though they were, and to rely on the
general views of the main protagonists-landlords,
tenants and governments- which were expressed in
the interviews that were carried out.

The results, which are not extensive and are
sometimes rather specualtive, do nevertheless bring
to light a number of important findings. First, we
shall examine security of tenure, referring back to
material from chapter five, then a number of other
aspects will be considered. Next the recent growth
of local housing activism will be discussed before
attempting to summarise what can be learnt from
this brief review of an extremely complex topic.

SECURITY OF TENURE

In most countries the original form of tenancy
agreement often provided for the rent to be paid on
a weekly or monthly basis (although payment at
longer intervals was not uncommon, especially in
higher rented property). Tenants had little security
beyond this term. But with the imposition of rent
controls some provision had to be made for security,
in order to prevent eviction by landlords whose
rents were suddenly controlled. The security
provisions were often lifted or eased as rent
controls diminished in the inter-war period, only
to be reimposed during the second world war. Since
1945 there has been a more extensive development
of tenants' rights and, increasingly, some degree
of security of tenure has been made available, in
theory at least, to many tenants.

In France even at the end of the seventies
tenants in the old and by now small scale controlled
sector still had lifetime security of tenure and
on their death members of their family living with
them could 'inherit' the tenancy (and this could
happen an indefinite number of times). This
provision was sometimes manipulated to 'bequeath'
tenancies to people who did not legally qualify for
them. When units left the controlled sector the
sitting tenants lost this lifetime security but
were supposed to be given three year leases. No
research had been done to assess whether this
usually occurred in practice (Duclaud-Williams,

1978, 88).
In other cases security was limited to the
length of the contract which was (more or less)
freely negotiated between the landlord and the
tenant. If the tenant was left in possession at the
end of the contract the law assumed that, tacitly,
a new contract had been agreed. If the landlord
sold the property the new owner could not obtain
vacant possession until the end of the contract,
unless there was a specific contractual clause
allowing an earlier notice to quit, and this was
rare. Nevertheless there was considerable freedom
for the landlord to determine what was contained
in a contract. So in practice landlords often had a
good deal of freedom to remove tenants and the
grounds for ending a tenancy were largely a matter
for agreement by the two parties to the contract,
rather than being severely limited by generally
applicable laws (CNL, n.d). A more secure regime
existed in the aided private sector. Thus tenants
of an SII normally had three year contracts and
could only be evicted during its term on specific
and rather limited grounds, such as rent arrears
(CNL, 1974, 1975). In all disputes between landlord
and tenants redress could only be sought via the
normal court system, there were no special
intitutions regulating the private rented sector.
In 1966 in Denmark a distinction was made
between legislation which regulated rents, which was
regarded as 'provisional', and other aspects of
the relationship between landlords and tenants,
concerning which a more permanent Landlord and
Tenant Act was passed in 1967. This Act covered
all tenancies, except boarding houses and hotels,
and was operative throughout the country (having
been extended to the non-regulated areas in 1975).
The act explicitly declared that its purpose was to
protect the tenant who was regarded as the weaker
of the two parties to a rental contract. It covered
the full range of duties and responsibilities of
both parties and provided a model tenancy
agreement (whose full adoption was optional). The
central feature of the act was the mandatory
limitation of acceptable grounds for eviction.
These were:-
1. demolition of the unit;
2. a service tenancy where employment had
ended;
3. the landlord wished to occupy the unit;
4. bad behaviour;
5. rent arrears;

6. neglect of the dwelling;
7. subletting without the landlord's
   permission.

As was noted in chapter five, the first
recourse regarding most contractual disputes was to
the Rent Boards in the controlled areas and to the
housing courts elsewhere. Courts could defer
possession orders, normally from between three
months to a year, depending on circumstances. But
tenants of single rooms (whose rent was basically
unregulated, although the Landlord and Tenant Act
said that it should be 'reasonable') usually only
got two weeks notice.

The landlords' and tenants' associations both
seemed satisfied that these arrangements worked
reasonably well, although the tenants'
representatives would have liked to improve security
for the tenants of single rooms. Nevertheless
several unauthorised ways of removing tenants were
practiced, although noone   could say how extensive
such practices were. These included trying to
force out tenants in the non-regulated sector by
excessive rent increases (although in theory there
was legal redress for this via the 'reasonable rent'
provision of the Landlord and Tenant Act). More
common, especially when the landlord wanted to sell
with vacant possession, was neglect of repair and
maintenance in order to try to drive tenants out.
Again there was some possibility of legal redress
in this situation, but these rights were limited
and rarely exercised (Rent Boards could only force
landlords to carry out urgent maintenance, in other
cases they could defer work until it was
'financially feasible').

Germany had had a particularly interesting
recent history of legislation regarding security
of tenure (Federal Minister for Regional Planning
etc., n.d., 38). As discussed in chapter five, in
the early sixties it was decided to decontrol
rents. As, area by area, rents were freed, landlords
were also free to serve   notices to quit. The
courts had a limited power to defer possession
orders, for up to a year. Further extensions of
this time could be granted if the courts were
satisfied that enforcing the order would cause the
household undue hardship. This law did create a
good deal of hardship and the national tenants'
organistion and the labour movement campaigned for
new restrictions. Small changes were made in 1967
and a new protection from eviction act was passed
in 1971. At first this was regarded as a temporary

departure from the civil code provisions which had previously been in force but in 1974 it was made a permanent part of the legal code. This was apparently generally accepted, there was only one vote against it in the Bundestag (in contrast the rent controlling legislation was still a temporary and controversial measure - so the situation was rather similar to that which existed in Denmark).

The basic principle was that tenants had security of tenure. Landlords had to go to court to obtain possession. This was only granted on one of three grounds; first, that the tenant had broken a clause in the contract; second, that the unit was required for the landlord or his/her family; and third, that the present use of the land on which the accommodation was sited was uneconomic and that it could be converted to a more economic use (a rarely used case). However, as in Denmark, some accommodation was excluded. This included most rented rooms (where all arrangements were negotiated freely), holiday lets and student accommodation (where similar provisions applied, with some safeguards against 'bogus' holiday and other lets), and most significantly, tenants in 'special tenements'. This was the description for the rented units which were contained in the two unit housing which, it will be recalled, owner occupiers had been encouraged to build. If such a landlord wished to remove a tenant this could be achieved either on one of the three grounds stated above or by simply giving the required notice as stated in the contract plus an additional three months. So tenants in this accommodation were only weakly protected.

Little was known about how often recourse was made to these provisions but, as elsewhere, it was suggested that informal methods were resorted far more frequently. Little was known either about how insecure tenants really were but there was plenty of incidental evidence of insecurity, especially among the groups which were only weakly protected by the law. More generally, ignorance and the cost and difficulties of access to the courts prevented the law from being as widely used as it might have been.

A complex and often amended body of law governed security in Britain, where the legal provisions affecting rent determination also affected security of tenure (for a brief review see House of Commons Environment Committee, 1982, II, 245-6). But in general no tenant or licensee could be evicted without due process of law.

Usually a written notice to quit for a date not
less than four weeks ahead was required.
 Tenants who had protected or restricted
tenancies had further rights. In most cases
protected tenants had to be given a notice to quit
which stated that possession would only be granted
on a fairly long list of specified grounds, some
of which were mandatory and some discretionary (1).
In the discretionary cases the courts could suspend
or postpone a possession order if the tenant's
circumstances made this desirable. In the mandatory
cases they could not do this but usually gave
tenants four weeks to go. Tenants with restricted
contracts could ask Rent Tribunals to postpone
notices to quit. Normally up to six months of stay
of possession could be granted, in exceptional
cases this might be extended.
 In fact Tribunals dealt with rather few
disputes about security because the sector of
the market for which they had responsibility, i.e.
mainly lettings where there was a resident landlord,
was so highly 'informal'. Thus, in 1977 there were
only about 5,600 decisions which affected security
taken by Tribunals (2). But rather few actions
concerning any kind of private rented tenancy were
taken in the courts. In the same year only 6-7,000
actions were taken by private (mainly absentee)
landlords and most involved the discretionary
grounds for possession which applied to protected
tenancies. These figures suggest that many tenants
either moved of their own accord or went when they
got a notice to quit or when pressure was put
upon them. Only a minority of landlords had
recourse to the courts but the figures show that
when they did possession was almost always
obtained. Nor apparently did the courts make much
use of their power to suspend the operation of
possession orders. Informal pressure, even
amounting to harassment (against which there was a
rather ineffectual law) was probably regarded as
more effective, cheaper and faster (3).
 The 1976 survey of densely rented areas
provided some interesting additional details
(Paley, 1978). Most landlords stated that legal
provisions had not affected their letting policies
but the proportion saying this varied according to
the type of landlord. Thus only 20% of resident
landlords said that they had been affected by the
security provisions, this supports the view that
this sector was dominated by 'informal'

arrangements. However, 40% of non-resident
individual landlords and almost 50% of company
landlords said that they had been affected by the
security laws. Of those who were affected, many had
as a result become more selective in their choice
of tenants or reluctant to relet vacant property.
But a significant minority of company landlords had
decided to relet in ways which avoided or evaded
the security provisions, for example by arrangements
which created licences to occupy rather than
tenancies or which created 'holiday lets'. And other
evidence suggests that, especially in larger cities
(above all in London) such arrangements eventually
become virtually the rule, at least for most
advertised vacancies (Bovaird, et. al., 1982a). The
survey also showed that many landlords, especially
the resident ones, were ignorant of the legal
provisions governing security in their accommodation.
But these provisions were anyway thought to be less
of a problem than low rents. About 60% of those
landlords who said they would not relet vacant
units cited low rents as the main reason, compared
to only 14% who mentioned security.
    In the Netherlands, as elsewhere, the informal
matter in which most landlord/tenant matters were
settled was stressed by those interviewed. Until
the reform of rent legislation in the late
seventies, repossession was fairly easy in the
liberalised zones. Notices to quit could be
disputed in the courts where landlords had to argue
a case on one of four grounds; first, that the
tenant had in fact agreed to leave; second, bad
conduct and more generally breaking contract terms;
third, that the contract was for a fixed period
which had now expired (normally contracts were given
for 2 - 5 years at the start of a tenancy and then
left to run on indefinitely, but in the controlled
zones fixed term contracts were forbidden); or,
fourth, that the landlord could prove that he/she
needed the accommodation more urgently than the
tenant. 'Urgency' was a matter for judicial
interpetation, and this ground was apparently often
used to get vacant possession in order to sell.
In the controlled zones landlords always had to go
to court to end tenancies. Four grounds were again
possible, two of these were similar to the second
and fourth cases noted above. In addition the
landlord could argue, first, that the tenant could
obtain an alternative and equivalent dwelling
(usually this meant that the landlord had to offer

272

one) or, second, that, acting within the rules for
rent setting, the landlord wanted to raise the rent,
that this was a reasonable increase in the view of
the judge but that the tenant had refused to pay.
A rather large number of cases came to court but
most concerned disagreements over what rent should
be legally payable. The most common ground for
possession was that the unit was required for the
landlord's own use. In both zones, if the courts
accepted this case they could defer possession for
up to three years. Tenants in rent arrears were not
usually evicted if they paid up.

In the controlled zones landlords could only
proceed in the courts if the Rent Committee had
failed to resolve the problem. In the other areas
landlords could go directly to the courts but the
latter had to seek the advice of the Committees.
At the end of a fixed term contract in the
liberalised zones, if tenants paid what the court
regarded as a reasonable rent landlords found it
difficult to repossess, unless he/she could argue
for eviction on other grounds. Sub tenants were in
a much weaker position regarding security, as in
the other countries in this survey.

Despite the law there was evidence that, in a
situation where many landlords had much to gain by
selling vacated units, pressure was put on tenants
to leave. Methods used, including the payment of
inducements and harrassment, were similar to those
which had become familiar in Britain from the early
sixties onwards. Also, as in Denmark, some landlords
had allowed property to become dilapidated in order
to force tenants out.

Some of these provisions were altered by the
reform of rent legislation in 1979. This extended
the provisions for possession which formerly applied
to the controlled zones to the whole country but in
modified form. The main change affected the fourth,
most frequently used, case for possession. In
future the court was to decide not only whether
the landlord 'urgently' needed the unit but also,
in such a case, whether the landlord's interests
outweighed those of the tenant. If possession was
granted the court could order that the tenant was
compensated for the costs of removal. This
legislation clearly strengthened the tenants'
position.

As with many other housing matters, landlord/
tenant legislation in the USA was a matter of local
and state rather than federal concern (except laws
outlawing racial discrimination in letting which

dated from the sixties and were rather ineffective
(Polikoff, 1978)). So it is not possible to make
more than a few general points, although some more
detailed reference will be made to New York City,
which had an especially well developed set of legal
provisions. Originally, as elsewhere, many tenants
had verbal agreements with their landlords, paying
rent on a monthly or weekly basis and having the
same periods of security. Most of the power to
impose terms was in the landlords' hands especially
if the local rental market was tight. Despite the
existence of a growing body of legislation, the
impression was that this state of affairs had not
greatly altered in some localities (Garrity, 1973).
But the fairly rapid growth of building and housing
codes had at least placed landlords under formal
obligations to provide minimal standards of
accommodation. In addition, where there had been
controls there had also been security laws.
     Thus in New York City tenants in
stabilised and controlled apartments had special
rights to security of tenure (as already noted in
chapter five). Other tenants usually only had
security for the contract term but no right to a
renewed contract (Striker and Shapiro, 1978; City of
New York, 1974). Tenants in New York City could
only be legally evicted through the courts. There
were two types of procedure. The first was an
action for the non-payment of rent, eviction could
be avoided at any stage by paying the arrears due.
The second type was a 'holdover action', so called
because the landlord declared that the lease was
terminated and that he/she was taking action to
remove a tenant remaining in occupancy. In such
cases possession orders were often granted by the
courts. The most common grounds for a holdover
action were; if the tenant remained in occupation
after the ending of the normal term of a lease
(tenants of controlled and stabilised tenancies
could not be in this position, having no fixed
term); if there was a substantial violation of the
lease; if there was persistent rent arrears; if
the tenant was a nuisance or damaged the apartment;
if illegal activities were carried out on the
premises; or if the tenant refused the landlord
reasonable access to the apartment. Retaliatory
eviction was illegal, as was harrassment. As
elsewhere, the effectiveness of these provisions
was unknown.

274

Landlord/Tenant Relations

OTHER MATTERS

In France contracts in the controlled sector were
governed by the relevant law (CNL, n.d., 1975;
Duclaud-Williams, 1978, 33-63). In the free rented
stock contracts could be verbal or written. They
were supposed to set out who was to pay taxes,
charges and so on. It was illegal to force tenants
to pay more than two months rent. Provisions could
be included for regular rent increases, it was
common to link these to the offficial construction
cost index (a formula the government itself often
used). Landlords had a legal duty to maintain their
property in a reasonable condition. If this did not
happen the tenants could seek redress in the courts,
do the work themselves and sue the landlord for
the costs or, in some cases retain part of the
rent. Tenants were not usually allowed to sublet.
Tenants in difficulty faced considerable obstacles
in getting help. The cost of going to court was
often prohibitive although some legal aid had been
available since 1970. There did not appear to be
any significant development of aid or advice
provided by voluntary agencies or local authorities
for tenants.
      Many of the rights of Danish tenants have been
noted elsewhere in this book, for example the right
to inspect landlords' budgets and the position
regarding repair and improvement. Contracts could
be written or verbal, but if the latter
all the provisions of the model agreement mentioned
earlier were regarded as being in force. Landlords
and tenants could agree variations to many of the
clauses in the model agreement but these had to be
incorporated in a written contract. In practice
this often occurred. In the regulated areas 75%
of all tenants in a building had to agree to any
such variations, and fewer were possible than in
other areas. Moreover, all tenants in a block had
to have similar contracts and pay the same rent (if
the units were identical).
      An interesting development was the provision
for 'tenant democracy' which followed the 1974
housing pact. In blocks of more than twelve units
tenants could elect representatives to deal with
the landlord. At least half the tenants had to be
present at the election meetings, which the
landlord could also attend. Representatives had
the right to see the balance sheet of the property,
discuss the budget and ask questions regarding rent
rises; had to be consulted on how funds set aside

for the running and maintenance of the building were used; had to be informed about the appointment and dismissal of staff; could work out house rules for the majority approval of tenants (although landlords could object, they had to have compelling reasons to have them changed); and make proposals for improvements (which, as mentioned in chapter seven, had to be accompanied by financing proposals). Since 1976 these provisions had also been applied to tenants in freehold flats if the building contained more than twelve rented dwellings before freehold conversion. These measures mainly involved rights of consultation and inspection, they did not result in tenant control. But at least tenants did have the right to organise, to obtain information and to seek to make the landlord justify his/her actions. Also if the landlord wanted to sell out, tenants representatives could negotiate in order to ensure that tenants had an opportunity to form a co-operative and buy the properties (4). Tenants also had the right to exchange dwellings with other tenants in the same block. But there were some restrictions, including when the landlord had a 'reasonable ground' to refuse the exchange.

In Germany, as elsewhere, the features of ignorance of the law, the cost and inaccessibility of legal help and so on were common. Written agreements were normal. Verbal contracts were possible but landlords tended to avoid them as they could only exclude certain rights (which the courts normally assumed tenants to have) by making written agreements. It was suggested that many contracts would in fact, if examined in court, be regarded as unfair to tenants (and on occasion, presumably, to landlords) (5). A law on general conditions of contract had recently been passed. It forbade any terms which might be unduly onerous to either party and provided the basis, for the first time, for tenants' organisations or other interested bodies to take 'class actions'. Contracts had to make provision for the supply of basic services, good repair and so on. If services were cut off the courts could compel the landlord to restore them. Tenants could reduce their rents if repairs and maintenance were not done. They could also go to court to compel the landlord to act or do the work themselves and reduce the rent to pay for it (after the landlord had been given a chance to do the work).

As elsewhere, in Britain agreements could be verbal or written. In either case the courts had the power to decide, regardless of the contract's contents and having regard to the relevant circumstances of the letting, what the respective rights and duties of landlords and tenants were in the light of the type of tenancy which had been created. There were several legal provisions which applied all or almost all tenants such as the right to a rent book, to know who their landlord was, and to be protected from harrassment and illegal eviction (Department of the Environment, 1977, d, e, f, g). Protected and some restricted contract tenants had certain other rights. For example, it was illegal to charge them 'key money', and incoming tenants could only be required to pay a 'reasonable' sum for fixtures and fittings. But there was evidence that many tenants did not understand that they had these rights and that in some cases the rights were hard to exercise (6).

As already described, rent officers, assessment panels and tribunals played an important role in the administration of the rent acts. In principle they were easily accessible to both tenants and landlords but the latter were more likely to use professional advisers to present their case. This could be costly and tenants, although they could plead their own cases, often needed help. In the county courts, which handled most matters not connected with regulated rents or the rents and security of restricted contracts, legal aid or advice was often needed. Low income tenants (or possibly low income landlords) could obtain some minor legal aid when appearing before a tribunal or assessment panel, but not in order to pay for representation. They might qualify for full (but means tested) legal aid in the county courts, although this was at the discretion of local legal aid committees. In addition, various legal and housing aid centres, financed by the local authorities or by voluntary bodies, had been established in recent years, mostly in the bigger cities. These gave free advice to tenants and, in many cases, to landlords. In some cases they had also taken up problems more actively.

An important right for tenants (or owner occupiers) made homeless was that, under the terms of the 1977 Housing (Homeless Persons) Act they might have a right to be rehoused by the local authority, if they fell into certain priority categories (such as having children) and had not made themselves 'intentionally homeless' (a term which had been interpreted widely by local authorities and the courts). Other homeless people had a right to information and advice from the local authorities. Before 1977, under welfare legislation, some homeless families in severe need had been rehoused, in other cases children were taken into local authority care, or mothers and children but not fathers housed in special blocks.

In the Netherlands the familiar features of ignorance of the law and widespread informal arrangements were reported by those who were interviewed. Many contracts were verbal, in which case the general provisions of the civil code were held to apply. If there was a verbal agreement containing special provisions evidence to this effect had to be supplied in any court case which arose. Larger landlords tended to use written contracts as these could be more restrictive than the civil code. In theory contracts could be set aside by the courts as unfair, although this rarely happened. Subletting was prohibited unless specifically permitted but, as elsewhere, this provision was often ignored by tenants. As in Britain, while harrassment was quite common the legal offence was hard to prove.

Tenants found legal assistance hard to get and few lawyers specialised in housing matters (a problem noted in other countries). But legal aid payments had recently increased, providing a greater incentive to lawyers to take on housing work. In addition in each large town a legal aid bureau had been established, financed by the Ministry of Justice and staffed by one or two full time lawyers with the assistance of others in private practice. There had been resistance to anyone other than the immediate parties to a dispute bringing proceedings (housing matters were dealt with in the municipal courts only, where individuals could represent themselves) but actions brought, for example, by tenants' organisations or other consumer bodies on behalf of tenants were beginning to be acceptable.

In the USA, the development of tenants' rights beyond the minimal levels implied by the sort of contracts derived from commercial practice has already been noted. In some areas tenants had been given protection concerning the possible contents of rental contracts (increasingly these were written rather than verbal). In some places the concept of a 'warranty of habitability' was slowly being developed and there was also legislation

which enabled tenants to enforce repairs, redress
included the right to withhold rent or to carry out
the repairs, reclaiming the costs from the rent (7).
There were very few specialist housing aid and
advice centres, although there were many other
bodies which gave assistance such as legal aid
centres.

New York City had developed one of the most
elaborate sets of laws governing landlord/tenant
relations of any US city (Striker and Shapiro, 1978,
City of New York, 1974). Some aspects of the New
York situation were covered in chapter 5 where it
was noted that landlord/tenant affairs were governed
by both city and state laws though, as in 1971
when the state passed a vacancy decontrol law,
state law took precedence. In New York as elsewhere,
the federal anti-discrimination laws were backed up
by the state's own human rights legislation. This
prohibited discrimination on, for example, grounds
of having children, or being an unmarried couple or
of being handicapped. Other legislation made key
money illegal and all tenants were entitled to a
fair lease, the right to enjoy their apartment (as
long as they did no harm to others), maintenance
and repairs and a building adequately protected
against crime. Several important new rights were
added in the seventies. First, that leases be
written in 'plain english'. Second, powers were
given to the courts to decide whether leases, even
after they had been signed by tenants, contained
clauses which were 'unconscionable' (this was
important because of the shortage of accommodation,
few tenants were in a position to bargain about
lease terms before signing). Third, the concept of
a warranty of habitability was introduced. This
borrowed from the law concerning consumer good
warranties and applied it to housing. It meant that
in every lease there was an implicit condition
guaranteeing that the unit was fit for human
habitation and free from hazardous or detrimental
conditions. These new laws were subject to judicial
interpretation but, especially in the last case,
the courts seemed to be interpreting the landlords'
duties broadly, for example, to encompass matters
such as failure to deal with noisy neighbours.
Tenants could sue landlords for damages but by far
the most common form of action had been withholding
of rent and a defence of the action on the grounds
that the warranty of habitability had been broken.

Various matters were covered by other laws.
For example, landlords could not stop tenant

organising and were not able to put security money
to their own uses (it had to be held in an interest
bearing account and repaid, with interest, to
tenants when they left, provided that they left
without rent arrears etc.). Other rights, including
subletting, were dependent on the lease provisions,
although if the landlord's consent was unreasonably
refused the tenant could end the contract. There
were additional provisions for the tenants of
controlled and stabilised units relating to
security, rent levels and the provision of certain
services. In addition the bodies which administered
rent control and stabilisation had enforcement
powers which tenants of other units had to rely on
the courts to exercise. (In fact uncertainties and
ignorance about who had jurisdiction over what
was a considerable problem.)

All tenancies in buildings with three or more
units were covered by the city's Housing Maintenance
Code which required the landlord to supply adequate
heat, hot water and sanitation. The requirements
were laid out in detail, for example the minimum
temperatures to be maintained during the winter
months at different times of the day. But
enforcement could be a tortuous business. After a
fairly long process landlords who failed to right
defects were subject to fines but the volume of
complaints was so enormous that by the late
seventies only very serious breaches of the law
were being pursued by the city officials (in this,
as in all other aspects of housing, the city's
staffing and programmes had been severely curtailed
as a result of the fiscal crisis).

Tenants could themselves take defaulting
landlords to the city's housing court (a division
of the civil courts). Access to this court was
cheap, tenants could present their own cases and
the atmosphere was inormal. Help was available from
the court clerks and from a special unit set up by
the city to educate tenant leaders in basic legal
and other housing matters. Being taken to court
often had some effect in inducing landlords to take
action and tenants were sometimes authorised to
carry out repairs and deduct the costs from their
rent. In some cases this could even be done before
getting permission from the court. Tenants could
also call a rent strike and pay their rents to a
court appointed administrator in order to provide
the necessary funds for maintenance and repairs.
Although the law was originally aimed at helping
less well off tenants, it was extensively used by

occupants of luxury accommodation who were dissatisfied with the quality of the services provided. At least one third of the tenants had to agree before any action could be started.

Landlords could also be sued in the civil courts for damages if they were in default of any of their obligations and landlords could also sue defaulting tenants. Many small claims were dealt with in small claims courts. In these courts the costs of bringing an action (a lawyer was not needed) could be under $5, cases were heard in the evening so that working people could attend and the atmosphere was informal, with the judge aiding the claimants in the presentation of their cases.

To summarise, New York had a highly developed series of legal provisions governing landlord/tenant relations. The fact that 75% of the city's population were tenants had obviously resulted in considerable and, over the years, rather effective pressure for new measures of protection. What had resulted was an extremely complex, often too complex, set of laws. But, perhaps offsetting this deficiency, New York did seem to have taken more effective steps than many other jurisdictions to make access to the courts relatively easy for those who lacked the normal skills or resources that are required for this purpose. However, it must be stressed that while many other United States cities had developed considerable measures of tenant protection, few - if any - had as elaborate or extensive a code as New York.

NEIGHBOURHOOD ORGANISATIONS AND THE PRIVATE RENTED SECTOR

We have noted that on a number of occasions tenant activism seems to have had some effect, for example in West Germany in the sixties. In fact in many countries there have been periods of intense struggle which involved tenants and tenants' organisations - particularly during the era of rapid urbanisation in the nineteenth century. Often these struggles went far beyond immediate housing issues to, for example, encompass demands for the extension of the franchise. Unfortunately research into such episodes is still very limited (for an important English study see Englander, 1979). However to illustrate the point, recent work by Heskin (1981, forthcoming) has examined the early history of tenants' conflict in the USA and shown how - very soon after Independence - urban tenants began to campaign on a platform which included universal male suffrage. And in the late nineteenth century Henry George's ideas were taken up by tenant organisations and in New York (in which 85% of the population were tenants) in 1886 they provided the basis for the formation of a labour party - with George as its mayoral candidate. In this century the issues which most tenants have organised around have usually been of lesser general importance. But tenant activism has tended to increase at times of more generalised turmoil - in the United States, Heskin suggests, peaks of activity occurred around the turn of the century, during both World Wars and in the sixties (see also Marcuse, 1973; Dreier, forthcoming).

However most tenant actions have been on a small scale, concerning individual landlords, properties or estates. Many tenants' movements have failed to survive for longer than the life of the immediate grievances which led to their formation and relatively few have made a significant impact on the more general conditions of private tenants by, for example, successfully promoting changes in the law. As we have seen national tenant organisations existed in all six countries. In the mainland European countries they had existed for many years and often had close links with socialist parties and the labour movement. They often seemed to be more effective in pressing for changes in the social rented sector - and perhaps more interested in focusing their energies on this tenure. In Britain the formation of a national tenants' organisation had only recently occurred, it too was more concerned with the social rented sector and had made little impact on the position of private tenants. By the late seventies the most active organisations of private tenants were to be found among the small and rapidly diminishing number of middle class tenants in better quality property - especially in central London - who were threatened by the activities of landlords eager to sell off these units for owner occupation. But even these able and articulate tenant activists were unable to obtain the passage of legislation to control this process.

Practical constraints limited the examination of tenant activism during the course of the project. But in the sixties there seemed to have been a significant increase in activity which took place largely outside the orbit of the established political parties and tenants' federations. The

broader causes of this development lie beyond the
immediate concerns of this chapter but tenant
activism was a part of the growing level of
community action and urban protest linked to other
forms of protest such as the Civil Rights movement
in the USA and left wing 'extra parliamentary'
action in Europe (8). Perhaps the single most
common cause of tenant activism was urban
redevelopment (and later rehabilitation) in central
city areas. But other issues, for example rent
control in several United States cities, were
important too.

Some of the problems faced by these movements
have already been noted. Recently two writers have
analysed these in the context of the USA and West
Germany. According to Dreier (forthcoming), the
United States tenants' movement of the sixties
tended to fade in the seventies as the general
turmoil of the former decade receded (9). It left
behind improved housing conditions for many low
income tenants, a body of trained organisers and
important changes in landlord/tenant laws in several
jurisdictions. But it did not result in stable
organisations, did not establish a permanent
presence in (i.e. pressure on) government, tended
to be crisis oriented and rather emphemeral. It
depended heavily on government support from the
urban programmes of the sixties. When these were
ended in the seventies, tenant organisations
suffered. Also, it focused on low income households who moved frequently and had little in the
way of resources to support permanent organisation.

According to Dreier, in the late seventies -
as grassroots protest on a wide range of issues
began to become more significant again - the
prospects for tenant organisation again improved,
in many cases aided by renewed federal funding. The
re-emergence of more ambitious tenants'
organisations was now paralleled by increased landlord organisation. Particularly effective tenant
action was taken in New Jersey and California. In
Santa Monica tenant action eventually led to the
election of a progressive city council, pursuing a
wider range of political objectives than those which
were solely concerned with rental housing (Heskin,
forthcoming). But there were still many problems.
Insofar as tenant organisations had broadened the
basis of their activities and their geographical
coverage they had been met by increasing landlord
organisation and the landlords had usually had far

more resources at their disposal to, for example,
influence legislatures and voters (10). Moreover,
in most areas tenants were in the minority, they
could probably only become a really significant
influence on major housing policy by allying with
other grassroots movements. For the moment it had
to be concluded that 'The general thrust for the
forseeable future will be more of the same - rent
control laws, eviction regulation, and improved
enforcement of housing codes. On the larger scale
of American politics, however, the tenants'
movement is still a minor actor. It is still
primarily a local phenomenon. The sum of its local
activities does not add up to a significant
political force at the national level, where major
housing policy decisions get made'.
    Mayer (1982; n.d.) in discussions of
neighbourhood movements in West Germany and the USA,
has outlined some futher problems. According to
her, in the USA many of these movements existed
to defend the interests of middle and moderate
income home owners (see also Miller, 1977). While
these organisations often opposed, for instance,
commercial urban renewal or mortgage redlining,
they were also often equally opposed to the
interests of lower income households - especially
when the latter seemed likely to 'invade' the
neighbourhoods concerned. This situation is
illustrated by the case of an area in inner
Baltimore visited just before the research project
began (see Harloe, 1978, 87-90; Kuttner, 1976).
In this locality neighbourhood organisations were
active but the results of their activities involved
the conversion of housing from a low income, rental
use to middle income owner occupation. In the
process tenants were displaced, landlords sold
out and the rental stock was significantly reduced
as a consequence (for a similar analysis, in London,
see Ferris, 1972). Mayer also noted that,
especially under the Carter Administration,
neighbourhood organisations began to play an
important role in Federal urban policies (11).

    'In the course this development goal
    displacement often occurred ...
    as the emphasis shifts from "social
    problems" to "economic development".
    Priority is increasingly placed on the
    technical mastery of grant administration
    and management while the problems of
    unemployment and blight are "solved" by

eliminating - displacing - the original
constitutency. Especially in multi-
class neighbourhoods with organisations
focussed on preservation ... the
bourgeois element is usually strengthened
and becomes the "representative" of the
whole community. This, in turn prepares
the way for organisational involvement
in gentrification'.

Mayer contrasts this situation with developments in
West Germany where some neighbourhood housing
movements, especially those which involved young
people in squatting accompanied by rehabilitation,
had made a considerable impact in the seventies -
often in the face of attack rather than support
from the authorities. This situation has been seen
in other countries too, for example in the
Netherlands - notably in Amsterdam - and in
Copenhagen (12). In London too, earlier in the
decade, there had been a growth of organised
squatting. The impact of such activities on the
existing private rented housing in the areas
affected and on the situation of existing landlords
and tenants must have varied considerably. In
London, for example, much of the squatting that
occurred was as a response to the existence of
vacant social - not private - rented housing
(Bailey, 1979). But in Amsterdam the conversion or
loss of private rented housing has more often been
among the squatters' main concerns.
     One of the most impressive and remarkable
results of tenant activism encountered during the
research project had occurred in Washington
D.C. (13). It will be recalled that this city had
an extremely tight housing market and that rent
control was introduced in the early seventies,
after much pressure from tenants. But this did
not stem the speculative conversion of low and
moderate income rented property for upper income
ownership by a variety of legal and illegal means.
In 1974 the council took action to control such
conversions. After a temporary moratorium tenants
were given first refusal if a landlord intended
to sell off for owner occupation (similar rights
existed in New York City where many landlords had
tried to sell off their properties to
co-operatives). Controls on rehabilitation were
also introduced. But large scale speculation
continued and community groups mounted a series
of militant anti-speculation demonstrations.

Eventually two councillors presented a draft bill to the council which would have heavily taxed the speculative gains, a rather remarkable development in United States housing policy and strongly opposed by property interests. By spring 1978 the proposal contained a requirement that dealers in property be licensed, that all transfers of residential property and vacant units be registered, that sales and purchase prices be disclosed and that the tenants' rights of first refusal be strengthened. These measures were quite untypical but they did show how, in certain circumstances tenants could have a considerable impact on local housing politics, especially when rental housing comprised a large part of the total stock (as was also the case in Santa Monica and New York City).

To summarise, there is evidence of a fluctuating growth in neighbourhood based organisations concerned with housing issues. To a considerable extent these new groups exist outside (although not necessarily without links to) the traditional organisations such as political parties and the established tenants' organisations. But the extent to which these new groups impinge on the private rental sector is unknown. Certainly several cases where there has been such an impact can be found. But the evidence is partial and fragmented. Moreover, even when there are effects on the private rental sector these may be negative, leading to the reduction of such accommodation - as for example appears to have occurred in many cases in the USA. In general, as Pickvance (1976, 1977) has suggested (in a discussion of urban protest in Britain and France), lower income households often face considerable barriers to achieving effective group action. Given the predominantly low income nature of private rented tenants, this conclusion has an obvious significance.

CONCLUSION

Several general conclusions emerge from this chapter. There had been a growth in the formality and complexity of the letting contract and, in most countries, a growth in tenant protection, especially with respect to their right to enjoy reasonably habitable living conditions. But the effectiveness of much of this law was doubtful. First, because such evidence as there was showed that many tenants and landlords remained in ignorance of legal provisions. Second, because, even if they knew that legal remedies were avilable, they often lacked the means to pursue them. The development of legal and housing aid had probably only made a marginal impact on removing this constraint.

But some countries had developed these rights more than others. Thus in France landlord/tenant law was still strongly marked by the concern to protect the ownership of private property that had been enshrined in the Napoleonic Code. (Interestingly in 1982, after the conclusion of this research, the new socialist government passed the Loi Quillot which ended the assumption that the right of the residential landlord over his/her property should be virtually absolute and introduced many rights similar to those available to tenants in other European countries, including provision for collective bargaining between landlords and tenants. See De Moor, 1983). Moreover, in most countries the rights enjoyed by some categories of tenants, for example those in rented rooms, remained minimal. But problems arose even where much more elaborate legal protection existed. Thus New York's housing law was so complex, and the burdens it put on a resource starved local government organisation so massive, that the effectiveness of the legal regulation of landlord/ tenant relations was questionable. A possible alternative to legal redress was political action (even though the end product might be more legislation) and direct action, such as rent strikes. The example of Washington DC showed that in some circumstances, especially when substantial proportions of the population still lived in rental housing, political pressure could be effective (as, it should be noted, could pressure from property interests too). But at the time of the research little evidence of this occurring on a significant scale existed outside the USA, although this had not always been the case.

From the sixties there had been a growth of neighbourhood based activity. Some of this was concerned with private rental housing, but not always to the advantage of the maintenance of this tenure or of improving the position of tenants. A good deal more research would be necessary to draw any very firm conclusions regarding the overall significance and effects of neighbourhood based activity but it was tentatively suggested that, in many cases, the sort of housholds now living in

private rented housing face considerable obstacles
when attempting to form or participate in such
organisations.

The principal feature of landlord/tenant
relations to which we must return was their
individualistic and informal nature or, more
accurately, the extent to which they operated in a
framework which was wholly or substantially
untouched by legal provisions. Despite legal
innovations, the relationship between landlords and
tenants was mainly governed by their relative
strengths in the market place or, in cases where
'rational' economic motives did not appear to
underly landlords' decisions to let, a variety of
more personal, non-instrumental factors. These
factors were so diffuse and unresearched that they
cannot be usefully discussed here but it would be
very interesting to know what proportion of the
rental market lies outside the boundaries of a
reasonably 'rational' market system.

In cases where economic factors were important
and where the position of the two parties to a
letting agreement depended on the respective
levels of demand for and supply of accommodation,
relations were likely to vary according to the
sector of the market concerned (and therefore the
tenants' means) and by the location. In general,
those at the bottom of the shrinking rental market
were likely to find themselves involved in contracts
and relations with landlords which were less
satisfactory than those encountered by the better
off who had a greater freedom to choose alternative
accommodation. This is not universally true, as
we saw in New York tenants of luxury properties
had protested at the decline in the services which
their contracts had promised them and in some ghetto
areas it has been suggested that landlords faced
slackening demand for their properties. But in this
latter situation tenants who pressed for
improvements in their living conditions often found
the exercise counter-productive as landlords did
not have the available resources. Indeed such
pressure could bring about abandonment with the
consequent loss of even the minimal level of
services which had earlier been provided.

In sections of the rental housing market which
were still relatively crisis free the impression
was that the vast majority of tenants and landlords
co-existed fairly harmoniously. But in the
circumstances of decline and lack of resources

which was coming to characterise a very substantial
proportion of the market, and where either
landlords could no longer afford reasonable
standards of management and maintenance or where
exploitation of poor tenants occurred, scattered
but culminatively substantial evidence existed of
widespread and often bitter conflict. Moreover,
several informants were clear that elaborate legal
frameworks were often ineffective in regulating
and resolving such situations. In short the
economics of the market place defined the real, as
opposed to the theoretical, limits of the law.

Landlord/Tenant Relations

NOTES

1. The court had to give possession if the
landlord had lived there in the past and wanted the
property back to live there again or for one of his
or her family, who had lived there with the
landlord in the past, to live there again; if the
house had been bought as a retirement home and was
now needed for the landlord's retirement; if the
premises had normally been used as a holiday
letting; if it was let by an educational
establishment to students; and various other minor
cases. The court might grant possession if the
landlord offered suitable alternative accommodation
(which might be local authority housing); if the
tenant was in rent arrears or had broken other
tenancy conditions; if there had been unauthorised
subletting; if the letting had been in connection
with employment, this had now ended and the
housing was wanted for another worker; if the
accommodation was required for the landlord or a
family member (but not if it was brought with the
tenant already in occupation) and various other
minor cases.
2. The figures in this paragraph are taken
from Department of the Environment, quarterly.
3. A number of government reports had examined
the question of harassment and illegal eviction
which, it was often claimed, was common especially
in areas such as inner London where property could
be sold with vacant possession at far higher prices
than its tenanted value. See, for example,
Committee on Housing in Greater London, 1965;
Committee on the Rent Acts,1971, House of Commons
Environment Committee I, 1982. Legislation on
harassment and illegal eviction dated from the mid
sixties, it was only used in a very few cases -
difficulties of proof being one of the main
obstacles.
4. The election of representatives was made
a precondition for the duty placed on the landlord
to give 'first refusal' to the tenants on seeking
to sell out.
5. I am indebted to Rolph Neiderberger
(member of the Legal Board of the Deutschen
Mieterbund) for most of the information in this
section.
6. For instance a survey of tenants published
in 1970 found that many tenants did not know that
Rent Act protection was available, others declined

to use it and a significant minority, especially
in furnished accommodation, feared retaliation from
the landlord if they sought the Act's protection
(Committee on the Rent Acts, 1971, 241-315).

7. One commentator, writing in 1969, noted
that laws which enabled rent witholding pending
property repairs had been passed in seven states
including New York, Pennsylvania and Massachusetts.
He also noted that six states had passed laws
which enabled tenants to carry out repairs
themselves and deduct the costs from the rent, in
some cases such laws were of long standing (Meador,
1969). Since this date there had been a growth of
such legislation.

8. There is now a vast literature on these
organisations or 'urban social movements' as they
were called by Manuel Castells. For example, see
Castells et. al., 1974; Castells, 1978; 1983;
Saunders, 1979; and the discussion on the
international literature in Lebas, 1982.

9. Lebas (1982) also notes 'In Europe by the
mid seventies the study of urban social movements
appeared to have noticeably declined, as did
movements themselves'. For a similar point see also
Ceccarelli, 1982.

10. See, for example, the considerable
resources devoted by the landlords and other
property interests to attempting to defeat a
referendum on rent control in Santa Monica - as
discussed in Heskin, forthcoming and Shearer, 1982a.
In the case of the Washington DC antispeculation
campaign Richards and Rowe (1977, 60) noted 'The
irony is that if the antispeculation proposal
accomplishes nothing else, it has molded the
rehabilitation industry into a political force. A
year and a half ago rehabbers were a loose
assortment of staunch individualists'. In cities,
such as New York, where there was an extended
history of tenant activism, landlord organisation
was longer established and considerably more
influential than in these former two cities. See,
for example, Rust, 1977; Tumolillo, 1977; Newfield
and Du Brul, 1978, passim.

11. During the course of the research, in
March 1978, President Carter announced his 'new
partnership to conserve America's communities'
which stressed the need for there to be a
co-operative effort between federal/state and local
government, business and neighbourhood
organisations to preserve and develop the areas of
the older inner cities. Governmental resource

constraints were one of the main reasons why the
government now sought to tap 'community' resources
to carry out its urban policies (see President
Jimmy Carter, 1978).

12. The conflict has been particularly intense
in the Netherlands. See, for example, Anderiesen,
1981; Bijlsma and Salverda, 1978; Priemus, 1983;
Draaisma and van Hoogstraten, 1983.

13. The account of developments in Washington
is based on interviews carried out in 1978 and
Committee on Finance and Revenue, 1976; Richards
and Rowe, 1977; Council of the District of Columbia
1979.

Chapter Nine

THE FUTURE OF THE PRIVATE RENTED SECTOR

In this final chapter we summarise the conclusions
which we have drawn from the detailed examination
of the private rented sector contained in the
previous chapters. Clearly, the sector is in decline
but the rate of decline varies considerably. We
shall highlight some of the reasons for this as
well as considering some recent political and
policy responses to it. Finally the prospects for
the tenure are discussed.

THE DECLINE OF PRIVATE RENTING

As we have seen, the decline in private rented
housing is not confined, as some allege, to
countries with 'anti-landlord' policies such as
strict rent controls. While such policies have of
course had their impact the reasons for decline are
more complex and deep rooted and in some respects
pre-date the first imposition of controls. Moreover
decline has continued and even accelerated when
controls have been eased or lifted altogether.
    The growth of rental housing was a consequence
of developments which occurred at varying rates and
times in the six countries from the early
nineteenth century onwards. With the move to an
urban based, capitalist economy housing was
increasingly provided, like other essentials, as a
market commodity. In housing (and consumption
generally), as in production, the previous social
relations which determined housing provision were
replaced by the new limited and calculative
relationships of the capitalist social formation.
(This probably occurred less rapidly and completely
in the countryside, but this is a topic which is
very under-researched).
    The form which the market provision of housing

293

took - private renting - was shaped by the
circumstances of the time. On the one hand, there
was the rapid growth of a mass of wage labourers,
lacking capital or land, with low and uncertain
earnings, in densely populated cities (and so cut
off from traditional rural housing solutions) and
requiring to reside close to sources of employment.
On the other hand, there was the growth of new
forms of land and property development and
speculation. As we have seen, the provision of
rented housing brought together large land owners,
speculative - mainly small-builders, finance capital
and small investors in new and complex
relationships - the outcome of which was substantial
profits for themselves and inadequate and costly
housing for the mass of the new working class (1).
As today, the poorest paid the highest proportion
of their incomes for the worst housing. In fact the
profitability of low income housing was probably
often higher than that of better middle and upper
income quality housing. Furthermore, in several
countries the problem of low income housing costs
seemed to worsen as urban growth continued (2).
     The inability of the unassisted private market
to provide adequate housing at a bearable cost for
a large proportion of the population is one of the
root causes of the eventual decline of private
renting. The consequences of this failure began to
be seen as a serious threat to social stability and
an obstruction to economic development - because,
for example, of its ill-effects on the workforce
and/or its potential for increasing the pressure
for higher wages. Therefore, from a fairly early
stage, private rented housing was in some
countries on the defensive. In the long term the
ability of private landlords to resist the pressure
from other major economic and political interests
for limits to be placed on their activities has
been weak. While much more work needs to be done on
the detailed history of this pressure and
resistance, the relative powerlessness of the
private landlord is likely to have resulted from
the small scale, fragmented and unorganised nature
of this form of property capital, the growth of
much larger scale and better organised groups -
both of workers and capital - elsewhere in the
economy, and the declining significance of local
political power, with the growth of central
government which has more strongly reflected the
political and economic interests of these more
powerful groups. The point is illustrated with

respect to politics, in the case of Britain, by the
conclusions of a recent study of property and
politics in the late Victorian and Edwardian era.

> 'The small owner of weekly property did not
> recover from the Edwardian slump. Rent
> control in wartime transformed the pre-war
> slump into a capital levy on the small
> landlord. And the Tory champions of property
> did not rush, post-war, to salvage this
> most self-effacing of political interests.
> Was it because rent control was numbing one
> of the most painful of social interfaces,
> the relation between landlord and urban
> working-class tenant?' (Offer, 1981, 405).

The economic issue is illustrated by the Chairman
of the London County Council's Housing of the
Working Classes Committee, writing at the end of
the nineteenth century, 'The Housing problem ...
provokes the vexed question of the relation between
rent and wages, which easily slides into that of
capital and labour' (Quoted by Pahl in the
introduction to Harloe, Issacharoff and Minns, 1974,
viii). As Daunton has written, in a study of
Victorian housing published after this study was
completed, the sacrifice of the British landlord
was a consequence of the sector's marginal position
in the social and political formation (he states
that elsewhere in Europe and in the USA the position
was very different - but the conclusion of this
study must be that, while the timing and extent of
such marginalisation has varied, its existence has
been far more common than Daunton suggests)
(Daunton, 1983, 3).
    State intervention was at first wholly
regulatory and, when it finally began to be
effective, did little to solve the mass housing
problem and a good deal to make it more evident and
even more acute. At first regulation mainly
affected the provision of the very worst housing
for the least well off. Indeed we saw that in some
cases the housing developers and up-market landlords
supported increased regulation when the demand for
new housing was sluggish. The increasing
difficulties that faced the profitable provision of
low quality housing as regulation began to take
effect, coupled with the growth of suburban housing
and of more profitable and legitimate uses for
central city land all helped to reduce the supply
of reasonable low income housing.

The Future of the Private Rented Sector

Of course the details of this general pattern
varied from country to country. First, the timing
and pace of the industrial/urban transition varied
- for example, occurring earliest and over the
longest period in Britain and much later and more
rapidly in Germany. Second, the nature and
relationship of the major class interests and
ideologies involved in this transition varied. As
more general analyses have shown,(3) the nature and
limits of state welfare policies were conditioned
by such factors, and we have seen how, in housing,
attitudes and policies varied considerably.
Third, there was of course a close relationship
between the economic position of the population and
its housing conditions. As the surveys of working
class housing standards and costs of living carried
out by the British government in the 1900's showed,
American workers could afford better housing than
their European counterparts and, within Europe,
housing conditions in those countries which were
only developing slowly - such as France - were
particularly poor (Board of Trade, 1908a, 1908b,
1909, 1911, 1913).
By 1914 state intervention had achieved little
in the way of a positive solution to the mass
housing problem. The first world war and its
aftermath brought about the first major change in
this situation. For both political and economic
reasons, all six governments accepted new, if
sometimes temporary, responsibilities for low
income housing. The most significant developments
were the imposition of rent controls and the
provision of state subsidised rental housing. The
extent to which these changes persisted varied
according to the postwar situation of each country.
Broadly, the greater the economic and political
crisis, the greater the intervention so that, for
example, in the twenties the German housing market
was almost wholly dependent on state aid and
regulation whereas the American housing market
rapidly reverted to private enterprise with the
minimum of regulation.
Throughout the interwar period we can again
see how the interplay of broad political and
economic factors determined the situation of
private rental housing. We noted, for example, the
varying influence of social democratic parties on
housing policies, the impact of the economic crisis
of the thirties and of economic growth both before
and after this crisis (4). But, by 1939, with
perhaps the exception of parts of the USA, private

rented housing still dominated urban housing markets. But very little had changed in the inability of the private landlord to provide adequate lower income housing. The slums of the previous century still provided the main solution to much of this demand.

We shall consider the political context of private renting since 1945 below, but the background to its fortunes has been shaped by nationally varying factors which include the immediate post-war circumstances of each country, the pace and scale of economic growth and the growth of incomes, the nature and objectives of state intervention and - most directly - by the growth of social rented and owner occupied housing. But, regardless of individual national circumstances, the declining significance of this tenure has become ever more apparent. At the end of the second world war about 60-75% of the population of the five European countries lived in private rented housing. In the USA just under 50% were housed in this tenure. But by the end of the seventies only West Germany still had more than a third of its housing stock in this sector. Moreover, the production of private rented housing, perhaps the most sensitive indicator of the prospects for the sector, had shrunk even further, down to less than a quarter of all new building in West Germany and the USA and to negligible proportions elsewhere (Bovaird et. al., 1982a, 59).

The details of this decline were examined in chapters 3 - 8. The principal conclusions of these chapters were:

1. Much of the private rental stock was located in the inner areas of the older cities and was built at high densities. It tended to consist of small units which lacked modern facilities - much of it having been built at a time when standards and incomes were far lower than today. It usually offered far worse value for money than social rented housing.
2. There was a significant amount of newer rented accommodation in most countries. But this was often let at rather high rents to middle income households and (in the French case most clearly) was almost as expensive to rent as it would have been to buy. The output of new rented housing had, in recent years, been minimal in several countries.

3. Increasingly, the sector was becoming
   polarised, housing the elderly and the
   young. Both these groups were relatively
   disadvantaged in the housing market,
   containing many low income households.
   Aided by subsidies, social rented and -
   later - owner-occupied housing siphoned off
   much of the demand arising from the rest of
   the population.
4. Many private tenants had incomes which
   over time rose more slowly than the
   average. In an era of rapid inflation in
   landlords' costs this was a serious
   situation as the gap between revenue and
   cost narrowed. While some middle and upper
   income demand remained, even those who had
   had continued for many years to invest in
   rental housing began to withdraw from this
   activity.
5. Especially in the larger cities some -
   mainly small - landlords continued to make
   good profits by providing poor quality
   'housing of last resort' to those who
   could not gain access to better quality
   housing. Such groups included racial
   minorities, guest workers, large/low
   income families, single parent families,
   the young, the elderly, and others who
   were - in some respects - 'marginal'
   categories with limited economic and/or
   political power.
6. The impact of rent controls was far from
   simple and self-evident. In some countries
   the most rapid decline in the sector
   occurred after 1960, at a time when rigid
   controls were giving way to decontrol or to
   more flexible controls which attempted to
   relate rent levels to quality and costs.
7. The principal reasons for this decline were
   that the growth of inflation from the
   sixties onwards sharply raised costs at a
   time when an increasing proportion of those
   housed by the sector had a severely limited
   ability to pay higher rents. The rising
   demand for owner occupation which
   stimulated the sales and prices of older
   property added a positive incentive to the
   negative features which were encouraging
   landlords to sell off their holdings. Data
   from West Germany, England and the USA

clearly documented the declining returns
experienced during this period. In some
cases political pressures caused by the
rising rent burdens on tenants led to a
reimposition or a strengthening of rent
controls and added to the pressure to leave
the sector.

8. With the exception of Britain, all of the
countries had offered substantial subsidies
to encourage new private rental
construction after 1945. But, especially in
comparison with subsidies to the other main
tenures, this assistance had become less
generous over time. In Denmark, for example,
this was because there had always been
substantial political opposition to aiding
private landlords, so assistance was seen
as a temporary post-war expedient. More
generally, as for example in Germany,
emphasis switched away from private renting
as the objective of encouraging owner
occupation became more important to
governments committed to private market
housing solutions (5). Increasingly,
subsidies to the private rental sector
focussed on the provision of housing
allowances for low income households.
Although this was an aspect of a more
general movement from 'institutional' to
'residual' welfare in housing and,
especially in the seventies, pressures to
withdraw or sharply reduce generaly
subsidies to social rented housing were
also noticeable, it was not, however,
applied to owner occupied housing. In
several countries, the taxation treatment
of private rental housing had also become
less favourable in relation to the other
tenures.

9. One important consequence of the decline of
the private rented sector was that it
formed the hard core of the problem of
older, dilapidated housing which became the
object of increasing government action
from the fifties onwards. At first policies
concentrated on demolition and rebuilding
but later shifted to rehabilitation.
Neither did much to improve conditions
within the private rented sector. In fact
they probably accelerated the decline of

the sector as, in the first phase, units
were demolished and, in the second phase,
improvement was often accompanied by a
change of tenure. While the position varied
many landlords could not afford or manage
the process of rehabilitation and many
tenants could not afford the increased
rents that usually resulted. Rehabilitation
subsidies mainly benefitted owner
occupation, and, in some instances, social
rented housing.

10. The legal regulation of landlord/tenant
relations was of limited effectiveness.
Many landlords and tenants coexisted
without recourse to the law. But in a
declining sector, in which many landlords
could not sustain reasonable standards of
management and maintenance and in which
some were able to exploit the lack of
alternative low income accommodation, there
was evidence of considerable conflict
which existing laws did little to help
resolve. One indicator of this conflict
was the growth of protest movements,
especially in the inner urban areas of
major cities. In a few instances these
groups had obtained major gains but their
overall impact was probably marginal.

FUTURE PROSPECTS

All those interviewed during the research were
certain that the decline of private renting would
continue. This contention will be questioned
later but we shall first consider the prospects
in each country as they appeared at the time of the
research.

As we have seen, in France there was a clear
division between the older private rented units and
the newer, often subsidised, units constructed
since 1948. The first sub-sector tended to house
the elderly and poor while the second served better
off households who preferred to rent or who
could only afford to buy property located at a
considerable distance from the centres of the
larger cities. It did not seem likely that the HLM
sector would be able to take over the role of the
older private rented housing. On the contrary, new
proposals for higher rents and an increasing
emphasis on HLM housing for sale seemed more likely

300

to reduce the supply of low income social housing.
At the same time the rapid inflation of building
and land costs increased the incentives - for those
who could afford it - to buy rather than to rent
and the output of new rental housing was falling.
In many rural areas housing abandonment was likely
to continue as demand fell due to depopulation.
Some of this stock would also be sold off, or
rented out, as second homes. Landlords in
'unpopular' rural areas would often not be able to
raise rents as rapidly as they wished for fear of
not finding tenants. So a further deterioration in
the condition of this property seemed likely. In
towns and some rural areas where there was greater
demand there would be incentives to upgrade
property in order to sell it off. This had already
occurred but not so extensively as in some other
countries. One reason was that in some towns good
returns were made from letting to mobile middle and
upper income households who continued to rent
rather than to buy. As noted already, economic
circumstances were increasing the attraction of
owner occupation, so the future size of this submarket was open to question. However, the rapid
inflation of house prices meant that the owners of
this property had, besides receiving adequate rents,
also been able to benefit from considerable capital
appreciation.

The elderly small scale and frequently low
income landlords who owned much of the older
property seemed likely to gradually disappear. The
new improvement policies did not offer much
assistance to them and so would not make a big
impact on the quality of this stock. As the older
and cheaper stock disappeared, the average rent/
income ratio was likely to rise. This would be
accentuated by the policy of raising direct housing
costs for most households.

Nevertheless, despite the general signs of
decline, there was still a considerable demand for
private rental housing in France. But the tenure
was gradually becoming confined to the poor and
those with special needs plus a small high quality
sector, as, for instance, in Britain, Denmark and
the Netherlands. The development of the movement
towards ownership and out of renting would depend
on the interaction of several factors including
the inflation of house prices, the rate of
increase of real incomes, the success of the policy
of raising rents and its impact on the various
market subsectors and the relative degree of

The Future of the Private Rented Sector

government assistance for investors in and occupants of housing in the main tenures. At the time of the research the competitive advantage of owner occupied over rental housing was still less pronounced in France than in many other developed capitalist economies and there was perhaps, in comparison with some of these countries, less general political acceptance of the declining significance of private renting (6).

In Denmark there was a far clearer acceptance of the decline of rental housing and its lack of significance for future housing provision, although there were different ideas about what should then occur. The conservatives wanted to see a great expansion of owner occupation with sales of private and social rented housing. The socialists wanted to maintain the social housing sector and end all commercial letting. The most contentious development was the growth of extensive sales of private rented property either to tenant co-operatives or, more advantageously for the landlords, by creating freehold flats, i.e. creating a legal form of ownership of individual flats in a block which then enabled them to be sold off.

No statistics on the growth of co-operatives were available but it was known that their numbers had increased in the late sixties and early seventies when a rapid increase in the 'break up' and selling off of blocks of flats had led to new laws restricting this operation. Many of the so-called co-operatives then established were unsound and the co-operators were often persuaded to pay too high a price for their units and to accept onerous financial responsibilities.

The legal powers enabling freehold conversion to occur were an innovation contained in the 1966 housing pact. At first all private rented property built after 1890 could be sold off. Between 1966/67 and 1976 over 100,000 freehold flats were created (although many of these were still occupied by tenants - as the landlords had to wait until they were vacant, or until the sitting tenants agreed to buy, before disposing of the units). Conversion was heavily concentrated in the Copenhagen area and sales were mostly not to sitting tenants. So this development was beginning to have a major impact on the already fast declining private rental sector.

In 1976 a new policy to regulate freehold conversion was agreed between the major political parties. The topic was intensely political with the left and the tenants' movement wanting to encourage co-operatives and the conservatives and the landlords' association wanting to promote freehold conversion. As normal in the fragmented Danish political system, the outcome was a compromise policy. Before freehold conversion landlords were now required to give their tenants an opportunity for co-operative purchase. Regulations governed the constitution of co-operatives and sales prices. But experience so far had shown that many tenants were unable to afford co-operative ownership, at least without the provision of some subsidies. The government seemed to be moving towards such a policy in the late seventies (7).

The main advantage for landlords was the opportunity to obtain enhanced capital values. The purely legal process of freehold conversion was likely to add about 20% to capital values and when a sale occurred far higher gains might be made. Informants estimated that capital values might increase by about four to six times their former (tenanted) levels. Tenants who could afford to buy were often able to do so at below market prices (the cost to the landlord of their security of tenure) and then resell and also realise a capital gain. This new source of smaller, relatively cheap second-hand property had opened up ownership opportunities for those who could not afford the traditionally available, larger and more expensive owner-occupied stock. After the rapid rent rises which had occurred many tenants seemed eager to buy. Ownership was probably also becoming more attractive for other households who were finding it difficult to obtain good private rented accommodation in a shrinking market and, as newcomers, would be faced with high rents in social housing.

To summarise, in many respects the situation in Denmark seemed close to that which existed in Britain, with the private rental sector having undergone a rapid decline and with little belief that it would ever play a major role in housing provision. As in Britain, most young households only remained in the sector for a few years before moving to social housing or in owner occupation. Developments such as freehold conversion and the growing numbers of families able to draw on two incomes to meet mortgage repayments, together with the assistance for owner occupation and rising rents had resulted in a rapid growth in the demand

for ownership. The residual private rented sector
was likely to house an increasingly high proportion
of poorer tenants living in the worst stock.
Without new and extensive subsidies improvements
in their position were unlikely. But there seemed
to be little political support for such subsidies.

As we have shown, West Germany has retained a
substantial private rented sector. With the aid of
considerable government assistance, many new units
have been produced since 1945. But by the late
seventies it seemed that this expansion was over
and that new investment was rapidly declining. The
landlords' association stated that few companies
were still building units, that banks had become
unwilling to finance rental development and that
new activity seemed to be confined to small
investors. These people were probably interested
in owning property as a hedge against inflation
and as a provision for their old age. In addition
there was some conversion of better quality
property in desirable areas for upper income
rental (Einem, 1982).

In contrast to other countries such as Britain,
the Netherlands and Denmark, it seemed that rather
few sales of rented property for owner occupation
had occurred in Germany - up till the late seventies
at least. Moreover, as we saw in chapter five, when
the Social Democrats came to power in 1969 they had
made important changes in rent and security policy
which had benefitted tenants. But, increasingly,
this government was mainly concerned to encourage
owner occuaption. In 1977 it extended owner occupier
subsidies, until then only available for new
housing, to older housing units. This was resulting
in an increase in sales, in particular a growth in
speculative activity involving the surface
improvement and resale of formerly privately rented
properties. This was aided by legislation which
enabled owners who wanted to improve to remove
sitting tenants. There were also reports of payments
to induce tenants to vacate property and harassment
to achieve the same end.

Landlords insisted that the reintroduction of
permanent tenant protection in 1974 had provided
a major disincentive to investment. But the decline
which was beginning to occur could not be viewed in
such a narrow light. The post war expansion of
rental housing has to be seen in the context of the
rather special situation that West Germany was in
immediately after the last war and the actions that
were taken by its government. The low level of

The Future of the Private Rented Sector

owner occupation which had persisted was unlikely
to continue, given the growth in prosperity in the
sixties and seventies, the encouragement which all
parties gave to the expansion of owner occupation,
and the reduction of fiscal and other inventives
for the production of new rental units. In addition
rapidly rising house prices and rents, coupled with
the new help for the purchase and improvement of
older housing, seemed likely to increase the
propensity of middle income households - who had
long remained in private rented housing - to buy.
The increasingly negative attitude to new rental
investment adopted by the financial institutions was
an important indicator of the changing prospects
for the tenure. It seemed likely that the private
rental sector would, as elsewhere, begin to
polarise, with a small, high quality, sector meeting
the needs of mobile, better off households and a
larger, poor quality sector providing accommodation
for those who could not afford owner occupation or
the high rents of new social housing (8). As
elsewhere too, current policies did not appear to
have found an answer to the problem of improving
conditions in this part of the sector.
    The decline of the British private rented
sector preceded that which was occurring in the
other countries. Its causes relate in particular to
the early development of a substantial social
housing sector and of owner occupation. Also the
growth of owner occupation probably had an effect
on the flow of funds into private renting because
the building societies which financed this growth
provided a more secure investment medium than
private rented housing for many smaller investors.
A significant feature of British housing politics
was the lack of any effective support for private
renting by either of the major political parties
from 1945 onwards. The first post-war Labour
government had favoured council housing and in the
fifties the Conservative government, while paying
lip-service to the need to encourage the private
landlord, had not provided the subsidies which
would have been essential if the sector was to be
sustained. Instead, from the fifties onwards the
main objective had been to expand owner occuaption.
This was an aim fully shared by the Labour Party by
the time it regained power in the sixties.
    As elsewhere, the rented sector was
increasingly confined to providing poor quality
housing for low income households. So it was
increasingly 'insolvent' (9). However, this

305

conclusion did not apply to the small luxury sector, nor to some lettings in housing stress areas which were made available at high rents and with minimal security under a variety of arrangements which avoided or evaded legal controls. This part of the market was becoming even more significanℴ as the traditional providers of rented housing left the market. In 1982 a Parliamentary committee reported that, on the basis of the evidence which it had received, it seemed likely that most new lets were not in practice protected by the Rent Act (House of Commons Environment Committee, 1982, I, xx).

Among those who were able to let largely free of controls were resident landlords - many of them owner occupiers letting rooms for a temporary period in order to meet initially high mortgage repayments. A survey had shown that such landlords when ceasing to let were being replaced by others, whereas non-resident landlords (individuals and companies) were steadily disappearing from the sector (Paley, 1978). Future prospects for resident landlords were less affected by legislation or by the attractiveness of alternative investments than by their own economic circumstances. It seemed that this part of the market might remain reasonably buoyant as real incomes stagnated due to the economic recession, as housing policy tended to force people to buy even when incomes were limited and as the number of elderly underoccupying lower income owners rose.

But there was no sign that the decline in the rest of the sector would stop. As in the past, much of the worst property would eventually be purchased by local authorities or housing associations and demolished or improved, although cuts in public expenditure were slowing this process down. The better property would continue to be sold off to owner occupiers and also some of the poorer property to low income households. Research in inner city areas had shown that poor quality housing was often sold to lower income households unable to gain access to alternative housing and that a variety of 'fringe' financial institutions had provided loans - often at extortionate interest rates (Harloe, Issacharoff and Minns, 1974; Karn, 1979). As in Denmark, there had been a lucrative trade, especially in London, of the speculative 'break up' and selling off of rented flats with the development of a few tenant co-operatives. As in this country too, the only change which might have stemmed the decline was the provision of large scale subsidies but, once again, no political party seemed likely to adopt such a policy (10).

Until the seventies it seemed as if the Netherlands had a relatively active and healthy private rented sector. The size of the tenure was gradually declining but new units were being added to it. But by the late seventies new building for private landlords had almost disappeared and the sector was declining by about 50,000 units per annum. The very sharp decline in new building was precipitated by the introduction of the dynamic cost subsidy system but, as elsewhere, more fundamental factors were also at work.

Since 1945 new building by small investors had virtually disappeared as the social housing sector had expanded. Up to the seventies the institutions, interested in longer term returns from higher rented property, maintained some new production. However, even they found unsubsidised production unprofitable as it was in competition with subsidised social rented housing and, from the sixties, with subsidised owner occupation. So the proportion of private rented unsubsidised units fell to a very low level. In the seventies rapid inflation and high interest rates finally made almost all new production unprofitable. So institutional investors switched, as in West Germany, France and elsewhere, into building for sale. In addition, sales of rented property accelerated, together with all the consequences of this activity noticeable elsewhere. Particularly in the housing stress areas of the Randstadt this was causing considerable stress and political conflict, with a large scale, well-organised squatting movement. The various rent control and allocation measures were breaking down under the increasing pressures which were being put upon them. With the exception of Rotterdam, alternatives which involved the public take-over of low income rental housing were not seriously considered by the major parties.

The prospects for improvement appeared to be poor and it was suggested that the condition of much of the lower rented stock was likely to deteriorate. Some of this property was being acquired by speculators, being held by a succession of owners on short-term mortgages and providing inadequate and insecure accommodation at high rents in relation to their quality. Conditions were likely to worsen as there was considerable evidence of intensifying housing stress and exploitation, especially in the inner areas of the Randstad and among certain vulnerable groups. While in government both left and right wing parties had promoted owner occupation and done little to stem the decline of private renting (although, when in opposition at the end of the seventies, the left again stressed their earlier support for social rented housing). As elsewhere, the economic weakness of private renting was compounded by its political weakness.

The private rental sector in the USA was larger and more complex than those of the other five countries. Moreover, it seemed likely to continue to house very many people, given the lack of a significant social rented sector. It also retained considerable economic and political significance. Indicators of this included the continued building that was occurring in some regions and the ability which property interests still had to influence state and local policies regarding matters such as rent control. But despite these strengths, many of the general symptoms of crisis and decline were evident here too.

Thus, even in the sunbelt states where there was still extensive new investment, many better off households of types which had traditionally provided the more solvent demand for this tenure were turning to owner occupation. Despite the rapid growth in 'renter prone' households, a growing proportion of these were opting to buy rather than to rent. As elsewhere, this change was occurring at a time of rapid inflation in house prices and other costs. Indeed, in the USA it was occurring at a time when homeowner costs were rising more rapidly than renter costs. Evidently, as elsewhere, inflation had merely increased the desire to buy. Rapidly rising real incomes (for some) plus the growth of second earnings had enabled the expansion of owner occupation to be sustained.

While there was a relatively slow growth in rents, a consequence of the lack of demand for new and better quality units, operating costs and the cost of new building had risen sharply and the combination of inflation and stagnating demand was adversely affecting the prospects for the whole sector. But, in the short term at least, the really acute crisis concerned low income renting. There was a growing gap between incomes, and therefore rent paying capacity, and costs. In many central areas conventional loans were unobtainable, forcing landlords, if they wished to remain in business, to

308

borrow from 'fringe' banks at high interest rates.
This was crucial as refinancing to realise increased
capital values had often been an important source
of income for landlords. Furthermore, in many cases
capital values were falling, ruling out any
possibility of realising capital gains. Another
adverse factor was the inability of many localities
to supply adequate services to inner city areas.
At the same time the burden of ever-increasing
dependency and social need had to be supported by a
narrowing tax base. This resulted in sharply rising
local property tax payments by landlords.

Possible solutions to some of these problems
were a massive transfer of financial
responsibilities from the localities to the federal
government (especially for the growing burden of
welfare payments), the curtailing of suburban
autonomy, greater control over industrial location
and, more generally, increased economic growth which
would reduce high central city unemployment rates.
These changes would have improved the viability of
low income rental housing but neither of the main
political parties seemed remotely likely to adopt
such policies. A more possible response would have
been to increase subsidies by, for example, an
expanded section 8 programme. But at the time
of the research government support was on a very
small scale relative to needs and was unlikely to
expand significantly in future (11).

There were several dramatic indicators of these
problems. For example, there was the growth in
abandonment and of units whose tenants were
subjected to the 'sweating' tactics discussed
earlier and the increase in mortgage default (12).
A government commissioned analysis showed that even
subsidised projects were in trouble (Stegman, 1978;
Wye, et. al., 1978). Thus, at the end of 1976 about
29% of all multifamily federally subsidised rental
projects were in mortgage default or assignment or
had already reverted to government ownership
through foreclosure. About 13% of the much larger
number of non-subsidised federally insured projects
were in similar difficulties and the default rate
was rising rapidly. Defaults and foreclosures on
multifamily mortgages in the non-federally insured
and/or subsidised sector were also rising sharply.
Moreover, as noted above, the capital value of
older rental property in inner city areas was
falling. According to a study in New York City,
values began to fall in the sixties. Before this
time buildings traded at six times their current

309

rent rolls but by the late seventies the multiplier
was as low as one or two (13). In real terms the
sales prices of New York elevator buildings fell by
about 65% between the mid-sixties and the mid-
seventies. This had seriously reduced the city's
property tax base.
    Existing government policies were unlikely to
make much impact on these trends. As we have seen,
there was an extraordinary range of federal, state
and local programmes but few of them operated on a
large scale. Some of these programmes had
stimulated new investment in private renting, but
at a cost. For example, the federal tax benefits for
certain upper income earners encouraged investment
but in the longer term produced considerable
instability of ownership and financial difficulty.
Rehabilitation, even when government aided, had
been ineffective in keeping property within the
rental sector, or at least within the low income
rental sector and, as elsewhere, had resulted in
the displacement of many poorer households.
    At the upper end of the market there would
probably be a gradual drying up of new investment
and an increase in sales in the form of
co-operatives or, more commonly, condominiums.
Initially most condominiums were newly built but
by 1980 it was estimated that more units were
leaving the rental stock in this way than the
numbers being added to the rental stock by new
building. The number of units coverted tripled
between 1977 and 1979 - from 50,000 to 145,000. It
was estimated that 80% of tenants were forced to
leave their buildings when conversion occurred and
the rate of increase in conversion in the larger
cities in all regions was very rapid indeed
(Legates and Murphy, 1981, 267-8 - but for a more
optimistic view see Kain, 1983, 142-4. Both of
these accounts draw on the results of a large
scale national survey carried out in 1979, US
Department of Housing and Urban Development, 1980b).
Developments in the seventies in neighbourhood
revitalisation in cities such as Baltimore, where
much of the housing was not in blocks of apartments,
involved the conversion of rented property to forms
of ownership.
    At the lower end of the market, despite many
small-scale initiatives involving, for example, the
formation of low income co-operatives in abandoned
properties (with some governmental support) growing
numbers of tenants were likely to face deteriorating
neighbourhood and housing conditions and increasing

310

The Future of the Private Rented Sector

rent/income ratios (Kolodny, 1973) (14). Yet
many lower income tenants had surely reached the
limits of their ability to pay higher rents, even
though such rents might still not be enough to
induce landlords to remain in business. As we saw
earlier in this book, the classic response to such
a situation has been for tenants to consume less
space. It seemed possible that this might be one
response in at least some United States urban
centres in future (15). Politically, the growth of
local conflicts over rent and other housing
controls was one of the most interesting
developments. Controls provided another solution to
low income rental housing problems, albeit one
that would not improve the long term prospects for
sustained investment.

THE END OF PRIVATE RENTING?

By the time this book was completed in 1982 it was
widely accepted that private renting was in a
seemingly   inevitable decline and that it would no
longer provide the 'normal' lifetime tenure for a
large proportion of the population. In this year a
House of Commons Committee reviewed the state of
the British private rental sector and its report
included a chapter on the situation in other
countries. The Committee concluded:

> '...private renting is now in decline at least
> in proportional, and, in the majority of
> countries, in absolute terms. Inflation,
> stagnating incomes and support for other
> tenures are all playing a part in bringing
> about the decline ... Indeed a recent United
> States Government report states: "Concern
> has been expressed about the future of the
> rental housing inventory, given the
> preference for home-ownership among those
> who can afford to buy, the conversion of
> rental units to condominium or other
> ownership forms by property owners who are
> squeezed between rising operating costs and
> the inability of the remaining lower income
> renters (after higher income renters have
> moved to home-ownership) to pay the higher
> rents needed, and the relatively low
> production levels of new rental housing due
> to high construction and operating costs and
> the prospect of inadequate rental incomes"'

The Future of the Private Rented Sector

(House of Commons Environment Committee, 1982, I, xxxv) (16).

If we recall the conditions in which rental housing first developed - minimal government regulation; the rapid growth of demand from a new workforce which had low and uncertain earnings; the emergence of a class of small investors and various speculative, landed, financial and building interests; the lack of alternative forms of tenure, especially state subsidised housing for rent or sale; and so on - it may readily be seen that from the late nineteenth century onwards changes began to occur in these circumstances which eventually resulted in the decline which the House of Commons Committee notes has occurred in many countries. In short, there have been major changes in what Ball (1982) has referred to as the social relations of tenure, and in the political, economic and social significance of private renting.

In the emerging capitalist economies the private rented sector provided a major investment opportunity and essential housing for the majority of the population. Its economic and social significance was matched by the considerable political influence of those who owned, financed and built it. But the economic, political and social circumstances changed and with this change the private rented sector lost the dominant role that it had had in the early phase of capitalist urbanisation to the other two main tenures. The growth of these other tenures will be the subject of a future publication but in general terms it may be suggested it relates to some important changes in the economic and political relationships and position of the major class interests which are concerned, directly or indirectly, with the production and consumption of housing. Among these have been;

1. The increase in the political power of the organised working class, resulting in Europe in particular in the promotion (by social democratic parties and others) of social legislation (Rimlinger, 1971; Heidenheimer,et. al., 1975). In housing this interest has supported the expansion of subsidised social housing and, latterly, subsidised owner occupation. The fact that much of the socialist critique of the market provision of housing has focused on distribution and access rather than on the

whole system of the capitalist production
of housing has resulted in considerable
opposition to private landlordism but far
less scrutiny of the continued significance
of private finance, construction and
land ownership in all tenures (17).

2. The attractiveness of investment in owner
occupation rather than rental housing
for major property and financial interests
(given adequate subsidies and increasing
real incomes for a significant section of
the population). The long term nature of
investment in private renting and the
many difficulties it has increasingly
faced have reduced the likelihood that
large scale capital will consider such
investment worthwhile. In addition in every
country (even for a very brief period in
the USA) social rented housing offered
certain advantages to dominant non housing
interests. For example, in France we saw
that social housing was developed to
provide accommodation for expanding firms,
in the Netherlands housing policy was also
closely connected with economic policy
objectives and in most countries large
scale builders benefitted from contracts
to build social housing, especially when
the demand for private housing and other
private development was weak.

3. In contrast, the political and economic
position of the private rented sector has
steadily weakened, especially since 1945.
Most landlords are small scale capitalists
whose ability to organise themselves and
make an impact on the politics of housing
has declined, especially as it has
increasingly become the preserve of
natonal rather than local government. The
loss of much of the middle income demand
for housing to owner occupation and of the
skilled working class (in Europe) to the
social rented sector has had an economic
and a political effect. Economically, it
has meant that the sector predominantly
houses those on low to moderate incomes
with all the consequences that have been
examined in this study. Politically, it
has meant that the impact which private
tenants have been able to make on housing
policy has been limited. In most countries

the claims of the other main tenures are
now far more significant factors in
national housing politics than those
of the private rented sector. The point
is, in a way, illustrated by the somewhat
exceptional case of the USA where, to a
greater extent than in Europe, private
renting remains the main alternative to
owner occupation, much housing policy
has continued to be determined at local
level and local landlord/tenant struggles
over matters such as rent control can
still make a considerable, if localised,
impact.

But any explanation, such as the one given above,
which relates the decline of private renting and
the growth of the other tenures to an analysis of
the changing social relations of housing must also
acknowledge that some of the conditions which
bought about the growth of social rented and owner
occupied housing are now undergoing major changes.
There is nothing inevitable about the rise of these
tenures or their continued significance - despite
the popularity of naturalistic explanations of their
growth which suggest that, for example, this is
based on 'deep-seated aspirations' for owner
occupation or that this tenure 'satisfies a deep
and natural desire' or a 'basic and natural desire'
or a need for 'ontological security' (18). Their
future is dependent on the maintenance of the
political and economic circumstances which have led
to their growth (or of successful adaptions to
changes in these circumstances).
    Recently some of these circumstances have
altered. These include:

1. Increasing signs of weakening political
    support for social housing, the loss of
    some of its function as a source of
    housing for the better-off working class
    (to the owner occupied sector), the growth
    of low income 'problem' estates and its
    use as housing of last resort for some
    of those at the bottom of the housing
    market. In short tendencies - more
    developed in some countries than in others
    - for social rented housing to become
    marginal or welfare housing, limited in
    supply and beset with problems. Even in
    countries where such developments are less

advanced, social housing has been an early
target (and this reflects its political
weakness) for reductions in government
subsidies and production and sharp rent
increases which have served to reduce its
availability to many who still require
rental housing and its attractiveness to
those who can exercise some choice in the
housing market and afford to buy. It
hardly needs adding that such trends have
been accelerated by the growth of
inflation from the late sixties
onwards (19).

2. In the case of owner occupied housing the
signs of change are perhaps less
immediately evident. Owner occupation has
after all emerged as the dominant tenure
in political and economic terms. But some
of the circumstances which underlay this
emergence are now changing. One of the
pre-conditions for mass owner occupation,
in its modern form at least, was the
sustained economic growth, full employment
and rising real incomes which characterised
the post-war period. But, to a degree
which varies from country to country, none
of these preconditions are now guaranteed
or even being met. In particular the
growth of real incomes which underlay the
expansion of home ownership - and even
the ability of existing owner occupiers
to maintain mortgage repayments is
threatened. More generally, throughout the
the seventies there have been increasing
signs of instability in the home
ownership market with fluctuating and at
times extremely depressed rates of new
building, high interest rates, increased
competition for credit, and so on. In
several countries, notably the USA and
Britain, the special circuits of housing
finance which to some extent sheltered
home buyers from commercial interest rate
fluctuations are now breaking down.
Moreover, while governments have continued
to provide extensive subsidies, questions
have begun to be raised in several
countries about the desirability or the
possibility of maintaining such a high
level of support, especially as house
price inflation results in higher and

higher subsidies (and such subsidies, in turn encourage further inflation) (20). In short, while owner occupation has continued to expand there must now be serious doubt about the ability of an increasing number of households to afford this tenure and about the likelihood that national governments will be able to provide ever more financial support for it.

So the belief that social rented and owner occupied housing would be able to meet most future housing needs must be now open to doubt because the conditions which underlay their expansion are changing. After a period in which many people claimed that countries such as those discussed in this book had 'solved' the problem of mass housing shortages, that in future problems would be local and sectoral, concerned with raising housing quality rather than its quantity and so on, there are new signs of a more generalised shortage of reasonable and affordable housing (21).

In such circumstances there are of course demands for government action to give assistance to the owner occupied sector or to social housing. The nature of these demands varies from country to country but two general points should be noted. First, demands for the support of one or other of the major tenures are not only advanced by those who have traditionally been thought to support such tenures. As we saw earlier, social housing has at times been supported by conservative and capitalist interests and in recent years owner occupation has been strongly promoted by social democratic parties. And it is interesting to note that, for example, for a period in the early eighties, conservative governments in the Netherlands and West Germany were expanding social rented housing construction because of immediate political and economic pressures, despite their ideological commitments to the reverse of this policy (Wollmann, forthcoming; Harloe and Martens, 1983).

Second, however, at the time of writing the governments of all six countries were attempting to reduce public expenditure and some were pursuing a more general attempt to withdraw from state responsibility for social policy. In the USA and Britain in particular there has been a major reduction of direct housing subsidies and an attempt to leave housing provision increasingly to the

The Future of the Private Rented Sector

market (Hartman, 1982; Harloe and Paris, 1984). In
such circumstances the prospects for many poorer
households getting increased government housing
assistance seem dim (22). Of course the situation
may change if the crisis of housing costs and
availability worsens, if key sections of the
electorate begin to be badly affected and if the
need for more housing becomes an important political
issue. It is also possible that the stronger
economies among the six countries may overcome some
of their worst difficulties and that here conditions
may revert, to some degree at least, to those of
greater stability, employment and economic growth.
   But, as Pahl has recently noted, 'Employment
in the formal economy in advanced industrial
societies such as Britain or the United States
seems certain to decline ... Economists approaching
the problem from sharply differing ideological
perspectives agree that it seems extremely
improbable that full-time employment in the formal
economy will expand in the next decade' (Pahl,
1980, 1). Pahl and many others have pointed to the
growth of the 'informal economy', especially in
areas hard hit by a loss of jobs in the formal
economy. Szelenyi has outlined some of the features
of this development,

> 'With increasing structural employment,
> with the possibility of an absolute decline
> in living standards, with an increasing
> environmental and energy crisis, large
> scale industrial work organisations may
> have reached their limits. Working hours
> may in the future be gradually reduced,
> employment by large scale organisations
> diminish and activities which were
> previously commodified might be
> "decommodified", perhaps permanently.
> Smaller, informal productive organisations,
> amongst these domestic organisations,
> might gain in significance ... Sharing
> employment between members of the family,
> sharing household tasks, increasing the
> importance of domestic production - some-
> times for cash, sometimes to meet direct
> consumption needs - might become an integral
> part of life strategies' (Szelenyi, 1981, 9).

   Clearly, such developments will affect housing
as they will affect other sections of the economy.

The Future of the Private Rented Sector

To some degree the major housing tenures may contract because of a stagnation or even a decline in effective demand and because of state retrenchment. If Pahl, Szelenyi and others are right it seems probable that new patterns of housing provision linked to the growth of the informal economy may arise. One could for example envisage, as in the informal economies of the Third World (and in areas in Europe and the USA in the past), the growth of self-build activities resulting in a low income, owner occupied sector existing outside most state regulation and support (23). Other possibilities, which might perhaps be viewed as new forms of social rented housing and which we have already seen are occurring, are the growth of low income tenant co-operatives (such as those in New York City) and of large scale squatting (24).

But the growth of certain forms of private renting may also occur. There is unlikely to be any revival of the large scale, organised capitalist provision of rental housing. Indeed, its decline will continue and even accelerate in those countries where substantial commercially provided rental housing remains (25). But, as we have seen in the case of Britain, there has in recent years been a fairly constant number of resident landlords - basically people letting out parts of their own homes for a time in order to meet their own housing costs. We also noted that in the nineteenth century one of the main ways in which the poor were able to meet their housing costs was by subletting. And, insofar as some of the conditions of the nineteenth century economy and society (or perhaps those of contemporary Third World cities) are now being reproduced, one of the solutions to the housing problem may be an expansion of small scale provision of rented accommodation by resident landlords and others. This form of housing might become the normal lifetime housing tenure for increasing numbers of households whose opportunity to gain access to the formal, organised and state subsidised housing sector is poor (26).

The poverty and squalor of nineteenth century cities accompanied the growth of the private rented sector; the gradual fading of these conditions accompanied the decline of the sector in this century; the economic and political changes now occurring may result in some revival of private renting. If so, the form that this housing takes will not be exactly the same as it was in the nineteenth century but it will be a consequence of

318

The Future of the Private Rented Sector

many of the same social, economic and political deprivations which attended the tenure's earlier expansion.

NOTES

1. This very general statement does of course ignore the fact that the combination of these agents varied considerably. For example, as we saw, finance capital seems to have been much more involved in small scale landlordism in Germany than in Britain.

2. While the cost of other essential items, especially food, tended to become less of a burden.

3. Most notably - in the case of Russia, France, Britain, Germany and the USA - in Rimlinger, 1971.

4. The latter factor having a big impact on the growth of suburban housing in the USA in the twenties and in southern England in the mid to late thirties (see Warner, 1972; Jackson, A.A., 1973).

5. As we saw, the sequence of events was more complicated in the USA, where social renting only provided a marginal solution to low income housing supply and where - in the late sixties and early seventies - there was a considerable expansion of heavily subsidised new private rented housing - essentially a response to the social turmoil of the sixties. In the early seventies, under President Nixon, this programme was virtually ended and was later replaced by the Section 8 programme for new and existing housing. After the election of President Reagan in 1980 it was proposed to end all construction subsidies (including those for 'traditional' public housing), except for a few low income rental units for the elderly, to raise rent payments for the existing subsidised stock and to replace Section 8 (existing housing) by a limited scheme of housing vouchers (Rayner, 1982; Hartman, 1982).

6. After the research was completed there was a dramatic change in the nature of the French government with the election of President Mitterand and, later, a socialist majority in the National Assembly. At the time of completion of this chapter (early 1983) the new government's housing policies did not appear to be radically different from those which went before and it did not seem likely that they would be any more favourable to the prospects for private renting. The one major development, which was potentially of great benefit to existing tenants, were the extensive new protections (regarding rents and security) contained in the Loi Quillot (1982). But, at least at first, this seems to have sharply reduced the attractiveness of continued investment in private renting (De Moor,

(1983).

7. In fact after the research ended, in 1979, the government announced a total ban on any more freehold conversion. At the same time there was a new scheme for the co-operative ownership of new housing with direct rather than indirect subsidies, this seemed likely to be expanded in future. I am indebted to Hedvig Vestergaard for this information.

8. These rent levels were, as we have seen, only partially abated by the housing allowance system.

9. Although, as in Denmark, it was a lucrative source of capital gains in some circumstances. See for example Hamnet and Randolph, 1981, on the rapid disappearance of middle income rented property in central London in the seventies due to 'break up' operations.

10. This was, however, the general conclusion reached by the House of Commons Environment Committee (1982) after the only recent comprehensive review of the sector in Britain carried out by an official body.

11. In fact it was later cut back. See note 5 above.

12. See Home Front, 1977 for a very full discussion of the factors leading to abandonment in New York City.

13. I am indebted to Professor Emanuel Tobier for this information. See also Real Estate Research Corporation, 1975 for earlier trends.

14. However, co-operative conversion was on a very small scale. The national survey of condominium and co-operative conversion already referred to found that between 1970 and 1979 only 18,000 units were converted to co-operatives. In the same period almost 350,000 units were converted to condominiums (US Department of Housing and Urban Development, 1980b).

15. According to one recent commentator (a former president of the Levitt volume house building company), declining standards and space were likely to occur more generally in the United States housing market in the eighties, 'Just as ... horizons soared in the last half of the 1970's, they may be severely limited int he 1980's. If this occurs, the existing housing stock will be used more intensely - sharing, sub-dividing existing houses, and so on; new houses will be smaller and more often high density town houses and multi-storey buildings; and more young families will rent. Absent controls, rents will rise dramatically' (Eichler, 1983, 43).

16. The Committee was quoting from the United
States government's 1980 National Housing Report to
Congress (US Department of Housing and Urban
Development, 1980a, 41).

17. This limited concern with distribution is
not exclusive to housing policies but is a central
feature of the socialist (and non socialist)
reformism. Generally, the role of the welfare state
as a support rather than a substitute for market
capitalism has been stressed by a number of recent
writers (for example, Gough, 1979; O'Connor, 1973;
Miliband, 1973). The consequences of the
limitations of this reformism for individual policy
areas require more research but it is likely that
the concentration on reforming distribution and
access will be a common theme. For recent British
examples of work which comes to this conclusion, see
Centre for Contemporary Cultural Studies, 1981 (on
education) Navarro, 1978 and Doyal, 1979 (on health).

18. The first three quotations are from
Britain, and were made by Conservative and Labour
governments in recent years (Cited in Short, 1982,
119). The last quotation derives from Giddens (1981)
recent critique of historical materialism but is
applied to homeownership specifically by Saunders
(1984, 223). For a critique of the latter see
Harloe, 1984a, 228-37.

19. A detailed examination of these trends in
social rented housing in the six countries is now
being carried out. It is clear that, as in the case
of private rented housing, while the pressures on
this tenure are widespread their effects in
practice are varied. For example, towards the end of
the seventies Conservative governments in both
Britain and the Netherlands aimed to radically
reduce the role of social rented housing and the
subsidies to this sector. But only the former
government was immediately able to achieve this
aim. Detailed analysis of the historical development
of Dutch housing and of its broader economic and
political context provides an insight into the
reasons why material circumstances made the
ideological objective of curtailing this tenure more
difficult to achieve in the Netherlands than in
Britain (Harloe and Martens, 1983).

20. These trends in owner occupation are also
one of the main themes in the further research now
being carried out in the six countries. Recent
discussions of the problems of this tenure include,
for example, some of the contributors to Smith
1983 and LeGates and Murphy, 1981 (on the USA);

The Future of the Private Rented Sector

Ball, 1982 (on Britain); Priemus, 1981 (on the
Netherlands); and Wollman, forthcoming (on Germany).
Problems were also evident in France and Denmark.
In the former country, the attempt in the sixties
and early seventies to develop an effective
mortgage market based on private finance capital
had suffered a reverse as had the associated move
towards large scale owner occupied housing
development. The annual rate of increase of owner
occupier households was, from the mid-seventies
onwards, at its lowest annual rate since before the
mid-fifties (information supplied by Christian
Topalov). In the latter country the production of
new owner occupied units fell from 28,000 in 1977
to about 5,000 in 1981, many houses remained
unsold and prices were falling, mortgage defaults
had risen sharply and a combintion of the previous
inflation of housing costs and falling real incomes
had made access to this tenure increasingly
difficult (information supplied by Hedvig
Vestergaard).
    21. By the early eighties all six countries
had suffered to varying degrees from difficulties
that included collapsing house-building output,
high interest rates and escalating housing costs,
cut backs in subsidies to social rented housing and
a crisis in the owner occupied market. But the
exact combinations of conditions varied
considerably from country to country. For example,
in Britain investment and subsidies for social
rented housing were severly reduced while in the
Netherlands the market for owner occupation
collapsed and the (conservative) government was
forced to expand social housing production while
at the same time attempting to reduce the degree to
which individual tenants were subsidised. In the
USA output slumped and there was considerable chaos
in the housing finance market. In Denmark and West
Germany and the situation was similar to that
occurring in the Netherlands (Harloe and Martens,
1983; Wollmann forthcoming; Smith, 1983). For a
survey of the crisis in social rented housing in
the OECD countries generally see Harloe 1984b.
    22. This is most evident in the USA and
Britain. But in the other four countries too there
are attempts to increase the proportionate
contribution that rents make to the costs of this
housing. The problem of the high costs of new
social rented housing in relation to the incomes
of those in the greatest housing need (somewhat
less of a problem in Britain due to rent pooling)

has been increasing in the four mainland European
countries in recent years. Therefore it is far from
clear that new programmes of social rented housing
will improve the position of those who are worst
off (see Harloe, 1984b).

23. The existence of self build housing in
rural areas in Europe has been quite widespread.
But shanty dwelling on the urban fringe, or even in
cities by low income households has been quite
common too. For example, in France in the inter-war
period there was large scale development of such
housing by low income rural-urban migrants
especially in the Paris area. The inhabitants of
these 'lotissments' agitated for an improvement in
their conditions and helped to establish the so-
called 'red belt' round central Paris (for an
account of conditions see Dennery, 1935). In
England there was a similar, though less
significant development of 'plotlands', especially
to the east of London (the subject of recent
research soon to be published by Colin Ward. See
also Ward, 1983, 80-7). In America too in the
Depression of the thirties there was a growth of
shanty towns (for an account of one in Seattle see
Roy, 1979). After the Second World War, in the
immediate condtions of post-war housing crisis,
much shelter took this form - especially in German
cities (and squatting was common too). Later on
many of the foreign workers migrating to France,
especially those from North Africa, found their
first accommodation in bidonvilles. Ardagh reports
that these still existed in the seventies. At this
time 50,000 lived in these shanty towns, four-
fifths in the Paris area. They were mainly occupied
by Portuguese and Algerians and were slowly being
resettled by the government. Many of these single
workers resisted resettlement (Ardagh, 1977, 460).
On squatting and self-help housing generally see
Ward, 1983. It is of course a mistake to regard
self build housing as necessarily or permanently
of a poor quality, as sensitive accounts of Third
World housing make clear. Much of this housing has,
over time, been upgraded and integrated with the
'conventional' stock. It is also important to note
that both in Europe and the USA there has been small
scale self build housing for many years, but this
is often carried out by those who could afford
conventional housing but prefer to obtain better
quality units by investing some 'sweat equity'.
This is not the type of low income self build

which is being referred to in this paragraph.

24. There is, as yet, very little recognition of the possibility of such a prospect let alone research on its nature. However, there are a wide variety of, usually small scale, changes occurring which - if taken together - could be seen as providing some support for the speculations contained in this paragraph. Examples include the growth of squatting in major urban centres in several countries (for a recent survey see Kearns, 1980), some forms of self-build housing (which Pahl's continuing work on the informal economy has shown may accompany this situation), and a wide variety of what might be seen as low quality (often) low cost (to governments) and low income housing solutions - which include devices such as 'sweat equity' homesteading, tenant management and ownership of ex-public or privately owned housing and so on. Many of these latter ideas originated in American cities in the seventies. These cities, notably New York, faced economic collapse and a 'fiscal crisis'. In the circumstances local housing programmes were drastically curtailed, to be replaced (sometimes) by programmes with minimal subsidisation which relied to a great extent on the self help activities of low income households. (See, for example, Harloe, 1978; Kolodny, 1973; Urban Homesteading Assistance Board, 1977; Home Front, 1977; Real Estate Research Corporation, 1975b). In the seventies some of these ideas began to be taken up by central and local government in Britain.

25. There is one circumstance in which larger scale private renting could revive - if governments decided to provide substantial subsidies to the sector. In this context it is interesting to note that two recent analyses of rental housing, the first in Britain and the second in the USA, come to much the same conclusions. These are:

(i)   that for the economic reasons we have already described private renting is in decline;

(ii)   that the increasing loss of the more solvent demand to other tenures makes the future chances of profitable large scale provision remote;

(iii)   that only large scale government subsidisation could meet the gap between profit making rents and what most tenants could afford to pay;

(iv)   that, in the current circumstances, this could probably only occur by a redistribution of housing subsidies away from owner occupation in the USA and from this tenure and perhaps social rented housing in Britain. But, given the political strength of owner occupation in particular, the chances of this occurring seem remote (House of Commons Environment Committee, 1982; Downs, 1983).

26. The extent to which there may be growing similarities between the housing situation of the Third World urban poor and the situation of some in the developed countries is a topic which needs further research. But a number of interesting issues may arise. These include the links between forms of low income housing and the informal economy , whether and in what ways housing offers significant opportunities for income and capital generating activities in the petty commodity production of this sector and the extent to which self help housing is viewed positively as encouraging dweller control, freedom and enterprise or the extent to which it is merely a form of exploitation of the poor. In the Third World situation this debate is particularly associated with the writings of John Turner. But Turner and his associates are also suggesting that self help housing is of growing applicability to the developed countries too (see Turner and Fichter, 1972; Turner, 1976; Ward, 1983). For a critique see Burgess, 1978 with the reply by Turner, and Ward, 1982. Incidentally, the intense discussion of squatter housing in the Third World has rather obscured the fact that the very poorest in these societies are often housed in inner city rented slum property (see, for example, the comments on this in Butterworth and Chance, 1981, 148 regarding Latin America). It would be interesting to know more about the landlords of such property and whether there are any parallels with emergent forms of inner city landlordism in the developed societies. In one of the relatively few studies which has looked at other forms of Third World housing Leeds identified (in Rio), among other types, the existence of rooming houses, small apartments with shared facilities and large areas of private rented slum housing in apartments, single houses and rooms (Leeds, 1974). Studies of

326

slum landlordism in the six countries discussed
in this book are rare but in Britain there is some
work on inner city housing which distinguishes
betwen small absentee landlords - letting outside
the Rent Act to low income households under
exploitative conditions - and multiple occupation
of housing bought by low income households
(especially ethnic minorities) for their own
occupation, in which rooms are let to help meet
mortgage repayments (often these mortgages have
been obtained from 'fringe' financiers at very high
interest rates) (Harloe, Issacharoff and Minns,
1974, 126-7; Rex and Moore, 1967, 133-46;
Sawbridge, 1982). In the United States Sternlieb's
classic study also showed the existence, in inner
city areas, of owner occupier landlords (often
black) and speculative absentee landlordism.
Unconventional and expensive housing finance was
also common (Sternlieb, 1966).

APPENDIX

THE ORGANISATION OF THE STUDY

As noted in the Introduction, this study is partly
based on research originally carried out as an
input to a governmental review of the private
rented sector in Britain.

The survey was later extended to include
Britain (the initial research was limited to the
USA, France, West Germany, France and the
Netherlands), to add historical and political
material to the initial, limited examination of
current aspects of the private rented sector and to
develop the questions discussed in the Introduction
and the final chapter.

But the initial survey of conditions in the
contemporary private rented sector presented most
problems in terms of organisation and methodology.
Some of these touched on in the Introduction. In
this study they were added to by the very tight
time schedule which was allowed for the research in
order to meet deadlines set by the governmental
policy process.

The selection of countries to be surveyed was
not determined by a single criterion. But important
factors included,

> (i)   the wish to focus on the development of
>   the tenure in advanced capitalist
>   societies with, broadly speaking,
>   similar levels of economic development,
>   political structures, and structures of
>   housing provision;
>
> (ii) within this broad similarity the wish,
>   to consider a selection of countries in
>   which there appeared to be considerable
>   variation in the detailed position of
>   the tenure and in specific policies

towards it. In short, the concern with exploring both broader structural determinants and also specific national differences, discussed in the Introduction, helped to determine the selection of countries;

(iii) Specific policy interests such as, for example, the policy of encouraging small scale landlords in Germany, the reasons why this country and the USA still seemed to be maintaining a rather large private rented sector and so on.

(iv) A variety of practical considerations such as the availability and accessibility of research findings and information.

Following the selection of the five countries a consultant was engaged in each country. These consultants prepared initial reports, following detailed brief which they were provided with. The consultants' brief concentrated on obtaining statistical and descriptive information on the private rented sector, including details of the historical development of the tenure, its economic position, social composition and physical state. The major policies described included those designed to protect tenants, subsidy policies and those concerned with the maintenance and improvement of the stock. The brief included a detailed list of basic data requirements. As far as possible the consultants were asked to provide data for specific years and according to specific definitions in order to achieve as much comparability as possible. There were of course considerable limitations in the extent to which this could be done. These are discussed in the main text when they arise.

There followed a series of visits to each country during the course of which interviews with key government and non-government organisations and individuals were carried out. During these visits far more detail about matters such as the processes at work in the sector, political attitudes to its development and current problems were obtained. Discussions were also held with each consultant to clarify and add to the material presented in their reports. Then a lengthy report was produced for each country and this was reviewed by each of the consultants before a final, comparative report was submitted to the Department of the Environment.

The next stage of the research (supported by

the Nuffield Foundation) involved the preparation
of a similar report on Britain (no consultant was
necessary here) and the revision, updating and
bringing together in a single draft of the six
individual country reports. The final stage involved
library based research to provide the historical
and broader political, economic and demographic
material for chapters one and two.

The principal organisations visited and
individuals interviewed during the course of the
research (and in earlier visits to the USA and West
Germany in preparation for the project) were:

Denmark
Individuals: L. Østergaard, Mr. Halvorsen,
Organisations: Boligministeriet, Lejernes
                  Landsorganisation, Copenhagen Rent
                  Board, National Federation of
                  Landlords.

Netherlands
Individuals: J. van der Schaar, P. Bekker,
                  Mr. Visser, Mr. Bruinsma, A. Bjilsma,
                  N. de Vreeze, P. Kuenzli, Mr. Baazen,
                  Mr. de Haan, Mr. Samson,
                  Mr. Adrianseens, W. Hayge,
                  A. v. Leeuwen, Mr. Stykerman,
                  Mr. Liedup.
Organisations: Technische Hogeschool Delft,
                  Amsterdam City Council Planning
                  Department, Landelijke Organisatie
                  Belanengroepen Huisvesting,
                  Landelijke Ombudsteam
                  Stadsvernieuwing, Ministerie van
                  Volkshuisvesting en Ruimtelijke
                  Ordening, City of Rotterdam Housing
                  Department.

France
Individuals: C. Topalov, S. Magri, M. du Puis,
                  M. Dumoulin, J. Carassus, P. Strobel,
                  S. Nora, M. Lattez, M. Platon,
                  M. Val.
Organisations: Centre de Sociologie Urbaine,
                  Ministère de l'Équipement et de
                  l'Aménagement du Territorie, Cofimeg,
                  Confédération Nationale du Logement.

West Germany
Individuals: U. Pfeiffer, Dr. Kampfmeyer,
                  Mr. Illies, Frau Winter-Effinger,
                  Professor M. Einsele, W. Kroning,
                  Professor H. Harms, Dr. U. Wullkopf,
                  S. Lemmelsen, Dr. R. Neiderberg,

Appendix

	Dr. E. Mühlich, I. Mühlich-Klinger, Dr. Carter, Herr Gerth,
Organisations:	Deutscher Stadetag, Bundesminterium für Raumordnung, Bauwesen und Stadtebau, Deutscher Verband, Deutscher Mieterbund, Baubeborde Freie und Hansestadt Hamburg, VEBA-Siedlung, Institut für Wohnen und Umwelt, Stadt Darmstadt Burgomasters Office, Zentralverband der Deutschen Haus-Wohnungs-und Grundeigentumer e.v.

United States
Individuals: C. Fox, Professor R. Kolodny, Professor P. Marcuse, Professor E. Tobier, L. Winnick, A. Miller, N. Hardy, R. Schur, B. Higher, R. Embry, Mr. Sroge, Mr. Witte, E. Glatt, J. Khadduri, K. Kollias, T. Black, R. Struyk, M. Isler.

Organisations: US Department of Housing and Urban Development Office of Policy Development and Research, New York Settlement House Foundation, Graduate School of Architecture and Planning Columbia University, The Ford Foundation, Association of Neighbourhood Housing Developers, New York City Housing and Development Administration, New York City Rent Stabilisation Association, National Association of Housing and Redevelopment Officials, Urban Institute, Urban Land Institute, Metropolitan Council on Housing, Baltimore Department of Housing and Community Development.

Thanks are also due to the many other organisations and individuals who answered more limited queries during the course of the research.

BIBLIOGRAPHY

ABRAMS, C. 1965, The City is the Frontier, Harper
    and Row, New York.
AARON, H. 1972, Shelter and Subsidies, Brookings
    Institution, Washington DC.
AHLBRANDT, R. and BROPHY, P. 1976, 'Neighbourhood
    Housing Services', Journal of Housing, No. 1,
    pp. 36-9.
ALCALY, R. and MERMELSTEIN, D. (eds.), 1977,
    The Fiscal Crisis of American Cities, Vintage
    Books, New York.
ANDERIESEN, G. 1981, 'Tanks in the streets: the
    growing conflict over housing in Amsterdam',
    International Journal of Urban and Regional
    Research, vol 5, no 1, pp. 83-95.
ANSIDEI, M., CARASSUS, J. and STROBEL, P. 1978,
    Logement: Pourquoi La Hausse des Prix?, La
    Documentation Francaise, Paris.
ARDAGH, J. 1977, The New France, (3rd edn.),
    Penguin, Harmondsworth.
ASHFORD, D. 1980a, 'A Victorian drama: the fiscal
    subordination of British local government' in
    D. Ashford (ed.), Financing Urban Government
    in the Welfare State, Croom Helm, London,
    pp. 71-96.
    1980b, Financing Urban Government in the
    Welfare State, Croom Helm, London.
BAILEY, P. 1977, 'Housing for people' in M.
    Loney and M. Allen (eds.), The Crisis of the
    Inner City, Macmillan, London, pp. 97-109.
BALL, M. 1981, 'The development of capitalism in
    housing provision', International Journal of
    Urban and Regional Research, vol 5, no 2,
    pp. 145-77.
    1982, 'Housing provision and the economic
    crisis', Capital and Class, 17, pp.66-77.
BALLERSTEDT, E. and GLATZER, W. 1975, Soziologischer

332

Bibliography

Almanach, Herder and Herder, Frankfurt/New York

BAUER, C. 1934, Modern Housing, Houghton Mifflin, Boston and New York.

BERGLUND, S. and LINDSTROM, U. 1978, The Scandanavian Party Systems, Studentlitteratur, Lund.

BIJLSMA, A. and SALVERDA, F. 1978, 'Speculaties', Vrij Nederland, 20 Mei, p. 57.

BLACK, J. 1976, Prospects for Rental Housing Production Under Rent Control: A Case Study of Washington, DC, Urban Land Institute, Washington DC.

BLANKESPOOR, G. and JAFFEE, S. 1978, 'The New Construction Programme' in U.S. Department of Housing and Urban Development, Office of Policy Development and Research, Lower Income Housing Assistance Program (Section 8) Interim Findings of Evaluation Research, HUD, Washington DC, pp. 159-81.

BLONDEL, J. and GODFREY, E.G. 1968, The Government of France, Methuen, London.

BLOOMBERG, L. (with H. Lamale) 1976, The Rental Housing Situation in New York City, 1975, City of New York, New York.

BOARD OF TRADE, 1908a, Cost of Living of the Working Classes, HMSO, London.
1908b, Cost of Living in German Towns HMSO, London.
1909, Cost of Living in French Towns, HMSO, London.
1911, Cost of Living in American Towns, HMSO, London.
1913, Cost of Living of the Working Classes, HMSO, London.

BOLIGMINISTERIET, 1965, Betaenkning om arbejdet i det af boligministeren nedsatte lejelovsudvalg af 1964, Copenhagen.
1975, Den bygge-og boligpolitiske udvikling 1974-75, Copenhagen.
1977, Bygge-og boligredegørelse, (mimeo), Copenhagen.

BOLLENS, J. and SCHMANDT, H. 1975, The Metropolis: the People, Politics and Economic Life (3rd edn), Harper and Row, New York.

BOVAIRD, A., HARLOE, M. and WHITEHEAD, C. 1982a, 'Avoidance, evasion, harassment and illegal eviction' in House of Commons Environment Committee, The Private Rented Housing Sector, vol III, HMSO, London, pp. 43-52.
1982b, 'The private rented sector abroad' in House of Commons Environment Committee, The

Private Rented Housing Sector, vol III,
appendix 3, HMSO, London.
1982c, 'The current position' in House of
Commons Environment Committee, _The Private Rented
Housing Sector_, vol III, appendix I, HMSO, London.
BOWLEY, M. 1945, _Housing and the State, 1919-44_,
Allen and Unwin, London.
BRENNER, J. and FRANKLIN, H. 1977, _Rent Control in
North America and Four European Countries_,
Potomac Institute/Council for International
Urban Liaison, Washington DC.
BUILDING SOCIETIES ASSOCIATION 1983, _BSA Bulletin_,
No 23.
BURNETT, J. 1978, _A Social History of Housing_,
_1815-1970_, David and Charles, Newton Abbott.
BUTTERWORTH, D. and CHANCE, J. 1981, _Latin American
Urbanisation_, Cambridge University Press,
Cambridge.
CARLSON, D. 1978, _Revitalising North American
Neighbourhoods: A Comparison of Canadian and
US Programs for Neighbourhood Preservation and
Housing Rehabilitation_, The Urban Institute,
Washington DC.
CARLSON, D. and HEINBERG, J. 1978, _How Housing
Allowances Work_, Urban Institute, Washington DC.
CASTELLS, M. 1978, _City, Class and Power_, Macmillan,
London and Basingstoke.
1983, _The City and the Grass Roots_, Edward
Arnold, London.
CASTELLS, M., CHERKI, E., GODARD, F. and MEHL, D.
1974, _Sociologie des Mouvements Sociaux
Urbains Enquête sur la Région Parisienne_, 2
vols, Centre d'Etude des Mouvements Sociaux,
Paris.
CASTLES, S. and KOSACK, G. 1973, _Immigrant Workers
and Class Structure in Western Europe_, Oxford
University Press, New York.
CBS, 1964, _Woningbehoeftenoderzoek_,
Staatsuitgeverij, 's-Gravenhage.
1967, _Woningbehoeftenoderzoek_,
Staatsuitgeverij, 's-Gravenhage.
1970, _Woningbehoeftenoderzoek_,
Staatsuitgeverij, 's-Gravenhage.
1971, _Volkstelling annex Woningtelling_,
Staatsuitgeverij, 's-Gravenhage.
1975, _Woningbehoeftenonderzoek_,
Staatsuitgeverij, 's-Gravenhage.
Monthly a, _Maandstatistiek van de Prijzen_,
Staatsuitgeverij, 's-Gravenhage.
Monthly b, _Maandstatistiek Bouwnijverheid_,
Staatsuitgeverij, 's-Gravenhage.

Bibliography

CENTRAL DIRECTIE VAN VOLKSHUISINVESTING, 1975,
    Kwalitatief Woningonderzoek, Ministerie van
    Volkshuisinvesting en Ruimtelijke Ordening,
    's-Gravenhage.
CECCARELLI, P. 1982, 'Politics, Parties and Urban
    Movements: Western Europe' in N. & S. Fainstein
    (eds.), Urban Policy Under Capitalism, Sage,
    Beverly Hills and London, pp. 261-76.
CENTRE FOR CONTEMPORARY CULTURAL STUDIES, 1981,
    Unpopular Education, Schooling and Social
    Democracy in England since 1944, Hutchinson,
    London.
CHAPMAN, B. 1952, Introduction to French Local
    Government, Allen and Unwin, London.
CHAPUT DE SAINTONGE, R. 1961, Public Administration
    in Germany, Weidenfeld and Nicholson, London.
CITY OF NEW YORK, OFFICE OF THE MAYOR, 1974, The
    Housing Advocate, City of New York, New York.
CLAWSON, M. and HALL, P. 1973, Planning and Urban
    Growth: An Anglo-American Comparison, Johns
    Hopkins Press, Baltimore.
CNL, n.d., La CNL et la Réglementation des
    Conditions de Location pour les Logements
    Neufs non HLM et pour les Logements Anciens
    non Réglementes, Confédération Nationale du
    Logement, Paris.
    1974, Primes et Prêts, Confédération Nationale
    du Logement, Paris.
    1975, Project de Bail. Proposition de Loi,
    Confédération Nationale du Logement, Paris.
CNRC, 1978, Les Entreprises d'Assurances, Les
    Sociétés Immobilières d'Investissement, Les
    Caisses de Retraites, Les Sociétés Foncières
    Immobilières, mimeo, Paris.
COFIMEG, 1977, Exercice 1976, Paris.
COLE, W. and DEANE, P. 1965, 'The growth of
    national incomes', in H. Habbakuk and M. Postan
    (eds.), The Cambridge Economic History of
    Europe, Vol VI, The Industrial Revolutions and
    After: Incomes, Population and Technological
    Change (I), Cambridge University Press,
    London, pp. 1-55.
COMMISSION OF THE EUROPEAN COMMUNITIES, 1981,
    Report on Social Developments. Year 1980,
    Office for Official Publications of the
    European Communities, Luxembourg
COMMITTEE OF ENQUIRY INTO LOCAL GOVERNMENT FINANCE
    (Layfield Committee), 1976a, Appendix 5.
    Reports on Foreign Visits, HMSO, London.
    1976b, Appendix 8. Local Income Tax: Evidence

and Commissioned Work, HMSO, London, 1976b.
COMMITTEE ON FINANCE AND REVENUE, 1976, Partial
    Draft Report. Real Property Transaction Act of
    1976, mimeo, Washington D.C.
COMMITTEE ON HOUSING IN GREATER LONDON (Milner
    Holland Committee), 1965, Report, Cmnd 2605,
    HMSO, London.
COMMITTEE ON THE RENT ACTS (Francis Committee),
    1971, Report, Cmnd 4609, HMSO, London.
COMPTROLLER GENERAL OF THE UNITED STATES, 1974,
    Report to Congress. An Assessment of the
    Department of Housing and Urban Development's
    Experimental Housing Allowance Program, US
    Government Printing Office, Washington DC.
    1978, Report to Congress. Observations on
    Housing Allowances and the Experimental Housing
    Allowances Program, US Government Printing
    Office, Washington DC.
CONRADT, D. 1978, The German Polity, Longman, New
    York and London.
COUNCIL OF THE DISTRICT OF COLUMBIA, 1979,
    Residential Real Property Excise Tax Act of
    1979 and Draft Bill, mimeo, The Council,
    Washington DC.
CREP, 1976, Le Financement des Biens Immobiliers
    pour les Particuliers: Rapport de Synthèse
    Fascicule 3: Les logements de Rapport, CREP,
    Paris.
CSO, Annually, Economic Trends, HMSO, London.
CULLINGWORTH, J. 1977, Housing Allowances: The
    British Experience, Centre for Urban and
    Community Studies, Toronto.
    1979, Essays on Housing Policy, Allen and
    Unwin, London.
DANMARKS STATISTIK, 1925-77, Statistike
    Efterretninger, Danmarks Statistik, Copenhagen.
    1975, Folke-og Boligtaellingen 9 November
    1970. C2 Boligen, Danmarks Statistik,
    Copenhagen.
DAUNTON, M. 1983, House and Home in the Victorian
    City, Edward Arnold, London.
DAWSON, W. 1914, Municipal Life and Government in
    Germany, Longman, Green and Co., London.
DeMOOR, A. 1983, 'Landlord and tenant in French law:
    a recent statute', Oxford Journal of Legal
    Studies, vol 3, no 3, pp.425-31.
DE VRIES, J. 1976, 'Benelux 1920-1970' in C. Cipolla
    (ed.) The Fontana Economic History of Europe,
    Contemporary Economies - 1, Collins/Fontana
    Books, Glasgow, pp. 1-71.
DENBY, E. 1938, Europe Rehoused, George Allen and

Unwin, London.

DENNERY, E. 1935, La Question de l'Habitation Urbaine En France, Société des Nations, Geneve.

DEPARTMENT OF THE ENVIRONMENT, SCOTTISH DEVELOPMENT DEPARTMENT, WELSH OFFICE, Quarterly, Housing and Construction Statistics, HMSO, London.

DEPARTMENT OF THE ENVIRONMENT, 1977a, Housing Policy Review. Technical Volume, Part 1, HMSO, London.
1977b, Housing Policy, HMSO, London.
1977c, Housing Policy. Technical Volume, Part III, HMSO, London.
1977d, The Review of the Rent Acts. A Consultative Paper, DoE, London.
1977e, Landlords and the Law, HMSO, London.
1977f, Regulated Tenancies, HMSO, London.
1977g, Rooms to Let, HMSO, London.
1978a, National Dwelling and Housing Survey, HMSO, London.
1978b, English House Condition Survey 1976. 1. Report of the Physical Condition Survey, HMSO, London.
1979, English House Condition Survey 1976. 2. Report of the Social Survey, HMSO, London.

DER BUNDESMINISTER FUR RAUMORDNUNG, BAUWESEN UND STADTEBAU, 1975, Das Wohnen in der Bundesrepublic, Bonn-Bad Godesberg.
1976, Wohngeld '76, Presse-und Informationsamt der Bundesregierung, Bonn.

DET ØKONOMISKE RAD, 1970, Boligmarkedet og Boligbyggeriet, Copenhagen.

DET STATISTISKE DEPARTMENT, 1949, Husleje og Boligforhold, November 1945, Det Statistike Department, Copenhagen.
1953, Husleje Boligforhold, November 1950, Det Statistike Departement, Copenhagen.
1959, Boligtaellingen, Oktober 1955, Det Statistike Departement, Copenhagen.
1964, Folke-og Boligtaellingen, 26 September 1969, C. Bolig-og Husstendsundersøgelse 1960, Det Statistike Department, Copenhagen.

DIW, 1976, Wochenbericht 40-41/76, Berlin, p.371.

DONNISON, D. 1967, The Government of Housing, Penguin, Harmondsworth.

DOWNS, A. 1983, 'The coming crunch in rental housing', The Annals of the American Academy of Political and Social Science, vol 465, pp.76-85.

DOYAL, L. 1979, The Political Economy of Health, Pluto, London.

DRAAISMA, J. and VAN HOOGSTRATEN, P. 1983, 'The squatter movement in Amsterdam', International Journal of Urban and Regional Research, vol 7,

no 3, pp.406-16.
DREIER, P. Forthcoming, 'The tenants movement in the
    United States', International Journal of Urban
    and Regional Research.
DRURY, H. et al, 1978, Lower Income Housing
    Assistance Program: (Section 8) Interim Findings
    Findings of Evaluation Research, HUD: Office of
    Policy Development and Research, Washington DC.
DRURY, H., LEE, O., SPRINGER, H. and YAP, L. 1978,
    Lower Income Housing Assistance Program:
    (Section 8) Nationwide Evaluation of the
    Existing Housing Program, HUD: Office of Policy
    Development and Research, Washington DC.
DUCLAUD-WILLIAMS, R. 1978, The Politics of Housing
    in Britain and France, Heinemann Educational
    Books, London.
DYOS, H. and REEDER, D. 1973, 'Slums and suburbs',
    in J. Dyos and H. Wolff (eds.) The Victorian
    City, vol 1, Routledge and Kegan Paul, London
    and Boston, pp.359-86.
ECONOMIC COMMISSION FOR EUROPE, 1972, The EEC Region
    in Figures, UN, New York.
    1979, Labour Supply and Migration in Europe
    (Economic Survey of Europe in 1977: Part II),
    UN, New York.
EDSON, C. (ed.), 1974, A Working Guide to the
    Housing and Community Development Act 1974,
    Section 23 Leased Housing Association,
    Washington DC.
EICHLER, N. 1983, 'House building in the 1980s',
    The Annals of the American Academy of Political
    and Social Science, vol 465, pp.35-44.
VON EINEM, E. 1982, 'Comparing urban revitalisation
    in the United States and West Germany' in
    G. Hellstern, F. Spreer and H. Wollmann,
    Applied Urban Research, Vol III, BLR, Bonn.
EMMERICH, L. 1976, The Dynamic Cost-Price Rent,
    IFHP, Luxembourg.
ENGELS, F. 1920, The Condition of the Working Class
    in England in 1844, Allen and Unwin, London.
ENGLANDER, A. 1979, Landlord and Tenant in Urban
    Britain: The Politics of Housing Reform,
    1838-1924, Ph.D. thesis, Warwick University.
ENGLISH, J. and NORMAN, P. 1974, One Hundred Years
    of Slum Clearance in England and Wales -
    Policies and Programmes 1868 to 1970,
    University of Glasgow.
ENQUÊTE-LOGEMENT 1955. Results published as (1)
    'Une enquete par sondage sur le logement
    (October 1955)', Etudes statistiques, no 2,
    Avril-Juin 1957, pp. 35-48. (2) 'La demande de

logements en France', Annales du CREDOC, no 2,
Avril-Juin 1957.
1961. Results published as (1) 'Les conditions
de logement des Francais en 1961', Annales du
CREDOC, no 2, Juillet-Septembre 1962. (2) 'La
situation du logement en 1961', Bulletin
statistique du Ministère de la Construction,
Septembre 1962. (3) 'Quelques resultats d'une
enquête sur le logement', Etudes et
conjoncture, 17, no 10, Octobre 1962, pp. 839-
58.
1963. Results published as (1) 'Aspects du
logement en France en 1963', Bulletin
statisque du Ministère de la Construction
various issues, Janvier-Juin 1965. (2) 'Une
etude sur les loyers en 1963. Resultats d'une
enquête generale sur le logement', Etudes et
conjoncture, 13, no 11, Novembre 1966.
1967. Results published as (1) 'Aspects du
logement en France en 1967', Statistiques de
la construction. Ministère de l'Equipement et
du Logement, various issues, Janvier 1969 -
Février 1970. (2) 'Le niveau des loyers en
1967 et leur évolution depuis 1963', Etudes
et conjoncture, 15, no 9, Septembre 1968,
pp. 115-218. (3) 'Propriétaires et loctaires en
1967', Economie et statistique, no 3, Juillet-
Août 1971, pp. 3-25.
1970. Results published as 'Les conditions de
logement des ménages en 1970', Les Collections
de l'INSEE, M28, no 110, Novembre 1973.
1973, Results published as (1) 'Les conditions
de logement des ménages en 1973', Les
Collections de l'INSEE, M42, no 149, Avril 1975.
(2) 'Les conditions de logement des ménages en
1973 (résultats régionnaux)', Les Collections
de l'INSEE, Décembre 1975.
EUROSTAT, 1977, Social Indicators for the European
Community 1960-75, Statistical Office for the
European Communities, Luxembourg.
1981, Review 1970-79, Statistical Office of the
European Communities, Luxembourg.
FASSBINDER, H. and KALLE, E. 1982, A Comparative
Study of Urban Renewal Policy, Netherlands
National Committee for the European Urban
Renaissance Campaign, The Hague.
FEAGIN, J. 1982, Social Problems, Prentice Hall,
Englewood Cliffs, N.J.
FEDERAL MINISTER FOR REGIONAL PLANNING, BUILDING AND
URBAN DEVELOPMENT, n.d., Habitat: National
Report for the United Nations Conference on

Human Settlements, Federal Republic of Germany, Bonn.

FERRIS, J. 1972, Participation in Urban Planning: The Barnsbury Case, Bell, London.

FLOOR, J. 1972, Rents, Subsidies and Dynamic Cost, Ministry of Housing and Physical Planning, The Hague.

FOHLEN, C. 1976, 'France 1920-70' in C. Cipolla (ed.), The Fontana Economic History of European Contemporary Economies - 1, Collins/Fontana Books, Glasgow, pp.72-127.

FOSTER, J. 1979, 'How imperial London preserved its slums', International Journal of Urban and Regional Research, vol 3, no 1, pp.93-114.

FRIEDMAN, L. 1968, Government and Slum Housing, Rand McNally and Company, Chicago.

FUERST, J. (ed.), 1974, Public Housing in Europe and America, Halsted, New York

GARRITY, P. 1973, 'Redesigning landlord-tenant law for an urban society', in J. Pynoos, R. Schafer and C. Hartman (eds.) Housing Urban America, Aldine, Chicago, pp.75-86.

GAULDIE, E. 1974, Cruel Habitations, Allen and Unwin London.

GELFAND, M. 1980, 'How cities arrived on the national agenda in the United States' in D. Ashford (ed.) Financing Urban Government in the Welfare State, Croom Helm, London, pp.28-49

GIDDENS, A. 1981, A Contemporary Critique of Historical Materialism, Macmillan, London.

GILBERT, B. 1970, British Social Policy, 1914-39, Batsford, London.

GLATT, E. 1978, Findings and Lessons from the Experimental Housing Allowance Program, mimeo (paper delivered to the National Conference of American Society for Public Administration, Phoenix, Arizona).

GLASS, R. 1960, Newcomers, Centre for Urban Studies and George Allen and Unwin, London.

GOLDSTON, E. 1973, 'BURP and make money' in J. Pynoos, R. Schafer and C. Hartman (eds.) Housing Urban America, Aldine, Chicago.

GORDON, D. 1973, City Limits, Charterhouse, New York.

GOUGH, I. 1979, The Political Economy of the Welfare State, Macmillan, London.

GOUREVITCH, P. 1981, 'Local government reform in France' in A. Gunlicks (ed.), Local Government Reform and Reorganisation, Kennikat Press, Port Washington, NY, pp. 131-50.

GRESSEL, D. 1976, Financing Techniques for Local

Rehabilitation Programs, NAHRO, Washington DC.
GUNLICKS, A. 1981a, 'The reorganisation of local
government in the Federal Republic of Germany'
in A. Gunlicks (ed.), Local Government Reform
and Reorganisation, Kennikat Press, Port
Washington, NY, pp. 169-81.
1981b, 'Problems, politics and prospects of
local government reorganisation in the United
States' in A. Gunlicks (ed.), Local Government
Reform and Reorganisation, Kennikat Press, Port
Washington, NY, pp. 7-29.
HALL, P. 1979, The World Cities, (2nd edn), McGraw-
Hill, New York.
1980, Urban and Regional Planning, Penguin,
Harmondsworth.
1981, 'The inner city worldwide' in P. Hall
(ed.), The Inner City in Context, Heinemann
Educational Books, London, pp. 64-70.
HALLETT, G. 1977, Housing and Land Policies in West
Germany and Britain, Macmillan, London.
HAMNETT, C. and RANDOLPH, B. 1981, 'Flat break-ups'
Roof, vol 6, no 3, pp. 18-19, 24.
HANDLIN, D. 1976, 'Housing and city planning in the
United States, 1910-45', Transactions of the
Martin Centre for Architectural and Urban
Studies, no 1, pp. 317-334.
HARDACH, K. 1976, 'Germany 1914-70' in C. Cipolla
(ed.), The Fontana Economic History of Europe.
Contemporary Economics - 1, Collins/Fontana
Books, Glasgow, pp. 180-265.
HARLOE, M. 1977a, 'Will the Green Paper mean better
housing', Roof, vol 2, no 5, pp. 143-8.
1977b, (ed.) Captive Cities, Wiley, Chichester
and New York.
1978, Housing Management and New Forms of
Tenure in the United States, Centre for
Environmental Studies, London.
1979, 'Marxism, the state and the urban
question: critical notes on two recent French
theories' in C. Crouch (ed.), State and Economy
in Contemporary Capitalism, Croom Helm, London,
pp. 122-56.
1981, 'The recommodification of housing' in
M. Harloe and E. Lebas (eds.) City, Class and
Capital, Edward Arnold, London, pp.17-50.
1982, 'Towards the decommodification of
housing? A comment on council house sales',
Critial Social Policy, vol 2, no 1, pp.39-42.
1984a, 'Sector and class: a critical comment',
International Journal of Urban and Regional
Research, vol 8, no 2, pp.228-37.

1984b, Social Housing in the OECD Countries - A
Selective Review of Developments and Problems,
mimeo, University of Essex.
HARLOE, M., ISSACHAROFF, R. and MINNS, R. 1974,
The Organisation of Housing, Heinemann
Educational Books, London.
HARLOE, M. and MARTENS, M. 1983, 'The housing
crisis in Britain and the Netherlands', mimeo,
University of Essex (to appear, revised in
Environment and Planning).
Forthcoming, 'Comparative Housing Research',
Journal of Social Policy.
HARLOE, M. and PARIS, C. 1984, 'The decollect-
ivisation of consumption. Housing and local
government finance in Britain, 1979-81' in
I. Szelenyi (ed.) Cities in Crisis: Public
Policies, Sage, Beverly Hills and London.
HARTMAN, C. 1974, Yerba Buena, Glide Publications,
San Francisco.
1982 'Housing' in A. Gartner, C. Greer and
F. Reissman (eds.), What Reagan is Doing to Us,
Harper and Row, New York, pp.141-62.
HARTMAN, C., KESSLER, R. and LE GATES, R. 1974,
'Municipal housing code enforcement and low-
income tenants', AIP Journal, March, pp.90-104.
HARVEY, D. 1977, 'Government policies, financial
institutions and neighbourhood change in United
States cities' in M. Harloe (ed.) Captive
Cities, Wiley, Chichester and New York,
pp.123-39.
HEARDER, H. 1966, Europe in the Nineteenth Century,
1830/1880, Longman, London and New York.
HEIDENHEIMER, A., HECLO, H. and ADAMS, C. 1975,
Comparative Public Policy, Macmillan, London.
HEINBERG, J. 1971, Tax Incentives and Housing
Rehabilitation: A Policy Analysis, The Urban
Institute, Washington DC.
HENNOCK, E. 1973, Fit and Proper Persons, Edward
Arnold, London.
HEPWORTH, N. 1980, Local Government Finance (5th
edn), Allen and Unwin, London.
HESKIN, A. 1981, 'The history of tenants in the
United States, struggle and ideology',
International Journal of Urban and Regional
Research, vol 5, no 2, pp. 178-203.
Forthcoming, Tenants and the American Dream.
HINSLEY, F. (ed.), 1962, The New Cambridge Modern
History - Vol XI, Material Progress and World-
wide Problems 1870-1898, Cambridge University
Press, Cambridge.
HOLE, J. 1866, The Homes of the Working Class,

Longmans, Green and Co., London.

HOME FRONT, 1977, Housing Abandonment in New York City, Home Front, New York City.

HOUSE COMMITTEE ON BANKING, CURRENCY AND HOUSING, 1975, Evolution of the role of the Federal Government in housing and community development: a chronology of legislative and selected executive actions, 1892-1974, US Government Printing Office, Washington DC.

HOUSE OF COMMONS ENVIRONMENT COMMITTEE, 1982, The Private Rented Housing Sector (First report, Session 1981-2), 3 vols, HMSO, London.

IBANEZ, R. 1975, 'Le financement du logement: investisseurs institutionnels et groupes financiers', Dossiers GRECOH, no 9, pp.1-12.

INDENRIGSMINISTERIETS, BYGGEUDVALG AF 1940, 1945, Det Fremtidige Boligbyggeri, Indenrigsministeriet, Copenhagen.

INSEE, 1974, 'Les revenues des ménages en 1970', Les Collections de l'INSEE, M40, no 147.

INSTITUTE OF POLITICAL SCIENCE. 1977, Public Involvement in Denmark, University of Aarhus, Aarhus.

INTERNATIONAL LABOUR OFFICE. 1923, The European Housing Problem Since the War, 1914-23, International Labour Office, Geneva.

JACKSON, A. 1976, A Place Called Home, MIT Press, Cambridge.

JACKSON, A.A. 1973, Semi-Detached London, Allen and Unwin, London.

JORBERG, L. 1973, 'The Nordic countries 1850-1914' in C. Cipolla (ed.) The Fontana Economic History of Europe 4(2): The Emergence of Industrial Societies, Collins/Fontana Books, Glasgow, pp.375-485.

JORBERG, L. and KRANTZ, O. 1976, 'Scandinavia 1914-1970' in C. Cipolla (ed.), The Fontana Economic History of Europe 6(2): Contemporary Economies -2, Collins/Fontana Books, Glasgow, pp.377-459.

KAIN, J. 1983, 'America's persistent housing crises: errors in analysis and policy', The Annals of the American Academy of Political and Social Science, vol 465, pp.136-48.

KARN, V. 1979, 'Pity the poor homeowners', Roof, vol 4, no 1, pp. 10-14.

KASARDA, J. 1980, 'The implications of contemporary redistribution trends for national urban policy', Social Science Quarterly, vol 61, nos 3 & 4, pp. 373-400.

KEARNS, K. 1980, 'Urban squatting', Social Policy,

Bibliography

vol 11, no 2, pp.21-9.
KEMP, T. 1972, The French Economy, 1913-39, Longman,
    London.
KERR, C. et al, 1965, Industrialisation and
    Industrial Man, Penguin, Harmondsworth.
KEYES, L. 1969, The Rehabilitation Planning Game,
    MIT Press, Cambridge, Mass. and London.
    1970, The Boston Rehabilitation Program: An
    Independent Analysis, Joint Center for Urban
    Studies, Cambridge, Mass.
KILROY, B. 1978, Housing Finance. Organic Reform?,
    LEFTA, London.
KOHLER, P. and ZACHER, H. in collaboration with
    PARTINGTON, M. 1982, The Evolution of Social
    Insurance 1881-1981, Frances Pinter, London.
KOLODNY, R. 1973, Self Help in the Inner City: A
    Study of Low Income Co-operative Housing
    Conversion in New York, United Neighbourhood
    Houses of New York, New York.
KONUKIEWITZ, H. and WOLLMANN, H. 1982, 'Physical
    planning in a federal system: the case of West
    Germany' in D. McKay (ed.) Planning and
    Politics in Western Europe, Macmillan, London
    and Basingstoke, pp.71-110.
KRANE, R. (ed.) 1979, International Labour Migration
    to Europe, Praeger, New York.
KRISTOF, B. 1976, 'Housing and the people in New
    York City', City Almanac, vol 10, no 5.
KUTTNER, B. 1976 'Ethnic renewal', New York Times
    Magazine, May 9th, pp.18-32.
LEAGUE OF NATIONS, ECONOMIC INTELLIGENCE SERVICE,
    1939, Urban and Rural Housing, League of
    Nations, Geneva.
LEAGUE OF NATIONS, HEALTH COMMITTEE, 1939, Rural
    Housing and Planning, League of Nations,
    Geneva.
LEBAS, E. 1982, 'Urban and regional sociology in
    advanced industrial societies: a decade of
    Marxist and critical perspectives', Current
    Sociology, vol 30, no 1.
LEEDS, A. 1974, 'Housing settlement types,
    arrangements for living, proletarianisation
    and the social structure of the city', in
    W.Cornelius and F. Trueblood (eds.), Latin
    American Urban Research, 4, Sage, Beverly Hills
    and London, pp.67-99.
LEGATES, R. and MURPHY, K. 1981, 'Austerity, shelter
    and social conflict in the United States',
    International Journal of Urban and Regional
    Research, vol 5, no 2, pp.255-75.
LEE, J. 1978, 'Labour in German industrialisation'

344

in P. Mathias and M. Postan (eds.), The
Cambridge Economic History of Europe: Vol VII
The Industrial Economies: Capital, Labour and
Enterprise, Part I Britain, France, Germany
and Scandinavia, Cambridge University Press,
Cambridge, pp.442-491.

LETT, M. 1976, Rent Control, Concepts, Realities
and Mechanisms, Center for Urban Policy
Research, Rutgers.

LÉVY-LEBOYER, M. 1978, 'Capital investment and
economic growth in France 1820-1930' in
P. Mathias and M. Postan (eds.), The Cambridge
Economic History of Europe: Vol VII The
Industrial Economies: Capital, Labour and
Enterprise, Part I Britain, France, Germany
and Scandinavia, Cambridge University Press,
Cambridge, pp.231-95.

LIJPHART, A. 1968, The Politics of Accommodation,
University of California Press, Berkeley and
Los Angeles.

LOWRY, I. et al, 1972, Welfare Housing in New York
City, Rand Corporation, New York.

LUBOVE, R. 1962, The Progressives and the Slums:
Tenement House Reform in New York City 1890-
1917, University of Pittsburg Press, Pittsburg.

LYDALL, H. 1968, The Structure of Earnings, Oxford
University Press, Oxford.

MAGRI, S. 1972, Politique du Logement et Besoins
en Main-d'oeuvre, CSU, Paris.
1977, Logement et Reproduction de
L'Exploitation, CSU, Paris.

MANDELKER, D. 1973, Housing Subsidies in the United
States and England, Bobbs-Merrill, Indianapolis.

MARCUSE, P. 1973, 'The rise of tenant organisation'
in J. Pynoos, R. Schafer and C. Hartman (eds.),
Housing Urban America, Aldine, Chicago,
pp.49-54.
1977, US Housing Policy, mimeo, Columbia
University, New York.
1978, 'The myth of the benevolent state: notes
towards a theory of housing conflict' in
M. Harloe (ed.), Urban Change and Conflict -
CES Conference, York 1977, CES, London, pp.397-
444.
1979, Rental Housing in the City of New York,
Supply and Condition 1975-1978, New York.
1981, 'The determination of state housing
policies' in O. Barteis and H. Frank (eds.),
The Crisis of Housing Policy, Technische
Universitat, Hamburg, pp.104-45.
1982, 'Building housing theory: notes on some

recent work', International Journal of Urban
and Regional Research, vol 6, no 1, pp.115-21.

MARRIS, P. 1982, Community Planning and Conceptions
of Change, Routledge and Kegan Paul, London.

MASSU, C. 1977, Une Politique Du Logement Pour la
France, Éditions de la Courtille. Paris.

MATHIAS, P. and POSTAN, M. (eds.) 1978, The
Cambridge Economic History of Europe: Vol VII
The Industrial Economies: Capital, Labour and
Enterprise, Part I Britain, France, Germany
and Scandinavia, Cambridge University Press,
Cambridge.

MAYER, M. 1982, 'The profile of contemporary
neighbourhood movements' in G. Hellstern,
F. Spreer and H. Wollmann (eds.) Applied Urban
Research, Volume II, BLR, Bonn, pp.233-42.
N.d. Precis on Neighbourhood Discontent and
State Policy: A Comparative Approach, mimeo,
Amerika-Institut der Universitaet Frankfurt/
Institute of Urban and Regional Development,
UC, Berkeley.

McCOY, D. 1973, Coming of Age, Penguin,
Harmondsworth.

McDERMOTT, R. 1981, 'The functions of local levels
of government in West Germany and their
internal organisation' in A. Gunlicks (ed.),
Local Government Reform and Reorganisation,
Kennikat Press, Port Washington, NY, pp.182-
201.

McKAY, D. 1980, 'The rise of the topocratic state:
US intergovernmental relations in the 1970s' in
D. Ashford (ed.), Financing Urban Government
in the Welfare State, Croom Helm, London,
pp.50-70.

McKAY, D. and COX, A. 1979, The Politics of Urban
Change, Croom Helm, London.

McKELVEY, B. 1963, The Urbanisation of America,
Rutgers University Press, New Brunswick.

McLENNAN, D. 1982, Housing Economics, Longman,
London and New York.

MEADOR, D. 1969, Comments to the Colloquium on the
Statutory Control of the Letting of Dwelling
Houses, mimeo, UK National Committee of
Comparative Law, Durham.

MÉNY, Y. 1980, 'Financial transfer and local
government in France: national policy despite
36,000 communes' in D. Ashford (ed.), Financing
Urban Government in the Welfare State, Croom
Helm, London, pp.142-58.

MILIBAND, R. 1973, The State in Capitalist Society,
Quartet, London.

MILLER, K. 1968, Government and Politics in
    Denmark, Houghton Mifflin, Boston.
MILLER, S. 1977, 'Economic crisis and oppositional
    movements in the USA', International Journal
    of Urban and Regional Research, vol 1, no 1,
    pp.126-31.
MILLER, S. and REIN, M. 1975, 'Can income
    redistribution work?' Social Policy, May/June,
    pp.3-18.
MILWARD, A. and SAUL, S. 1973, The Economic
    Development of Continental Europe 1780-1870,
    Allen and Unwin, London.
MINISTERIE VAN VOLKSHUISVESTING EN RUIMTELIJKE
    ORDENING, 1977, Individuele Huursubsidie voor
    Gezinnen en Alleenstaanden van 30 jaar en ouder,
    Centrale Afeling Voorlichting en Externe
    Betrekkingen, Den Haag.
MINISTRY OF HOUSING, 1974, Housing in Denmark,
    Ministry of Housing, Copenhagen.
MISRA, R. 1977, Society and Social Policy,
    Macmillan, London and Basingstoke.
MITCHELL, B. 1976, 'Statistical appendix' in
    C. Cipolla (ed.), The Fontana Economic History
    of Europe 6(2): Contemporary Economies - 2,
    Collins/Fontana Books, Glasgow.
    1980, European Historical Statistics 1750-1975
    (2nd revised edn), Macmillan, Facts on File,
    Sitjhoff and Noordhoff, London etc.
MORLAN, R. 1981a, 'Local government reorganisation
    in the Netherlands' in A. Gunlicks (ed.), Local
    Government Reform and Reorganisation, Kennikat
    Press, Port Washington, NY, pp.42-53.
    1981b, 'Territorial reorganisation and
    administration reform in Denmark' in A. Gunlicks
    (ed.) Local Government Reform and
    Reorganisation, Kennikat Press, Port Washington,
    NY, pp.31-41.
NATIONAL CENTER FOR HOUSING MANAGEMENT, 1973 Task
    Force on Improving the Operation of Federally
    Insured or Financed Housing Programs, Report.
    Volume III Multi-family Housing, The Center,
    Washington DC.
NATIONAL COMMISSION ON URBAN PROBLEMS (Douglas
    Commission) 1968, Building the American City,
    US Government Printing Office, Washington DC.
NAVAL INTELLIGENCE DIVISION 1944, Netherlands,
    HMSO, London.
NAVARRO, V. 1978, Class Struggle, the State and
    Medicine, Martin Robertson, London.
NEVITT, A. 1966, Housing, Taxation and Subsidies,
    Nelson, London.

Bibliography

NEWFIELD, J. and DU BRUL, P. 1978, The Abuse of
    Power: The Permanent Government and the Fall
    of New York, Penguin, Harmondsworth.
NORA, S. and EVENO, B. 1975, L'Amélioration De
    L'Habitat Ancien, 2 vols, La Documentation
    Francaise, Paris.
O'CONNOR, J. 1973, The Fiscal Crisis of the State,
    St. Martins Press, New York.
ODLING-SMEE, J. 1975, The Impact of the Fiscal
    System on Different Tenure Sectors, mimeo, LSE,
    London.
OFFER, A. 1981, Property and Politics, 1870-1914,
    Cambridge University Press, Cambridge.
OPCS 1974, Census 1971. England and Wales.
    Housing: Part I Households, HMSO, London.
    1979, The General Household Survey 1977, HMSO,
    London.
PAHL, R. 1977, 'Managers, technical experts and
    the state: forms of mediation, manipulation
    and dominance in urban and regional development
    in M. Harloe (ed.), Captive Cities, Wiley,
    Chichester and New York, pp.49-60.
    1980, 'Employment, work and the domestic
    division of labour', International Journal of
    Urban and Regional Research, vol 4, no 1,
    pp.1-20.
PALEY, B. 1978, Attitudes to Letting in 1976, HMSO,
    London.
PARIS, C. and BLACKABY, B. 1979, Not Much Improve-
    ment, Heinemann Educational Books, London.
PERRY, D. and WATKINS, A. (eds.), 1977, The Rise
    of the Sun Belt Cities, Sage, Beverly Hills.
PICKVANCE, C. 1976, 'On the study of urban social
    movements', in C. Pickvance (ed.), Urban
    Sociology: Critical Essays, Methuen, London,
    pp.198-218.
    1977, 'From "social base" to "social force":
    some analytical issues in the study of urban
    protest' in M. Harloe (ed.), Captive Cities,
    Wiley, Chichester and New York.
POLLARD, S. and HOLMES, C. 1968, Documents of
    European Economic History. Vol I The Process
    of Industrialisation 1750-1870, Edward Arnold,
    London.
    1972, Documents of European Economic History.
    Vol II Industrial Power and National Rivalry
    1870-1914, Edward Arnold, London.
    1973, Documents of European Economic History.
    Vol III The End of Old Europe 1914-39, Edward
    Arnold, London.
POLIKOFF, A. 1978, Housing the Poor: The Case for

Bibliography

Heroism, Ballinger, Cambridge Mass.
PRESIDENT JIMMY CARTER. 1978, New Partnership to
    Conserve America's Communities, Office of the
    White House Press Secretary, Washington DC.
PRESIDENT OF THE UNITED STATES. 1976, Eighth Annual
    Report on the National Housing Goal, US
    Government Printing Office, Washington DC.
PRICE, R. 1981, An Economic History of Modern
    France 1730-1914, Macmillan, London.
PRICE, WATERHOUSE AND CO. 1973, A Study of the
    Effects of Real Estate Property Tax Incentive
    Programs Upon Property Rehabilitation and New
    Construction, US Government Printing Office,
    Washington DC.
PRIEMUS, H. 1981, 'Rent and subsidy policy in the
    Netherlands during the seventies', Urban Law
    and Policy, 4, pp.299-355.
    1983, 'Squatters in Amsterdam: urban social
    movement, urban managers or something else?',
    International Journal of Urban and Regional
    Research, vol 7, no 3, pp.417-27.
PYNOOS, J., SCHAFER, R. and HARTMAN, C. (eds.),
    1973, Housing Urban America, Aldine Press,
    Chicago.
RAYNER, G. 1982, 'U.S. housing cuts', Roof, vol 7,
    no 5, p.6.
REED, J. 1976, 'Housing and Social Reform in France
    1894-1935', Transactions of the Martin Centre
    for Architecture and Urban Studies, no 1,
    pp.297-315.
REAL ESTATE RESEARCH CORPORATION 1975a, A Policy
    Review of Rented Housing in New York City,
    Coalition to Save New York, New York.
    1975b, Neighbourhood Preservation: A Catalog
    of Local Programs, US Government Printing
    Office, Washington DC.
RECENSEMENT DE 1954, 1957, Recensement général de
    la Population de Mai 1954. Résultats du
    sondage au 1/20°. Menages, Logements, INSEE,
    Paris.
RECENSEMENT DE 1962, 1965, Recensement Général de
    la Population de 1962. Résultats du Sondage
    au 1/20° pour la France Entiere. Logements,
    Immeubles, INSEE, Paris.
REISSERT, B. 1980, 'Federal and state transfers to
    local government in the Federal Republic of
    Germany: A case of political immobility', in
    D. Ashford (ed.), Financing Urban Government in
    the Welfare State, Croom Helm, London, pp.158-
    78.
REX, J. and MOORE, R. 1967, Race, Community and

Bibliography

    Conflict, Oxford University Press, Oxford.
RHODES, R. 1981, 'The changing pattern of local
    government in England' in A. Gunlicks (ed.)
    Local Government Reform and Reorganisation,
    Kennikat Press, Port Washington NY, pp. 93-111.
RICHARDS, C. and ROWE, J. 1977, 'Restoring a City:
    Who pays the price?', Working Papers, Winter,
    pp. 54-61.
RIDLEY, F. and BLONDEL, J. 1969, Public Adminis-
    tration in France, Routledge and Kegan Paul,
    London.
RIMLINGER, G. 1971, Welfare Policy and
    Industrialisation in Europe, America and Russia,
    Wiley, New York.
ROBBINS, I. 1966, 'Housing achievements', in
    W. Wheaton, G. Milgram and M. Meyerson, Urban
    Housing, Free Press, New York, pp. 9-13.
ROBERTS, J. 1970, Europe 1880-1945, Longmans,
    London and New York.
ROTTERDAM CITY DEVELOPMENT DEPARTMENT N.d.,
    Rotterdam on the Road to Renewal, City of
    Rotterdam Press and Information Services,
    Rotterdam.
ROY, D. 1979, 'Hooverville - community of homeless
    men' in J. Abu-Lughod and R. Hay Jr. (eds.),
    Third World Urbanisation, Methuen, New York and
    London, pp. 300-6.
RUST, D. 1977, 'The tenant movement pulls one out
    of the fire', Network, June, pp. 28-35.
SAUNDERS, P. 1979, Urban Politics: A Sociological
    Interpretation, Hutchinson, London.
    1984, 'Beyond housing classes: the
    sociological significance of private property
    rights in means of consumption', International
    Journal of Urban and Regional Research, vol 8,
    no 2, pp. 202-27.
SAWBRIDGE, B. 1982, 'Pity the poor landlord', Roof,
    vol 7, no 4, p. 9.
SCHAUFELBERGER, F. 1980, Guide Du Financement Du
    Logement Neuf ou Ancien, Editions du Moniteur,
    Paris.
SCHNEIDER, K. and KORNEMANN, R. 1977, Soziale
    Wohnungs marktwirtschaft: Studien zur
    Kommunalpolitik, Band 20, Eichholz-Verlag, Bonn.
    Bonn.
SECRETARIAT OF THE ECONOMIC COMMISSION FOR EUROPE.
    1979, Labour Supply and Migration in Europe,
    UN, New York.
SEFIMEG. 1977, Exercice 1976, Paris.
SENATE COMMITTEE ON BANKING, HOUSING AND URBAN
    AFFAIRS. 1976, Comparative Costs and Estimated
    Households Eligible for Participation in

Certain Federally Assisted Low Income Housing
Programs, US Government Printing Office,
Washington DC.
SHAC. 1981, Good Housekeeping: An Examination of
Housing Repair and Improvement Policy, SHAC,
London.
SHEARER, D. 1982, 'How the progressives won in
Santa Monica', Social Policy, Winter, pp.7-14.
SHELTER. 1982, Housing and the Economy, Shelter,
London.
SHORT, J. 1982, Housing in Britain. The Post-War
Experience, Methuen, London and New York.
SKOVSGAARD, C.J. 1982, Consequences of Reforming
Central-Local Relations: The Changing Role of
Local Government in Denmark, mimeo, Institute
of Political Science, Aarhus.
SMITH, W. (ed.), 1983, 'Housing America', The Annals
of the American Academy of Political and Social
Science, vol 465.
SOCIALT TIDSSKRIFT (ed.) 1947, Social Denmark,
Socialt Tidsskrift, Copenhagen.
STATISTISCHES JAHRBUCH. Annually, Bundesrepublik
Deutschland, Bonn.
STEDMAN, M. 1975, Urban Politics (2nd edn), Winthrop
Publishers, Cambridge, Mass.
STEGMAN, M. 1978, 'Trouble for multi-family housing:
its effects on conserving older neighbourhoods',
Occasional Papers in Housing and Community
Affairs, vol 2, US Department of Housing and
Urban Development, Washington DC, pp.233-71.
STERNLIEB, G. 1966, The Tenement Landlord, Rutgers
University Press, New Brunswick.
STERNLIEB, G. and HUGHES, J. 1976, Housing and
Economic Reality: New York City, 1976, Center
for Urban Policy Research, Rutgers.
STERNLIEB, G. and HUGHES, J. 1977, 'Metropolitan
decline and inter-regional job shifts' in
R. Alcaly and D. Mermelstein (eds.) The Fiscal
Crisis of American Cities, Vintage Books, New
York, pp.145-64.
STERNLIEB, G., ROISTACHER, E. and HUGHES, J. 1976,
Tax Subsidies and Housing Investment: A Fiscal
Cost-benefit Analysis, Center for Urban Policy
Research, Rutgers.
STILL, B. 1974, Urban America. A History with
Documents, Little, Brown and Company, Boston.
STOLPER, G. et al. 1967, The Germany Economy, 1870
to the Present, Weidenfeld and Nicolson, London.
STREICH, P. and CLARKE, L. 1980, Multi-family
Federal Rental Assistance Programs in Canada and
the United States, US Department of Housing and

Bibliography

Urban Development/Canada Central Mortgage and
Housing Corporation, Washington DC.
STRIKER, J. and SHAPIRO, A. 1978, Super Tenant (rev.
edn), Holt, Rinehart and Winston, New York.
SUTCLIFFE, A. 1970, The Autumn of Central Paris,
Edward Arnold, London.
SWENARTON, M. 1981, Homes Fit For Heroes, Heinemann
Educational Books, London.
SZELENYI, I. 1981, 'Structural Changes in and
alternatives to capitalist development in the
contemporary urban and regional system',
International Journal of Urban and Regional
Research, vol 5, no 1, pp.1-14.
TARN, J. 1973, Five Per Cent Philanthropy, Cambridge
University Press, London.
TOPALOV, C. 1973, Les Promoteurs Immobiliers,
Mouton, Paris La Haye.
TOWNSEND, P. 1979, Poverty in the United Kingdom,
Penguin, Harmondsworth.
TRUTKO, J., HETZEL, O. and YATES, A. 1978, A
Comparison of the Experimental Housing Allowance
Program and Great Britain's Rent Allowance
Program, Urban Institute, Washington DC.
TUMOLILLO, A. 1977, 'Industry misregulation: rent
stabilisation', Network, June, pp.44-49.
UFIMEG, 1977, Exercice 1975-6, Paris.
UNITED NATIONS. 1968, Compendium of Social
Statistics 1967, UN, New York.
1981, 1979-80 Statistical Yearbook, UN, New York.
URBAN HOMESTEADING ASSISTANCE BOARD. 1977, Sweat
Equity Homesteading of Multi-family Housing in
New York City, US Department of Housing and
Urban Development, Washington DC.
URBAN PLANNING AID INC. 1973, 'An evaluation of the
Boston rehabilitation program', in J. Pynoos,
R. Schafer and C. Hartman (eds.), Housing Urban
America, Aldine, Chicago.
US BUREAU OF THE CENSUS. 1961, Historical Statistics
of the United States Colonial Times to 1957, US
Government Printing Office, Washington DC.
1965, Historical Statistics of the United States
Continuation to 1962 and Revisions, US
Government Printing Office, Washington DC.
1979, Statistical Abstract of the United States,
1979, US Government Printing Office, Washington
DC.
US BUREAU OF THE CENSUS AND US DEPARTMENT OF HOUSING
AND URBAN DEVELOPMENT. 1976, Annual Housing
Survey: 1974. Part B - Advance Report, US
Government Printing Office, Washington DC.
1977, Annual Housing Survey 1975, General

Housing Characteristics. Part A - United States and Regions, US Government Printing Office, Washington DC.
1978, Annual Housing Survey 1976, General Housing Characteristics. Part A - United States and Regions, US Government Printing Office, Washington DC.
1979a, Annual Housing Survey 1977, General Housing Characteristics. Part A - United States and Regions, US Government Printing Office, Washington DC.
1979b, Annual Housing Survey 1977: Part B, US Government Printing Office, Washington DC.
US DEPARTMENT OF COMMERCE, BUREAU OF ECONOMIC ANALYSIS. 1973, Long Term Economic Growth 1860-1970, US Government Printing Office, Washington DC.
US DEPARTMENT OF HOUSING AND URBAN DEVELOPMENT.
1973, Housing in the Seventies, pre-publication mimeo, Washington DC.
1976a, Housing for Low Income Families. HUD's New Section 8 Housing Assistance Payments Program, HUD, Washington DC.
1976b, Community Development Block Grant Program. Second Annual Report, US Government Printing Office, Washington DC.
1977, 1976 Statistical Yearbook, US Government Printing Office, Washington DC.
1978, HUD Challenge, March, HUD, Washington DC.
1980a, 1980 National Housing Production Report, US Government Printing Office, Washington DC.
1980b, The Conversion of Rental Housing into Condominiums and Co-operatives, US Government Printing Office, Washington DC.
US DEPARTMENT OF HOUSING AND URBAN DEVELOPMENT, OFFICE OF POLICY DEVELOPMENT AND RESEARCH. 1975, Experimental Housing Allowance Program. Initial Impressions and Findings, HUD, Washington DC.
1976, Housing Allowances: The 1976 Report to Congress, US Government Printing Office, Washington DC.
1978, A Summary Report of Current Findings from the Experimental Housing Allowance Program, HUD, Washington DC.
1979, Experimental Housing Allowance Program. A 1979 Report of Findings, HUD, Washington DC.
1980, Experimental Housing Allowance Program. Conclusions - The 1980 Report, HUD, Washington DC.
VAN DER KAA, H. 1935, La Question de l'Habitation aux Pays-Bas, Société des Nations, Genève.

Bibliography

VAN DER SCHAAR, J. 1979, Sektor-indeling en
    woningmarkt-processen, s'Gravenhage.
    1982, Housing Costs in the Netherlands: Trends
    in the Period 1950-1980 and the Distribution
    of Housing Costs in 1977, mimeo, Delft.
VAN WEESEP, J. 1982, Production and Allocation of
    Housing. The Case of the Netherlands, Vrije
    Universiteit, Amsterdam.
WALTON, J. 1982, 'Economic crisis and urban
    austerity: issues of research and policy in
    the 1980s', in T. Bottomore, S. Nowak and
    M. Sokolowska (eds.) Sociology. The State of
    the Art, Sage, London and Beverly Hills, pp.
    pp.277-98.
WARD, C. 1983, Housing. An Anarchist Approach,
    Freedom Press, London.
WARD, P. (ed.) 1982, Self-help Housing: A Critique,
    Mansell, London.
WARNER, S. 1962, Streetcar Suburbs: The Process of
    Growth in Boston 1870-1900, Harvard University
    Press, Cambridge.
    1972, The Urban Wilderness, Harper and Row,
    New York.
WEBER, A. 1963, The Growth of Cities in the
    Nineteenth Century, Cornell University Press,
    Ithaca.
WEIL, G. 1970, The Benelux Nations, Holt, Rinehart
    and Winston, New York.
WELFELD, I. 1972, European Housing Subsidy Systems,
    US Government Printing Office, Washington DC.
WELLS, R. 1932, German Cities, Princeton University
    Press, Princeton.
WENDT, P. 1962, Housing Policy: The Search for
    Solutions, University of California Press,
    Berkeley and Los Angeles.
WHITBREAD, M. 1975, Housing Finance Policies. An
    International Review, mimeo, Centre for
    Environmental Studies, London.
WICKS, M. 1975, The Non Take-up of Rent Rebates and
    Allowances, mimeo, Home Office Urban
    Deprivation Unit, London.
WILDING, P. 1972, 'Towards exchequer subsidies for
    housing 1906-14', Social and Economic
    Administration, vol 6, no 1, pp.3-18.
WILENSKY, H. and LEBEAUX, C. 1965, Industrial
    Society and Social Welfare, Free Press, New
    York.
WILLIAMS, O. and COLIJN, G. 1980, 'Territorial
    political resource transfer in the Netherlands',
    in D. Ashford (ed.), Financing Urban Government
    in the Welfare State, Croom Helm, London,

pp.179-203.

WOHL, A. 1977, The Eternal Slum, Edward Arnold, London.

WOLLMANN, H. Forthcoming, 'Housing policies in West Germany - between state intervention and market mechanism' in K. von Beyme and H. Schmidt (eds.), Policy Making in the Federal Republic of Germany, Sage, Beverly Hills and London.

WOLMAN, H. 1975, Housing and Housing Policy in the U.S. and the U.K., Lexington Books, Lexington.

WOMEN'S CITY CLUB OF NEW YORK. 1977, With Love and Affection. A Study of Building Abandonment, The Club, New York.

WOOD, E. 1966, 'A century of the housing problem', in W. Wheaton, G. Milgram and M. Meyerson (eds.), Urban Housing, Free Press, New York.

WYE, C., PICKERING, J. and KAMINSKY, D. 1978, 'HUD's insured multi-family housing: the problems of financially troubled subsidised projects', Occasional Papers in Housing and Community Affairs, vol 2, US Department of Housing and Urban Development, Washington DC, pp.168-232.

YOUNG, K. and KRAMER, J. 1978, Strategy and Conflict in Metropolitan Housing, Heinemann Educational Books, London.

ZAPF, W. 1977, Lebensbedingungen in der Bundesrepublik Sozialer Wandel und Wohlfahrtsentwicklung, Campus, Frankfurt/Main.

ZELDIN, T. 1973, France 1848-1945. Vol 1, Oxford University Press, Oxford.
1977, France 1848-1945. Vol 2, Oxford University Press, Oxford.

INDEX

Index

Index

Index

Index

Index

362

Index

For Product Safety Concerns and Information please contact our EU
representative GPSR@taylorandfrancis.com
Taylor & Francis Verlag GmbH, Kaufingerstraße 24, 80331 München, Germany

www.ingramcontent.com/pod-product-compliance
Lightning Source LLC
Chambersburg PA
CBHW070715280326
41926CB00087B/2152

9 780367 680152